# the essential
# asian
## cookbook

# the essential
# asian
## cookbook

This edition produced specially for Borders Group, Inc. by arrangement with
Murdoch Books Pty Limited. Printed 2005.

First published by Murdoch Books Pty Limited.

Chief Executive: Juliet Rogers
Publisher: Kay Scarlett

ISBN 1-74045-770-6

Printed by 1010 Printing International Limited.
PRINTED IN CHINA

IMPORTANT: Those who might be at risk from the effects of salmonella food poisoning
(the elderly, pregnant women, young children and those suffering from immune deficiency diseases)
should consult their GP with any concerns about eating raw eggs.

OUR STAR RATING: When we test recipes, we rate them for ease of preparation.
The following cookery ratings are used in this book:
☆ A single star indicates a recipe that is simple and generally quick to make—perfect for beginners.
☆☆ Two stars indicate the need for just a little more care, or perhaps a little more time.
☆☆☆ Three stars indicate special dishes that need more investment in time,
care and patience—but the results are worth it. Even beginners can make these
dishes as long as the recipe is followed carefully.

# UNIQUE ASIA

Although it's been around for thousands of years, Asian food is suddenly the smart new food. Restaurant chefs from Vancouver to London are introducing Asian ingredients and cooking techniques into their repertoire, suburban greengrocers and supermarkets are stocking fresh coriander and lemon grass, and no wonder... Asian food is fresh and colourful, full of flavour, and never boring or bland. With its emphasis on grains and vegetables, it is also healthy, cheap and often quick to prepare. Yet it's dangerous to generalise. Asian food is as multi-faceted and diverse as European food. While neighbours share some common ingredients and cooking styles, Asian countries have developed cuisines that are uniquely their own. Sampling the food of each is truly an adventure.

*Selamat makan.*

# CONTENTS

## SPECIAL FEATURES

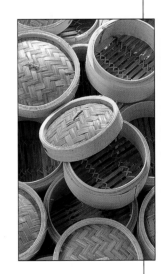

# YOUR ASIAN KITCHEN

Although the countries of Asia are spread over half the globe, the various Asian cuisines have many things in common. Spices and herbs are used  extensively, rice is a staple, and many ingredients, such as noodles, soy sauce and tofu, have crossed borders from one country to another and continue to do so. Stir-frying, deep-frying and steaming are techniques used in most Asian countries and there is one utensil, the wok, that is found, in various forms and with different names, throughout Asia.

## THE WOK

No-one contemplating cooking a range of Asian dishes should be without a wok. With its large surface area and high sides it is ideal for stir-frying, and for deep-frying it requires less oil than a straight-sided pan. A wok is also ideal for steaming. Its sloping sides allow bamboo and metal steamers to fit firmly into place. There are many types of woks available today. They vary in size and shape and the materials from which they are made. The traditional wok has a round base and is made from rolled steel. Woks are also made from stainless steel, cast iron and aluminium, and some have nonstick surfaces. A wok with a flat base is the best one to use on an electric stove because it will sit more directly and securely on the heating element, allowing a more even conduction of heat. Round-based woks work best on gas stoves; however a stand may be necessary to provide stability. Choose a stand which is open because this allows sufficient air to flow through, thus providing optimum heat. Gas stoves are ideal for wok cooking as the heat is delivered instantly and can be more easily controlled than it can with electric stoves.

## SEASONING AND CLEANING A WOK

Rolled steel woks—the standard inexpensive ones available from Chinese and Asian stores—are coated with a thin film of lacquer to stop them rusting while they are being shipped and stored before being sold. This film has to be removed before the wok can be used. The best way to do this is to place the wok on the stove top, fill it with cold water and add 2 tablespoons of bicarbonate of soda. Bring the water to the boil and boil rapidly for 15 minutes. Drain, scrub off the varnish with a plastic scourer, and repeat the process if any lacquer remains. Then rinse and dry the wok.

The wok is now ready to be seasoned. This is done to create a smooth surface which stops the food sticking to it or discolouring. Place the wok over low heat. Have a small bowl of oil, preferably peanut oil, nearby and scrunch a paper towel into a wad. When the wok is hot,

*A hot wok is seasoned by rubbing peanut oil into it with paper towels until the towels come away clean.*

wipe it with the wadded paper dipped into the oil. Repeat the process with fresh paper until it comes away clean and without any trace of colour.

A seasoned wok should not be scrubbed. To wash a wok after cooking, use hot water and a sponge, or soak the wok in warm water and detergent if food is stuck to it. Dry it well after washing by heating it gently over low heat, and rubbing it all over with an oiled paper towel. Store the wok in a dry, well-ventilated place. Long periods in a dark, warm, airless cupboard can cause the oil coating to turn rancid. Using the wok frequently is the best way to prevent it from rusting.

## OTHER ESSENTIALS

### FOR GRINDING

No Asian kitchen would be without some sort of grinding apparatus, usually a mortar and pestle. Ground spices quickly lose their flavour and aroma, so it is best to grind small amounts of whole spices when needed. While it is generally considered that a mortar and pestle gives the best results, an electric coffee grinder is ideal for this task: the motor, designed for hard beans, is strong enough to take the strain of grinding spices, the blades are low down and the bowl is appropriately small in size. If you cannot set aside a coffee grinder just for spices, grind a little rice to remove coffee flavours, and again after spices have been processed to remove curry aromas.

Pounding the ingredients in a mortar and pestle is the best way to make curry and spice pastes, but if the paste is wet enough, a blender or food processor can be used.

### FOR CUTTING

Sharp, good-quality knives are essential as so much Asian cooking involves cutting up raw ingredients. For most jobs, a Western chef's knife is the easiest to handle. A medium-weight cleaver is useful when chopping a chicken Chinese-style. If preferred, a heavy-bladed chef's knife can be used. However, once you are used to the feel of it, a cleaver can be a very versatile instrument.

## STEAMING TIPS

Food that is steamed is cooked by the moist heat given off by steadily boiling water. To get the best results:
● Fill your wok or pan about one-third full with water. Stand the steamer over the water to check that it is the correct height before you bring the water to the boil. It is important that you have enough, and not too much water, in your wok or pan. If there is too much water, it will boil up into the food and if you have too little water, it will quickly boil dry during cooking.
● When the water is boiling, arrange the food in the steamer and place it carefully in the wok.

*Bamboo steamers placed over water in a wok are ideal for steaming dishes such as won tons and fish parcels.*

*Whole fish can be steamed on a serving plate placed on a wire rack in a wok.*

● Cover the wok and maintain the heat so the water boils rapidly, allowing the steam to circulate evenly around the food.

When lifting the lid on a wok while steaming is in progress, always lift it up and away from you like a shield so the skin on your wrist is not exposed to a blast of scalding steam.

## STIR-FRYING TIPS

Stir-frying involves cooking small pieces of food over medium to high heat for a short period of time. To get the best results:
● Prepare all the ingredients before you start to cook. The meat is often cut into even, paper-thin slices, fast-cooking vegetables are evenly sliced or cut into small pieces, and slower-cooking vegetables are cut thinly or blanched before being added to the stir-fry. Once the slicing and cutting are done, all the ingredients for the sauce should be measured out. If rice or noodles are part of the dish, these should be ready to be added as well.
● Heat the wok before adding the oil.
● Heat the oil before adding the food. This ensures that the cooking time will be short and that the ingredients, especially meat, will be

seared instantly, sealing in the juices and the flavour.
● Toss and turn the food carefully while it cooks. Keeping the food constantly moving ensures even cooking and prevents burning. Stir-fried vegetables should be crisp and the meat tender and succulent.

## DEEP-FRYING TIPS

It is very important to make sure that the wok or pan you are using for deep-frying is very stable and secure on the stove top, and you should never leave the kitchen while the oil is heating as it can quickly overheat and ignite. To get the best results:
● Add the oil, never filling the pan or wok more than half full, and heat over high heat. When the oil is the required temperature for deep-frying (180°C/350°F), it will start to move and a 3 cm (1¼ inch) cube of bread lowered into it will brown in just 15 seconds. Lower the heat to medium if that is all that is needed to maintain the right temperature.
● Carefully add the food to the oil with tongs and move small pieces around, gently turning them to ensure even cooking.

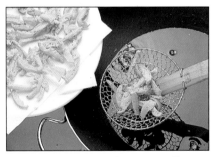

*A traditional wire mesh strainer allows the oil to drip away from deep-fried food.*

● When ready, carefully lift out the food with tongs, a wire mesh strainer or a slotted spoon and drain it on a tray covered with several layers of paper towels.
● If you are frying in batches, keep the cooked food warm in a moderate 180°C (350°F/Gas 4) oven.
● When frying food in batches, make sure you reheat the oil to the required temperature after each batch. Use a slotted spoon to remove any small fragments of food left in the oil as these will burn.

## CURRY PASTES

In Thai and Indian markets, mounds of colourful curry pastes, made fresh each day, await the home cook. Red (from fresh or dried red chillies), yellow (turmeric) and green (fresh green chillies and fresh green herbs), they come in a range of strengths and blends. In the West, imported curry pastes are available in jars and cans, but making your own will give you the best results. Make a batch of your favourite pastes and store them in the refrigerator. This will save you a lot of time when you are preparing a meal. Fresh paste will keep for up to 3 weeks in an airtight container in the refrigerator. Alternatively, place tablespoons of paste in an ice cube tray, cover and freeze. When the paste is frozen, release the cubes into a freezer bag, and store in the freezer until required. Allow the cubes to defrost for 30 minutes at room temperature before using them. Frozen paste will keep for up to 4 months.

## SPICES AND BLENDS

Ground spices quickly lose their flavour and aroma, so it is best to grind small amounts of whole spices when needed. Dry-roasting whole spices brings out their flavour and makes them easier to grind. You can dry-roast each spice individually in the pan or, if doing small quantities, dry-roast them together. Heat a clean, dry, heavy-based frying pan over low heat. Add the spices, stir constantly until fragrant and lightly browned, then turn onto a plate to cool. Ground spices can be dry-roasted to make them more aromatic, but they will burn more quickly and so need the very lowest heat.

*Dry-roasting spices whole maximises their flavour and makes grinding easier.*

*A mortar and pestle is an essential part of the Asian kitchen.*

While freshly prepared spices produce the best results, it may often be convenient to prepare a quantity of spice blends such as garam masala (see page 127) or Ceylon curry powder (see page 126). These will last well if stored in airtight glass jars away from sunlight and heat.

## BASIC STOCKS

A number of recipes in this book include a stock in the ingredients. The following list of ingredients used in a basic stock recipe can be modified to produce a beef, chicken or seafood stock by varying the type of carcassses, bones or trimmings used and by following the cooking instructions for the type of stock you need. For example, for a chicken stock use chicken necks, feet or wings; for a seafood stock, use fish heads or prawn heads and shells or lobster shells; and for a beef stock, use bones, oxtail or shanks. Stock can be stored in the refrigerator for up to a week and in the freezer for up to 6 months.

*1 kg (2 lb) carcasses, bones or trimmings with fat removed*
*2 litres cold water*
*3 red Asian shallots or 3 spring onions, roughly chopped*
*5 cm (2 inch) piece fresh ginger, sliced*
*1 medium carrot, roughly chopped*
*5 black peppercorns*
*2 cloves garlic, sliced*

### BEEF STOCK

1 Bake the beef bones in a baking dish, at 230°C (450°F/Gas 8) for 40 minutes, adding the carrots and shallots to the dish halfway through the cooking time.
2 Deglaze the baking dish with a little water and transfer the contents to a stockpot or large saucepan, with the remaining ingredients, including the water, and bring to the boil. Remove any scum that has risen to the surface of the liquid.
3 Reduce the heat and simmer gently for 3 hours (or longer if you prefer a more concentrated stock). Remove any scum that rises to the top during simmering.
4 Strain the stock through a fine sieve, pressing the solids to extract all the liquid and then allow to cool. Remove any fat from the surface.

### CHICKEN STOCK

1 Place the carcass or bones in a stockpot or large saucepan with the remaining ingredients and bring to the boil. Remove any scum that has risen to the surface of the liquid.
2 Reduce the heat and simmer for 1 hour. Remove any scum that rises to the top during simmering.
3 Strain the stock through a fine sieve and allow to cool. Remove any fat from the surface.

### FISH STOCK

1 Cut the bones and fish trimmings into pieces, discard the eyes and gills. (Soak the bones and trimmings in cold salted water for about 10 minutes to remove any blood.) Break up prawn or lobster shells.
2 Place the bones and trimmings in a stockpot or large saucepan with the water and the remaining ingredients and bring to the boil.
3 Simmer for 20 minutes, skimming off the scum as it rises to the surface.
4 Strain the stock through a fine sieve and allow to cool.

### VEGETABLE STOCK

For vegetable stock, increase the number of red Asian shallots to eight and use two extra carrots.
1 Put the chopped vegetables in a stockpot or large saucepan with the water and remaining ingredients. Bring to the boil and simmer for up to 1 hour.
2 Strain the stock through a fine sieve, pressing the vegetables with a ladle to extract all the liquid. Set aside to cool.

# USEFUL PREPARATION TECHNIQUES

## CHOPPING A CHICKEN OR DUCK, CHINESE-STYLE

When cutting the chicken, bring the cleaver or knife down sharply in one clean stroke. With a dense bone mass, you may need to lift the blade with the food attached to it and bring it down sharply on the board again until the food is cleanly cut.

*Cut the chicken in half by cutting along the breast bone, continuing down through the backbone.*

*Remove the wings, drumsticks and thighs. If you don't have a cleaver, use a heavy-bladed chef's knife.*

*Chop each large segment, such as the breasts or legs, into two or three pieces. The pieces must be a manageable size for handling with chopsticks.*

## PREPARING MEAT

Many Asian dishes call for the meat to be very thinly sliced. If the meat is partially frozen, this makes it firmer and much easier to slice.

*Trim all the fat and sinew from the meat and cut it across the grain.*

## PEELING PRAWNS

Don't throw prawn heads and shells away but reserve them for use in stocks. They can be stored in the freezer for up to 6 months.

*To peel prawns, break off the head then snap the shell away from the underbody. Depending on the recipe, either leave the tail intact or remove it by gently squeezing it off the body.*

*Cut down the back of the prawn with a sharp knife, then gently remove the vein.*

## HANDLING CHILLIES

Take great care when chopping or seeding chillies. Capsaicin, the pungent substance that gives chillies their hot taste, can cause severe skin irritation and remains active even in dried chillies. Wear rubber gloves and handle the chilli, especially the membrane and seeds, as little as possible. Don't touch your face, eyes or any other sensitive part of your body. Immediately after preparing chillies, wash the gloves, your hands and the board and utensils. If you like a hot flavour, leave the seeds and membrane (the hottest parts) in, but for a milder flavour, remove them.

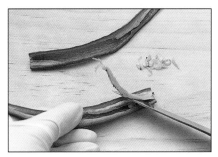

*To seed a chilli, use a sharp knife to cut off the stalk, slit open the pod and scrape out the central membrane and seeds.*

## PREPARING VEGETABLES

A number of vegetables are used time and time again in Asian recipes. The way they are prepared depends on the dish. Some common methods are shown here.

*Fresh ginger should be peeled, then grated, cut crossways into thin slices or, for shredded ginger, sliced lengthways and cut into very thin strips.*

*Use the white part only of lemon grass. If used whole in a recipe, bruise it with the back of a knife to release the flavour.*

Many fresh herbs are essential in Asian cooking. Wrap any leftover herbs in a damp paper towel and refrigerate them in a sealed plastic bag in the vegetable crisper for up to a week.

# GLOSSARY

Today many of the herbs, spices, vegetables and other items needed to create authentic Asian dishes are readily available, often in local supermarkets. The more unusual ingredients can be found in Asian food stores.

## ASIAN GREENS

BOK CHOY, also known as *Chinese chard* and *Chinese white cabbage*, has fleshy white stems and leaf ribs and green flat leaves. It has a slightly mustardy taste. Separate the leaves, wash well and drain. The white stems can be sliced thinly and eaten raw. Look for firm stems and unblemished leaves. A smaller type is called *baby bok choy* or *Shanghai bok choy*.

CHINESE CABBAGE, also known as *celery cabbage* and *napa cabbage*, has a long shape and closely packed broad, pale green leaves with wide white stems. It has a delicate mustard-like flavour. This is the vegetable which is always used in cabbage rolls and Kim Chi.

CHOY SUM, also known as *Chinese flowering cabbage*, is slimmer than bok choy and has smooth green leaves and pale green stems with clusters of tiny yellow flowers on the tips of the inner shoots. The leaves and flowers cook quickly and have a light, sweet mustard flavour; the stems are crunchy and juicy.

GAI LARN, also known as *Chinese broccoli* or *Chinese kale*, has smooth, round stems sprouting large dark green leaves and small, white flowers. The juicy stems, trimmed of most of their leaves, are the piece of the plant which is most commonly eaten. Gai larn has a similar flavour to Western broccoli, but without the characteristic large flower heads.

## BAMBOO SHOOTS

Crunchy in texture and with a subtle, refreshing taste, these are the edible young shoots of certain types of bamboo. Spring bamboo shoots are pale, fibrous and chunky; winter shoots are thinner with a finer texture and more pronounced flavour. Fresh bamboo shoots are hard to get and, if not already prepared, must be peeled then parboiled to remove toxic hydrocyanic acid— boil whole or in chunks for 5 minutes or more until they no longer taste bitter. Canned and bottled bamboo shoots are the ones most often used.

## BANANA LEAVES

The large flexible leaves of the banana plant are used throughout Asia to wrap foods for steaming or baking. They keep the food moist and impart a mild flavour. Remove the thick central stalk, rinse the leaves well and blanch in boiling water to soften. Foil can be used instead.

## BARBECUED CHINESE PORK

Also known as *cha siew*, these are strips of pork fillet which have been marinated in five spice powder, soy sauce, sugar and red colouring (usually from annatto seeds) then barbecued over charcoal.

## BASIL

Three varieties of basil are used in Asian cooking; all of which are very aromatic. If any are unavailable, substitute fresh sweet basil or fresh coriander in cooked dishes and fresh mint in salads.

THAI BASIL (*bai horapha*) has slightly serrated green leaves on purple stems. It has a sweet anise flavour and is used in stir-fries, red and green curries, shredded in salads and as a garnish for soups.

LEMON BASIL (*bai manglaek*) has small green leaves with a lemony scent and peppery flavour. It is usually sprinkled over salads or used in soups. Its seeds (*luk manglak*) are used in desserts and drinks.

PURPLE or HOLY BASIL (*bai kaphrao*) has narrow, dark, purple-reddish tinged leaves with a pungent, clove-like taste. It is added to stir-fries and strong flavoured curries.

## BLACK BEANS

One of the most popular flavours in the cooking of southern China, black beans are dried soy beans that have been cooked and fermented with salt and spices. They are soft with a sharp, salty taste. Wash before use and lightly crush or chop to release the aroma. Black beans are available in cans or packets; once opened, refrigerate in an airtight container.

## BLACK FUNGUS

Also known as cloud ear, this tree fungus has little flavour of its own, but is valued for its crunchy texture. It is most commonly available in its dried form, which looks like wrinkled black paper. Before use, soak in warm water for 15–30 minutes, until the fungus swells to about five times its size.

## CANDLENUTS

These hard, waxy, cream-coloured nuts are similar in shape to macadamia nuts, but have a drier texture. Roasted, then ground, they are used to thicken and enrich curries and sauces. They should be stored in the freezer to prevent them becoming rancid. Candlenuts should not be eaten raw as the oil is thought to be toxic. They are quite safe once cooked.

## CARDAMOM

This very aromatic spice of Indian origin is available as whole pods, whole seeds or ground. The pale green oval pods, each up to 1.5 cm (⁵⁄₈ inch) long, are tightly packed with sweetly fragrant brown or black seeds. When using whole pods, lightly bruise them before adding to the dish.

## CHILLIES, DRIED

CHILLI FLAKES are dried red chillies that have been crushed, usually with the seeds (leaving in the seeds increases the hotness). Store in a cool, dark place in an airtight container.

COMMON DRIED RED CHILLIES will vary in size and degree of heat, depending on which type has been dried (it is not usually specified). Soak in hot water until soft, then drain well before adding to dishes. If preferred, remove the seeds before soaking to reduce the fieriness. The tiny chillies are very hot.

CHILLI POWDER is made by finely grinding dried red chillies and can vary in hotness from mild to fiery. Chilli flakes can be substituted, but not Mexican chilli powder, which is mixed with cumin.

## CHILLIES, FRESH

BIRD'S EYE CHILLIES are the hottest chillies of all. From 1–3 cm (¹⁄₂–1¹⁄₄ inches) long, they are available fresh, dried or pickled in brine.

SMALL RED CHILLIES, approximately 5 cm (2 inches long) and also very hot, are the chillies used to make chilli powder and chilli flakes.

MEDIUM CHILLIES, 10–15 cm (4–6 inches) long, are the most commonly used in Indonesian and Malaysian cooking. Long thin chillies, these are hot but not overpowering.

LARGE RED AND GREEN CHILLIES, 15–20 cm (6–8 inches) long, are thicker than medium chillies. The ripe red ones are very hot.

## COCONUT CREAM AND MILK

COCONUT CREAM, also known as thick coconut milk, is extracted from the flesh of fresh coconuts and has a thick, almost spreadable consistency. It is very rich.

COCONUT MILK is extracted from fresh coconut flesh after the cream has been pressed out and has a much thinner consistency. Once opened, the milk or cream does not keep, so freeze any leftovers. (Coconut milk is not the clear, watery liquid found in the centre of fresh coconuts—this is coconut water or coconut juice.)

## CORIANDER

Also known as *cilantro* (in the United States) and *Chinese parsley*, all parts of this aromatic plant—seeds, leaves, stem and root—can be eaten. The leaves add an earthy, peppery flavour to curries and are used in salads and as a garnish, and the stems and roots are ground for curry pastes. Dried coriander cannot be used instead. Store a bunch of fresh coriander by standing in a glass of water, tying a plastic bag over the top of the plant and glass and refrigerating.

## CRISP FRIED GARLIC AND ONION

These are very thin slices of garlic cloves and onions or red Asian shallots that that have been deep-fried until crisp. They are used as a garnish, and can be added to peanut sauce. Available in packets or they can be prepared at home (see page 131).

## CUMIN

These small, pale brown, aromatic seeds have a warm, earthy flavour. In its ground form cumin is an essential component of curry pastes and many other spice mixes. Black cumin is smaller and darker than common cumin and sweeter in taste.

## CURRY LEAVES

These small, shiny, pointed leaves from a tree native to Asia have a spicy fragrance and are used in southern India, Sri Lanka and Malaysia to impart a distinctive flavour to curries and vegetable dishes. Use as you would bay leaves, and remove before serving.

## DAIKON

Much used in Japanese and Chinese cooking, some varieties of this carrot-shaped white radish can grow up to 30 cm (12 inches) long. It has a similar taste and texture to ordinary radish and is grated and added to stewed dishes or mixed with finely chopped chillies as a relish.

## DASHI

Made from dried kelp (*kombu*) and dried fish (*bonito*), this is the basic stock used in Japanese cooking. It is available as granules or a powder which are dissolved in hot water to make up stock.

## EGGPLANT (AUBERGINE)

Native to Asia, eggplants come in a variety of shapes, sizes and colours. Tiny PEA EGGPLANTS are small, fat, green balls which grow in clusters and can be bitter in flavour. They are used whole in Thai curries or raw in salads.

SLENDER EGGPLANTS, also called *baby* and *Japanese eggplants*, are used in Indian curries and vegetarian cooking, where they readily absorb the flavours; the common eggplant used in Western cooking can be substituted.

## FENUGREEK

An important ingredient in Indian cooking, the dried seeds from this plant of the pea family are small, oblong and orange-brown. They are usually gently dry-fried, then ground and added to a curry paste. In Sri Lanka a few seeds are often used whole in seafood curries. Use sparingly, as the flavour can be bitter.

## FISH SAUCE

This thin, clear, brown, salty sauce, with its characteristic 'fishy' smell and pungent flavour, is an important ingredient in Thai, Vietnamese, Laotian and Cambodian cooking. It is made from prawns (shrimp) or small fish that have been fermented in the sun. Its strong flavour diminishes when cooked with other ingredients.

## FIVE SPICE POWDER

This fragrant, ready-mixed ground spice blend is used extensively in Chinese cooking. It contains star anise, Szechwan peppercorns, fennel, cloves and cinnamon. Use sparingly, as it can overpower lesser flavours.

## FLOURS

ASIAN RICE FLOUR is ground from short-grain rice. It has a fine, light texture and is used in noodles, pastries and sweets. It gives a crunch to fried foods if used in a batter or as a coating.
ATTA FLOUR, also known as *chapatti flour*, is a finely milled, low-gluten, soft-textured, wholemeal wheat flour used for making Indian flatbreads, especially parathas and chapattis. Plain wholemeal flour can be used instead—sift first and discard the bran—but may result in heavier, coarser bread.
BESAN is a pale yellow, finely milled flour made from dried chickpeas (garbanzo beans). Used in Indian cooking to make batters, doughs, dumplings and pastries, it has a slightly nutty aroma and taste. It is unleavened, so produces a heavy texture.

## GALANGAL

Galangal root is similar in appearance to its close relative ginger, but it is a pinkish colour and has a distinct peppery flavour.

Use fresh galangal if possible. When handling take care not to get the juice on your clothes or hands, as it stains. Dried galangal, sold in slices, must be soaked in hot water before it can be used. Galangal can also be bought sliced and bottled in brine. Galangal powder is also known as Laos powder.

## GARAM MASALA

This is a mixture of ground spices which usually includes cinnamon, black pepper, coriander, cumin, cardamom, cloves and mace or nutmeg, although it can sometimes be made with mostly hot spices or with just the more fragrant spices. Commercially made mixtures are available, but garam masala is best freshly made (see page 127). Unlike other spice mixtures, it is often added close to the end of the cooking time.

## GARLIC

Garlic is used in large quantities in all Asian cooking except Japanese. Asian varieties are often smaller and more potent. Pickled garlic is used as a garnish and relish.

## GARLIC CHIVES

Also known as *Chinese chives*, these thick, flat, garlic-scented chives are stronger in flavour than the slender variety used in Western cooking. The plump flowerbud is edible.

## GINGER

This spicy tasting root, used fresh, is an indispensable ingredient in every Asian cuisine. Look for firm, unwrinkled roots and store them in a plastic bag in the refrigerator. The brown skin is usually peeled off before use. Ground ginger cannot be substituted for fresh.

## GOLDEN MOUNTAIN SAUCE

This thin, salty, spicy sauce is made from soy beans and is used as a flavouring in Thai cooking.

## HOISIN SAUCE

From China, this thick, red-brown sauce is made from soy beans, garlic, sugar and spices and has a biting, sweet-spicy flavour. It is used in cooking and as a dipping sauce, usually with meat and poultry dishes.

## KECAP MANIS

Also known as sweet soy sauce, this thick, dark, sweet soy sauce is used in Indonesian cooking as a seasoning and condiment, particularly with satays. If it is not available, a substitute can be made by gently simmering 1 cup (250 ml/8 oz) dark soy sauce with 6 tablespoons treacle and 3 tablespoons soft brown sugar until the sugar has completely dissolved.

## LEMON GRASS

This long, grass-like herb has a citrus aroma and taste. Trim the base, remove the tough outer layers and finely slice, then chop or pound the white interior. For pastes and salads, use the tender, white portion just above the root. The whole stem, trimmed, washed thoroughly and bruised with the back of a knife, can be added to simmering curries and soups (remove before serving). Dried lemon grass is rather flavourless so it is better to use lemon rind, although this will not duplicate the unique flavour.

## MISO

A staple of the Japanese diet, this is a protein-rich, thick, fermented paste made from soy beans and a variety of other ingredients, including wheat, rice or barley. It has a pungent, wine-like taste. The many varieties include red, brown, light brown, yellow and white, each having a distinctive flavour and varying in texture from smooth to chunky. Lighter coloured miso is usually milder and sweeter. Miso is used in soups, sauces, marinades and dips. Can only be bought from Asian food and health stores.

## MUSHROOMS

### CHINESE DRIED MUSHROOMS,
also called *Chinese dried black mushrooms,* grow on fallen decaying trees. Their distinctive woody, smoky taste is intensified by the drying process and they are rarely eaten fresh.

### STRAW MUSHROOMS
are named for their growing environment—straw—and are cultivated throughout Asia. They have globe-shaped caps, are stemless and have a musty flavour. They are available in cans but need to be drained and rinsed before use.

### SHIITAKE MUSHROOMS
are closely related to the Chinese black mushroom and are the most commonly used mushrooms in Japan. They have a rich smoky flavour, are grown on the bark of a type of oak tree, and are used fresh and dried. The fresh mushroom has a fleshy, golden-brown cap and a woody stem. Only buy shiitake mushrooms as you need them, as they tend to become slimy when stored in the refrigerator.

## NOODLES

### DRIED MUNG BEAN VERMICELLI,
also known as *cellophane noodles* and *glass noodles,* are wiry, threadlike, translucent noodles made from mung beans. They are tough and difficult to break and may need to be soaked in warm water so they can be cut into shorter lengths for boiling or adding to stir-fries. Small bundles of unsoaked noodles can be deep-fried for use as a garnish.

### DRIED RICE STICK NOODLES
are short, translucent flat noodles. They need to be soaked in hot water until soft, then cooked briefly in boiling water until just tender.

### DRIED RICE VERMICELLI
are thin translucent noodles. They need to be soaked in hot water until tender, then drained thoroughly before being used in stir-fries and soups. Small bundles of unsoaked noodles, quickly deep-fried until they expand, can be used as a garnish.

### DRIED SOBA (BUCKWHEAT) NOODLES
are a speciality of northern Japan. These are beige-coloured noodles, made from a mixture of buckwheat and wheat flours; some are even lightly flavoured with green tea or beetroot. They are cooked in simmering water, then rinsed in cold water to cool before use. The noodles are served either hot in a broth or cold with a dipping sauce.

### FRESH EGG NOODLES
are made from egg and wheat flour and are pale yellow. Before use they need to be shaken apart and cooked in boiling water until tender and then drained well. Fresh egg noodles are sold in a range of widths. The noodles are dusted lightly with flour before packing to stop them sticking together. Store in the refrigerator.

### FRESH RICE NOODLES
are made from a thin dough of rice flour. This is steamed, giving it a firm, jellylike texture, then lightly oiled

and packaged ready for use—the pearly white noodles need only to be rinsed in hot water to loosen and separate, then drained. They come in thick or thin varieties, or in a sheet that can be cut. Used in stir-fries or added to simmering dishes near the end of cooking. Store in the refrigerator.

### HARUSAME NOODLES
are very fine, white, almost transparent Japanese noodles. They are made from mung bean flour and are very similar to dried mung bean vermicelli—use in the same way.

### HOKKIEN NOODLES,
also known as *Fukkien* and *Singapore noodles,* are thick, yellow, rubbery-textured noodles made from wheat flour. They are packaged cooked and lightly oiled and need no preparation before use—simply stir-fry or add to soups or salads. Store in the refrigerator.

### POTATO STARCH NOODLES,
also known as *Korean vermicelli,* are long, fine, green-brown, translucent dried noodles. Cook in rapidly boiling water for about 5 minutes or until plump and gelatinous; overcooking will make them gluggy.

SHANGHAI NOODLES are white noodles made from wheat flour and water, similar to the somen noodles of Japan. They can be thick or thin. Cook in boiling water before use. Fresh noodles are dusted lightly with flour before packing to stop them sticking together. Store in the refrigerator. Dried wheat flour noodles are also available.

SHIRATAKI NOODLES are a basic ingredient in the Japanese dish sukiyaki. Thin, translucent and jelly-like, they are made from the starchy root of a plant known in Japan as devil's tongue. They have a crunchy texture, but little flavour and are available fresh or dried. Store the fresh noodles in the refrigerator.

SOMEN NOODLES are fine, white, dried wheat flour noodles used in Japanese cooking. Before use, cook in boiling water for 1 to 2 minutes, then rinse in cold water.

UDON NOODLES are white, wheat flour noodles used in Japanese cooking. They may be round or flat. Cook in boiling water or miso soup before use. Udon noodles are used in Japanese soups and simmered dishes, or can be braised and served with a sauce.

## NORI

This is the most common form of dried seaweed used in Japanese and Korean cooking. It comes in paper-thin sheets, plain or roasted. Before use it can be toasted lightly over a naked flame to freshen and produce a nutty flavour. Keep in an airtight container or in the freezer.

## OKRA

Also known as *ladies' finger*, this vegetable of African origin is a narrow, 5-sided seed pod, pointed at one end and containing small white seeds; it has a gelatinous quality when it is cooked. It is much used in Indian cooking where it is added to curries and stir-fries, stuffed with spices and deep-fried, or pickled.

## OYSTER SAUCE

This is a thick, smooth, deep brown sauce with a rich, salty, slightly sweet flavour. Although it is made from oysters and soy sauce, it does not have a fishy taste.

## PALM SUGAR

Made from the boiled down sap of several kinds of palm tree, including the palmyra palm and the sugar palm of India, palm sugar ranges in colour from pale golden to deep brown. It is sold in block form or in jars. Palm sugar is thick and crumbly and can be grated or gently melted before use. Soft brown sugar can be used as a substitute.

## PAWPAW, GREEN

Green pawpaw is an underripe pawpaw. It is commonly used in Asian salads and some soups, or as a snack with sugar and chilli. To shred green pawpaw, peel and slice finely. Sometimes lightly blanched before shredding.

## PLUM SAUCE

This sweet-sour, jam-like sauce is used in Chinese cooking and as a dip with fried meats and snacks. It is made from plums, garlic, ginger, sugar, vinegar and spices.

## RICE WINE

CHINESE RICE WINE, also known as *Shaosing,* is amber-coloured with a rich, sweetish taste. Dry sherry can be substituted, but grape wines are not suitable.

MIRIN is a golden-coloured, sweetened rice wine. Sweet sherry can be substituted.

SAKE is a clear-coloured Japanese liquor made from fermented rice. It should be used within a year of manufacture and, once a bottle is opened, as soon as possible or it will begin to lose its flavour.

## RICE VINEGAR

This clear, pale yellow, mild and sweet-tasting vinegar is made from fermented rice. Diluted white wine vinegar or cider vinegar can be substituted.

## SAFFRON POWDER AND THREADS

Made from the dried, thread-like stigmas of the saffron crocus, this costly spice adds a vivid yellow colour and subtle flavour to food. It is available as bright orange threads (sealed in small glass jars or tiny plastic packets) or ground into powder (the powder is often adulterated and of inferior quality). Saffron threads are usually soaked in a little warm water before use, then squeezed out to release the colour into the water. The threads and liquid are then both added to the dish to give the characteristic saffron colouring.

## SAMBAL OELEK

This is a hot paste made from fresh red chillies, mashed and mixed with salt. It is used as a relish in Indonesian and Malaysian cooking and can be used as a substitute for fresh chillies in most recipes. Covered, it will keep for months in the refrigerator.

## SESAME OIL

This dark amber, very aromatic oil is pressed from toasted white sesame seeds and has a strong, rich, nutty flavour. It is used as a flavouring in Chinese, Korean and Japanese dishes and is not used for frying. Store in a cool dark place, but not in the refrigerator where it will turn cloudy. Cold-pressed sesame oil, pressed from the raw seed, has little flavour and cannot be used as a substitute.

## SESAME SEEDS

The tiny, oval, oil-rich seeds of an annual herb, sesame seeds are used throughout Asia for their flavour and their high protein content.

WHITE SESAME SEEDS are the most common. Toasted and crushed, they are an essential ingredient in Japanese and Korean dressings, dipping sauces and marinades. Whole seeds are used as a garnish for both savoury and sweet dishes and breads, and pressed seeds are made into a variety of pastes. Japanese sesame seeds are plumper and have a nuttier flavour than other sesame seeds.

BLACK SESAME SEEDS have a more earthy taste. They are used in sesame and seaweed sprinkle, a Japanese condiment, and in some Chinese desserts.

## SHALLOTS, RED ASIAN

Small reddish-purple onions, these grow in bulbs, like garlic, and are sold in segments that look like large cloves of garlic. They have a concentrated flavour and are easy to slice and grind. If unavailable, substitute French shallots or brown or red onions.

## SHRIMP PASTE

Also known as *blachan,* this type of shrimp paste is used in the cooking of Thailand, Malaysia and Indonesia. It is made from prawns or shrimps that have been dried, salted and pounded. Sold in blocks, it has a very pungent odour and, when opened, should be wrapped in plastic, sealed in an airtight container and stored in the refrigerator or freezer (this is to reduce the smell as the paste itself does not require refrigeration). Use sparingly; always roast or fry before adding to a dish.

BAGOONG, also known as shrimp sauce, is a soft, thick paste made from shrimps or prawns that have been salted and fermented in earthenware pots. It has a strong odour and taste, and is used in cooking and as a condiment, particularly in the Philippines.

## SNAKE BEANS

Also called *long beans* and *yard-long beans*, this legume grows wild in tropical Africa, where it probably originated. Growing to 38 cm (15 inches) and more long, with a crunchy texture and similar taste to green beans, they are available in two varieties: pale green with slightly fibrous flesh, and darker green with firmer flesh. Use when as fresh as possible; just snip off the ends and cut into bite-sized pieces. Stringless green beans can be used instead.

## SOY SAUCE

Soy sauce is made from fermented soy beans, roasted grain (usually wheat, but sometimes barley or rice) and salt. Dark-coloured with a rich, salty flavour, it is widely used in Asian cooking, and is essential for flavour and colour in many dishes.

JAPANESE SOY SAUCE, also known as *shoyu,* is less salty and much lighter and sweeter than standard soy sauce. Because it is naturally brewed, it must be refrigerated after opening.

## SPRING ONIONS

Also called *green onions* and *scallions*, these are immature onions which are pulled before the bulb has started to form and sold in bunches with the roots intact. Discard the roots and base of the stem, and wash the stem leaves well before use. Spring onions add colour and a mild onion flavour and they need little cooking.

## STAR ANISE

The dried, star-shaped seed pod of a tree native to China, star anise adds a distinctive aniseed taste to long-simmered meat and poultry dishes and is one of the components of five spice powder. Available whole or ground.

## TAMARIND

The tropical tamarind tree bears fruit in pods like large, brown beans. The fruit is tart-tasting and has fibrous flesh and a flat stone at the centre. An essential flavour in many Asian dishes, tamarind is available in bottles as tamarind concentrate (also known as tamarind purée), a rich brown liquid, and as blocks of compressed pulp that has to be soaked, kneaded and seeded.

## TOFU

Also called *bean curd*, tofu is a processed extract of soy beans. It is an excellent source of protein, and is available fresh or deep-fried. FRESH TOFU comes in two forms: a soft, white variety, also known as *silken tofu*, which is cut into cubes and used in Japanese dishes; and a firmer variety which is cut into cubes, wedges or slices and deep-fried. Both are available in blocks sealed in plastic; once opened, store in the fridge in water (change daily) and use within a few days.

TOFU POUCHES, also known as *inari,* are deep-fried, thin slices of tofu, crisp on the outside and dry on the inside, that can be cut open to form bags. In Japan inari are stuffed with vegetables or vinegar-seasoned rice; they can also be added whole or shredded to soups and other dishes.

TOFU PUFFS are cubes of tofu that have been deep-fried until they are puffed and golden.

## TURMERIC

This is a bitter-tasting spice which comes from the root of a plant related to ginger. It is used for its intense, bright yellow-orange colour and, dried and ground, it is the main ingredient in many curry powders. The fresh root is used in the same way as fresh ginger root. Store in a plastic bag in the refrigerator.

## VIETNAMESE MINT

Also called *laksa leaf* and *Cambodian mint*, this trailing herb with narrow, pointed, pungent-tasting

leaves does not belong to the mint family, despite its common name. Its flavour resembles coriander but slightly sharper, and it is eaten raw in salads.

## WASABI

Also known as Japanese horseradish, this is a pungent paste made from the knobbly green root of the wasabi, a plant native to Japan. It is used as a condiment with seafoods and is extremely hot, so use sparingly.

## WATER CHESTNUTS

These white-fleshed roots of a variety of water grass are prized for their semi-sweet taste and crisp texture, which is retained when cooked. They are used throughout China and Southeast Asia in both savoury and sweet dishes. Available canned and sometimes fresh; cut off the woody base, peel away papery skin, and cover in water to stop discolouring.

## WATERCRESS

Introduced into Asia by the British, its peppery flavour is added to soups and steamed vegetables in Chinese cooking, and it is used in salads in Thailand, Laos and Vietnam and as a garnish in Japan.

## WRAPPERS

These are thin pieces of dough used to wrap bite-sized savoury fillings. They are available fresh and frozen; defrost before use. When filling, work with one at a time and keep the others covered with a damp cloth to prevent them from drying out.

WON TON WRAPPERS are thin squares of a wheat flour and egg dough.

SPRING ROLL WRAPPERS are square or round, and made from a wheat flour and egg dough.

GOW GEE WRAPPERS are round and made from a wheat flour and water dough.

DRIED RICE PAPER WRAPPERS are paper-thin, and made from a dough of rice flour, water and salt. Brush with water before use to make them pliable.

# CHINA

Chinese cuisine uses the freshest meats and
vegetables in an endless variety of ways
to create dishes in perfect balance. The
Cantonese cooking of the south makes use of
the abundant natural ingredients, steamed
or stir-fried over high heat and flavoured with
just a little soy sauce, ginger or spring onion.
Peking cuisine struggles with the harsher
climate and geography of the north, but
the result is wonderfully warming hotpots,
dumplings and the famous Peking duck.
Szechwan food is flavoured with vibrant
chillies and spices, while ingredients
in Shanghai are braised slowly to create
rich meat and fish dishes.

PRAWN OMELETTE
WITH OYSTER SAUCE

Finely slice the soaked
mushrooms.
(Everything should be
ready before you begin
cooking.)

Swirl the wok so the
egg mixture coats the
sides. (Make sure the
wok is extremely hot
before adding the egg
as the heat produces
the traditionally lacy
appearance of the
omelette.)

Divide the omelette into
4 or 5 sections with a
spatula, and turn each
section over to cook the
other side.

Above: Prawn
Omelette with
Oyster Sauce

# PRAWN OMELETTE
# WITH OYSTER SAUCE

•

**Preparation time:** 30 minutes
**Total cooking time:** 25 minutes
Serves 4

☆ ☆ ☆

2 dried Chinese mushrooms
400 g (12²/₃ oz) raw prawns
3 tablespoons oil
5 cm (2 inch) piece fresh ginger,
   finely grated
¹/₂ cup (125 g/4 oz) drained, canned
   bamboo shoots, roughly chopped
6 spring onions, chopped
5 eggs
2 tablespoons water
¹/₂ teaspoon salt
¹/₂ teaspoon ground white pepper
3 tablespoons oyster sauce
2 tablespoons soy sauce
2 tablespoons Chinese rice wine
2 teaspoons cornflour
1 tablespoon water
finely sliced spring onion, for garnish

•

1 Soak the mushrooms in hot water for
20 minutes or until softened; drain and slice
finely, discarding the hard stem.
2 Peel and devein the prawns; roughly chop the
meat.
3 Heat 1 tablespoon of the oil in a wok and
stir-fry the ginger and prawn meat over very high
heat for 2 minutes; transfer to a plate. Add the
bamboo shoots, spring onion and mushrooms
and stir-fry for 1 minute. Transfer to a plate and
wipe the wok clean with paper towels.
4 Beat the eggs, water, salt and pepper in a bowl
until foamy. Add the remaining oil to the wok,
swirling it around to coat the base and sides.
Heat the wok until it is extremely hot and the oil
is slightly smoking. Give the egg mixture a quick
whisk again and pour it into the very hot wok,
swirling the wok a little so the egg mixture coats
the side to ¹/₂ cm (¹/₄ inch) thickness. Cook for
1 minute. Using a slotted spoon to drain away
any juices, carefully and quickly spoon the
prawn and bamboo shoot mixture over the
omelette. Gently lift the edge of the omelette
with a spatula and tilt the wok so some of the
uncooked egg from the centre runs underneath.
Repeat this at a couple of different places around
the omelette. Cook for about 2 minutes until the
base is a crisp brown and has set. Divide the
omelette into 4 or 5 sections, cutting it with the
spatula, and turn each section over to cook the
other side. When each section is lightly set
underneath, transfer it to a platter, arranging the
slices as they were in the wok.
5 Add the oyster sauce, soy sauce and rice wine
to the wok. Mix the cornflour and water and add
to the wok, stirring constantly until the sauce
boils and thickens slightly. Spoon over the
omelette, garnish with spring onion and serve.

NUTRITION PER SERVE: Protein 25 g; Fat 20 g;
Carbohydrate 10 g; Dietary Fibre 1 g; Cholesterol 425 mg;
1415 kJ (335 cal)

## CANTONESE LEMON CHICKEN

•

*Preparation time:* 15 minutes
  +10 minutes standing
*Total cooking time:* 25 minutes
*Serves 4*

★ ★

500 g (1 lb) chicken breast fillets
1 egg yolk, lightly beaten
1 tablespoon water
2 teaspoons soy sauce
2 teaspoons dry sherry
3 teaspoons cornflour
¹/₂ cup (60 g/2 oz) cornflour, extra
2¹/₂ tablespoons plain flour
oil, for deep-frying

•

*Lemon Sauce*
¹/₃ cup (80 ml/2³/₄ fl oz) fresh lemon
  juice
2 tablespoons water
2 tablespoons sugar
1 tablespoon dry sherry
2 teaspoons cornflour
1 tablespoon water, extra
4  spring onions, very finely sliced

•

1 Cut the chicken into long strips, about 1 cm (¹/₂ inch) wide, and then set aside. Combine the egg, water, soy sauce, sherry and cornflour in a small bowl and mix until smooth. Pour the egg mixture over the chicken, mixing well, and set aside for 10 minutes.

2 Sift the extra cornflour and plain flour together onto a plate. Roll each piece of chicken in the flour, coating each piece evenly, and shake off excess. Place the chicken in a single layer on a plate ready to be fried.

3 Heat the oil for deep-frying in a wok or pan. It is hot enough to use when a cube of bread turns brown in it in 30 seconds. Carefully lower about 4 pieces of chicken into the oil and cook until golden brown. Remove the chicken with a slotted spoon and drain it on paper towels. Repeat with the remaining chicken. Let the chicken stand while preparing the sauce.

4 To make Lemon Sauce: Combine the lemon juice, water, sugar and sherry in a small pan. Bring to the boil over medium heat, stirring until the sugar dissolves. Stir the cornflour into the extra tablespoon water and mix to a smooth paste; add it to the lemon juice mixture, stirring constantly until the sauce boils and thickens. Set the sauce aside.

5 Just before serving, reheat the oil in the wok to very hot; add all the chicken pieces and fry for 2 minutes until very crisp and a rich golden brown. Remove the chicken with a slotted spoon and drain well on paper towels. Pile the chicken onto a serving plate, drizzle over the sauce, sprinkle with spring onion and serve immediately.

NOTE: The first frying can be done several hours in advance.

*NUTRITION PER SERVE WITH SAUCE: Protein 30 g; Fat 10 g; Carbohydrate 40 g; Dietary Fibre 1 g; Cholesterol 105 mg; 1515 kJ (360 cal)*

CHINESE RICE WINE
*China's best known rice wine is Shaosing, from Chekiang (Zhejiang) province in the north-east of the country, where for more than 2000 years it has been made from a mixture of glutinous rice, millet, yeast and local spring water. In China it is known as 'carved flower', for the pattern on the urns in which it is stored, and also as 'daughter's wine', because traditionally some is put away at the birth of a daughter to be drunk at her wedding. Shaosing is aged for at least 10 years and sometimes as long as 100 years. As a drink to accompany food it should be served warm in small cups without handles.*

*Above: Cantonese Lemon Chicken*

*Above: Beef with Mandarin*

## BEEF WITH MANDARIN

•

*Preparation time:* 15 minutes
+ 15 minutes standing
*Total cooking time:* 5 minutes
*Serves 4*

★

350 g (11¼ oz) rib eye steak, finely
   sliced
2 teaspoons soy sauce
2 teaspoons dry sherry
1 teaspoon chopped fresh ginger
1 teaspoon sesame oil
1 tablespoon peanut oil
¼ teaspoon ground white pepper
2 teaspoons finely chopped dried
   mandarin or tangerine peel
2 teaspoons soy sauce, extra
1½ teaspoons caster sugar
1½ teaspoons cornflour
⅓ cup (80 ml/2¾ fl oz) beef stock

1 Place the beef in a bowl. Mix the soy sauce, sherry, ginger and sesame oil together; stir through the meat to coat it. Set aside for 15 minutes.
2 Heat the peanut oil in a wok or heavy-based frying pan, swirling gently to coat the base and sides. Add the beef and stir-fry over high heat for 2 minutes, until meat changes colour.
3 Add the pepper, peel, extra soy sauce and sugar; stir-fry briefly.
4 Dissolve the cornflour in a little of the stock; add the remaining stock. Add the cornflour mixture to the wok and stir until the sauce boils and thickens. Serve with rice.

*NUTRITION PER SERVE: Protein 30 g; Fat 15 g; Carbohydrate 3 g; Dietary Fibre 0 g; Cholesterol 70 mg; 1025 kJ (245 cal)*

## CHICKEN AND SWEET CORN SOUP

•

*Preparation time:* 15 minutes
*Total cooking time:* 10 minutes
*Serves* 4

★

200 g (6½ oz) chicken breast fillets
1 teaspoon salt
2 egg whites
3 cups (750 ml/24 fl oz) chicken stock
1 cup (250 g/8 oz) creamed corn
1 tablespoon cornflour
2 teaspoons soy sauce
2 spring onions, diagonally sliced

•

1 Wash the chicken under cold water and pat dry with paper towels. Place the chicken in a food processor and process until finely chopped. Add the salt.
2 Lightly beat the egg whites in a small bowl until foamy. Fold the egg whites into the chicken mince.
3 Bring the chicken stock to the boil and add the creamed corn. Dissolve the cornflour in a little water and add to the soup, stirring until the mixture thickens.
4 Reduce the heat and add the chicken mixture, breaking it up with a whisk. Allow to heat through, without boiling, for about 3 minutes. Season to taste with soy sauce. Serve immediately, sprinkled with the spring onion.

*NUTRITION PER SERVE: Protein 15 g; Fat 2 g; Carbohydrate 15 g; Dietary Fibre 2 g; Cholesterol 25 mg; 540 kJ (128 cal.)*

•

## WON TON SOUP

•

*Preparation time:* 40 minutes
*Total cooking time:* 5 minutes
*Serves* 6

★ ★

250 g (8 oz) raw prawns
4 dried Chinese mushrooms
250 g (8 oz) pork mince
1 teaspoon salt
1 tablespoon soy sauce
1 teaspoon sesame oil
2 spring onions, finely chopped
1 teaspoon grated fresh ginger
2 tablespoons finely sliced water chestnuts
1 x 250 g (8 oz) packet won ton wrappers
5 cups (1.25 litres) chicken or beef stock
4 spring onions, very finely sliced, for garnish

1 Peel, devein and finely chop the prawns.
2 Cover the mushrooms with hot water and soak them for 20 minutes. Drain and squeeze to remove excess liquid. Remove stems and chop the caps finely. Thoroughly combine the prawn meat, mushrooms, pork, salt, soy sauce, sesame oil, spring onion, ginger and water chestnuts.
3 Work with 1 won ton wrapper at a time, keeping the remainder covered with a clean, damp tea towel to stop them drying out. Place heaped teaspoons of mince mixture in the centre of each square. Moisten the edges of the wrapper, fold it in half diagonally and bring the 2 points together. Place the won tons on a plate dusted with flour to prevent sticking.
4 Cook the won tons in rapidly boiling water for 4 to 5 minutes. Bring the stock to the boil in a separate pan. Remove the won tons from the water with a slotted spoon and place them in a serving bowl. Garnish with the extra spring onion and pour the simmering stock over them. Serve immediately.
NOTE: The won tons can be prepared 1 day ahead up to Step 4 and stored, covered, in the refrigerator. Cook just before serving. A 250 g (8 oz) packet of won ton wrappers contains 60 small sheets—wrap any leftover sheets in clingwrap and freeze.

*NUTRITION PER SERVE: Protein 20 g; Fat 3 g; Carbohydrate 35 g; Dietary Fibre 0 g; Cholesterol 60 mg; 945 kJ (225 cal)*

*WON TON SOUP*

*Place a heaped teaspoon of mixture in the centre of each wrapper.*

*Moisten the edges of the wrapper, fold it in half diagonally and bring the two points together.*

*Below: Won Ton Soup (top); Chicken and Sweet Corn Soup*

it. Cover the steamer tightly and steam the scallops for 1 minute. If they aren't cooked, they may need about 30 seconds more. Remove and set aside to keep warm. Repeat with the remaining scallops. Serve at once.

*NUTRITION PER SERVE: Protein 5 g; Fat 10 g; Carbohydrate 1 g; Dietary Fibre 0 g; Cholesterol 15 mg; 510 kJ (120 cal)*

## CRYSTAL PRAWNS

*Preparation time:* 15 minutes
  + 30 minutes marinating
*Total cooking time:* 10 minutes
*Serves 4*

750 g (1¹/₂ lb) medium raw prawns
2 spring onions, roughly chopped
2 teaspoons salt
1 tablespoon cornflour
1 egg white, lightly beaten
125 g (4 oz) sugar snap peas or snow
  peas (mange tout)
1 small red pepper (capsicum)
1 tablespoon oyster sauce
2 teaspoons dry sherry
1 teaspoon cornflour, extra
1 teaspoon sesame oil
oil, for deep-frying
¹/₂ teaspoon crushed garlic
¹/₂ teaspoon finely grated fresh ginger

1 Peel and devein the prawns. Place the shells, heads and the spring onion in a pan with enough water to cover them. Bring the water to the boil; simmer, uncovered, for 15 minutes. Strain the liquid into a bowl, discarding the shells. Reserve ¹/₂ cup (125 ml/4 fl oz) of the prawn liquid. Place the prawns in a glass bowl. Add 1 teaspoon of the salt and stir briskly for a minute. Rinse under cold, running water. Repeat the procedure twice, using ¹/₂ teaspoon salt each time. Rinse the prawns thoroughly the final time. Pat dry with paper towels.
2 Combine the cornflour and egg white in a bowl, add the prawns and place in the refrigerator, covered, for 30 minutes.
3 Wash and string the sugar snap peas. Cut the red pepper into thin strips. Combine the reserved prawn liquid, oyster sauce, sherry, extra cornflour and sesame oil in a small bowl. Heat the oil in a wok and deep-fry the prawns in batches, cooking for 1 to 2 minutes or until lightly golden. Carefully remove the prawns from the oil with tongs or a slotted spoon. Drain on paper towels and keep warm.

## FRIED AND STEAMED
## SCALLOPS WITH GINGER

*Preparation time:* 10 minutes
*Total cooking time:* 10 minutes
*Serves 4 as a starter*

12 scallops attached to the shell
¹/₄ teaspoon ground white pepper
2 tablespoons soy sauce
2 tablespoons dry sherry
2 tablespoons oil
8 cm (3 inch) piece fresh ginger, shredded
1 spring onion, white part only, cut into
  long shreds

1 Sprinkle the scallops with the pepper. Mix together the soy sauce and sherry in a bowl.
2 Heat the oil in a large, heavy-based pan until very hot. Carefully add several shells, scallop-side-down, and cook for 30 seconds to sear. Turn face-up and place in a shallow dish. Repeat with the remaining scallops.
3 Sprinkle the scallops with sherry–soy mixture and scatter a few shreds of ginger and spring onion over them.
4 Fill a wok about one-third full of water and bring to a simmer. Put a steamer lined with baking paper in the wok and place 6 scallops on

*Above: Fried and Steamed Scallops with Ginger*

4 Carefully pour off all but 2 tablespoons of the oil (if you are keeping it to re-use, only use it for fish, as the prawn flavour will have permeated). Add the garlic and ginger to the wok and stir-fry for 30 seconds. Add the peas and pepper and stir-fry over high heat for 2 minutes. Add the combined sauce ingredients and cook, stirring, until the sauce boils and thickens. Add the prawns and stir to combine. Serve immediately.

NUTRITION PER SERVE: Protein 20 g; Fat 3 g; Carbohydrate 10 g; Dietary Fibre 2 g; Cholesterol 175 mg; 560 kJ (130 cal)

## CRISPY FRIED CRAB

*Preparation time:* 30 minutes
  + 2 hours freezing
  + overnight marinating
*Total cooking time:* 15 minutes
*Serves* 4 as a starter

★ ★ ★

*1 x 1 kg (2 lb) live mud crab*
*1 egg, lightly beaten*
*1 red chilli, finely sliced*
*1/2 teaspoon crushed garlic*
*1/2 teaspoon salt*
*1/4 teaspoon ground white pepper*
*oil, for deep-frying*

*Seasoning Mix*
*4 tablespoons plain flour*
*4 tablespoons rice flour*
*3 teaspoons caster sugar*
*1 teaspoon ground white pepper*

•

1 Place the crab in the freezer for 2 hours or until it is absolutely immobile and dead (this is the most humane way to kill crab or lobster).
2 Scrub the crab clean of any mossy bits. Pull back the apron from the underbelly and snap off. Twist off the legs and claws. Pull the body apart and remove the feathery gills and internal organs. Using a cleaver, chop the body into 4 pieces. Crack the claws with a good hit with the back of the cleaver.
3 Combine the egg with the chilli, garlic, salt and pepper in a large bowl. Put the crab pieces in the mixture; cover and refrigerate overnight.
4 To make Seasoning Mix: Sift all the seasoning ingredients together on a large plate. Dip all the crab segments in the seasoning and dust off excess.
5 Heat the oil in a wok and deep-fry the claws for 7 to 8 minutes, the body portions for 3 to 4 minutes and the legs for 2 minutes. Drain on paper towels and serve.
NOTE: Eat the crab with your fingers. This dish should be served on its own, without rice.

NUTRITION PER SERVE: Protein 20 g; Fat 2 g; Carbohydrate 25 g; Dietary Fibre 1 g; Cholesterol 150 mg; 810 kJ (190 cal)

*Pull back the apron from the under belly and snap it off.*

*Pull the body apart.*

*After removing the internal organs, remove the feathery gills.*

*Use the back of the cleaver to crack the claws, or you may break the blade.*

*Left: Crispy Fried Crab*

# CHILLI SPARE RIBS

•

*Preparation time:* 20 minutes
*Total cooking time:* 1 hour
*Serves* 4

★

750 g (1½ lb) pork spare ribs
1 tablespoon peanut oil
2 teaspoons finely chopped garlic
¼ cup (60 ml/2 fl oz) dry sherry
1 tablespoon chilli bean paste
   or sambal oelek
2 cups (500 ml/16 fl oz) water
2 teaspoons hoisin sauce
3 teaspoons caster sugar
1 tablespoon soy sauce,
   preferably dark

•

1 Place the pork in a large pan with water to cover. Bring to the boil, reduce heat, simmer for 5 minutes; drain well.
2 Place all the remaining ingredients and the pork ribs in a wok or deep, heavy-based pan. Cover and simmer for 45 minutes. Drain, reserving 1 cup (250 ml/8 fl oz) of liquid. Heat a clean wok or heavy-based frying pan and sear the pork pieces to brown them.
3 Add the reserved cooking liquid and cook over medium heat until it forms a glazed coating for the pork.
4 Chop the pork pieces into 3 cm (1¼ inch) pieces and serve with the sauce poured over them.

*Below: Chilli Spare Ribs*

NUTRITION PER SERVE: Protein 30 g; Fat 60 g; Carbohydrate 5 g; Dietary Fibre 1 g; Cholesterol 190 mg; 2920 kJ (695 cal)

# STIR-FRIED BEEF AND SNOW PEAS (MANGE TOUT)

•

*Preparation time:* 15 minutes
*Total cooking time:* 5 minutes
*Serves* 4

★

400 g (12⅔ oz) rump steak, finely sliced
2 tablespoons soy sauce
½ teaspoon grated fresh ginger
2 tablespoons peanut oil
200 g (6½ oz) snow peas (mange tout),
   topped and tailed
1½ teaspoons cornflour
½ cup (125 ml/4 fl oz) beef stock
1 teaspoon soy sauce, extra
¼ teaspoon sesame oil

•

1 Place the beef in a dish. Mix the soy sauce and ginger and stir through the meat to coat it.
2 Heat the oil in a wok or heavy-based frying pan, swirling gently to coat the base and sides. Add the beef and snow peas and stir-fry over high heat for 2 minutes, or until the meat changes colour.
3 Dissolve the cornflour in a little of the stock. Add the cornflour to the wok with the remaining stock, extra soy sauce and the sesame oil. Stir until the sauce boils and thickens. Serve with steamed rice.
NOTE: If time allows, place the meat in the freezer for 30 minutes before slicing. This will firm it and make slicing it finely much easier.

NUTRITION PER SERVE: Protein 25 g; Fat 15 g; Carbohydrate 5 g; Dietary Fibre 1 g; Cholesterol 65 mg; 980 kJ (235 cal)

CHILLI BEAN PASTE
*A thick, red-brown sauce made from soy beans, dried red chilli, garlic and spices, chilli bean paste has a hot, nutty, salty taste and is much used in the fiery dishes of Szechwan and Hunan in central western China. Available in jars from Asian food stores and some supermarkets. Sambal oelek has a different flavour but can be used as a substitute.*

## NOODLES WITH PRAWNS AND PORK

•

***Preparation time:*** 20 minutes
***Total cooking time:*** 10 minutes
***Serves*** 4

★

*10 large raw prawns*
*200 g (6¹/₂ oz) Chinese barbecued pork*
*500 g (1 lb) Shanghai noodles*
*¹/₄ cup (60 ml/2 fl oz) peanut oil*
*2 teaspoons finely chopped garlic*
*1 tablespoon black bean sauce*
*1 tablespoon soy sauce*
*1 tablespoon white vinegar*
*¹/₄ cup (60 ml/2 fl oz) chicken stock*
*125 g (4 oz) fresh bean sprouts,*
  *scraggly ends removed*
*3 spring onions, finely sliced*
*fresh coriander leaves, for garnish*

1 Peel and devein the prawns. Cut the pork evenly into thin slices.
2 Cook the noodles in a large pan of rapidly boiling water until just tender. Drain and set aside.
3 Heat the oil in a wok or heavy-based frying pan, swirling gently to coat the base and sides. Add the garlic and cook, stirring, until pale gold. Add the prawns and pork, and stir for 3 minutes, or until the prawns are pink. Add the noodles to the wok with the black bean sauce, soy sauce, vinegar and stock. Stir-fry over high heat until the mixture has heated through and the sauce has been absorbed.
4 Add the bean sprouts and spring onion and cook for 1 minute. Place in a serving dish and garnish with coriander.
NOTE: Barbecued pork can be bought ready-cooked from speciality Chinese stores. If you enjoy a little 'fire' in your food, add a garnish of fresh chopped chillies or a splash of chilli oil at the end of cooking.

*NUTRITION PER SERVE: Protein 35 g; Fat 30 g; Carbohydrate 100 g; Dietary Fibre 10 g; Cholesterol 105 mg; 3340 kJ (795 cal)*

*Above: Noodles with Prawns and Pork*

## CHINESE FRIED RICE

•

*Preparation time:* 15 minutes
*Total cooking time:* 10 minutes
*Serves* 4

★

2 eggs, lightly beaten
1 medium onion
4 spring onions
1 x 250 g (8 oz) piece of ham
2 tablespoons peanut oil
2 teaspoons lard, optional
1¹/₃ cups (265 g/8¹/₂ oz) long-grain rice,
    cooked and cooled (see note)
¹/₄ cup (40 g/1¹/₃ oz) frozen peas
2 tablespoons soy sauce
250 g (8 oz) cooked small prawns, peeled

•

1 Season the eggs with salt and pepper.
2 Cut the onion into 8 wedges. Cut the spring onions into short lengths on the diagonal. Cut the ham into very thin strips.
3 Heat 1 tablespoon oil in a wok or large frying pan and add the eggs, pulling the set egg towards the centre and tilting the pan to let the unset egg run to the edges. When the egg is almost set, break it up into large pieces so it resembles scrambled eggs. Transfer to a plate and set aside.

*Below: Chinese
Fried Rice*

4 Heat the remaining oil and lard in the wok, swirling to coat the base and side. Add the onion and stir-fry over high heat until it starts to turn transparent. Add the ham and stir-fry for 1 minute. Add the rice and peas and stir-fry for 3 minutes until the rice is heated through. Add the eggs, soy sauce, spring onion and prawns. Heat through and serve.
NOTE: If possible, cook the rice a day ahead and refrigerate it overnight. This makes the grains separate and means the fried rice is not gluggy.

*NUTRITION PER SERVE: Protein 30 g; Fat 20 g; Carbohydrate 55 g; Dietary Fibre 3 g; Cholesterol 250 mg; 2195 kJ (520 cal)*

•

## STIR-FRIED PRAWNS WITH LEEKS

•

*Preparation time:* 15 minutes
*Total cooking time:* 4–5 minutes
*Serves* 6

★

800 g (1 lb 10 oz) raw king prawns
2 young leeks, white parts only
1 fresh red chilli
3 cm (1¹/₄ inch) piece fresh ginger
3 tablespoons oil
2 teaspoons light soy sauce
1 tablespoon mirin
¹/₃ cup (80 ml/2³/₄ oz) chicken stock
1 teaspoon cornflour

•

1 Peel and devein the prawns, leaving the tails intact.
2 Rinse the leeks well. Cut them first into 4 cm (1¹/₂ inch) lengths and then lengthways into fine shreds. Slit open the chilli, remove and discard the seeds and cut the flesh into fine shreds. Cut the ginger into fine shreds.
3 Heat a little of the oil in a wok and stir-fry the prawns in batches until just pink; remove from the wok. Add the remaining oil and stir-fry the leek, chilli and ginger over high heat for 40 seconds, then push to one side of the wok. Return the prawns to the wok and stir-fry for about 1¹/₂ minutes, or until just cooked through.
4 Add the soy sauce and mirin to the pan. Mix the chicken stock and cornflour and pour in. Cook on high heat, stirring, until thickened. Serve immediately.

*NUTRITION PER SERVE: Protein 15 g; Fat 10 g; Carbohydrate 3 g; Dietary Fibre 1 g; Cholesterol 100 mg; 670kJ (160 cal)*

## CLAY POT CHICKEN
## AND VEGETABLES

•

**Preparation time:** 20 minutes
+ 30 minutes marinating
**Total cooking time:** 25 minutes
Serves 4

★

500 g (1 lb) chicken thigh fillets
1 tablespoon soy sauce
1 tablespoon dry sherry
6 dried Chinese mushrooms
2 small leeks
250 g (8 oz) orange sweet potato
2 tablespoons peanut oil
5 cm (2 inch) piece fresh ginger, shredded
1/2 cup (125 ml/4 fl oz) chicken stock
1 teaspoon sesame oil
3 teaspoons cornflour

•

1 Wash the chicken under cold water and pat it dry with paper towels. Cut the chicken into small pieces. Place it in a dish with the soy sauce and sherry, cover and marinate for 30 minutes in the refrigerator.
2 Cover the mushrooms with hot water and soak for 20 minutes. Drain and squeeze to remove excess liquid. Remove the stems and chop the caps into shreds. Wash the leeks thoroughly to

remove all grit. Cut the leeks and sweet potato into thin slices.
3 Drain the chicken, reserving the marinade. Heat half the oil in a wok or heavy-based frying pan, swirling it gently to coat the base and sides. Add half the chicken pieces and stir-fry briefly until seared on all sides. Transfer the chicken to a flameproof clay pot or casserole. Stir-fry the remaining chicken and add it to the clay pot.
4 Heat the remaining oil in the wok; add the leek and ginger and stir-fry for 1 minute. Add the mushrooms, remaining marinade, stock and sesame oil and cook for 2 minutes. Transfer to the clay pot with the sweet potato and cook, covered, on the top of the stove over very low heat for about 20 minutes.
5 Dissolve the cornflour in a little water and add it to the pot. Cook, stirring, until the mixture boils and thickens. Serve the chicken and vegetables at once with steamed brown or white rice or with noodles.
NOTE: Like all stews, this is best cooked 1 to 2 days ahead and stored, covered, in the refrigerator to allow the flavours to mature. It can also be frozen, but omit the sweet potato. Steam or boil the potato separately when the dish is reheating and stir it through.

*NUTRITION PER SERVE: Protein 30 g; Fat 10 g; Carbohydrate 15 g; Dietary Fibre 3 g; Cholesterol 85 mg; 1160 kJ (275 cal)*

*Above: Clay Pot Chicken and Vegetables*

*PEKING DUCK WITH MANDARIN PANCAKES*

*Remove the seeds from the cucumber and slice into matchsticks. Slice the spring onion sections and place in iced water to form brushes.*

*Roll the dough balls into circles. Lightly brush one circle with sesame oil and place another circle on top.*

*When cool enough to handle, peel the two halves of the double pancake apart.*

*Opposite page:
Peking Duck with
Mandarin Pancakes*

# PEKING DUCK WITH MANDARIN PANCAKES

•

*Preparation time:* 1 hour
+ 5 hours standing
*Total cooking time:* 1 hour 15 minutes
*Serves* 4 as a main course or 6 with other dishes

1 x 1.7 kg (3¾ lb) duck
3 litres boiling water
1 tablespoon honey
½ cup (125 ml/4 fl oz) hot water
1 Lebanese cucumber
12 spring onions
2 tablespoons hoisin sauce

•

*Mandarin Pancakes*
2½ cups (310 g/9¾ oz) plain flour
2 teaspoons caster sugar
1 cup (250 ml/8 fl oz) boiling water
1 tablespoon sesame oil

•

1 Wash the duck and remove the neck and any large pieces of fat from inside the carcass. Hold the duck over the sink and very carefully and slowly pour the boiling water over it, rotating the duck so the water scalds all the skin. You may need another kettle of boiling water at this stage.

2 Put the duck on a rack placed in a baking dish. Mix the honey and hot water together and brush 2 coats of this glaze over the duck, making sure it is entirely covered. Dry the duck, preferably by hanging in a cool, airy place for about 4 hours. Alternatively, you could use an electric fan on a cool setting, positioned a metre or so away. The skin is sufficiently dry when it feels papery.

3 Remove the seeds from the cucumber and slice the flesh into matchsticks. Cut an 8 cm (3 inch) section from the white end of each spring onion; make fine parallel cuts from the top of the section towards the white end. Place the spring onion pieces in iced water; they will open into 'brushes'.

4 Preheat the oven to hot 210°C (415°F/Gas 6–7). Roast the duck on the rack in the baking dish for 30 minutes. Turn the duck over carefully without tearing the skin; roast it for another 30 minutes. Remove the duck from the oven and let it stand for a minute or two, then place it on a warm dish.

5 To make Mandarin Pancakes: Place the flour and sugar in a medium bowl and pour over the boiling water. Stir the mixture a few times and leave until lukewarm. Knead the mixture on a lightly floured surface to make a smooth dough. Cover and set aside for 30 minutes.

6 Take 2 level tablespoons of dough; roll each one into a ball. Roll out to circles 8 cm (3 inches) in diameter. Lightly brush one of the circles with sesame oil and place the other circle on top. Re-roll to make a thin pancake about 15 cm (6 inches) in diameter. Repeat with the remaining dough and oil to make about 10 'double' pancakes.

7 Heat a frying pan and cook the pancakes one at a time. When small bubbles appear on the surface, turn the pancake over and cook the second side, pressing the surface with a clean tea towel. The pancake should puff up when done. Transfer the pancake to a plate. When cool enough to handle, peel the 2 halves of the double pancake apart. Stack them on a plate and cover them at once to prevent them drying out.

8 To serve: Finely slice the duck. Place the pancakes and duck on separate serving plates. Arrange the cucumber sticks and spring onion brushes on another serving plate. Place the hoisin sauce in a small dish. Each diner helps themselves to a pancake, spreads a little sauce on it and adds a couple of pieces of cucumber, a spring onion brush and finally a piece of duck. The pancake is then folded over into a neat envelope shape for eating.

NOTE: If you do not have a roasting rack on which to cook the duck, try a cake cooling rack, sitting in or over a baking dish.

The pancakes can be made a few hours ahead and kept covered in a cool place. Reheat briefly just before serving; you can either steam them in a colander lined with a clean tea towel or wrap them securely in aluminium foil and place in a moderate oven for 2 minutes.

*NUTRITION PER SERVE (4): Protein 45 g; Fat 15 g; Carbohydrate 75 g; Dietary Fibre 5 g; Cholesterol 200 mg; 2635 kJ (625 cal)*

# CHICKEN AND ALMONDS

•

*Preparation time:* 30 minutes
*Total cooking time:* 20 minutes
*Serves* 4

★★

1 cup (250 ml/8 fl oz) oil
125 g (4 oz) blanched almonds
1 tablespoon soy sauce
2 teaspoons cornflour
300 g (9²/₃ oz) chicken breast fillets, sliced
    diagonally
1 medium onion, chopped
1 stick celery, thinly sliced diagonally
50 g (1²/₃ oz) thin green beans, sliced
¹/₄ cup (60 g/2 oz) drained, canned
    bamboo shoots
2 cm (³/₄ inch) piece fresh ginger, grated
3 tablespoons chicken stock
2 tablespoons Chinese rice wine or
    medium sherry
2 tablespoons water
1 teaspoon sesame oil
2 teaspoons cornflour, extra
¹/₄ teaspoon salt
¹/₄ teaspoon ground white pepper

1 Heat the oil in a small pan and deep-fry the almonds for about 1 minute only, tossing them in the oil until they are a pale golden colour. Remove immediately with a slotted spoon and drain on paper towels. Reserve the oil.
2 Combine the soy sauce and cornflour and stir until smooth. Mix well with the chicken and leave for 5 minutes. Heat 2 tablespoons of the oil used to cook the almonds in a wok until it is extremely hot. Stir-fry the chicken over high heat for 2 minutes, then remove from the wok.
3 If there is very little oil in the wok, add another tablespoon of the almond oil. Reheat the wok and stir-fry the onion and celery for 4 minutes. Add the beans, bamboo shoots and ginger and cook for 1 minute further. Add the chicken stock, wine or sherry, water and sesame oil, cover and steam for 30 seconds. Combine the extra cornflour with 1 tablespoon water and mix until smooth. Stir into the sauce and bring to the boil. Return the chicken and almonds to the pan, tossing well to combine, and allow to just heat through. Season with the salt and pepper and serve immediately.

*NUTRITION PER SERVE: Protein 25 g; Fat 35 g; Carbohydrate 5 g; Dietary Fibre 4 g; Cholesterol 40 mg; 1870 kJ (445 cal)*

## MONGOLIAN INFLUENCE

*The Mongols ruled China for 100 years from the late thirteenth century. Dubbed the 'devil's horsemen', these invaders from the north were never really accepted by the Chinese, who looked down upon them as barbarians and shunned the goat's milk, smelly cheese, and strong-tasting lamb's meat they brought with them. However some dishes were adopted, notably Mongolian hotpot (in which diners dip paper-thin strips of raw lamb and other ingredients into a central bowl of simmering broth), stewed lamb dishes and poultry dishes served with full-flavoured sauces.*

*Right: Chicken and Almonds*

## MONGOLIAN LAMB

•

**Preparation time:** 15 minutes
+ 1 hour marinating
**Total cooking time:** 15 minutes
**Serves** 4

★

*1 kg (2 lb) lamb fillets*
*2 cloves garlic, crushed*
*1 tablespoon grated fresh ginger*
*1 tablespoon hoisin sauce*
*1 tablespoon sesame oil*
*1 tablespoon sesame seeds*
*2 tablespoons peanut oil*
*4 onions, cut into wedges*
*3 teaspoons cornflour*
*3 tablespoons soy sauce*
*¼ cup (60 ml/2 fl oz) sherry*

•

**1** Trim the meat of any excess fat and sinew and slice it across the grain into thin slices. Combine the garlic, ginger, hoisin sauce and sesame oil in a bowl, add the meat and stir to coat. Cover and refrigerate for 1 hour.

**2** Toast the sesame seeds in a dry pan over medium heat for 3 to 4 minutes, shaking the pan gently, until the seeds are golden brown; remove from the pan immediately to prevent burning.
**3** Heat the peanut oil in a wok or heavy-based frying pan; add the onion and stir fry over medium heat for 10 minutes or until soft and golden brown. Remove the onion from the wok and keep warm.
**4** Reheat the wok and cook the meat in batches over high heat until browned but not cooked through. Return all the meat to the wok.
**5** Mix together the cornflour, soy sauce and sherry until smooth. Add to the wok and stir-fry over high heat until the meat is cooked and the sauce has thickened.
**6** Serve the meat on a bed of the onions and sprinkle with the toasted sesame seeds.

*NUTRITION PER SERVE: Protein 60 g; Fat 25 g; Carbohydrate 10 g; Dietary Fibre 3 g; Cholesterol 165 mg; 2190 kJ (520 cal)*

*Above:*
*Mongolian Lamb*

# YUM CHA
Meaning literally 'to drink tea', this morning ritual is accompanied in tea houses throughout China with tiny steamed or fried parcels of dim sum, stuffed with fresh seafood, meats and vegetables.

### CRABMEAT DIM SIMS
In a bowl, combine 200 g (6½ oz) drained and flaked crabmeat, 250 g (8 oz) raw prawns, peeled, deveined and chopped, 4 finely chopped spring onions, 3 soaked and chopped dried Chinese mushrooms, 3 tablespoons finely chopped bean sprouts, a tablespoon teriyaki sauce, 2 crushed cloves garlic and 2 teaspoons grated fresh ginger. Working with 1 won ton wrapper at a time (you will need about 20), place 1 tablespoon filling in the centre, gather up the corners and pinch together to seal. Keep the other won ton wrappers covered with a damp tea towel until needed. Line the base of a bamboo or metal steamer with a circle of baking paper. Arrange the dim sims on the paper, making sure they are not touching (you may need to cook them in batches). Cover and steam for 8 minutes. Serve immediately. Makes about 20.

*NUTRITION PER DIM SIM: Protein 5 g; Fat 1 g; Carbohydrate 10 g; Dietary Fibre 1 g; Cholesterol 20 mg; 260 kJ (60 cal)*

### CHICKEN MONEYBAGS
In a bowl, combine 375 g (12 oz) chicken mince, 90 g (3 oz) finely chopped ham, 4 finely chopped spring onions, 1 finely chopped stick of celery, 3 tablespoons chopped bamboo shoots, 1 tablespoon soy sauce, 1 crushed clove garlic and 1 teaspoon grated fresh ginger. Working with 1 won ton wrapper at a time (you will need about 40), place 2 teaspoons filling in the centre, gather up the corners and pinch together to form a pouch, leaving a

frill at the top. Cut 15 chives in half and place in a heatproof bowl. Cover with boiling water for 1 minute; rinse and drain. Deep-fry moneybags in hot oil for 4–5 minutes until crisp and golden; drain on paper towels. Tie a chive around each moneybag. Serve immediately. Makes about 40.

*NUTRITION PER MONEYBAG: Protein 3 g; Fat 3 g; Carbohydrate 5 g; Dietary Fibre 0 g; Cholesterol 10 mg; 230 kJ (55 cal)*

## PRAWN GOW GEES
In a bowl, mix 500 g (1 lb) raw prawns, peeled, deveined and chopped, 4 finely sliced spring onions, 1 tablespoon grated fresh ginger and 2 tablespoons chopped water chestnuts. Blend 3 teaspoons cornflour, 2 teaspoons sesame oil, 1 teaspoon soy sauce, 1/2 teaspoon caster sugar and a little salt and pepper until smooth, and stir into the

prawn mixture. Working with 1 gow gee wrapper at a time (you will need about 40), put 1 rounded teaspoon of mixture in the centre and press the edges together to form a semicircle. Twist the corners down to form a crescent shape. Line the base of a bamboo or metal steamer with a circle of baking paper. Arrange the gow gees on the paper, making sure they are not touching (you may need to cook them in batches). Steam, covered, for 8 minutes. Makes about 40.

*NUTRITION PER GOW GEE: Protein 2 g; Fat 1 g; Carbohydrate 5 g; Dietary Fibre 0 g; Cholesterol 10 mg; 140 kJ (35 cal)*

## STUFFED PEPPERS
(CAPSICUMS)
Mix together 500 g (1 lb) peeled, deveined and finely chopped raw prawns, 300 g (9 2/3 oz) lean pork

mince, 1 teaspoon salt, 3 finely chopped spring onions, 3 tablespoons finely chopped water chestnuts, 3 teaspoons soy sauce and 2 teaspoons dry sherry. Cut 3 peppers (capsicums) lengthways into 3–4 segments and remove the seeds and membrane. Fill the pepper wedges with filling and cut in half. Heat 1 tablespoon oil in a wok. Cook the pepper pieces in 2 batches over medium-high heat for 3–4 minutes, or until well browned. Turn over and cook for a further 3 minutes. Repeat with remaining pieces. Serve immediately. Makes about 24.

*NUTRITION PER PIECE: Protein 5 g; Fat 1 g; Carbohydrate 1 g; Dietary Fibre 0 g; Cholesterol 45 mg; 190 kJ (45 cal)*

*Clockwise from top left: Prawn Gow Gees; Crabmeat Dim Sims; Stuffed Peppers; Chicken Moneybags*

4 Remove the pan from the heat. Add the tomato sauce, soy sauce, vinegar, sesame oil and spring onion. Season with salt and black pepper to taste. Serve topped with extra spring onion, if desired.
NOTE: Add a few drops of chilli oil to the recipe if a more fiery soup is desired.

*NUTRITION PER SERVE (8): Protein 10 g; Fat 4 g; Carbohydrate 5 g; Dietary Fibre 1 g; Cholesterol 50 mg; 390 kJ (90 cal)*

•

## BLACK SATIN CHICKEN

*Preparation time:* 25 minutes
   + 20 minutes soaking
*Total cooking time:* 1 hour
*Serves* 10

★ ★

3 dried Chinese mushrooms
$1/2$ cup (125 ml/4 fl oz) hot water
$1/2$ cup (125 ml/4 fl oz) dark soy sauce
3 tablespoons soft brown sugar
2 tablespoons Chinese rice wine
1 tablespoon soy sauce
1 teaspoon sesame oil
$1/4$ teaspoon ground star anise or 1 whole
   star anise
1 x 1.4 kg (2 lb 12$2/3$ oz) chicken
4 cm (1$1/2$ inch) piece fresh ginger, grated
1 teaspoon salt
2 spring onions, finely sliced

•

1 Soak the mushrooms in the hot water for 20 minutes. Drain and reserve the liquid. Put the dark soy sauce, sugar, wine, soy sauce, sesame oil, star anise and reserved liquid in a small pan and bring to the boil, stirring continuously.
2 Rub the inside of the chicken with ginger and salt. Place the chicken in a large pan. Cover with the soy marinade and mushrooms, turning the chicken over so it is evenly coated. Cover and cook the chicken over low heat, turning regularly, for 55 minutes or until the juices run clear when pierced with a skewer. Remove the chicken and allow it to cool briefly. Boil the sauce over high heat until thick and syrupy. Discard the mushrooms.
3 Chop the chicken Chinese-style (see page 10). Arrange the chicken pieces on a serving platter, brush lightly with the syrupy sauce and sprinkle over the spring onion. Alternatively you could serve the sauce separately, for dipping.
NOTE: Dark soy sauce is available from Asian food stores.

*NUTRITION PER SERVE: Protein 15 g; Fat 3 g; Carbohydrate 5 g; Dietary Fibre 0 g; Cholesterol 40 mg; 450 kJ (105 cal)*

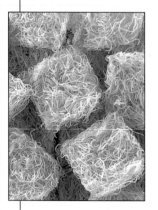

## SZECHWAN SOUP

•

*Preparation time:* 20 minutes
   + 40 minutes soaking
*Total cooking time:* 15 minutes
*Serves* 6–8

★

4 dried Chinese mushrooms
45 g (1$1/2$ oz) thick dried rice stick noodles
4 cups (1 litre) chicken stock
1 cup (175 g/5$2/3$ oz) chopped cooked
   chicken
230 g (7$1/3$ oz) can bamboo shoots,
   drained and chopped
1 teaspoon grated fresh ginger
1 tablespoon cornflour
$1/3$ cup (80 ml/2$3/4$ oz) water
1 egg, lightly beaten
1 teaspoon tomato sauce
1 tablespoon soy sauce
1 tablespoon vinegar
2 teaspoons sesame oil
2 spring onions, finely chopped

•

1 Cover the mushrooms with hot water and soak for 20 minutes; drain thoroughly and chop. Soak the noodles in hot water for 20 minutes; drain and cut into short lengths.
2 Heat the stock in a large pan and bring to the boil. Add the mushrooms, noodles, chicken, bamboo shoots and ginger. Reduce the heat and simmer gently.
3 Combine the cornflour and water in a small bowl and mix to a smooth paste. Add the cornflour mixture to the soup and stir until clear. Add the egg to the soup in a fine stream, stirring the mixture constantly.

*Above: Szechwan Soup*

# HONEY PRAWNS

•

*Preparation time:* 20 minutes
*Total cooking time:* 12 minutes
*Serves 4*

★

16 raw king prawns
1/4 cup (30 g/1 oz) cornflour
1/4 cup (40 g/1 1/3 oz) white sesame seeds
oil, for deep-frying
1/4 cup (90 g/3 oz) honey

•

*Batter*
1 cup (125 g/4 oz) self-raising flour
1/4 cup (30 g/1 oz) cornflour
1 cup (250 ml/8 fl oz) water
1/4 teaspoon lemon juice
1 tablespoon oil

•

1 Peel and devein the prawns, leaving the tails intact. Pat the prawns dry with paper towels, then lightly dust them with the cornflour.
2 Toast the sesame seeds in a dry pan over medium heat for 3 to 4 minutes, shaking the pan gently, until the seeds are golden brown; remove from the pan at once to prevent burning.
3 To make Batter: Sift the flour and cornflour into a medium bowl. Combine the water, lemon juice and oil. Make a well in the centre of the flour and gradually add the liquid, beating well to make a smooth batter.
4 Heat the oil in a large, deep frying pan until moderately hot. Working with a few at a time, dip the prawns in the batter; drain excess. Using tongs or a slotted spoon, place the prawns in the hot oil. Cook for 2 to 3 minutes or until the prawns are crisp and golden. Drain on paper towels and keep warm.
5 Place the honey in a large pan and warm over very low heat. (Don't overheat the honey or it will caramelise and lose some of its flavour.)
6 Place the cooked prawns in the pan with the warmed honey; toss gently to coat. Transfer to a serving plate and sprinkle over the sesame seeds. Serve immediately.

*NUTRITION PER SERVE: Protein 20 g; Fat 10 g; Carbohydrate 55 g; Dietary Fibre 2 g; Cholesterol 115 mg; 1675 kJ (390 cal)*

## SZECHWAN COOKING

*The immense geographical and climatic diversity of China has led to the development of many distinct and varied regional cuisines. There are four major styles: Peking, Cantonese, Shanghai and Szechwan. The distinctive hot and spicy Szechwan cuisine is a medley of many influences, one of the most important being the traders and Buddhist missionaries from India, who more than 2000 years ago brought cooking techniques, tangy spices and herbs, and a tradition of vegetarian dishes. Szechwan cooking makes liberal use of fiery chillies and most dishes include vinegar, sugar, salt and the unique spice, Szechwan pepper (which has a numbing effect on the tongue, rather than a bite).*

*Left: Honey Prawns*

1 Trim the meat of any fat and sinew, and slice it evenly across the grain into long, thin strips. Combine the soy sauce, egg white, cornflour and pepper; add the meat, stirring to coat.

2 Heat 1 tablespoon oil in a wok or heavy-based pan, swirling gently to coat the base and sides. Add the ginger, five spice powder, peppers, celery and corn and stir-fry over high heat for 2 minutes or until just beginning to soften. Remove from wok and keep warm.

3 Heat the remaining oil in the wok, swirling gently to coat the base and sides. Cook the meat quickly in small batches over high heat until browned but not cooked through.

4 Return all the meat to the wok with the vegetables and add the oyster sauce. Stir-fry over high heat until the meat is cooked and the sauce is hot. Remove from heat and serve immediately, sprinkled with the spring onion.

*NUTRITION PER SERVE: Protein 25 g; Fat 10 g; Carbohydrate 5 g; Dietary Fibre 3 g; Cholesterol 85 mg; 865 kJ (205 cal)*

## CHINESE BARBECUED PORK

*Preparation time:* 15 minutes
 + 30 minutes marinating
*Total cooking time:* 35 minutes
*Serves* 6

★

*1/4 cup (60 ml/2 fl oz) tomato sauce*
*1 tablespoon hoisin sauce*
*2 tablespoons honey*
*1 tablespoon malt extract or molasses*
*1 tablespoon chopped garlic*
*2 tablespoons caster sugar*
*1 teaspoon five spice powder*
*2 teaspoons cornflour*
*1 tablespoon water*
*750 g (1 1/2 lb) pork neck or fillet*

1 Combine the tomato sauce, hoisin sauce, honey, malt extract, garlic, sugar and five spice powder in a small pan. Dissolve the cornflour in the water and add to the mixture. Bring to the boil, then reduce to a simmer and stir for 2 minutes. Allow to cool.

2 If using pork neck, cut it in half lengthways. Pork fillets do not need to be cut. Place the meat in the sauce, turning to coat; cover and marinate in the refrigerator for at least 30 minutes.

3 Preheat the oven to hot 210°C (415°F/ Gas 6–7). Lift the pork from the marinade with a slotted spoon and reserve the marinade. Place the pork on a wire rack over a baking tray half-filled with hot water and cook for 15 minutes.

## BEEF WITH PEPPERS AND OYSTER SAUCE

*Preparation time:* 15 minutes
*Total cooking time:* 8 minutes
*Serves* 6

★

*500 g (1 lb) rump steak*
*1 tablespoon soy sauce*
*1 egg white, lightly beaten*
*1 tablespoon cornflour*
*1/4 teaspoon ground black pepper*
*2 tablespoons peanut oil*
*1 tablespoon grated fresh ginger*
*1/4 teaspoon five spice powder*
*1 small green pepper (capsicum), cut in diamond shapes*
*1 small red pepper (capsicum), cut in diamond shapes*
*2 sticks celery, thinly sliced*
*425 g (13 1/2 oz) can whole baby corn, drained*
*2 tablespoons oyster sauce*
*2 spring onions, diagonally sliced*

*Above: Beef with Peppers and Oyster Sauce*

4 Reduce the oven to moderate 180°C (350°F/ Gas 4) and cook the pork for a further 15 minutes, basting it occasionally with the reserved marinade. Remove the pork from the oven and let it stand for 5 minutes before slicing and serving.

*NUTRITION PER SERVE: Protein 30 g; Fat 2 g; Carbohydrate 25 g; Dietary Fibre 1 g; Cholesterol 60 mg; 940 kJ (225 cal)*

## CRISP-SKINNED CHICKEN

**Preparation time:** 20 minutes
+ 20 minutes refrigeration
**Total cooking time:** 25 minutes
Serves 4

★ ★ ★

1 x 1.3 kg (2¾ lb) chicken
1 tablespoon honey
1 star anise
1 strip dried mandarin or tangerine peel
1 teaspoon salt
oil, for deep-frying
2 lemons, cut into wedges

*Five Spice Salt*
2 tablespoons salt
1 teaspoon white peppercorns
½ teaspoon five spice powder
½ teaspoon ground white pepper

1 Wash the chicken in cold water. Place the chicken in a large pan and cover with cold water. Add the honey, star anise, peel and salt and bring to the boil. Reduce heat to low and simmer for 15 minutes. Turn off the heat and leave the chicken, covered, for a further 15 minutes. Transfer chicken to a plate and cool.
2 Cut the chicken in half lengthways. Place it on paper towels, uncovered, in the refrigerator for 20 minutes.
3 Heat the oil in a wok or deep, heavy-based pan. It is hot enough to use when a piece of bread turns brown in it in 30 seconds. Very gently lower in half the chicken, skin-side-down. Cook for 6 minutes, turn and cook another 6 minutes, making sure all the skin comes in contact with the oil. Drain on paper towels. Repeat with the second chicken half.
4 To make Five Spice Salt: Place the salt and peppercorns in a small pan and dry-fry until the mixture smells fragrant and the salt is slightly browned. Crush the mixture with a mortar and pestle or wrap in foil and crush it with a rolling pin. Mix with the five spice powder and white pepper and place in a tiny, shallow dish.

5 Chop the chicken Chinese-style (see page 10). Sprinkle over the Five Spice Salt and serve with lemon wedges.
NOTE: Any leftover Five Spice Salt can be stored in a dry, airtight container for several months.

*NUTRITION PER SERVE: Protein 25 g; Fat 25 g; Carbohydrate 5 g; Dietary Fibre 0 g; Cholesterol 110 mg; 1365 kJ (325 cal)*

*Above: Crisp-Skinned Chicken*

3 Place a pair of wooden chopsticks in a cross in the base of a large wok (to act as a rack) and fill the wok with about 7 cm (2¾ inches) of water. Score the fattest part of the fish three times, place on a heatproof dinner plate and sit the plate on top of the chopsticks. Cover and bring the water to the boil over high heat. Cook for 15–20 minutes; turn off the heat, scatter over the vegetables and leave, covered, for 3 minutes.
4 Slide the steamed fish onto a warmed serving platter. Heat the oil in a small pan until it is very hot and slightly smoking, then carefully pour it over the vegetables. The vegetables or fish skin may crackle. Serve with small bowls of soy and chilli sauce and plenty of steamed white rice.
NOTE: The oil must be very hot so it just crisps and brightens the vegetables. If desired, the oil can be poured over the fish at the table so the guests can watch; the crackling is quite spectacular.

*NUTRITION PER SERVE: Protein 25 g; Fat 35 g; Carbohydrate 2 g; Dietary Fibre 1 g; Cholesterol 80 mg; 1860 kJ (440 cal)*

## WHOLE STEAMED FISH WITH CRISP FINISH
•

*Preparation time:* 25 minutes
*Total cooking time:* 20 minutes
*Serves* 4

★ ★

*1 whole snapper or bream, approximately
  1 kg (2 lb), cleaned and scaled
½ teaspoon salt
½ teaspoon white pepper
3 cm (1¼ inch) fresh ginger, very finely
  sliced
1 tablespoon sesame oil
1 tablespoon soy sauce
3 spring onions
1 stick celery
½ red pepper (capsicum)
½ cup (125 ml/4 fl oz) oil*

•

1 Thoroughly wash the fish inside the cavity and out and pat dry with paper towels. Sprinkle the fish with the salt and pepper and place the ginger inside the cavity. Combine the sesame oil and soy sauce and lightly brush over the fish.
2 Cut the spring onions and celery into 4 cm (1½ inch) lengths, then finely shred them into long fine strips. Cut the red pepper into fine matchsticks 4 cm (1½ inches) long.

*Above: Whole Steamed
Fish with Crisp Finish*

## SWEET AND SOUR PORK
•

*Preparation time:* 35 minutes
*Total cooking time:* 25 minutes
*Serves* 4

★ ★

*½ teaspoon salt
350 g (11¼ oz) pork loin, cut into
  bite-sized pieces
2 eggs, lightly beaten
4 tablespoons cornflour
oil, for deep-frying
1 medium carrot, very thinly sliced
1 medium onion, cut into fine wedges
1 cup (160 g/5¼ oz) chopped fresh
  pineapple
½ medium red pepper (capsicum), cut into
  bite-sized pieces
½ medium green pepper (capsicum), cut
  into bite-sized pieces
1 stick celery, sliced
⅓ cup (75 g/2½ oz) sweet pickled Chinese
  vegetables, roughly chopped
3 tablespoons white vinegar
3 tablespoons soy sauce
2 tablespoons tomato paste (tomato purée,
  double concentrate)
2 tablespoons caster sugar
2 tablespoons orange juice
2 teaspoons cornflour, extra, mixed with
  1 tablespoon water*

1 Mix the salt through the pork. Dip each piece of pork in the egg, then roll it in the cornflour. Place the pork on a plate in a single layer.

2 Heat the oil in a wok over medium heat, drop in 4 pieces of pork and cook for about 3 minutes or until golden brown. Remove the pork with a slotted spoon and drain it on paper towels. Repeat with the remaining pork.

3 Remove all but 1 tablespoon oil from the wok, reheat and stir-fry the carrot, onion and pineapple for 2 minutes or until the carrot is just tender. Add the red and green pepper, celery and pickled vegetables and cook for a further 2 minutes.

4 Combine the vinegar, soy sauce, tomato purée, sugar and orange juice in a small bowl; stir in the cornflour mixture and mix well. Pour the sauce into the vegetables and stir constantly until the mixture boils and thickens slightly. Add the pork to the pan, stirring well to lightly coat the meat with the sauce. Arrange on a serving plate and serve immediately.

NOTE: Be sure to fry the pork quickly after coating it with the cornflour so it does not become sticky on standing.

NUTRITION PER SERVE: Protein 25 g; Fat 4 g; Carbohydrate 30 g; Dietary Fibre 3 g; Cholesterol 135 mg; 1135 kJ (270 cal)

•
## SMOKED FIVE SPICE CHICKEN
•

**Preparation time:** 30 minutes
+ 4 hours marinating
**Total cooking time:** 35 minutes
**Serves** 6

★ ☆

1 x 1.7 kg (3¾ lb) chicken
¼ cup (60 ml/2 fl oz) soy sauce
1 tablespoon finely grated ginger
2 medium pieces dried mandarin or
    tangerine peel
1 star anise
¼ teaspoon five spice powder
3 tablespoons soft brown sugar

•

1 Wash the chicken in cold water. Pat it dry with paper towels. Discard any large pieces of fat from inside the chicken.

2 Place the chicken in a large non-metallic bowl with the soy sauce and ginger. Cover and marinate for at least 4 hours or leave overnight in the refrigerator, turning occasionally.

3 Place a small rack in the base of a pan large enough to hold the chicken. Add water to the level of the rack. Place the chicken on the rack. Bring water to the boil, cover tightly, reduce heat and steam for 15 minutes. Turn off the heat and allow the chicken to stand, covered, for another 15 minutes. Transfer the chicken to a bowl.

4 Wash the pan and line it with 3 or 4 large pieces of aluminium foil. Pound the dried peel and star anise in a mortar and pestle until the pieces are the size of coarse breadcrumbs, or process in a food processor. Add the five spice powder and sugar. Spread the spice mixture over the foil.

5 Replace the rack in the pan and place the chicken on it. Place the pan over medium heat and, when the spice mixture starts smoking, cover tightly. Reduce the heat to low; smoke the chicken for 20 minutes. Test if the chicken is cooked by piercing the thigh with a skewer; the juices should run clear. Remove the chicken from the pan and chop it Chinese-style (see page 10). It is important to remember that the heat produced in this final step is very intense. When the chicken is removed from the pan, leave the pan on the stove to cool before handling it.

NUTRITION PER SERVE: Protein 25 g; Fat 15 g; Carbohydrate 0 g; Dietary Fibre 0 g; Cholesterol 95 mg; 980 kJ (235 cal)

SMOKED FIVE
SPICE CHICKEN

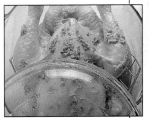

Place a small rack in a pan, add water to the level of the rack and place the chicken on the rack.

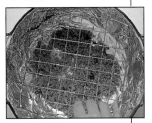

Spread the spice mixture over the foil-lined pan and replace the rack.

Above: Smoked Five Spice Chicken

## CHINESE GREEN VEGETABLES

*There are a number of Chinese green vegetables available in your fruit and vegetable market. Choy sum, bok choy and Chinese broccoli are all easily prepared by cutting off the base, separating the leaves and rinsing in cold water. Roughly chop the vegetables into large pieces. The whole plant is used, including the stem—this requires longer cooking than the leaves, but don't overcook or it will lose its lovely vibrant green colour.*

## CHINESE VEGETABLES

•

*Preparation time:* 10 minutes
*Total cooking time:* 5 minutes
*Serves* 4

☆

500 g (1 lb) Chinese green vegetables
  (see note)
2 teaspoons peanut oil
1/2 teaspoon finely chopped garlic
1 tablespoon oyster sauce
1/2 teaspoon caster sugar
2 tablespoons water
1 teaspoon sesame oil

•

1 Bring a large pan of water to the boil.
2 Wash Chinese greens. Remove any tough leaves and trim stems. Chop greens into 3 equal portions.
3 Add the greens to the pan of boiling water. Cook for 1 to 2 minutes, or until just tender but still crisp. Use tongs to remove greens from the pan, drain well and place on a heated serving platter.
4 Heat the peanut oil in a small pan and cook the garlic briefly. Add the oyster sauce, sugar, water and sesame oil and bring to the boil. Pour over the greens and toss to coat. Serve immediately.
NOTE: Use choy sum, bok choy or Chinese broccoli (gai larn), or a combination of any two.

*NUTRITION PER SERVE: Protein 1 g; Fat 3 g; Carbohydrate 2 g; Dietary Fibre 1 g; Cholesterol 0 mg; 180 kJ (40 cal)*

*Above: Chinese Vegetables*

## PORK WITH PLUM SAUCE

•

*Preparation time:* 15 minutes
*Total cooking time:* about 15 minutes
*Serves* 4

☆

3 tablespoons oil
2 cloves garlic, finely chopped
1 large onion, cut into fine wedges
500 g (1 lb) pork loin, cut into thin slices
2 tablespoons cornflour
1/2 teaspoon sugar
3 tablespoons plum sauce
1 tablespoon soy sauce
2 teaspoons hoisin sauce

•

1 Heat 1 tablespoon oil in a wok and cook the garlic and onion until softened. Transfer to a plate and remove the wok from the heat.
2 Coat the pork lightly in the cornflour and season well with salt and pepper. Add the remaining oil to the wok and return to the heat. When the wok is extremely hot, stir-fry the pork in 2 batches until dark golden brown, then return all the meat and its juices to the pan.
3 Add the plum sauce, soy sauce and hoisin sauce and onion to the wok. Toss well to coat the meat with the sauce and serve immediately.

*NUTRITION PER SERVE: Protein 30 g; Fat 15 g; Carbohydrate 15 g; Dietary Fibre 1 g; Cholesterol 60 mg; 1380 kJ (330 cal)*

## STIR-FRIED VEGETABLES
•
*Preparation time:* 5 minutes
*Total cooking time:* 4 minutes
*Serves* 4

⭐

1 carrot
1 red pepper (capsicum)
125 g (4 oz) green beans
1 tablespoon oil
1 teaspoon finely chopped garlic
200 g (6½ oz) straw mushrooms
1½ teaspoons cornflour
⅓ cup (80 ml/2¾ oz) chicken stock
1 teaspoon sesame oil
1 teaspoon caster sugar
2 teaspoons soy sauce
•

1 Slice the carrot finely. Seed the red pepper and cut it into 4 cm (1½ inch) pieces. Top and tail the beans and cut them in half.
2 Heat the oil in a wok or heavy-based frying pan, swirling gently to coat the base and sides. Add the carrot and stir-fry over high heat for 30 seconds. Stir in the garlic; add the remaining vegetables and stir-fry them over high heat for 2 minutes—they should be very crisp and firm.
3 Dissolve the cornflour in a little of the stock; mix with the remaining stock, sesame oil, sugar and soy sauce. Add the cornflour mixture to the wok and stir until the sauce boils and thickens. Serve immediately with steamed rice.

*NUTRITION PER SERVE: Protein 4 g; Fat 5 g;*
*Carbohydrate 5 g; Dietary Fibre 4 g; Cholesterol 0 mg;*
*420 kJ (100 cal)*

•
## SWEET GARLIC EGGPLANT (AUBERGINE)
•
*Preparation time:* 5 minutes
*Total cooking time:* 15 minutes
*Serves* 4

⭐

3 medium eggplants (aubergines)
7 tablespoons oil
1½ teaspoons finely chopped garlic
6 teaspoons caster sugar
6 teaspoons soy sauce
6 teaspoons cider vinegar
1 tablespoon dry sherry
•

1 Cut the eggplants in half lengthways and then slice into wedges about 3 cm (1¼ inches) wide. Cut the wedges into pieces about 3 cm (1¼ inches) long.

2 Heat 3 tablespoons oil in a wok or heavy-based frying pan, swirling gently to coat the base and sides. Add half the eggplant and stir-fry over high heat for 5 minutes, or until browned and all the oil is absorbed. Transfer to a plate. Repeat the cooking procedure with another 3 tablespoons oil and the remaining eggplant.
3 Heat the remaining oil in the wok, swirling gently to coat the base and sides. Add the garlic and cook slowly until just golden. Add the sugar, soy sauce, vinegar and sherry. Bring to the boil, stirring. Add the eggplant and simmer for 3 minutes to allow it to absorb the sauce. Serve with white rice.
NOTE: This dish can be cooked up to 2 days ahead and refrigerated until required. Serve it at room temperature.

*NUTRITION PER SERVE: Protein 2 g; Fat 35 g;*
*Carbohydrate 10 g; Dietary Fibre 4 g; Cholesterol 0 mg;*
*1520 kJ (360 cal)*

ADDING CORNFLOUR
*Cornflour will thicken a sauce without affecting the flavour. Mix the cornflour with a little cold water or stock to make a thin, smooth paste. Remove the wok or pan from the heat for a minute or so, then add the cornflour mixture, stirring again immediately before adding as the cornflour does not stay in suspension for long. Return the wok to the heat and, while stirring, quickly bring the sauce to the boil.*

*Left: Sweet*
*Garlic Eggplant*

2 Heat 1 tablespoon of the oil in a wok, swirling gently to coat. Add the garlic, black pepper, onion and red and green pepper and stir-fry over high heat for 1 minute; remove from the wok.
3 Add the remaining oil to the wok, swirling gently to coat the base and sides. Add the beef and stir-fry over high heat for 2 minutes, until it changes colour. Add the black beans, cornflour mixture and vegetables. Stir until the sauce boils and thickens. Serve with rice.

NUTRITION PER SERVE: Protein 25 g; Fat 10 g; Carbohydrate 5 g; Dietary Fibre 1 g; Cholesterol 65 mg; 980 kJ (235 cal)

## SAN CHOY BAU

**Preparation time:** 30 minutes
  + 20 minutes soaking
**Total cooking time:** about 12 minutes
Serves 4

✦

2 dried Chinese mushrooms
2 tablespoons oil
200 g (6½ oz) pork mince, not too lean
100 g (3⅓ oz) chicken mince
2 cloves garlic, finely chopped
3 cm (1¼ inch) piece fresh ginger, finely grated
1 stick celery, finely chopped
50 g (1⅔ oz) green beans, finely sliced
¼ red pepper (capsicum), finely chopped
⅓ cup (50 g/1⅔ oz) water chestnuts, chopped
2 tablespoons oyster sauce
1 tablespoons soy sauce
2 teaspoons Golden Mountain sauce
¼ teaspoon sugar
1 iceberg lettuce

1 Soak the mushrooms in hot water for 20 minutes. Drain and finely chop, discarding the hard stem.
2 Heat half the oil in a wok and stir-fry the pork, chicken, garlic and ginger until the meat changes colour, breaking up any lumps. Add the celery, beans, red pepper and cook for 3 minutes. Add the water chestnuts, oyster, soy and Golden Mountain sauces, sugar, and salt and pepper.
3 To serve, tear the lettuce into cups and place a heaped tablespoon of the filling into each cup. Roll up and eat with your fingers.
NOTE: If the pork mince is too lean the filling will be dry.

NUTRITION PER SERVE: Protein 20 g; Fat 15 g; Carbohydrate 5 g; Dietary Fibre 3 g; Cholesterol 45 mg; 965 kJ (230 cal)

## BEEF IN BLACK BEAN SAUCE

**Preparation time:** 10 minutes
**Total cooking time:** 10 minutes
Serves 4

✦

2 tablespoons canned black beans
1 medium onion
1 small red pepper (capsicum)
1 small green pepper (capsicum)
2 teaspoons cornflour
½ cup (125 ml/4 fl oz) beef stock
2 teaspoons soy sauce
1 teaspoon sugar
2 tablespoons oil
1 teaspoon finely crushed garlic
¼ teaspoon ground black pepper
400 g (12⅔ oz) rump or fillet steak, finely sliced

1 Rinse the black beans in several changes of water; drain and mash them. Cut the onion into wedges. Halve the peppers, discard seeds and cut them into small pieces. Dissolve the cornflour in the stock, add the soy sauce and sugar.

*Above: Beef in Black Bean Sauce*

## BEEF AND BOK CHOY

•

*Preparation time:* 20 minutes
*Total cooking time:* 10 minutes
*Serves* 4

☆

600 g (1¼ lb) bok choy
2 tablespoons oil
2 cloves garlic, crushed
250 g (8 oz) rump steak,
   thinly sliced
2 tablespoons soy sauce
1 tablespoon sweet sherry
2 tablespoons chopped fresh basil
2 teaspoons sesame oil

•

1 Wash the bok choy and drain it. Cut the leaves into thin strips. Heat 1 tablespoon oil in a frying pan or wok; add the garlic and stir-fry for 30 seconds.

2 Heat the remaining oil; add the meat in small batches and stir-fry for 3 minutes over high heat until the meat has browned but is not cooked through. Remove the meat from the pan.
3 Stir-fry the bok choy for 30 seconds or until it is just wilted. Add the meat, soy sauce and sherry. Stir-fry for 2 to 3 minutes or until the meat is tender.
4 Add the basil and sesame oil and toss well. Serve immediately. Garnish with strips of red pepper, if desired.
NOTE: The Asian vegetable choy sum has a similar flavour to bok choy and could be substituted in this dish. It has a longer leaf and a shorter stem. Baby bok choy could also be used.

*NUTRITION PER SERVE: Protein 15 g; Fat 15 g; Carbohydrate 1 g; Dietary Fibre 1 g; Cholesterol 40 mg; 825 kJ (195 cal)*

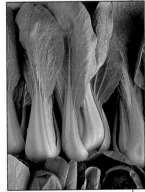

*Above: Beef and Bok Choy*

# INDONESIA

The cuisine of Indonesia is rich and
varied, a reflection of the many diverse
influences which have shaped the country's
history. Indonesian cooking combines
the spicy flavours of chillies, herbs and other
aromatic seasonings with the sweetness of
fresh coconut, palm sugar and peanuts,
and the sourness of limes, lemon grass
and tamarind. Meals are often served
with small bowls of sambal, spicy relishes
made from combinations of coconut,
chilli and shrimp paste.

*NASI GORENG*

*Remove the omelette from the pan with a spatula.*

*Process the garlic, onion, chilli, shrimp paste, coriander and sugar into a paste.*

*Stir-fry the steak and prawns until they change colour.*

*Stir-fry the rice, breaking up any lumps with a wooden spoon.*

# NASI GORENG
(FRIED RICE)

•

*Preparation time:* 35 minutes
*Total cooking time:* 30 minutes
Serves 4

2 eggs
1/4 teaspoon salt
1/3 cup (80 ml/2 3/4 fl oz) oil
3 cloves garlic, finely chopped
1 onion, finely chopped
2 red chillies, seeded and very finely
    chopped
1 teaspoon shrimp paste
1 teaspoon coriander seeds
1/2 teaspoon sugar
400 g (12 2/3 oz) raw prawns, peeled
    and deveined
200 g (6 1/2 oz) rump steak, finely sliced
1 cup (200 g/6 1/2 oz) long-grain rice,
    cooked and cooled
2 teaspoons kecap manis
1 tablespoon soy sauce
4 spring onions, finely chopped
1/2 lettuce, finely shredded
1 cucumber, thinly sliced
3 tablespoons crisp fried onion

•

1 Beat the eggs and salt until foamy. Heat a frying pan and lightly brush with a little of the oil; pour about one-quarter of the egg mixture into the pan and cook for 1 to 2 minutes over medium heat until the omelette sets. Turn the omelette over and cook the other side for 30 seconds. Remove the omelette from the pan and repeat with the remaining egg mixture. When the omelettes are cold, gently roll them up and cut them into fine strips; set aside.

2 Combine the garlic, onion, chilli, shrimp paste, coriander and sugar in a food processor or mortar and pestle, and process or pound until a paste is formed.

3 Heat 1 to 2 tablespoons of the oil in a wok or large deep frying pan; add the paste and cook over high heat for 1 minute or until fragrant. Add the prawns and steak and stir-fry for 2 to 3 minutes, or until they change colour.

4 Add the remaining oil and the cold rice to the wok. Stir-fry, breaking up any lumps, until the rice is heated through. Add the kecap manis, soy sauce and spring onion and stir-fry for another minute.

5 Arrange the lettuce around the outside of a large platter. Place the rice in the centre, and garnish with the omelette strips, cucumber slices and fried onion. Serve immediately.

NUTRITION PER SERVE: *Protein 25 g; Fat 25 g; Carbohydrate 20 g; Dietary Fibre 3 g; Cholesterol 240 mg; 1765 kJ (420 cal)*

*Right: Nasi Goreng*

## BEEF FILLET IN COCONUT

•

***Preparation time:*** 15 minutes
   + 1 hour marinating
***Total cooking time:*** 10 minutes
***Serves*** 4

✩

*500 g (1 lb) beef eye fillet*
*2 cloves garlic, crushed*
*2 teaspoons finely grated lemon rind*
*1 teaspoon grated fresh ginger*
*2 teaspoons ground coriander*
*1/2 teaspoon ground turmeric*
*2 teaspoons grated palm sugar or soft*
   *brown sugar*
*3 tablespoons peanut oil*
*1/2 cup (45 g/1 1/2 oz) desiccated coconut*
*3 spring onions, cut into thin strips*
*1/2 cup (125 ml/4 fl oz) coconut milk*

•

1 Cut the beef into thin slices. Mix together the garlic, lemon rind, ginger, coriander, turmeric, palm sugar and 2 tablespoons oil, add the beef and toss well to coat. Cover and chill for 1 hour.
2 Heat the remaining oil in a wok or frying pan; add the beef and stir-fry in batches until well browned. Add the coconut and spring onion and stir-fry for 1 minute more. Return all the meat to the pan; add the coconut milk and stir until heated through. Serve with rice.

*NUTRITION PER SERVE: Protein 30 g; Fat 35 g;*
*Carbohydrate 5 g; Dietary Fibre 0 g; Cholesterol 85 mg;*
*1780 kJ (425 cal)*

## DEEP-FRIED SPICED TOFU

•

***Preparation time:*** 10 minutes
***Total cooking time:*** 10 minutes
***Serves*** 4

✩ ✩

*375 g (12 oz) firm tofu*
*1/2 cup (90 g/3 oz) rice flour*
*2 teaspoons ground coriander*
*1 teaspoon ground cardamom*
*1 clove garlic, crushed*
*1/2 cup (125 ml/4 fl oz) water*
*oil, for deep-frying*

1 Drain the tofu and cut it into 1 cm (1/2 inch) thick slices.
2 Combine the flour, coriander, cardamom and garlic in a bowl; add the water and stir until smooth.
3 Heat the oil in a large pan. Dip the tofu slices into the spice mixture and coat thickly. Place the tofu slices into the oil, 3 at a time, and cook over medium heat for about 2 minutes, or until crisp and golden brown. Drain on paper towels.
NOTE: Serve the tofu with stir-fried vegetables and any sauce of your choice; for example, peanut, chilli or soy sauce—the tofu soaks up the flavours.

*NUTRITION PER SERVE: Protein 10 g; Fat 25 g;*
*Carbohydrate 20 g; Dietary Fibre 1 g; Cholesterol 0 mg;*
*1320 kJ (315 cal)*

### TOFU

*Tofu, or bean curd, is said to have been discovered more than 2000 years ago by a Chinese emperor who, while working with a group of scientists on new medicines, discovered the art of coagulating soy milk. In a region which has no tradition of dairy product consumption, tofu has long been valued for its high calcium and protein content. In addition, it is cheap to produce and extremely versatile.*

*Above: Beef Fillet*
*in Coconut*

## BAKED LEMON CHICKENS

•

*Preparation time:* 30 minutes + 1 hour
   marinating
*Total cooking time:* 40 minutes
*Serves* 4

*4 baby chickens, about 500 g (1 lb) each*
*2 medium onions, chopped*
*1 spring onion, chopped*
*2 red chillies, chopped*
*2 cloves garlic, crushed*
*1/4 cup (60 ml/2 fl oz) peanut oil*
*1/4 cup (60 ml/2 fl oz) lemon juice*

•

1 Cut the chickens in half along the breast and backbone. Press down on each half to flatten it slightly.
2 Combine the onion, spring onion, chilli, garlic, oil and lemon juice in a food processor and process until smooth. Spoon the mixture over the chickens; cover and marinate for 1 hour or overnight in the refrigerator.

*Below: Baked
Lemon Chickens*

3 Preheat the oven to moderate 180°C (350°F/Gas 4). Using tongs, remove the chickens from the marinade, reserving the marinade. Place the chickens in a baking dish in a single layer. Bake for 40 minutes, or until cooked and browned, brushing occasionally with the marinade. Serve with rice or noodles, and a vegetable dish.

NUTRITION PER SERVE: *Protein 40 g; Fat 40 g; Carbohydrate 5 g; Dietary Fibre 1 g; Cholesterol 165 mg; 2305 kJ (550 cal)*

•
## PINEAPPLE CURRY
•

*Preparation time:* 20 minutes
*Total cooking time:* 15 minutes
*Serves* 4

*1 medium pineapple*
*1 teaspoon cardamom seeds*
*1 teaspoon coriander seeds*
*1 teaspoon cumin seeds*
*1/2 teaspoon whole cloves*
*2 tablespoons oil*
*2 spring onions, cut in 2 cm (3/4 inch)*
   *pieces*
*2 teaspoons grated fresh ginger*
*4 candlenuts, roughly chopped*
*1 cup (250 ml/8 fl oz) water*
*1 teaspoon sambal oelek*
*1 tablespoon chopped fresh mint*

•

1 Peel and halve the pineapple, remove the core, and cut the pineapple into 2 cm (3/4 inch) chunks.
2 Grind the cardamom seeds, coriander seeds, cumin seeds and cloves in a mortar and pestle.
3 Heat the oil in a medium pan; add the spring onion, ginger, candlenuts and spice mixture, and stir-fry over low heat for 3 minutes.
4 Add the water, sambal oelek, mint and pineapple and bring to the boil. Reduce the heat to low, cover and simmer for 10 minutes, or until the pineapple is tender but still holding its shape. Serve as an accompaniment.
NOTE: If the pineapple is a little tart, add 1 to 2 teaspoons sugar. A 450 g (14 1/3 oz) can of drained pineapple pieces can be used instead of fresh pineapple.

NUTRITION PER SERVE: *Protein 5 g; Fat 10 g; Carbohydrate 35 g; Dietary Fibre 10 g; Cholesterol 0 mg; 1095 kJ (260 cal)*

# KING PRAWNS WITH PEANUTS

•

**Preparation time:** 20 minutes
  + 1 hour marinating
**Total cooking time:** 3 minutes
**Serves** 4

⭐

1.25 kg (2¹/₂ lb) raw king prawns
4 spring onions, chopped
1 clove garlic, crushed
1 teaspoon grated fresh ginger
1 teaspoon sambal oelek
1 teaspoon ground coriander
¹/₂ teaspoon ground turmeric
1 teaspoon grated lemon rind
1 tablespoon lemon juice
²/₃ cup (110 g/3²/₃ oz) chopped unsalted
  roasted peanuts
2 tablespoons peanut oil

•

1 Peel and devein the prawns, leaving the tails
intact.
2 Combine the prawns with the spring onion,
garlic, ginger, sambal oelek, coriander, turmeric,
lemon rind, lemon juice and peanuts. Cover and
refrigerate for 1 hour.
3 Heat the oil in a frying pan; add the prawn
mixture and stir-fry over high heat for about
3 minutes or until the prawns are cooked. Serve
with rice.

NUTRITION PER SERVE: Protein 30 g; Fat 25 g;
Carbohydrate 5 g; Dietary Fibre 2 g; Cholesterol 170 mg;
1515 kJ (360 cal)

•

# INDONESIAN
# SPICED CHICKEN

•

**Preparation time:** 25 minutes
**Total cooking time:** 1 hour
**Serves** 6

⭐ ⭐

1.5 kg (3 lb) chicken thighs
1 large onion, roughly chopped
2 teaspoons crushed garlic
1 teaspoon grated fresh ginger
¹/₂ teaspoon ground turmeric
¹/₂ teaspoon ground pepper
2 teaspoons ground coriander
1 teaspoon salt
3 strips lemon rind or 3 fresh kaffir lime
  leaves
1²/₃ cups (410 ml/13 fl oz) coconut milk
1 cup (250 ml/8 fl oz) water
2 teaspoons grated palm sugar or soft
  brown sugar

1 Wash the chicken under cold water. Pat it dry
with paper towels. Trim off any excess fat.
2 Place the onion, garlic and ginger in a food
processor and process until smooth, adding a
little water if necessary.
3 Place the chicken, onion mixture and
remaining ingredients in a large pan and slowly
bring to the boil. Reduce heat, cover and simmer
for 45 minutes or until the chicken is tender,
stirring occasionally. Transfer the chicken to a
plate, and remove and discard the lemon rind or
lime leaves.
4 Bring the sauce remaining in the pan to the
boil, increase the heat to moderately high and
cook, uncovered, until quite thick, stirring
occasionally.
5 Place the chicken on a lightly oiled grill tray
and cook under high heat, browning the pieces
on both sides. Serve the chicken with the sauce
poured over it or serve the sauce separately.

NUTRITION PER SERVE: Protein 35 g; Fat 20 g;
Carbohydrate 5 g; Dietary Fibre 0 g; Cholesterol 115 mg;
1460 kJ (350 cal)

### OUTSIDE
### INFLUENCES
*The Indonesian
archipelago has long
been subject to outside
influence—from India,
Arab traders, Chinese
merchants, and the
colonial Portuguese, Dutch
and British. The rich
and varied cuisine of
the coastal areas, in
particular, reflects this
contact. Elsewhere, a style
of cooking featuring
ingredients of local origin,
such as fresh roots and
herbs, sugar and coconut
milk, predominates.*

*Above: King Prawns
with Peanuts*

GADO GADO

Cut the block of tofu vertically and then into small cubes.

Place the potato slices in a medium pan and cover with water.

Plunge the cooked carrots and beans into iced water.

Add the kecap manis and tomato sauce.

*Above: Gado Gado*

## GADO GADO
### (VEGETABLES WITH PEANUT SAUCE)

•

**Preparation time:** 50 minutes
**Total cooking time:** 20 minutes
**Serves 4**

★★

250 g (8 oz) potatoes
2 medium carrots
200 g (6¹/₂ oz) green beans
¹/₄ cabbage, shredded
3 hard-boiled eggs
200 g (6¹/₂ oz) bean sprouts,
    scraggly ends removed
¹/₂ cucumber, sliced
150 g (4³/₄ oz) firm tofu,
    cut into small cubes
¹/₂ cup (80 g/2²/₃ oz) unsalted roasted
    peanuts, roughly chopped

*Peanut Sauce*
1 tablespoon oil
1 large onion, very finely chopped
2 cloves garlic, finely chopped
2 red chillies, very finely chopped
1 teaspoon shrimp paste, optional
250 g (8 oz) crunchy peanut butter
1 cup (250 ml/8 fl oz) coconut milk
1 cup (250 ml/8 fl oz) water
2 teaspoons kecap manis
1 tablespoon tomato sauce

•

1 Cut the potatoes into thick slices; place in a medium pan, cover with cold water and bring to the boil. Reduce the heat and simmer for about 6 minutes or until just tender. Drain and allow to cool.

2 Cut the carrot into thick slices. Top and tail the beans and cut into 4 cm (1¹/₂ inch) lengths. Bring a large pan of water to the boil, add the carrots and beans, and cook for 2 to 3 minutes. Remove the vegetables with a sieve and plunge briefly into a bowl of iced water. Drain well.

6 Drizzle a little of the Peanut Sauce over the salad, garnish with the chopped peanuts and serve the remaining sauce in a bowl.

NOTE: Fresh peanut butter, available from health food stores, will give the sauce the best flavour. Be sure not to overcook the vegetables—they should be tender yet still crisp.

*NUTRITION PER SERVE: Protein 35 g; Fat 65 g; Carbohydrate 25 g; Dietary Fibre 15 g; Cholesterol 160 mg; 3520 kJ (840 cal)*

•

## CHICKEN SOUP WITH VERMICELLI AND VEGETABLES
•

*Preparation time:* 15 minutes
*Total cooking time:* 45 minutes
*Serves* 4

⭐

1 kg (2 lb) chicken pieces (such as
    drumsticks and thighs)
1.5 litres water
6 spring onions, chopped
$^1/_4$ teaspoon salt
$^1/_4$ teaspoon pepper
2 cm ($^3/_4$ inch) piece fresh ginger,
    very finely sliced
2 bay leaves
2 tablespoons soy sauce
100 g (3$^1/_3$ oz) dried rice vermicelli
50 g (1$^2/_3$ oz) spinach leaves, roughly
    chopped
2 celery sticks, very thinly sliced
200 g (6$^1/_2$ oz) bean sprouts, scraggly ends
    removed
crisp fried onion, for garnish
chilli sauce, to serve

•

3 Plunge the shredded cabbage into the boiling water for about 20 seconds. Remove it from the pot and plunge it briefly into the iced water. Drain well.

4 Cut the eggs into quarters or halves. Arrange the eggs, potato, carrot, beans, cabbage, bean sprouts, cucumber and tofu in separate piles on a large serving platter. Cover the platter with plastic wrap and refrigerate while making the Peanut Sauce.

5 To make Peanut Sauce: Heat the oil in a heavy-based pan, add the onion and garlic and cook over low heat for 8 minutes, stirring regularly. Add the chilli and shrimp paste to the pan and cook for another minute. Remove the pan from the heat and mix in the peanut butter. Return the pan to the heat and slowly stir in the combined coconut milk and water. Bring the sauce to the boil, stirring constantly over low heat, and being careful the sauce does not stick and burn. Reduce the heat, add the kecap manis and tomato sauce, and simmer for another minute. Allow to cool.

1 Combine the chicken and water in a medium pan and bring to the boil; skim off any scum. Add the spring onion, salt, pepper, ginger, bay leaves and soy sauce, then reduce the heat and simmer for 30 minutes.

2 Place the vermicelli in a heatproof bowl. Cover it with boiling water and leave to soak for 10 minutes or until soft; drain.

3 Arrange the vermicelli, spinach, celery and bean sprouts on a platter. To serve, each diner places a serving of vermicelli and a selection of vegetables in large individual serving bowls; pour the chicken soup, including a couple of pieces of chicken, into each bowl. Sprinkle over the fried onion and season with chilli sauce.

*NUTRITION PER SERVE: Protein 40 g; Fat 5 g; Carbohydrate 25 g; Dietary Fibre 3 g; Cholesterol 115 mg; 1315 kJ (315 cal)*

GROW YOUR OWN
BEAN SPROUTS
*To grow your own sprouts, place $^1/_4$ to $^1/_2$ cup mung beans in a large glass jar (the sprouts will take up 10 times as much space as the beans). Rinse well, then soak the beans in cold water for 12 hours. Drain off water, cover the top of the jar with a piece of muslin held in place with a rubber band, and leave it in a dark place. Twice a day fill the jar with water, swirl, and then drain well, as any remaining water could cause the sprouts to rot. By the fourth or fifth day the beans should be well sprouted—about 2.5 cm (1 inch) long. Rinse again, transfer to a plastic bag and refrigerate.*

Cut the chicken
in half by cutting down
the backbone and along
the breastbone.

Combine the chilli,
garlic, peppercorns
and sugar in a food
processor.

Brush the spice mixture
all over the chicken.

*Above: Spicy
Roast Chicken*

## SPICY ROAST CHICKEN

•

*Preparation time:* 20 minutes
*Total cooking time:* 40 minutes
*Serves 4–6*

★

1.6 kg (3¹/2 lb) chicken
3 teaspoons chopped red chillies
3 cloves garlic
2 teaspoons peppercorns, crushed
2 teaspoons soft brown sugar
2 tablespoons soy sauce
2 teaspoons ground turmeric
1 tablespoon lime juice
30 g (1 oz) butter, chopped

•

1 Preheat the oven to moderate 180°C (350°F/ Gas 4).

2 Using a large cleaver, cut the chicken in half by cutting down the backbone and along the breastbone. To prevent the wings from burning, tuck them underneath. Place the chicken, skin-side-up, on a rack in a baking dish and bake for 30 minutes.

3 Meanwhile, combine the chilli, garlic, peppercorns and sugar in a food processor or mortar and pestle and process briefly, or pound, until smooth. Add the soy sauce, turmeric and lime juice, and process in short bursts, or stir if using a mortar and pestle, until combined.

4 Brush the spice mixture over the chicken, dot it with the butter pieces and bake it for another 25 to 30 minutes, or until cooked through and rich red. Serve warm or at room temperature.

*NUTRITION PER SERVE (6): Protein 25 g; Fat 10 g; Carbohydrate 2 g; Dietary Fibre 0 g; Cholesterol 90 mg; 775 kJ (185 cal)*

# BEEF SOUP WITH RICE NOODLES

•

***Preparation time:*** 30 minutes
+ 1 hour marinating
***Total cooking time:*** 1 hour
***Serves*** 4

★ ★

350 g (11¹/₄ oz) fillet steak
2 teaspoons soy sauce
¹/₄ cup (60 ml/2 fl oz) coconut milk
1 tablespoon crunchy peanut butter
1 tablespoon grated palm sugar or soft
  brown sugar
2 teaspoons sambal oelek
1 teaspoon oil
125 g (4 oz) dried rice vermicelli
1.5 litres beef stock
2 tablespoons grated palm sugar or soft
  brown sugar, extra
2 tablespoons fish sauce
1 small Lebanese cucumber
1 cup (90 g/3 oz) bean sprouts, scraggly
  ends removed
2 lettuce leaves, cut in small pieces
6 tablespoons finely chopped fresh mint
¹/₂ cup (80 g/2²/₃ oz) unsalted roasted
  peanuts, finely chopped

1 Trim the meat of any fat and sinew and slice it evenly across the grain into thin slices.
2 Combine the meat, soy sauce, coconut milk, peanut butter, sugar and sambal oelek. Cover and marinate in the refrigerator for 1 hour.
3 Heat the oil in a frying pan and cook the meat in small batches over high heat for 3 minutes, or until browned. Remove from heat and cover.
4 Soak the vermicelli in hot water for 10 minutes. Drain.
5 Place the stock in a large pan and bring to the boil. When the stock is boiling add the extra sugar and fish sauce.
6 Cut the cucumber in quarters lengthways and then into thin slices. Place about 1 tablespoon cucumber slices in each individual serving bowl; divide the bean sprouts, pieces of lettuce and mint leaves evenly between bowls. Place some vermicelli and then a ladleful of stock in each bowl. Top with slices of cooked beef, sprinkle with peanuts and serve immediately.

*NUTRITION PER SERVE: Protein 30 g; Fat 25 g;
Carbohydrate 45 g; Dietary Fibre 5 g; Cholesterol 65 mg;
2150 kJ (515 cal)*

*Above: Beef Soup
with Rice Noodles*

## BAKED SPICED
## FISH CUTLETS

•

*Preparation time:* 15 minutes
*Total cooking time:* 30 minutes
*Serves* 4

1 tablespoon oil
1 medium onion, very finely chopped
2 cloves garlic, finely chopped
5 cm (2 inch) piece fresh ginger, finely
    grated
1 teaspoon ground coriander
1 stem lemon grass (white part only),
    finely chopped
2 teaspoons tamarind concentrate
2 teaspoons very finely grated lemon rind
4 small fish cutlets, such as blue eye cod
lime wedges, to garnish

•

1 Preheat the oven to warm 160°C (315°F/
Gas 2–3).
2 Heat the oil in a frying pan; add the onion,
garlic, ginger, coriander and lemon grass, and
stir over medium heat for 5 minutes or until
aromatic.
3 Stir in the tamarind, lemon rind and season
with freshly ground black pepper to taste.
Remove from the heat and set aside until cool.
4 Line a baking dish with aluminium foil and
grease it lightly to prevent the fish from sticking.

*Below: Baked Spiced
Fish Cutlets*

Arrange the fish in the baking dish in a single
layer and bake for 10 minutes. Turn the fish over
gently, spread with the spice paste and bake for
another 8 minutes, or until the flesh flakes when
tested with a fork. Be sure not to overcook the
fish or it will become dry. Garnish with lime
wedges and serve with steamed rice.
NOTE: Adjust the cooking time if the cutlets are
thick.

NUTRITION PER SERVE: Protein 15 g; Fat 5 g;
Carbohydrate 2 g; Dietary Fibre 1 g; Cholesterol 180 mg;
520 kJ (125 cal)

•

## FIERY
## PRAWN CURRY

•

*Preparation time:* 45 minutes
*Total cooking time:* 35 minutes
*Serves* 4

★ ★

*Spice Paste*
6 small dried red chillies
1 teaspoon shrimp paste
1 teaspoon coriander seeds
1 large red (Spanish) onion, roughly
    chopped
6 cloves garlic
4 small red chillies, roughly chopped
2 green chillies, roughly chopped
4 cm (1½ inch) piece fresh galangal,
    roughly chopped
1 stem lemon grass (white part only),
    sliced
6 candlenuts
½ teaspoon ground turmeric
1 tablespoon oil

•

500 g (1 lb) medium raw prawns
250 g (8 oz) fresh pineapple
250 g (8 oz) potatoes
1 tablespoon oil
1 cup (250 ml/8 fl oz) coconut milk
½ cup (125 ml/4 fl oz) water
2 tablespoons tamarind concentrate
1 teaspoon sugar
1 teaspoon salt

•

1 To make Spice Paste: Soak the dried chillies in
hot water until soft, then drain. Wrap the piece
of shrimp paste in foil and grill for 1–2 minutes
under medium heat. Dry-fry the coriander seeds
in a small pan until aromatic. Place the onion,
garlic and drained dried red chillies in a food
processor and process until just combined. Add
the shrimp paste, coriander seeds, fresh red and
green chilli, galangal and lemon grass and

process until well combined, scraping down the sides of the bowl with a spatula. Add the candlenuts, turmeric and oil and process until a smooth paste is formed.

2 Peel and devein the prawns, leaving the tails intact. Cut the pineapple into bite-sized pieces. Cut the potatoes into slightly larger pieces.

3 Place the potato in a large pan with enough water to cover and cook for 5 minutes, or until just tender. Drain and set aside.

4 Heat the oil in a large frying pan or wok; add the Spice Paste and cook over medium heat for 5 minutes, stirring constantly. Add the pineapple, potato, coconut milk and water and bring to the boil. Reduce the heat, add the prawns and simmer for 5 minutes. Add the tamarind, sugar and salt. Serve with plenty of steamed rice.

NUTRITION PER SERVE: *Protein 15 g; Fat 25 g; Carbohydrate 20 g; Dietary Fibre 5 g; Cholesterol 120 mg; 1610 kJ (385 cal)*

## MEE GORENG
### (FRIED NOODLES)

***Preparation time:*** 45 minutes
***Total cooking time:*** 30 minutes
***Serves*** 4

★ ★

*1 kg (2 lb) raw prawns*
*250 g (8 oz) rump steak*
*1 large onion, finely chopped*
*2 cloves garlic, finely chopped*
*2 red chillies, seeded and very finely chopped*
*2 cm (3/4 inch) piece fresh ginger, grated*
*1/4 cup (60 ml/2 fl oz) oil*
*350 g (111/4 oz) Hokkien noodles, gently pulled apart*
*4 spring onions, chopped*
*1 large carrot, cut into 4 cm (11/2 inch) matchsticks*
*2 celery sticks, cut into 4 cm (11/2 inch) matchsticks*
*1 tablespoon kecap manis*
*1 tablespoon soy sauce*
*1 tablespoon tomato sauce*
*extra spring onions, to garnish*

1 Peel and devein the prawns. Finely slice the rump steak.

2 Combine the onion, garlic, chilli and ginger in a food processor or mortar and pestle, and process in short bursts, or pound, until a paste is formed, adding a little of the oil if necessary. Set aside until needed.

3 Heat about 1 tablespoon oil in a large wok; add the noodles and stir-fry over medium heat until they are plump and warmed through. Place the noodles on a serving plate and cover to keep warm.

4 Add another tablespoon of the oil to the wok; add the paste mixture and stir-fry until golden. Add the prawns, steak, spring onion, carrot and celery, and stir-fry for 2 to 3 minutes. Add the kecap manis, soy and tomato sauces, and season well with salt and pepper. Spoon the mixture over the noodles and garnish with the extra spring onion. Serve immediately.

NUTRITION PER SERVE: *Protein 45 g; Fat 20 g; Carbohydrate 70 g; Dietary Fibre 3 g; Cholesterol 280 mg; 2755 kJ (655 cal)*

MEE GORENG

*Gently prise apart the Hokkien noodles before adding them to the wok.*

*Stir-fry the paste mixture until golden.*

*Above: Mee Goreng*

# SATAYS & KEBABS To prevent the wooden

skewers used for satays and kebabs burning before the meat is cooked, soak

them in water for at least 30 minutes. The ends can also be wrapped in foil.

## CHICKEN SATAYS

Cut 500 g (1 lb) chicken tenderloins in half lengthways. In a shallow non-metallic dish, combine 1 tablespoon honey, ¼ cup (60 ml/2 fl oz) soy sauce, 2 teaspoons sesame oil, 1 teaspoon ground coriander, 1 teaspoon ground turmeric and ½ teaspoon chilli powder. Thread the chicken lengthways onto soaked wooden skewers and place the skewers in the marinade. Cover and refrigerate for at least 2 hours. To make Quick Satay Sauce, cook a small finely chopped onion in 1 tablespoon oil until softened and then stir in ½ cup (125 g/4 oz) crunchy peanut butter, 2 tablespoons soy sauce, ½ cup (125 ml/4 fl oz) coconut cream and 2 tablespoons sweet chilli sauce. Cook gently until smooth and heated through. To cook the satays, place the skewers on a preheated grill and cook for 5–7 minutes, turning and basting with the marinade frequently. Serve with warm Quick Satay Sauce. Makes 8 satays.

*NUTRITION PER SATAY: Protein 20 g; Fat 15 g; Carbohydrate 10 g; Dietary Fibre 2 g; Cholesterol 45 mg; 1090 kJ (260 cal)*

## TERIYAKI STEAK KEBABS

Cut 750 g (1½ lb) lean rump steak into thin strips, 15 cm (6 inches) long and thread the slices onto skewers. Combine ½ cup (125 ml/ 4 fl oz) soy sauce, ½ cup (125 ml/ 4 fl oz) sherry or sake, 1 crushed clove garlic and 1 teaspoon each ground ginger and sugar. Place the steak in a shallow non-metallic dish and marinate it for at least 1 hour in the refrigerator. Drain and place the skewers on a preheated, oiled grill tray or barbecue flatplate and cook for 3–4 minutes each side. Makes 24 kebabs.

*NUTRITION PER KEBAB: Protein 10 g; Fat 1 g; Carbohydrate 1 g; Dietary Fibre 0 g; Cholesterol 20 mg; 195 kJ (45 cal)*

## KOFTA ON SKEWERS

Combine 750 g (1½ lb) minced beef, 1 small grated onion, ½ cup (30 g/ 1 oz) chopped fresh parsley, 2 tablespoons chopped fresh coriander leaves, ½ teaspoon each ground cumin, nutmeg and cardamom, and ½ teaspoon each dried oregano and mint. Let stand for 1 hour. With wet hands, form the mixture into 24 sausage shapes; thread 2 koftas onto each skewer between wedges of lime. Place the koftas under a hot grill or on a preheated barbecue flatplate and cook for 10–12 minutes, turning frequently. Makes 12 skewers.

*NUTRITION PER SKEWER: Protein 15 g; Fat 5 g; Carbohydrate 0 g; Dietary Fibre 0 g; Cholesterol 40 mg; 470 kJ (100 cal)*

## MALAYSIAN LAMB SATAYS

Trim any fat or silver sinew from 500 g (1 lb) lamb fillets. Slice the meat across the grain into very thin strips (if you have time, leave the meat in the freezer for 30 minutes as this will make it easier to thinly slice.) In a food processor, combine 1 roughly chopped onion, 2 crushed cloves garlic, 2 cm (¾ inch) lemon grass (white part only), 2 slices fresh galangal, 1 teaspoon chopped fresh ginger, 1 teaspoon ground cumin, ½ teaspoon ground fennel, 1 tablespoon ground coriander, 1 teaspoon turmeric, 1 tablespoon soft brown sugar and 1 tablespoon lemon juice and process until a smooth paste is formed. Transfer the paste to a shallow non-metallic dish and add the lamb, stirring to coat well. Cover and refrigerate overnight. Thread the meat onto skewers and cook under a preheated grill for 3–4 minutes on each side, or until cooked. Brush regularly with the remaining marinade while cooking. Makes 8 satays.

*NUTRITION PER SATAY: Protein 15 g; Fat 2 g; Carbohydrate 3 g; Dietary Fibre 0 g; Cholesterol 40 mg; 380 kJ (90 cal)*

## CHILLI PORK KEBABS

Trim the fat and sinew from 500 g (1 lb) pork fillet and cut into small cubes. Combine 2 tablespoons sweet chilli sauce, 2 tablespoons tomato sauce, 2 tablespoons hoisin sauce, 2 crushed cloves garlic, 3 tablespoons lemon juice, 2 tablespoons honey and 2 teaspoons grated fresh ginger. Pour over the pork and stir well. Cover and refrigerate for several hours or overnight. Thread the pork onto skewers; cook on a lightly oiled grill or barbecue flatplate for 3–4 minutes each side, or until cooked. Brush with the remaining marinade while cooking. Serve with Quick Satay Sauce (opposite). Makes 8 kebabs.

*NUTRITION PER KEBAB: Protein 15 g; Fat 1 g; Carbohydrate 10 g; Dietary Fibre 1 g; Cholesterol 30 mg; 490 kJ (115 cal)*

*From left: Chicken Satays; Kofta on Skewers; Malaysian Lamb Satays; Chilli Pork Kebabs; Teriyaki Steak Kebabs;*

from the snow pea sprouts. Cut the red pepper into thin strips. Finely slice the onion.

2 Place the beans in a large pan of boiling water and cook for 1 minute to blanch; drain. Combine the beans, spinach, snow pea sprouts, bean sprouts, red pepper and onion in a bowl.

3 To make Spice Dressing: Heat the oil in a small pan; add the garlic, ginger, chilli and coconut, and stir-fry over medium heat for 1 minute. Add the vinegar and water, and simmer for 1 minute. Allow to cool.

4 To serve, add the dressing to the vegetables, and toss until combined.

NOTE: Snow pea sprouts are the growing tips and tendrils from the snow pea plant.

Any blanched vegetables can be used in this salad. Try to use a variety of vegetables which result in a colourful appearance.

The Spice Dressing can be added up to 30 minutes before serving.

*NUTRITION PER SERVE: Protein 10 g; Fat 10 g; Carbohydrate 5 g; Dietary Fibre 10 g; Cholesterol 0 mg; 725 kJ (170 cal)*

## PORK SAMBALAN

*Preparation time:* 10 minutes
*Total cooking time:* 6 minutes
*Serves* 4

☆

400 g (12²⁄₃ oz) pork fillet
1–2 tablespoons Indonesian Sambal Paste
  (page 126)
1 tablespoon oil
1¹⁄₂ cups (375 ml/12 fl oz) coconut milk
chopped spring onion, to garnish

1 Cut the pork fillet into thin strips. Place the strips in a bowl with the sambal paste and oil, and toss until well combined.

2 Heat a heavy-based wok to very hot; stir-fry the pork for about 2 minutes in 2 batches, until tender and lightly browned. Return all the meat to the wok.

3 Add the coconut milk and simmer, uncovered, for 2 minutes. Garnish with spring onion and serve with rice.

NOTE: 2 tablespoons of sambal paste will make this dish quite hot. Use less paste for a milder dish, if you prefer.

*NUTRITION PER SERVE: Protein 25 g; Fat 25 g; Carbohydrate 5 g; Dietary Fibre 0 g; Cholesterol 50 mg; 1440 kJ (340 cal)*

## COLD VEGETABLE SALAD WITH SPICE DRESSING

*Preparation time:* 15 minutes
*Total cooking time:* 8 minutes
*Serves* 4

☆

300 g (9²⁄₃ oz) green or snake beans
10 spinach leaves
80 g (2²⁄₃ oz) snow pea (mange tout)
  sprouts
1 red pepper (capsicum)
1 red (Spanish) onion
100 g (3¹⁄₃ oz) bean sprouts, scraggly ends
  removed

*Spice Dressing*
2 tablespoons peanut oil
1 clove garlic, crushed
1 teaspoon grated fresh ginger
1 small red chilli, chopped
2 tablespoons desiccated coconut
1 tablespoon brown vinegar
¹⁄₃ cup (80 ml/2³⁄₄ fl oz) water

1 Top and tail the beans and cut them into 10 cm (4 inch) lengths. Remove the stems from the spinach leaves and slice the leaves thinly. Remove about 1 cm (¹⁄₂ inch) of the long stems

*Above: Cold Vegetable Salad with Spice Dressing*

## BAKED FISH WITH SPICES

•

*Preparation time:* 15 minutes
*Total cooking time:* 30 minutes
*Serves* 2

✦

2 whole white fish, each about 300 g
  (9²/3 oz), such as bream or snapper
1 onion, chopped
1 clove garlic, crushed
1 teaspoon chopped fresh ginger
1 teaspoon chopped lemon rind
2 tablespoons tamarind concentrate
1 tablespoon light soy sauce
1 tablespoon peanut oil

•

1 Preheat the oven to moderate 180°C (350°F/ Gas 4).
2 Place the fish onto large pieces of foil. Make 3 deep incisions with a sharp knife on each side of the fish.
3 Place the onion, garlic, ginger, lemon rind, tamarind, soy sauce and oil in a food processor and process until a smooth paste is formed.
4 Spread the onion mixture on the inside of the fish and on both sides.
5 Wrap the foil around the fish and secure it firmly. Place the fish in a baking dish and bake for 30 minutes, or until the fish is just cooked.

NUTRITION PER SERVE: Protein 65 g; Fat 20 g; Carbohydrate 4 g; Dietary Fibre 1 g; Cholesterol 210 mg; 1820 kJ (435 cal)

## TAMARIND CHICKEN

•

*Preparation time:* 15 minutes
  + 2 hours marinating
*Total cooking time:* 30 minutes
*Serves* 4

✦

4 chicken thighs
4 chicken drumsticks
1/3 cup (80 ml/2³/4 fl oz) tamarind
  concentrate
2 teaspoons ground coriander
1 teaspoon ground turmeric
2 cloves garlic, crushed
2 tablespoons peanut oil
2 red chillies, finely chopped
6 spring onions, finely chopped
oil, for deep-frying

•

1 Remove the skin from the chicken pieces. Place the chicken in a large pan with enough water to cover it. Cover and simmer for 15 minutes, or until cooked through. Drain and cool.
2 Combine the tamarind, coriander, turmeric and garlic. Add the tamarind mixture to the chicken and toss well to coat. Cover and marinate in the refrigerator for at least 2 hours, or preferably overnight.
3 Heat the peanut oil in a frying pan; add the chilli and spring onion, and stir-fry over low heat for 3 minutes. Set aside.
4 Heat the oil for deep-frying in a large pan; cook the chicken in 3 batches over medium heat for 5 minutes, or until the chicken is golden brown and heated through. Drain the chicken on paper towels, and keep it warm while frying the remaining chicken. Serve the chicken pieces with a spoonful of the chilli mixture on the side.

NUTRITION PER SERVE: Protein 30 g; Fat 35 g; Carbohydrate 1 g; Dietary Fibre 1 g; Cholesterol 95 mg; 1775 kJ (420 cal)

*Below: Tamarind Chicken*

## GRATING COCONUT
*To make grated fresh coconut, gently prise the flesh away from the shell using a flat-bladed knife. Use a vegetable peeler to remove the tough skin and then grate the flesh or use the vegetable peeler to flake it. Roast in a slow oven for 10–15 minutes to dry out before using.*

## COCONUT VEGETABLE CURRY
•

*Preparation time:* 30 minutes
*Total cooking time:* 25 minutes
*Serves* 4

✫

2 tablespoons oil
1 large red (Spanish) onion, roughly
   chopped
3 cloves garlic, finely chopped
4 red chillies, finely chopped
1 teaspoon shrimp paste
2 bay leaves, torn
1 cup (250 ml/8 fl oz) coconut milk
1 tablespoon tamarind concentrate
2 teaspoons sugar
1/4 teaspoon salt
500 g (1 lb) combined chopped pumpkin,
   potato and carrot
125 g (4 oz) chopped green beans
125 g (4 oz) chopped zucchini (courgette)
2 large tomatoes, peeled and roughly
   chopped
150 g (5 oz) baby spinach leaves
2 tablespoons desiccated coconut
2 tablespoons lemon juice

•

1 Heat the oil in a large heavy-based pan; add the onion, garlic, chilli and shrimp paste, and cook over medium heat for 5 minutes, stirring regularly to mix in the shrimp paste. Add the bay leaves, coconut milk, tamarind, sugar and salt. Bring to the boil, then reduce the heat and simmer, uncovered, for 5 minutes.

*Above: Coconut Vegetable Curry*

2 Add the pumpkin, potato and carrot. Cover and cook for 7 minutes, stirring occasionally. Add the beans and zucchini and cook for another 5 minutes, or until the vegetables are tender. Stir in the tomato and spinach and cook, uncovered, for 2 minutes.
3 Just before serving, remove the bay leaves, stir in the coconut and sprinkle with lemon juice.
NOTE: If the curry becomes too thick, add 1/2 cup (125 ml/4 fl oz) of water.

*NUTRITION PER SERVE: Protein 10 g; Fat 25 g; Carbohydrate 20 g; Dietary Fibre 10 g; Cholesterol 0 mg; 1440 kJ (345 cal)*

•

## STEAMED FISH CAKES
•

*Preparation time:* 20 minutes
*Total cooking time:* 15 minutes
*Serves* 6 as a first course

✫

500 g (1 lb) boneless white fish fillets
1 tablespoon Indonesian Sambal Paste
   (page 126)
2 tablespoons chopped fresh lemon grass
   (white part only)
2 cm (3/4 inch) piece fresh ginger, finely
   grated
1 teaspoon ground cumin
3 spring onions, finely chopped
1 egg, lightly beaten
1 tablespoon chopped fresh mint
lemon wedges, to serve

1 Preheat the oven to moderate 180°C (350°F/Gas 4).

2 Place the fish, sambal paste, lemon grass, ginger, cumin and spring onion into a food processor and process until a smooth paste is formed.

3 Transfer the fish mixture to a bowl, and mix through the egg and mint.

4 Divide the mixture into 6 equal portions, and shape each portion into a sausage. Wrap each portion in a 15 x 25 cm (6 x 10 inch) piece of baking paper and bake for 15 minutes. Serve with a squeeze of lemon juice.

*NUTRITION PER SERVE: Protein 15 g; Fat 3 g; Carbohydrate 1 g; Dietary Fibre 0 g; Cholesterol 80 mg; 410 kJ (95 cal)*

## INDONESIAN RENDANG

*Preparation time:* 15 minutes
*Total cooking time:* 2 hours 30 minutes
*Serves* 6

*1.5 kg (3 lb) chuck steak*
*2 medium onions, roughly chopped*
*4 teaspoons crushed garlic*
*1²/3 cups (410 ml/13 fl oz) coconut milk*
*2 teaspoons ground coriander*
*¹/2 teaspoon ground fennel*
*2 teaspoons ground cumin*
*¹/4 teaspoon ground cloves*
*4 red chillies, chopped*
*1 stem lemon grass (white part only) or*
*  4 strips lemon rind*
*1 tablespoon lemon juice*
*2 teaspoons grated palm sugar or soft*
*  brown sugar*

1 Trim the meat of any fat and sinew, and cut it evenly into small (about 3 cm/1¹/4 inch) cubes.

2 Place the onion and garlic in a food processor and process until smooth, adding water if necessary.

3 Place the coconut milk in a large pan and bring it to the boil, then reduce the heat to moderate and cook, stirring occasionally, until the milk has reduced by half and the oil has separated out. Do not allow the milk to brown.

4 Add the coriander, fennel, cumin and cloves, and stir for 1 minute. Add the meat and cook for 2 minutes until it changes colour. Add the onion mixture, chilli, lemon grass, lemon juice and sugar. Cook, over moderate heat for about 2 hours, or until the liquid is reduced and the mixture is quite thick. Stir frequently to prevent catching on the bottom of the pan.

5 Continue cooking until the oil from the coconut milk begins to emerge again, letting the curry develop colour and flavour. The dish needs constant attention at this stage to prevent it from burning. The curry is cooked when it is brown and dry.

NOTE: Like most curries, this one benefits from being made ahead of time to allow the flavours to mature. Prepare 2 to 3 days in advance and store, covered, in the refrigerator. Reheat over low heat. The curry can also be completely cooled in the refrigerator and then frozen for 1 month.

*NUTRITION PER SERVE: Protein 55 g; Fat 25 g; Carbohydrate 5 g; Dietary Fibre 0 g; Cholesterol 170 mg; 1905 kJ (455 cal)*

*Above: Indonesian Rendang*

*Above: Balinese
Fried Rice*

# BALINESE
# FRIED RICE
•

**Preparation time:** 20 minutes
**Total cooking time:** 20 minutes
**Serves** 6

★

500 g (1 lb) raw prawns
2 teaspoons oil
2 eggs
2 medium onions, chopped
2 cloves garlic
3 tablespoons oil, extra
¼ teaspoon shrimp paste
125 g (4 oz) rump steak, finely sliced
1 cooked chicken breast, finely sliced
1½ cups (300 g/9²/₃ oz) long-grain rice,
  cooked and cooled
1 tablespoon soy sauce
1 tablespoon fish sauce
1 tablespoon sambal oelek
1 tablespoon tomato paste (tomato purée,
  double concentrate)
6 spring onions, finely chopped
sliced cucumber, to garnish

1 Peel and devein the prawns; chop the meat.
2 Heat the oil in a wok or heavy-based pan.
Lightly beat the eggs and season with salt and
pepper. Add the eggs to the pan and cook over
moderately high heat, pulling the cooked edges
of the egg towards the centre. When set, transfer
the omelette to a plate, cool, and cut into fine
strips. Set aside.
3 Place the onion and garlic in a food processor
and process until finely chopped.
4 Heat the extra oil in the wok; add the onion
mixture and cook over medium heat, stirring
frequently until it has reduced in volume and is
translucent. Add the shrimp paste and cook a
further minute. Add the prawns and steak and
cook over high heat for 3 minutes. Add the
cooked chicken and rice and toss until heated.
5 Combine the soy sauce, fish sauce, sambal
oelek, tomato paste and spring onion and add to
the rice mixture. Mix well. Remove the rice from
the heat and transfer to a serving platter. Top
with the omelette strips and garnish with sliced
cucumber.

*NUTRITION PER SERVE: Protein 30 g; Fat 20 g;
Carbohydrate 20 g; Dietary Fibre 2 g; Cholesterol 215 mg;
1495 kJ (355 cal)*

## BALINESE FRIED FISH

•

*Preparation time:* 25 minutes
*Total cooking time:* 30 minutes
*Serves* 4

★ ★

750 g (1¹/₂ lb) firm white fish fillets,
   such as jewfish or ling
¹/₂ teaspoon salt
¹/₂ teaspoon pepper
oil, for shallow frying
4 red Asian shallots, finely sliced
   lengthways
2.5 cm (1 inch) piece lemon grass
   (white part only), finely chopped
2 red chillies, finely chopped
2 cm (³/₄ inch) piece fresh ginger, grated
¹/₂ teaspoon shrimp paste
¹/₂ cup (125 ml/4 fl oz) water
2 tablespoons kecap manis
1 tablespoon grated palm sugar or soft
   brown sugar
2 teaspoons lime juice
3 spring onions, finely chopped

1 Preheat the oven to warm 160°C (315°F/
Gas 2–3). Cut the fish into bite-sized pieces;
sprinkle with the salt and pepper.
2 Heat the oil, about 2 cm (³/₄ inch) deep, in a
deep frying pan; add the fish 3 or 4 pieces at a
time, and fry over moderately high heat for
about 4 minutes, turning the pieces over, until
they are a light golden brown. Drain the fish
on paper towels and place in the oven to keep
warm.

3 In a small pan, heat 2 tablespoons of the fish
frying oil; add the shallots, lemon grass, chilli,
ginger and shrimp paste and cook for 3 minutes
over low heat, stirring occasionally. Add the
water, kecap manis and sugar, and stir until the
sauce boils and thickens. Stir in the lime juice
and spring onion. Drizzle the sauce over the fish
and serve immediately.
NOTE: The fish must have a solid meaty
texture or it will fall apart during the frying.
Kecap manis is Indonesian soy sauce, and is
slightly thicker and sweeter than Chinese
soy sauce.

*NUTRITION PER SERVE: Protein 40 g; Fat 30 g;
Carbohydrate 6 g; Dietary Fibre 1 g; Cholesterol 130 mg;
1850 kJ (440 cal)*

*Above: Balinese
Fried Fish*

## LAMB CURRY

•

*Preparation time:* 25 minutes
*Total cooking time:* 1 hour 45 minutes
*Serves* 4–6

★ ★

750 g (1½ lb) diced lamb
¼ teaspoon salt
¼ teaspoon pepper
2 large onions, chopped
3 tablespoons oil
2 stems lemon grass (white part only),
    sliced
6 cloves garlic
3 cm (1¼ inch) piece fresh galangal,
    roughly chopped
10 cm (4 inch) piece fresh ginger, roughly
    chopped
2½ teaspoons ground turmeric
2 red chillies, roughly chopped
1 teaspoon shrimp paste
2 tablespoons oil, extra
2 cinnamon sticks
⅛ teaspoon ground cloves
3 cups (750 ml/24 fl oz) coconut milk

•

1 Combine the lamb, salt, pepper, onion and oil.
Heat a wok or heavy-based pan until very hot;
add the lamb and onion mixture in several
batches and brown very well. Using tongs or a
slotted spoon, remove all the meat from the wok,
leaving any oil.
2 Combine the lemon grass, garlic, galangal,
ginger, turmeric, chilli and shrimp paste in a
food processor and process, adding the extra oil,
until a smooth paste is formed.
3 Reheat the wok; add the spice paste and cook
it over medium heat for 3 minutes, stirring
constantly (take care the paste does not burn).
Add the lamb and onion mixture, cinnamon,
cloves and coconut milk.
4 Simmer, uncovered, for 1½ hours, stirring
occasionally until the lamb is very tender. Serve
with steamed white rice.
NOTE: This curry is known as a 'gulai', which is
the richest of the Indonesian curries.

*NUTRITION PER SERVE (6): Protein 30 g; Fat 50 g;
Carbohydrate 5 g; Dietary Fibre 0 g; Cholesterol 85 mg;
2520 kJ (600 cal)*

## PRAWNS IN SPICES AND COCONUT CREAM

•

*Preparation time:* 15 minutes
*Total cooking time:* 10 minutes
*Serves* 4

★

1.25 kg (2½ lb) raw king prawns
¾ cup (185 ml/6 fl oz) coconut cream
1 teaspoon finely grated lime
    or lemon rind
1 tablespoon lime or lemon juice
2 teaspoons light soy sauce
½ teaspoon shrimp paste
1 tablespoon peanut oil
1 small onion, cut into 8 pieces
chopped spring onion, to garnish

•

1 Peel and devein the prawns, leaving the tails
intact.
2 Combine the coconut cream, rind, juice, soy
sauce and shrimp paste in a bowl.
3 Heat the oil in a frying pan; add the onion and
stir-fry over medium heat until soft. Add the
prawns and stir-fry for 2 minutes.
4 Add the coconut cream mixture and stir
for 2 to 3 minutes, until the sauce has
thoroughly heated through. Garnish with spring
onion and serve with rice.

*NUTRITION PER SERVE: Protein 25 g; Fat 15 g;
Carbohydrate 5 g; Dietary Fibre 0 g; Cholesterol 170 mg;
1020 kJ (240 cal)*

---

GINGER
*Tender young ginger, with
pink-tinged tips and skin
so soft and thin it can be
rubbed off between finger
and thumb, is fairly mild
in flavour. Mature ginger,
with thicker skin and more
fibrous flesh, is stronger in
flavour and heat. Ginger is
available grated in jars,
but fresh is always best.
Pickled young ginger is
sometimes used as a
garnish for grilled meats
or is served as a snack in
its own right.*

*Opposite page: Lamb
Curry (top); Prawns
in Spices and
Coconut Cream*

# SWEET KECAP PORK

•

*Preparation time:* 20 minutes
*Total cooking time:* 1 hour 10 minutes
*Serves* 4

500 g (1 lb) diced pork
¼ teaspoon each salt and pepper
2 tablespoons oil
1 large onion, finely chopped
3 cloves garlic, finely chopped
5 cm (2 inch) piece fresh ginger, grated
3 red chillies, finely chopped
2 tablespoons kecap manis
1 cup (250 ml/8 fl oz) coconut milk
2 teaspoons lime juice

•

1 Mix together the pork, salt, pepper and oil. Heat a wok or heavy-based pan and cook the pork in several batches over medium heat, until well browned. Remove all the meat from the wok and set aside.
2 Reduce the heat to low; add the onion, garlic, ginger and chilli and cook for 10 minutes, stirring occasionally, until the onion is very soft and golden.
3 Add the pork, kecap manis and coconut milk, and cook over low heat for 1 hour, stirring occasionally. Stir in the lime juice and serve with plenty of steamed rice and fresh chopped chilli.

*Below: Sweet Kecap Pork*

NUTRITION PER SERVE: Protein 30 g; Fat 25 g; Carbohydrate 5 g; Dietary Fibre 0 g; Cholesterol 60 mg; 1500 kJ (360 cal)

# STIR-FRIED HOT BEEF

•

*Preparation time:* 25 minutes
*Total cooking time:* 20 minutes
*Serves* 4

**Spice Paste**
5 red chillies
2 cm (¾ inch) piece fresh galangal, sliced
1 teaspoon shrimp paste
10 red Asian shallots, roughly chopped
4 cloves garlic
2 tablespoons oil

•

1 teaspoon coriander seeds
500 g (1 lb) sirloin, fillet or topside steak
½ teaspoon salt
1 tablespoon oil
2 tablespoons tamarind concentrate
2 teaspoons grated palm sugar or soft brown sugar
2 tablespoons coconut cream

•

1 To make Spice Paste: Place all the paste ingredients in a food processor and process until a smooth paste is formed, scraping down the sides of the bowl regularly.
2 Dry-fry the coriander over low heat for 1 minute in a frying pan, shaking the pan constantly. Grind the seeds in a mortar and pestle or food processor.
3 Slice the meat into thin pieces. Combine with the coriander and salt, mixing well. Set aside.

4 Heat the oil in a wok or frying pan; add the Spice Paste and cook over high heat for 3 minutes, or until very fragrant and a little oily. Remove the Spice Paste from the pan.
5 Reheat the the wok to high: add the meat in 2 batches and stir-fry for 2 to 3 minutes or until just cooked. Add the Spice Paste, tamarind, sugar and coconut cream. Toss over very high heat for 1 minute and serve immediately.

*NUTRITION PER SERVE: Protein 30 g; Fat 20 g; Carbohydrate 5 g; Dietary Fibre 0 g; Cholesterol 85 mg; 1370 kJ (325 cal)*

# BALINESE CHILLI SQUID

**Preparation time:** 25 minutes
**Total cooking time:** 10 minutes
**Serves** 4

✷ ✷

*750 g (1½ lb) calamari (squid) tubes*
*¼ cup (60 ml/2 fl oz) lime juice*
*2 tablespoons oil*
*1 large red chilli, seeded and sliced*
*3 spring onions, sliced*
*1 tablespoon oil, extra*
*1 tablespoon tamarind concentrate*
*1 stem lemon grass (white part only), finely sliced*
*1 cup (250 ml/8 fl oz) chicken stock*
*5 Thai basil leaves, shredded*

*Spice Paste*
*2 large red chillies, seeded and chopped*
*2 cloves garlic, chopped*
*2 cm (¾ inch) piece fresh turmeric, chopped*
*2 cm (¾ inch) piece fresh ginger, chopped*
*3 spring onions, chopped*
*1 tomato, peeled, seeded and chopped*
*2 teaspoons coriander seeds*
*1 teaspoon shrimp paste*

1 Cut the calamari into large pieces and score the tender inner flesh diagonally, in a criss-cross pattern, taking care not to cut all the way through. Place in a bowl with the lime juice and season to taste with salt and pepper. Cover and refrigerate.
2 To make Spice Paste: Place the chilli, garlic, turmeric, ginger, spring onion, tomato, coriander seeds and shrimp paste in a food processor and process until a smooth paste is formed.
3 Heat the oil in a wok and add the chilli and spring onion. Add the squid in batches and cook over moderate heat for 2 minutes. Remove from the wok.
4 Heat the extra oil in the wok, add the spice paste, tamarind and lemon grass and cook over moderate heat, stirring, for 5 minutes.
5 Return the squid to the wok and add the chicken stock. Season with pepper, to taste, and add the basil leaves. Bring to the boil, then reduce the heat and simmer for 20 minutes. Serve with rice.

*NUTRITION PER SERVE: Protein 35 g; Fat 15 g; Carbohydrate 3 g; Dietary Fibre 2 g; Cholesterol 375 mg; 1245 kJ (295 cal)*

*Above: Balinese Chilli Squid*

**2** Place the coconut milk in a medium pan, and heat until nearly boiling. Pour the milk over the rice, stirring constantly until the mixture comes to the boil. Add the salt and curry leaves. Cover with a tight-fitting lid, reduce the heat to very low and cook for 25 minutes.

**3** Remove the lid, stir well and leave to cool for 10 minutes. Remove the curry leaves and pile the rice onto a platter (traditionally lined with banana leaves). Arrange the egg, cucumber and chilli over the rice and scatter the fried onion over the top.

*NUTRITION PER SERVE: Protein 20 g; Fat 65 g; Carbohydrate 110 g; Dietary Fibre 4 g; Cholesterol 155 mg; 4680 kJ (1115 cal)*

## FRESH CORN SAMBAL

*Preparation time:* 25 minutes
*Total cooking time:* 10 minutes
*Serves* 8

☆ ☆

3 corn cobs
1 tablespoon coriander seeds
1 teaspoon shrimp paste, crumbled into
  pieces
1 clove garlic
1 medium onion, roughly chopped
3 red chillies
3 tablespoons tamarind concentrate
2 tablespoon water
¹/₂ teaspoon salt
3 teaspoons sugar

**1** Remove the husk and silks from the corn. Cut down the cobs with a sharp knife to remove the kernels. Dry-fry the corn kernels over medium heat for 5 minutes, in batches if necessary, shaking the pan regularly until the corn kernels turn golden but do not burn. Set aside.

**2** Dry-fry the coriander and shrimp paste in a frying pan for 3 minutes or until very fragrant. Roughly grind the coriander and shrimp paste in a mortar and pestle.

**3** Place the corn, ground coriander and shrimp paste, garlic, onion and chilli in a food processor and process until a rough paste is formed. Add the tamarind, water, salt and sugar and process again.

**4** Serve the sambal as an accompaniment to curries, fish and vegetable dishes with plenty of rice.

*NUTRITION PER SERVE: Protein 1 g; Fat 0 g; Carbohydrate 5 g; Dietary Fibre 1 g; Cholesterol 0 mg; 145 kJ (35 cal)*

## FESTIVE COCONUT RICE

*Preparation time:* 25 minutes
*Total cooking time:* 40 minutes
*Serves* 4

☆ ☆

3 tablespoons oil
1 medium onion, cut into thin wedges
4 cm (1¹/₂ inch) piece fresh ginger, grated
2 cloves garlic, finely chopped
2¹/₂ cups (500 g/1 lb) long-grain rice
1 teaspoon ground turmeric
4 cups (1 litre) coconut milk
1 teaspoon salt
6 curry leaves

### Garnishes
3 hard-boiled eggs, cut into quarters
1 Lebanese cucumber, thinly sliced
2 red chillies, thinly sliced
¹/₂ cup (35 g/1¹/₄ oz) crisp fried onion

**1** Heat the oil in a large heavy-based pan; add the onion, ginger and garlic and fry over low heat for 5 minutes. Add the rice and turmeric, and cook for 2 minutes, stirring well.

*Above: Festive Coconut Rice*

## MIXED VEGETABLES WITH TAMARIND

•

*Preparation time:* 25 minutes
*Total cooking time:* 30 minutes
*Serves 4*

★

250 g (8 oz) pumpkin
200 g (6¹/2 oz) potatoes
100 g (3¹/3 oz) beans
200 g (6¹/2 oz) cabbage
100 g (3¹/3 oz) English spinach leaves
2 cups (500 ml/16 fl oz) vegetable stock
¹/2 cup (125 ml/4 fl oz) tamarind
    concentrate
2 cinnamon sticks
2 bay leaves
4 cloves garlic, finely chopped
10 red Asian shallots, very finely sliced
5 cm (2 inch) piece fresh ginger, grated
200 g (6¹/2 oz) baby corn

1 Roughly chop the pumpkin. Cut the potatoes into thick slices. Top and tail the beans and cut them into short lengths. Shred the cabbage and spinach leaves.
2 Place the stock, tamarind, cinnamon, bay leaves, garlic, shallots and ginger in a large pan, and bring to the boil.
3 Add the pumpkin and potato and simmer for 5 minutes. Add the corn and beans and cook for another 5 minutes.
4 Add the cabbage and spinach and cook until just tender. Serve as an accompaniment to a main meal.

NUTRITION PER SERVE: Protein 5 g; Fat 1 g;
Carbohydrate 15 g; Dietary Fibre 5 g; Cholesterol 0 mg;
385 kJ (90 cal)

SHRIMP PASTE
*Shrimp paste is always cooked before it is eaten. This transforms its acrid flavour into an aromatic seasoning. If it is not to be fried with the spice paste, wrap it in aluminium foil and dry-fry in a pan or roast in the oven or under the grill—this will prevent its overpowering odour filling the entire house.*

*Above: Mixed
Vegetables with
Tamarind*

# SINGAPORE & MALAYSIA

Separated by only a narrow strip of water,
peninsula Malaysia and the island state
of Singapore have many dishes in common.
The Indian, Moslem and Chinese heritage of
both countries can be seen in Indian-hot
curries, Middle-Eastern inspired satays
and Chinese noodles, stir-fries and roasted
meats. These influences come together in
dishes like laksa, a creamy curry of seafood
or chicken simmered in coconut milk.
In Singapore, the mix of Malays and Chinese
has created Nonya food—an exciting blend
of  Chinese balance and Malaysian heat.

## SINGAPORE NOODLES

•

**Preparation time:** 45 minutes
**Total cooking time:** 20 minutes
**Serves 2–4**

★

300 g (9²/3 oz) dried rice vermicelli
600 g (1¹/4 lb) raw prawns
2 tablespoons oil
2 cloves garlic, finely chopped
350 g (11¹/4 oz) pork loin, cut into strips
1 large onion, cut into thin wedges
1 tablespoon mild curry powder
155 g (5 oz) green beans, cut into small
    diagonal pieces
1 large carrot, cut into fine matchsticks
1 teaspoon caster sugar
1 teaspoon salt
1 tablespoon soy sauce
200 g (6¹/2 oz) bean sprouts, scraggly ends
    removed
spring onion, cut into fine strips, to
    garnish

*Above: Singapore
Noodles*

1 Soak the vermicelli in boiling water for
5 minutes or until soft; drain well.
2 Peel and devein the prawns; chop the
prawn meat.
3 Heat 1 tablespoon oil in a wok and, when
hot, add the prawn meat, garlic and pork. Stir-fry
for 2 minutes or until just cooked; remove from
the wok.
4 Reduce the heat to medium and heat another
tablespoon oil; add the onion and curry powder
and stir-fry for 2 to 3 minutes. Add the beans,
carrot, sugar and salt, sprinkle with a little water
and stir-fry for 2 minutes.
5 Add the vermicelli and soy sauce to the wok;
toss with 2 wooden spoons. Add the bean
sprouts and pork mixture, season with salt,
pepper and sugar to taste, and then toss well.
Serve garnished with spring onion.

*NUTRITION PER SERVE (4): Protein 40 g; Fat 15 g;
Carbohydrate 70 g; Dietary Fibre 5 g; Cholesterol 185 mg;
2360 kJ (560 cal)*

## CHILLI CRAB

•

**Preparation time:** 30 minutes
**Total cooking time:** 45 minutes
**Serves** 2–4

★ ★ ★

2 fresh blue swimmer crabs,
  approximately 500 g (1 lb) each
½ cup (60 g/2 oz) plain flour
¼ cup (60 ml/2 fl oz) oil
1 medium onion, finely chopped
5 cm (2 inch) piece fresh ginger, finely
  grated
4 cloves garlic, finely chopped
3–5 red chillies, finely chopped
2 cups (500 ml/16 fl oz) ready-made
  tomato pasta sauce
1 cup (250 ml/8 fl oz) water
2 tablespoons soy sauce
2 tablespoons sweet chilli sauce
1 tablespoon rice vinegar
2 tablespoons soft brown sugar

•

1 Wash the crabs well and scrub the shells using a scourer. Using a large cleaver, cut the crabs in half and rinse well under cold water, carefully removing the yellow gills or spongy parts. Hit the legs and larger front nippers with the flat side of the cleaver to crack the shells (to make it easier to eat the meat inside).

2 Lightly and carefully coat the shells with a little flour. Heat about 2 tablespoons oil in a large wok, cook one crab half at a time, carefully turning and holding the crab in the hot oil until the shell just turns red. Repeat with the remaining crab halves.

3 Add the remaining oil to the wok; cook the onion, ginger, garlic and chilli for 5 minutes over medium heat, stirring regularly. Add the tomato sauce, water, soy sauce, chilli sauce, vinegar and sugar. Bring to the boil and cook for 15 minutes. Return the crab to the wok and simmer, turning carefully in the sauce for 8 to 10 minutes or until the crab meat turns white. Do not overcook. Serve with steamed rice and provide finger bowls.

NOTE: It is essential that only very fresh crabs are used so order them from your fishmonger the day before required, and insist on having crabs that have been freshly caught. Live crabs can be killed quickly by spearing them between the eyes—the fishmonger will do this for you if you prefer. Don't buy cooked crabs for this recipe, they must be fresh.

*NUTRITION PER SERVE (4): Protein 15 g; Fat 15 g;
Carbohydrate 40 g; Dietary Fibre 5 g; Cholesterol 52 mg;
1503 kJ (355 cal)*

*CHILLI CRAB*

*Hit the legs and larger
front nippers to crack
the shells.*

*Turn the crab and hold
it in hot oil until the
shell just turns red.*

*Above: Chilli Crab*

# MIXED VEGETABLES IN MILD CURRY SAUCE

•

*Preparation time:* 20 minutes
*Total cooking time:* 25 minutes
*Serves* 4

✫✫

250 g (8 oz) peeled pumpkin
2 medium orange sweet potatoes
125 g (4 oz) yellow squash
125 g (4 oz) green beans
125 g (4 oz) cabbage
6 teaspoons oil
1 large onion, finely sliced
1 clove garlic, crushed
1/2 cup (100 g/3 1/3 oz) peeled and chopped
    tomato
1 red chilli, chopped
3 strips lemon rind
4 kaffir lime leaves, dried or fresh
2 teaspoons grated palm sugar or soft
    brown sugar
1 teaspoon salt
1 tablespoon fish sauce
1 2/3 cups (410 ml/13 fl oz) coconut milk
1 cup (250 ml/8 fl oz) chicken stock
2 teaspoons lemon juice

•

1 Cut the pumpkin into small wedges and the sweet potato into 2 cm (3/4 inch) pieces. Quarter the squash; top and tail the beans, halving them if long; and cut the cabbage into 1 cm (1/2 inch) wide shreds.
2 Heat the oil in a medium pan; add the onion and garlic and cook over medium heat until soft and slightly golden.
3 Add the tomato, chilli, lemon rind, lime leaves, sugar, salt, fish sauce, coconut milk, stock and lemon juice; cook for 5 minutes until the flavour has intensified.
4 Add the sweet potato and pumpkin to the sauce and cook for 8 minutes. Add the beans, cabbage and squash and cook for 6 minutes. Serve with steamed rice.
NOTE: The sauce can be prepared a few hours ahead and reheated. Cook the vegetables just before serving.

*NUTRITION PER SERVE: Protein 10 g; Fat 30 g; Carbohydrate 45 g; Dietary Fibre 10 g; Cholesterol 0 mg; 1925 kJ (460 cal)*

# CURRIED NOODLES WITH PORK

•

*Preparation time:* 20 minutes
*Total cooking time:* 10 minutes
*Serves* 4

✫

125 g (4 oz) dried rice stick noodles
1 medium onion
2 tablespoons oil
2 teaspoons mild curry powder
1/2 teaspoon salt
1/2 cup (80 g/2 2/3 oz) frozen peas
1/4 cup (60 ml/2 fl oz) coconut milk or
    vegetable stock
2 teaspoons soy sauce
125 g (4 oz) Chinese barbecued pork or
    roast pork, thinly sliced

•

1 Place the rice noodles in a bowl, cover with hot water, and leave to soak for 20 minutes. Drain well in a colander. Cut the onion into eighths and separate the layers.
2 Heat the oil in a wok; add the onion and cook over high heat for 1 minute. Add the curry powder, salt and noodles; toss to coat.
3 Add the peas, coconut milk and soy sauce, tossing a few times to combine. Cover the wok tightly, reduce heat to very low and cook for 3 minutes. Gently stir the sliced pork through and heat for a further minute. Serve either as a course on its own or as a snack.

*NUTRITION PER SERVE: Protein 10 g; Fat 20 g; Carbohydrate 30 g; Dietary Fibre 5 g; Cholesterol 20 mg; 1355 kJ (325 cal)*

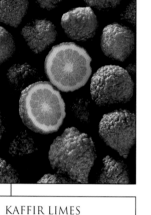

**KAFFIR LIMES**
*Native to Southeast Asia, this variety of lime tree has fragrant green leaves and bears a dark green, knobbly fruit. The leaves and fruit rind are added to curries and other dishes to give a citrus tang (the fruit is not very juicy and is seldom used). Remove the coarse central vein from the leaves and tear or shred them very finely. Pare or grate the rind. Both the leaves and limes are available fresh from Asian food stores. Leftover fresh leaves can be frozen in airtight plastic bags. Also available are dried leaves and dried rind; these must be soaked in water before use. Fresh young lemon leaves and strips of rind from a standard lime can be substituted, but the flavour will not be quite the same.*

*Opposite page: Mixed Vegetables in Mild Curry Sauce (top); Curried Noodles with Pork*

1 Toss together the pineapple, cucumber, tomatoes, beans and sprouts in a bowl, cover and refrigerate until chilled. Combine the vinegar, lime juice, chilli and sugar in a small bowl and stir until the sugar dissolves.

2 Dry-fry the shrimp in a frying pan, shaking the pan constantly until the shrimp are light orange and fragrant. Process the shrimp in a food processor until finely chopped.

3 Arrange the chilled salad on a serving platter, drizzle the dressing over the top and garnish with the chopped shrimp and mint leaves. Serve immediately.

*NUTRITION PER SERVE (6): Protein 5 g; Fat 0 g; Carbohydrate 10 g; Dietary Fibre 4 g; Cholesterol 30 mg; 270 kJ (65 cal)*

•

## GARLIC PRAWNS IN CHILLI SAUCE

•

***Preparation time:*** *40 minutes*
***Total cooking time:*** *10 minutes*
***Serves*** *4*

✬

*1 kg (2 lb) raw king prawns*
*2 cloves garlic, crushed*
*2 tablespoons peanut oil*
*3 teaspoons grated fresh ginger*
*1 stick celery, diced*
*1 red pepper (capsicum), seeded and diced*
*1 tablespoon sweet chilli sauce*
*1 tablespoon hoisin sauce*
*2 tablespoons lime juice*
*1 teaspoon sugar*

•

1 Peel and devein the prawns, leaving the tails intact. Place the prawns in a non-metallic bowl and mix in the garlic. Set aside.

2 Heat a wok and add 1 tablespoon oil. Add the ginger, celery and red pepper and cook until softened. Remove from the wok. Heat the remaining tablespoon oil and add the prawns. Cook over high heat until bright pink and cooked through. Spoon the celery and red pepper mixture back into the wok with the prawns and add the chilli sauce, hoisin sauce, lime juice and sugar. Season to taste with black pepper. Heat through for a minute or so then serve with steamed rice.

*NUTRITION PER SERVE: Protein 25 g; Fat 10 g; Carbohydrate 5 g; Dietary Fibre 2 g; Cholesterol 185 mg; 980 kJ (235 cal)*

## MIXED VEGETABLE SALAD

•

***Preparation time:*** *40 minutes*
***Total cooking time:*** *3 minutes*
***Serves*** *4–6*

✬

*300 g (9²/3 oz) chopped*
  *fresh pineapple*
*1 long cucumber, chopped*
*1 punnet cherry tomatoes, halved*
*155 g (5 oz) green beans, finely sliced*
*155 g (5 oz) bean sprouts, scraggly*
  *ends removed*
*1/3 cup (80 ml/2³/4 fl oz) rice vinegar*
*2 tablespoons lime juice*
*2 red chillies, seeded and very finely*
  *chopped*
*2 teaspoons sugar*
*30 g (1 oz) dried shrimp, to garnish*
*small fresh mint leaves, to garnish*

*Above: Mixed*
*Vegetable Salad*

# SIAMESE NOODLES IN SPICY COCONUT SAUCE

•

*Preparation time:* 1 hour 10 minutes
*Total cooking time:* 30 minutes
*Serves* 6

★ ★ ★

*Spice Paste*
10 dried red chillies, soaked in hot water
  until softened
10 red Asian shallots, chopped
1 stalk lemon grass (white part only),
  chopped
1 teaspoon shrimp paste
3 tablespoons peanut oil
1 teaspoon salt
1 tablespoon sugar

•

1 tablespoon dried tamarind pulp
1/2 cup (125 ml/4 fl oz) warm water
1.25 litres coconut milk
300 g (9²/3 oz) dried rice vermicelli
400 g (12²/3 oz) fried tofu
oil, for shallow frying
400 g (12²/3 oz) bean sprouts, scraggly
  ends removed
500 g (1 lb) cooked prawns, peeled with
  tails left on
1 cup (125 g/4 oz) chopped garlic chives
3 hard-boiled eggs, shells removed and cut
  into quarters
2 red chillies, seeded and finely sliced,
  optional
3 limes, quartered

•

1 To make Spice Paste: Drain and seed the soaked chillies, reserving the water, and chop. Place the chillies in a food processor along with the shallots, lemon grass and shrimp paste. Process until finely chopped, adding a little of the chilli water if necessary. Heat the peanut oil in a small frying pan and fry the paste over low heat for about 3 minutes. Add the salt and sugar. Set aside.
2 Soak the tamarind in the warm water for about 10 minutes.
3 Take half the spice paste and place it in a pan along with the coconut milk. Strain the soaked tamarind and water through a nylon sieve into the coconut milk and discard any seeds and fibre. Bring the mixture to the boil and simmer for 3 minutes. Set aside.
4 Soak the vermicelli in boiling water for 5 minutes, and drain. Cut the tofu into thick slices. Heat the oil in a small frying pan and fry the slices of tofu until golden on both sides. Remove and drain on paper towels.

5 When ready to serve the dish, heat the remaining spice paste in a large wok and add the bean sprouts. Turn the heat up high and cook for about a minute. Add half the prawns and half the garlic chives. Add the drained vermicelli to the wok; toss until heated through. Reheat the coconut sauce and keep it hot.
6 To serve, transfer the vermicelli mixture to a large warm serving platter and arrange the remaining prawns, the egg quarters and slices of tofu on top. Scatter over the sliced chilli and remaining garlic chives. Pour the coconut sauce into a large warm soup tureen. Provide deep bowls for diners to fill with the vermicelli mixture, then ladle over some coconut sauce and a squeeze of lime juice.

*NUTRITION PER SERVE: Protein 30 g; Fat 65 g; Carbohydrate 55 g; Dietary Fibre 5 g; Cholesterol 265 mg; 3840 kJ (915 cal)*

SPRING ROLLS
*Spring rolls were originally eaten in China at festivities to celebrate the Lunar New Year, which heralds the coming of spring. Because no work should be done at this time, the rolls—which traditionally contained fresh bamboo shoots— were made ahead. Varieties of spring roll are eaten throughout Southeast Asia.*

*Above: Siamese Noodles in Spicy Coconut Sauce*

# FINGER FOOD
Asia has a delicious range of finger food, served with fragrant tea in the middle of the day, a cooling beer in the evening or bought piping hot from a street stall.

## THAI SPRING ROLLS
Soak 30 g (1 oz) dried rice vermicelli in hot water until soft then drain well and cut into shorter lengths. Heat 1 tablespoon oil in a wok or pan and add 3 chopped cloves garlic, 2 teaspoons grated fresh galangal or ginger, 3 finely chopped coriander roots and 3 chopped spring onions. Stir-fry for 2 minutes. Add 200 g (6½ oz) pork mince and 2 sticks finely sliced celery and stir-fry for 3 minutes to brown the pork, breaking up any lumps. Add 1 cup (155 g/5 oz) grated carrot, ½ cup (25 g/¾ oz) chopped fresh coriander leaves, ¼ cup (45 g/1½ oz) finely chopped cucumber, 1 tablespoon sweet chilli sauce, 2 teaspoons fish sauce, 1 teaspoon brown sugar and the noodles and mix well. Cool completely. Place 1 spring roll wrapper at a time (you will need about 18), with a corner towards you, on a damp tea towel. Wet the edges with a little water. Spread about 1½ tablespoons filling in the centre of the wrapper. Fold the edges towards the centre, roll up the spring roll tightly and seal the edge with water. Repeat with the remaining wrappers and filling. Half fill a deep pan with oil and heat until moderately hot. Fry the rolls, in batches, for 2–3 minutes or until golden brown. Drain and serve with a sweet chilli sauce and soy sauce. Makes 18.

*NUTRITION PER SPRING ROLL: Protein 5 g; Fat 5 g; Carbohydrate 5 g; Dietary Fibre 1 g; Cholesterol 10 mg; 215 kJ (50 cal)*

## PRAWN TOASTS
Peel and devein 350 g (11¼ oz) raw prawns. Separate 2 eggs into small bowls and lightly beat the egg yolks. In a food processor, place the prawn meat, egg whites, 1 clove garlic, 75 g (2½ oz) drained, finely chopped,

canned water chestnuts, 1 tablespoon chopped fresh coriander leaves, 2 teaspoons fresh ginger, and ¼ teaspoon each white pepper and salt. Process for 20–30 seconds, or until the mixture is smooth. Trim the crusts from 6 slices of white bread, cut in half diagonally then cut the halves in half again to form small triangles. Brush the top of each bread triangle with egg yolk, spread the prawn mixture evenly over the triangles and sprinkle each with white sesame seeds—you will need about 1 tablespoon. Half fill a deep pan with oil and heat until moderately hot. Fry the triangles in small batches, with the prawn mixture face-down, for 10–15 seconds, or until golden and crisp. Drain on paper towels. Serve hot. Makes 24.

NUTRITION PER PIECE: Protein 5 g; Fat 5 g; Carbohydrate 4 g; Dietary Fibre 0 g; Cholesterol 30 mg; 240 kJ (55 cal)

## VEGETARIAN WON TONS

Heat 1 tablespoon oil in a wok or pan and cook 2 chopped cloves garlic, 4 chopped spring onions and 3 teaspoons grated fresh ginger for 2 minutes. Add 2 finely sliced sticks celery, 2 cups (150 g/4¾ oz) finely shredded cabbage, 2 cups (310 g/9¾ oz) grated carrot, 125 g (4 oz) finely sliced fried tofu, 1 cup (125 g/4 oz) chopped bean sprouts and 2 tablespoons chopped water chestnuts. Cover the pan and steam for 2 minutes. Blend 3 teaspoons cornflour with 1 tablespoon water, 2 teaspoons sesame oil, 2 teaspoons soy sauce and ½ teaspoon each of salt and white pepper and mix until smooth. Add to the vegetable mixture and stir for 2 minutes, or until the sauce has thickened. Cool completely. Place 1 tablespoon of filling in the centre of each won ton wrapper (you will need about 40). Brush the edges with a little water and gather around the filling to

form a pouch; twist and pinch the sides together. Deep-fry in hot oil for 4–5 minutes or steam in a bamboo or metal steamer for 25–30 minutes. Makes 40.

NUTRITION PER WON TON: Protein 2 g; Fat 2 g; Carbohydrate 10 g; Dietary Fibre 1 g; Cholesterol 0 mg; 305 kJ (70 cal)

## SEAFOOD WON TONS

Make as for vegetarian won tons but replace the celery, cabbage, carrot and tofu with 750 g (1½ lb) raw prawns, peeled, deveined and chopped. After steaming, stir in 170 g (5½ oz) drained canned crab meat and 2 tablespoons chopped fresh coriander leaves. Makes 50.

NUTRITION PER WON TON: Protein 5 g; Fat 1 g; Carbohydrate 10 g; Dietary Fibre 1 g; Cholesterol 15 mg; 260 kJ (60 cal)

From left: Thai Spring Rolls; Prawn Toasts; Vegetarian Won Tons; Seafood Won Tons

MALAY COOKING
*Malay dishes are usually rich with coconut milk, spiced with hot chillies and often flavoured with lemon grass. Over the centuries foreign traders have contributed culinary techniques and ingredients. From China came noodles, stir-frying and soy sauce, satay sticks are the legacy of Arab kebabs, the use of ghee, cumin and coriander came from India and chillies arrived with the Portuguese in the sixteenth century.*

# MALAYSIAN COCONUT CHICKEN

•

*Preparation time:* 25 minutes
*Total cooking time:* 45–60 minutes
*Serves* 4–6

★

1 x 1.6 kg (3½ lb) chicken
1 tablespoon oil
2 onions, sliced
3 cloves garlic, crushed
2 red chillies, seeded and chopped
½ cup (45 g/1½ oz) desiccated coconut
2 teaspoons ground turmeric
2 teaspoons ground coriander
2 teaspoons ground cumin
2 stems lemon grass (white part only), chopped
8 curry leaves
2 cups (500 ml/16 fl oz) coconut milk

•

1 Cut the chicken into 8 to 10 pieces.
2 Heat the oil in a large pan and cook the onion until soft. Add the garlic, chilli, coconut and turmeric. Stir mixture for 1 minute. Add the coriander, cumin, lemon grass, curry leaves and coconut milk. Stir until well combined.
3 Add the chicken pieces and stir until well coated with the sauce. Simmer, uncovered, for 45 to 60 minutes, or until the chicken is tender and the sauce has thickened. Serve with vermicelli noodles.

*Below: Malaysian Coconut Chicken*

NUTRITION PER SERVE (6): Protein 25 g; Fat 30 g; Carbohydrate 5 g; Dietary Fibre 0 g; Cholesterol 80 mg; 1600 kJ (380 cal)

# ROTIS WITH SPICY MEAT FILLING

•

*Preparation time:* 40 minutes
  + 2 hours resting
*Total cooking time:* 1 hour 30 minutes
*Makes* 12

★ ★

3 cups (375 g/12 oz) roti flour or plain flour
1 teaspoon salt
2 tablespoons ghee or oil
1 egg, lightly beaten
1 cup (250 ml/8 fl oz) warm water
oil, to brush
1 egg, extra, beaten
½ red (Spanish) onion, finely chopped

•

**Spicy Meat Filling**
1 tablespoon ghee
1 onion, finely chopped
3 cloves garlic, crushed
2 teaspoons ground cumin
1 teaspoon ground coriander
1 teaspoon ground turmeric
500 g (1 lb) lean beef or lamb mince
1 teaspoon finely chopped, seeded red chilli
1 tablespoon chopped fresh coriander leaves
extra ghee or oil, for frying

•

1 Sift the flour into a large bowl and stir in the salt. Rub in the ghee or pour in the oil. Add the egg and the water and mix together with a flat-bladed knife to form a moist mixture. Turn the mixture out on to a well-floured surface and knead for about 10 minutes until you have a soft dough, sprinkling with more flour as necessary. Form the dough into a ball and brush it with oil. Place it in an oiled bowl, cover with plastic wrap and leave to rest for a couple of hours.
2 To make Spicy Meat Filling: Heat the ghee in a large frying pan and add the onion. Cook over low heat for about 5 minutes until soft and golden. Add the garlic, cumin, coriander and turmeric and cook for a minute. Turn up the heat, add the mince and brown well, using a fork to break up any lumps. Carry on cooking until the meat is cooked through, adding the chilli in the last few minutes of cooking. Remove from the heat, stir in the coriander and season with salt to taste.
3 Working on a floured work surface (use a clean bench top), divide the dough into 12 pieces and roll it into balls. Take one ball and, working with a little oil on your fingertips, hold

the ball in the air and work around the edge pulling out the dough until a 15 cm (6 inch) round is formed. Lay the roti on a lightly floured surface and cover with plastic wrap so it doesn't dry out. Repeat with the other balls.

4 Heat a wide heavy pan or griddle and brush it with ghee or oil. Drape the roti over a rolling pin and carefully place the roti in the pan. Quickly brush the roti with some beaten egg and spoon over 2 heaped tablespoons of the meat filling. Cook until the underside of the roti is golden. This won't take long. Sprinkle the meat filling with some chopped onion, fold in 2 sides of the roti and then the other 2 sides, pressing to totally enclose the filling. Using an egg slice, slide the roti onto a plate and brush the pan with some more ghee or oil. Return the roti to the heat to cook the other side. Cook until that side is golden. Cook the remaining rotis with the filling in the same way. Serve warm.

NOTE: Roti flour is a creamy coloured flour available from Indian food shops. It is used in Indian unleavened breads. Plain flour can be used as a substitute.

*NUTRITION PER ROTI: Protein 15 g; Fat 15 g; Carbohydrate 25 g; Dietary Fibre 2 g; Cholesterol 85 mg; 1095 kJ (260 cal)*

•

## PRAWN AND NOODLE SOUP

•

*Preparation time:* 40 minutes
*Total cooking time:* 30 minutes
*Serves* 4

✵

300 g (9²/₃ oz) small cooked prawns
200 g (6¹/₂ oz) baby spinach leaves
500 g (1 lb) Shanghai noodles
1 tablespoon oil
1 large onion, finely chopped
5 cm (2 inch) piece fresh ginger,
    grated
2 red chillies, finely chopped
1.5 litres chicken stock
2 tablespoons soy sauce
2 teaspoons soft brown sugar
6 spring onions, chopped

•

*Garnishes*
2 tablespoons crisp fried garlic
2 tablespoons crisp fried onion
1 cup (90 g/3 oz) bean sprouts,
    scraggly ends removed
2 teaspoons chilli flakes
1 tablespoon chopped garlic chives

1 Peel the prawns, leaving the tails intact. Wash and drain the spinach and snap off any long stems; set aside. Add the noodles to boiling water and cook for 3 minutes, or until plump and tender. Drain and set aside.

2 Heat the oil in a large pan and cook the onion and ginger over medium heat, stirring regularly, for 8 minutes. Add the chilli, stock, soy sauce and sugar and bring to the boil. Reduce the heat and leave to simmer for 10 minutes. Add the spring onion.

3 Transfer the noodles to large soup bowls and top with the prawns and spinach leaves. Pour the boiling stock over the top and serve immediately. Place the garnishes in small bowls in the centre of the table, along with salt, pepper and sugar, for the diners to add according to their taste.

*NUTRITION PER SERVE: Protein 25 g; Fat 15 g; Carbohydrate 100 g; Dietary Fibre 10 g; Cholesterol 75 mg; 2590 kJ (615 cal)*

*Above: Prawn and Noodle Soup*

## FRIED RICE NOODLES

•

*Preparation time:* 20 minutes
*Total cooking time:* 15 minutes
*Serves* 4

★

2 Chinese dried pork sausages (see note)
400 g (12²/₃ oz) raw prawns
500 g (1 lb) thick fresh rice noodles
2 tablespoons oil
2 cloves garlic, finely chopped
1 medium onion, finely chopped
3 red chillies, seeded and chopped
250 g (8 oz) Chinese barbecued pork,
    finely chopped
150 g (4³/₄ oz) garlic chives, cut into short
    lengths
2 tablespoons kecap manis
3 eggs, lightly beaten
1 tablespoon rice vinegar
100 g (3¹/₃ oz) bean sprouts, scraggly ends
    removed

•

1 Diagonally slice the sausages into paper-thin
slices. Peel and devein the prawns. Gently
separate the noodles using your fingertips.
2 Heat the oil in a large wok or frying pan. Fry
the sausage slices, tossing regularly, until they
are golden and very crisp. Using a slotted spoon,

*Above: Fried
Rice Noodles*

remove from the wok and drain on paper towels.
3 Reheat the oil in the wok, add the garlic,
onion, chilli and barbecued pork and stir-fry for
2 minutes. Add the prawns and toss constantly
until they change colour. Add the noodles,
chives and kecap manis and toss. Cook for
1 minute or until the noodles begin to soften.
Pour the combined eggs and vinegar over the
top of the mixture and toss for 1 minute. Be
careful not to let the egg-coated noodles burn
on the base of the pan. Add the bean sprouts
and toss.
4 Arrange the noodles on a large serving platter,
scatter the drained pork sausages over the top
and toss a little to mix a few slices among the
noodles. Garnish with a few extra chives and
serve immediately.
NOTE: These spicy, dried sausages (lup chiang)
are available from Asian food stores. They will
keep for up to 3 months in the refrigerator.

*NUTRITION PER SERVE: Protein 35 g; Fat 30 g;
Carbohydrate 35 g; Dietary Fibre 5 g; Cholesterol 240 mg;
2370 kJ (565 cal)*

## PRAWN LAKSA

•

*Preparation time:* 1 hour
*Total cooking time:* 1 hour
*Serves 4*

★ ★

*Spice Paste*
*4–5 large dried red chillies*
*1 medium red (Spanish) onion, roughly*
  *chopped*
*5 cm (2 inch) piece fresh galangal,*
  *roughly chopped*
*4 stems lemon grass (white part only),*
  *sliced*
*3 red chillies, seeded and*
  *roughly chopped*
*10 candlenuts*
*2 teaspoons shrimp paste*
*2 teaspoons grated fresh turmeric*
*2 tablespoons oil*

•

*500 g (1 lb) raw prawns*
*1.5 litres water*
*1 tablespoon oil*
*2 cups (500 ml/16 fl oz) coconut milk*
*8 ready-made fried fish balls, sliced*
*500 g (1 lb) thin fresh rice noodles*
*1 Lebanese cucumber, cut into short, thin*
  *strips*
*100 g (3¹/₃ oz) bean sprouts, scraggly ends*
  *removed*
*¹/₂ cup (10 g/¹/₃ oz) Vietnamese mint leaves*

•

1 To make Spice Paste: Soak the chillies in hot water for 20 minutes. Drain the chillies and place them in a food processor with the onion, galangal, lemon grass, fresh chillies, candlenuts, shrimp paste, turmeric and oil. Process, wiping down the sides of the bowl regularly with a spatula, until very finely chopped.

2 Set aside 4 of the prawns, then peel and devein the remainder, reserving the heads and shells. Place all the heads and shells in a large, deep heavy-based pan and cook over medium heat for 10 minutes, shaking the pan occasionally. The prawn shells will turn a bright dark orange and become aromatic. Stir in 1 cup (250 ml/8 fl oz) of the water and, when it has boiled and almost evaporated away, add another cup and bring it to the boil before adding the remaining water. By slowly adding the water in the initial stages, the colour of the stock will be dark and rich and all the flavour from the base of the pan will be incorporated in the stock. Bring the stock to the boil and simmer gently for 30 minutes. Add the 4 reserved whole prawns and cook until they turn pink; remove with a slotted spoon and set

aside. Strain the stock and discard all the heads and shells—there should be about 2–3 cups (500–750 ml/16–24 fl oz) of stock.

3 Heat the oil in a wok and cook the Spice Paste over low heat for about 8 minutes, stirring regularly until the mixture is very aromatic. Stir in the prawn stock and coconut milk. Bring to the boil, then lower the heat and leave to simmer for 5 minutes. Add the peeled prawns and fish ball slices and simmer until the prawns have turned pink.

4 Gently separate the noodles using your fingertips. In a separate pan of boiling water, cook the noodles for about 30 seconds—don't overcook them or they'll fall apart. Drain well and divide the noodles among four deep soup bowls.

5 Reheat the stock and ladle it over the noodles. Garnish with a little of the cucumber, bean sprouts and mint and top each bowl with a cooked prawn. Serve immediately. Arrange the remaining garnishes on a plate so diners can add more of their favourite garnish to the laksa.

*NUTRITION PER SERVE: Protein 25 g; Fat 40 g; Carbohydrate 35 g; Dietary Fibre 5 g; Cholesterol 140 mg; 2490 kJ (595 cal)*

FISH BALLS
*These are small round balls made of finely minced fish, crab, prawns (shrimp) or scallops, and seasonings, bound with cornflour or egg white, then kneaded, formed into balls and cooked. They are added to soups and braised dishes. Available ready-made from Asian food stores, they should be stored in the refrigerator and used within 3 days of purchase, or frozen.*

*Below: Prawn Laksa*

## SPICY PRAWNS IN SARONGS

•

*Preparation time:* 30 minutes
+ 2 hours marinating
*Total cooking time:* 5 minutes
*Serves* 4 as a starter

★

*Spice Paste*
6 red Asian shallots, finely chopped
6 cloves garlic, crushed
3 candlenuts
2 teaspoons finely chopped fresh galangal
4 red chillies, seeded and finely chopped
1 teaspoon ground turmeric
1 teaspoon shrimp paste

500 g (1 lb) raw king prawns
1 tablespoon lime juice
1/4 teaspoon salt
2 teaspoons grated palm sugar or soft
  brown sugar
1/3 cup (80 ml/2³/4 fl oz) coconut milk
2 cm (³/4 inch) wide strips of banana leaf,
  long enough to wrap around each
  prawn
sweet chilli sauce, to serve

•

1 To make Spice Paste: Place the shallots, garlic, candlenuts, galangal, chilli, turmeric and shrimp paste in a food processor. Process until a rough-textured paste is formed.
2 Peel and devein the prawns. Place the prawns in a non-metallic bowl and sprinkle with the lime juice and salt. Add the sugar and coconut milk and then stir through the Spice Paste. Combine well, cover and place in the refrigerator to marinate for 2 hours.
3 Preheat the grill to as hot as it will go. Tie a strip of banana leaf around each prawn and cook under the hot grill for about 2 minutes on each side or until the prawns are cooked. Serve with sweet chilli sauce.
NOTE: Banana leaves are available from speciality fruit and vegetable shops or possibly from a friend who has a banana tree!

*NUTRITION PER SERVE: Protein 15 g; Fat 5 g; Carbohydrate 5 g; Dietary Fibre 0 g; Cholesterol 95 mg; 575 kJ (135 cal)*

## BARBECUED SEAFOOD

•

*Preparation time:* 20 minutes
+ 15 minutes marinating
*Total cooking time:* 18 minutes
*Serves* 4

★

*Spice Paste*
1 medium onion, grated
4 cloves garlic, chopped
5 cm (2 inch) piece fresh ginger, grated
3 stems lemon grass (white part only),
  chopped
2 teaspoons ground turmeric
1 teaspoon dried shrimp paste
1/3 cup (80 ml/2³/4 fl oz) oil
1/4 teaspoon salt

4 medium calamari (squid) tubes
2 firm white boneless fish fillets, each
  about 300 g (9²/3 oz)
8 raw king prawns
banana leaves, for serving
2 limes, cut into wedges

•

1 To make Spice Paste: Combine the onion, garlic, ginger, lemon grass, turmeric, shrimp paste, oil and salt in a food processor. Process in short bursts until a smooth paste is formed.
2 Cut the squid in half lengthways. Holding a sharp knife at a slight angle, make shallow, close cuts in one direction across the underside of each piece, then cut in the opposite direction, taking care not to cut all the way through. Then cut the squid into pieces about 4 x 3 cm (1¼ x 1½ inches).
3 Wash all the seafood under cold running water and pat dry with paper towels. Brush the seafood lightly with the Spice Paste. Place the seafood on a tray and allow to stand for 15 minutes.
4 Lightly brush a barbecue hotplate with the oil and heat gently. When the plate is hot, arrange the fish fillets and prawns side-by-side on the plate. Cook for about 3 minutes on each side, turning them once only, or until the fish flesh is just firm and the prawns turn bright pink to orange. Add the squid pieces and cook for about 2 minutes or until the flesh turns white and becomes firm. Take care not to overcook the seafood.
5 Arrange the seafood on a platter lined with the banana leaves, add the limes and serve immediately.

*NUTRITION PER SERVE: Protein 25 g; Fat 20 g; Carbohydrate 2 g; Dietary Fibre 1 g; Cholesterol 170 mg; 1200 kJ (285 cal)*

*BARBECUED SEAFOOD*

*Process all the ingredients for the spice paste until smooth.*

*Score a fine honeycomb pattern into the soft underside of the squid.*

*Opposite page: Barbecued Seafood*

## MALAYSIAN FISH CURRY

•

*Preparation time:* 25 minutes
*Total cooking time:* 25 minutes
*Serves* 4

★

*Spice Paste*
3–6 medium red chillies
1 medium onion, chopped
4 cloves garlic
3 stems lemon grass (white part only),
    sliced
4 cm (1½ inch) piece fresh ginger, sliced
2 teaspoons shrimp paste
1–2 tablespoons oil

•

1 tablespoon oil
1 tablespoon fish curry powder
1 cup (250 ml/8 fl oz) coconut milk
1 cup (250 ml/8 fl oz) water
1 tablespoon tamarind concentrate
1 tablespoon kecap manis
350 g (11¼ oz) firm white fish fillets,
    cut into bite-sized pieces
2 ripe tomatoes, chopped
1 tablespoon lemon juice

•

1 To make Spice Paste: Put the chillies, onion, garlic, lemon grass, ginger and shrimp paste in a food processor and roughly chop. Add enough oil to assist the blending and process until a smooth paste is formed, regularly scraping down the sides of the bowl with a spatula.
2 Heat the oil in a wok or heavy frying pan; add the curry paste and stir for 3 to 4 minutes over low heat, until very fragrant. Add the curry powder and stir for another 2 minutes.

3 Add the coconut milk, water, tamarind and kecap manis. Bring to the boil, stirring occasionally, then reduce the heat and simmer for 10 minutes. Add the fish, tomatoes and lemon juice and season to taste with salt and pepper. Simmer for about 5 minutes or until the fish is just cooked. Serve with steamed rice.

*NUTRITION PER SERVE: Protein 20 g; Fat 30 g; Carbohydrate 5 g; Dietary Fibre 5 g; Cholesterol 65 mg; 1625 kJ (390 cal)*

•

## MALAYSIAN RENDANG

•

*Preparation time:* 20 minutes
*Total cooking time:* 1 hour 30 minutes
*Serves* 4–6

★

2 onions, chopped
4 cloves garlic, crushed
5 red chillies, seeded
1 tablespoon grated fresh ginger
2 cups (500 ml/16 fl oz) coconut milk
1 tablespoon oil
1 tablespoon ground coriander
1 tablespoon ground cumin
1 teaspoon ground turmeric
1 teaspoon ground cinnamon
¼ teaspoon ground cloves
¼ teaspoon chilli powder
1 large strip lemon rind
1 kg (2 lb) chuck or skirt steak, cubed
1 tablespoon lemon juice
1 tablespoon soft brown sugar
1 teaspoon tamarind concentrate

•

1 Place the onion, garlic, chillies, ginger and 2 tablespoons coconut milk in a food processor, and process until a smooth paste is formed.
2 Heat the oil in a large pan, add the paste, coriander, cumin, turmeric, cinnamon, cloves, chilli powder, lemon rind and steak and stir until the meat is well coated with the spice mixture. Add the remaining coconut milk and bring to the boil, then simmer over low heat, stirring occasionally, for 1½ hours, or until the meat is tender and the mixture is almost dry.
3 When the oil starts to separate from the gravy, add the lemon juice, sugar and tamarind; stir until heated through. Serve with steamed rice.
NOTE: This recipe produces a 'dry' curry which does not have much liquid. The spicy flavours are absorbed by the meat as it cooks. It tastes even better if it is made a day in advance.

*NUTRITION PER SERVE (6): Protein 35 g; Fat 25 g; Carbohydrate 10 g; Dietary Fibre 0 g; Cholesterol 115 mg; 1765 kJ (420 cal)*

### FISH CURRY POWDER
*Fish curry powder is a blend of coriander, cumin, fennel seeds, turmeric, peppercorns and chillies, particularly suitable for using in fish curries. Specific curry powders such as this one are usually only found in Asian food stores. If fish curry powder is not available, simply use a freshly ground mixture of the spices above. Avoid curry powders that are sold in cardboard packaging as they tend to absorb the flavour and the aroma of the spice blend.*

*Below: Malaysian
Fish Curry*

## CHICKEN KAPITAN

•

**Preparation time:** 35 minutes
**Total cooking time:** 30 minutes
**Serves** 4–6

★

30 g (1 oz) small dried shrimp
4 tablespoons oil
4–8 red chillies, seeded and finely
   chopped
4 cloves garlic, finely chopped
3 stems lemon grass (white part only),
   finely chopped
2 teaspoons ground turmeric
10 candlenuts
2 large onions, chopped
1/4 teaspoon salt
500 g (1 lb) chicken thigh fillets,
   chopped
1 cup (250 ml/8 fl oz) coconut milk
1 cup (250 ml/8 fl oz) water
1/2 cup (125 ml/4 fl oz) coconut cream
2 tablespoons lime juice

1 Put the shrimp in a clean frying pan and dry-fry over low heat, shaking the pan regularly, for 3 minutes, or until the shrimp are dark orange and are giving off a strong aroma. Transfer the shrimp to a mortar and pestle and pound until finely ground. Alternatively, process in a food processor. Set aside.

2 Place half the oil with the chilli, garlic, lemon grass, turmeric and candlenuts in a food processor and process in short bursts until very finely chopped, regularly scraping down the sides of the bowl with a rubber spatula.

3 Heat the remaining oil in a wok or frying pan; add the onion and salt and cook over low heat for 8 minutes, or until golden, stirring regularly. Take care not to let the onion burn. Add the spice mixture and nearly all the ground shrimp meat, setting a little aside to use as a garnish. Stir for 5 minutes. If the mixture begins to stick to the bottom of the pan, add 2 tablespoons coconut milk to the mixture. It is important to cook the mixture thoroughly as it is this which develops the flavours.

4 Add the chicken to the wok and stir well. Cook for 5 minutes, or until the chicken begins to brown. Stir in the remaining coconut milk and water, and bring to the boil. Reduce the heat and simmer for 7 minutes, or until the chicken is cooked and the sauce is thick. Add the coconut cream and bring the mixture back to the boil, stirring constantly. Add the lime juice and serve immediately, sprinkled lightly with the reserved ground shrimp meat. Serve with steamed rice.

*NUTRITION PER SERVE (6): Protein 25 g; Fat 30 g; Carbohydrate 5 g; Dietary Fibre 0 g; Cholesterol 90 mg; 1670 kJ (400 cal)*

*CHICKEN KAPITAN*

*Pound the dry-fried shrimp in a mortar and pestle until finely ground.*

*Process the spice mixture in short bursts, regularly scraping down the sides of the bowl.*

*Stir-fry the onion, spice mixture and ground shrimp for 5 minutes, taking care not to let it stick to the pan.*

*Top: Malaysian Rendang*
*Left: Chicken Kapitan*

Serve drizzled with a little Chilli Sauce, and offer the rest of the sauce for dipping.

3 To make Chilli Sauce: Combine all the ingredients in a small pan, bring to the boil, reduce heat and simmer for 5 minutes or until the sauce thickens slightly.

NOTE: Tofu puffs are cubes of tofu which have been deep-fried and are puffed and golden. They are available from Asian food shops.

NUTRITION PER TOFU PUFF WITH SAUCE: Protein 2 g; Fat 3 g; Carbohydrate 1 g; Dietary Fibre 0 g; Cholesterol 0 mg; 170 kJ (40 cal)

## SPICY EGGS AND SNAKE BEANS

Preparation time: 20 minutes
Total cooking time: 15 minutes
Serves 4

✫

1 teaspoon sesame oil
1 tablespoon oil
2 cloves garlic, crushed
4 spring onions, chopped
300 g (9²/3 oz) snake beans, cut into
    5 cm (2 inch) lengths
200 g (6¹/2 oz) mixed mushrooms (see
    note)
8 eggs, lightly beaten
1 tablespoon kecap manis
2 teaspoons sambal oelek
3 tablespoons chopped fresh mint
3 tablespoons chopped fresh coriander
    leaves

1 Heat the combined oils in a wok or large frying pan, add the garlic and spring onion and cook over moderately high heat for 2 minutes.

2 Add the beans and mushrooms and stir-fry for a further minute. Remove from wok.

3 Add the combined eggs, kecap manis, sambal oelek, mint and coriander to the centre of the wok; allow to set for 2 minutes.

4 Return the vegetables to the wok and stir-fry, breaking up the egg, for 2 minutes or until the mixture is heated through. Serve with steamed rice.

NOTE: Use any combination of mushrooms up to the weight given. Some suitable mushrooms are button, oyster, shiitake or enoki.

NUTRITION PER SERVE: Protein 20 g; Fat 15 g; Carbohydrate 3 g; Dietary Fibre 5 g; Cholesterol 375 mg; 960 kJ (230 cal)

CRUNCHY STUFFED
TOFU PUFFS

Cut the tofu puffs in half and cut a small slit in each half.

Fill each pocket with some of the vegetable mixture.

## CRUNCHY STUFFED TOFU PUFFS

Preparation time: 30 minutes
Total cooking time: 5 minutes
Makes 24

✫

12 deep-fried tofu puffs
1 cup (90 g/3 oz) bean sprouts, scraggly
    ends removed
¹/4 cup (40 g/1¹/3 oz) unsalted roasted
    peanuts, chopped
1 carrot, grated
1 tablespoon chopped fresh coriander
    leaves

Chilli Sauce
2 small red chillies, finely chopped
2 cloves garlic, crushed
2 teaspoons soft brown sugar
1 tablespoon soy sauce
1 tablespoon vinegar
¹/2 cup (125 ml/4 fl oz) boiling water

1 Cut the tofu puffs in half. Cut a small slit in each half and open it up carefully to form a pocket.

2 Place the bean sprouts, peanuts, carrot and coriander in a bowl, and toss until well mixed. Fill each pocket with a portion of the mixture.

Above: Crunchy
Stuffed Tofu Puffs

## NONYA CHICKEN AND LIME CURRY

•

**Preparation time:** 30 minutes
**Total cooking time:** 1 hour
**Serves** 4

✿ ✿

*Spice Paste*
*1 large onion, roughly chopped*
*6 red chillies, seeded and finely chopped*
*4 cloves garlic, crushed*
*1 teaspoon finely chopped lemon grass*
   *(white part only)*
*2 teaspoons finely chopped fresh galangal*
*1 teaspoon ground turmeric*

•

*3 tablespoons oil*
*1 x 1.3 kg (2¾ lb) chicken, cut into*
   *8 pieces and skin removed*
*1 cup (250 ml/8 fl oz) coconut milk*
*2 limes, cut in half*
*5 lime leaves, stems removed and finely*
   *shredded*
*1 teaspoon salt*
*fresh coriander leaves, to garnish*
*2 limes, extra, cut in half, to serve*

1 To make Spice Paste: Place the onion, chilli, garlic, lemon grass, galangal and turmeric in a food processor and process for a few minutes until a thick rough paste is formed.
2 Heat the oil in a large heavy-based pan and add the Spice Paste. Cook over low heat for about 10 minutes, or until the paste is fragrant.
3 Add the chicken and stir-fry for 2 minutes, making sure that the chicken is covered with the paste. Add the coconut milk, lime halves and shredded leaves; cover and simmer for about 50 minutes, or until the chicken is tender. For the last 10 minutes of cooking remove the lid and allow the cooking liquid to reduce until it is thick and creamy. Add the salt, garnish with the coriander leaves and serve with the lime halves and steamed rice.

*NUTRITION PER SERVE: Protein 35 g; Fat 35 g; Carbohydrate 5 g; Dietary Fibre 0 g; Cholesterol 105 mg; 1900 kJ (455 cal)*

NONYA FOOD
*Nonya food is a mixture of Chinese ingredients with Malay spices and flavourings. The blending of the two cuisines evolved because Chinese merchants who settled in trading centres on the Straits of Malacca (Penang, Malacca and Singapore) were unable to bring Chinese women with them, so they married Malay wives. Nonya recipes are hot and spicy and often based on a rempah, a paste of hot chillies, shallots, lemon grass, candlenuts, galangal and turmeric. Coconut, unused in China, is an ingredient in many dishes, such as laksa, and the creamy coconut gravies of the Malacca region. To the north, around Penang, Nonya cooking shows Thai influences in the use of lime and tamarind.*

*Above: Nonya Chicken and Lime Curry*

# FISH AND HERB SALAD

•

*Preparation time:* 40 minutes
*Total cooking time:* 15 minutes
*Serves 4–6*

★ ★

500 g (1 lb) smoked cod
3 tablespoons lime juice
½ cup (30 g/1 oz) flaked coconut
1 cup (200 g/6 ½ oz) jasmine rice, cooked
    and cooled
½ cup (25 g/¾ oz) chopped fresh
    Vietnamese mint
3 tablespoons chopped fresh mint
½ cup (25 g/¾ oz) chopped fresh
    coriander leaves
8 kaffir lime leaves, very finely shredded

•

*Dressing*
1 tablespoon chopped fresh coriander root
2 cm (¾ inch) piece fresh ginger, finely
    grated
1 red chilli, finely chopped
1 tablespoon chopped lemon grass (white
    part only)
3 tablespoons chopped fresh Thai basil
1 avocado, chopped

⅓ cup (80 ml/2¾ fl oz) lime juice
2 tablespoons fish sauce
1 teaspoon soft brown sugar
½ cup (125 ml/4 fl oz) peanut oil

1 Preheat the oven to slow 150°C (300°F/
Gas 2). Place the cod in a large frying pan and
cover with water. Add the lime juice and simmer
for 15 minutes, or until the fish flakes when
tested with a fork. Drain and set aside to cool
slightly before breaking it into bite-sized pieces.
2 Spread the coconut onto an oven tray and
toast in the oven for 10 minutes or until it is
golden brown, shaking the tray occasionally.
Remove the coconut from the tray to prevent it
burning.
3 Place the fish, coconut, rice, Vietnamese mint,
mint, coriander and kaffir lime leaves in a large
bowl and mix to combine.
4 To make Dressing: Place the coriander root,
ginger, chilli, lemon grass and basil in a food
processor and process until combined. Add the
avocado, lime juice, fish sauce, sugar and peanut
oil and process until creamy.
5 Pour the dressing over the salad and toss to
coat the rice and fish. Serve immediately.

*NUTRITION PER SERVE (6): Protein 20 g; Fat 35 g;
Carbohydrate 30 g; Dietary Fibre 5 g; Cholesterol 45 mg;
2090 kJ (495 cal)*

*Below: Fish and
Herb Salad*

CHINESE FOOD
IN SINGAPORE
*The food of Singapore,
while sharing a similar
heritage to Malaysia,
also reflects the strong
influence of the island's
now predominantly
Chinese population.
Singapore–Chinese food is
mostly Cantonese-style,
with chicken, seafood and
vegetables in clear
sauces—a hint of chilli,
tamarind and shrimp paste
give it a Singaporean
touch. Pork is popular,
in contrast to largely
Moslem Malaysia
(converted to Islam in the
early fifteenth century),
where it is not eaten.*

## SINGAPORE SPARE RIBS

•

*Preparation time:* 20 minutes
  + 4 hours marinating
*Total cooking time:* 50 minutes
*Serves* 6

★

2 teaspoons sesame oil
1 teaspoon finely chopped fresh ginger
3 cloves garlic, crushed
2 tablespoons soy sauce
2 tablespoons Chinese rice wine
1/2 teaspoon five spice powder
2 tablespoons honey
1 teaspoon sambal oelek
1/2 teaspoon salt
1.5 kg (3 lb) pork spare ribs, cut into
  individual ribs (ask your butcher to
  do this), trimmed of excess fat
1 tablespoon chopped garlic chives
2 lemons, cut into wedges

1 In a large glass bowl combine the sesame oil, ginger, garlic, soy sauce, rice wine, five spice powder, honey, sambal oelek and salt. Mix well.
2 Add the pork spare ribs and stir until the ribs are totally coated in the marinade. Cover and refrigerate overnight or for at least 4 hours so they absorb the flavour of the marinade.
3 Preheat the oven to moderate 180°C (350°F/Gas 4). Place the ribs and marinade into an oiled baking dish and cook for 50 minutes, turning and basting with pan juices every 15 minutes. If the marinade begins to burn, add a few tablespoons of warm water to the pan during cooking.
4 Scatter the garlic chives over the spare ribs and serve with wedges of lemon and steamed rice.
NOTE: Line the baking dish with thick foil to make washing up easier.

*NUTRITION PER SERVE: Protein 35 g; Fat 75 g;
Carbohydrate 5 g; Dietary Fibre 0 g; Cholesterol 250 mg;
3630 kJ (865 cal)*

*Above: Singapore
Spare Ribs*

# THE PHILIPPINES

The 7000 islands of the Philippines owe
much of their exciting cuisine to the sea that
surrounds them. An abundance of fresh
fish is hauled to shore daily in wooden
outriggers and cooked in clay pots; Chinese
merchants arriving by sea brought spring rolls
and sticky noodles; while the Spanish,
who colonised and later named the islands
after their king, introduced foods such
as spicy chorizo and empanadas. Filipino
cooking often has a tart sharpness, with
its meats and fish being marinated in
vinegar or citrus fruit.

## BAGOONG

*Bagoong is a form of shrimp paste used mainly in the Philippines. The shrimps are salted and fermented in eathenware pots rather than being dried, as in other parts of Asia, and the paste has a runnier consistency.*

*Above: Prawn Fritters*

## PRAWN FRITTERS

•

*Preparation time:* 30 minutes
*Total cooking time:* 15 minutes
*Serves 4–6*

☆

*300 g (9²/3 oz) raw prawns*
*50 g (1²/3 oz) dried rice vermicelli*
*1 egg*
*³/4 cup (185 ml/6 fl oz) water*
*1 tablespoon fish sauce*
*1 cup (125 g/4 fl oz) plain flour*
*¹/4 teaspoon bagoong*
*3 spring onions, sliced*
*1 small red chilli, finely chopped*
*oil, for deep-frying*
*sweet chilli sauce, to serve*

•

1 Peel and devein the prawns. Place half the prawns in a food processor and process until smooth. Chop the remaining prawns, place them in a bowl with the processed prawns and mix to combine.
2 Place the vermicelli in a heatproof bowl, cover with hot water and soak for 1 minute. Drain and cut into short lengths.
3 In a small jug, beat the egg, water and fish sauce. Sift the flour into another bowl; make a

well in the centre, gradually add the egg mixture and stir until smooth.
4 Add the prawn mixture, bagoong, spring onion, chilli and vermicelli to the bowl and mix to combine.
5 Heat the oil in a large pan or wok; add tablespoons of the mixture to the pan and deep-fry for 3 minutes, or until the fritters are crisp and golden. Drain on paper towels. Repeat with the remaining mixture. Serve with sweet chilli sauce.

*NUTRITION PER SERVE (6): Protein 10 g; Fat 10 g; Carbohydrate 25 g; Dietary Fibre 1 g; Cholesterol 80 mg; 930 kJ (220 cal)*

•

## PRAWNS IN COCONUT

•

*Preparation time:* 20 minutes
*Total cooking time:* 20 minutes
*Serves 4–6*

☆

*1 kg (2 lb) raw king prawns*
*3 tablespoons desiccated coconut*
*1 cup (250 ml/8 fl oz) coconut cream*
*1 teaspoon finely chopped fresh ginger*
*8 cloves garlic, finely chopped*
*fresh coriander leaves, to garnish*

1 Preheat the oven to slow 150°C (300°F/Gas 2). Using small sharp scissors, snip down the back of the prawns, starting from behind the head. Using a toothpick or your fingers, pull out the intestinal tract. Leave the heads and shells on.
2 Spread the coconut on an oven tray and toast it in the oven for 10 minutes or until it is dark golden, shaking the tray occasionally. Remove the coconut from the tray immediately to prevent it from burning.
3 Place the coconut cream, ginger and garlic in a large pan and bring to the boil. Add the prawns, lower the heat and simmer, uncovered, for about 5 minutes or until the prawns are cooked. Stir every few minutes so the mixture doesn't catch on the bottom of the pan.
4 Season with salt and freshly ground black pepper to taste, and garnish with the toasted coconut and coriander leaves. Serve with rice.

*NUTRITION PER SERVE (6): Protein 20 g; Fat 10 g; Carbohydrate 2 g; Dietary Fibre 0 g; Cholesterol 125 mg; 755 kJ (180 cal)*

### RICE WITH CHICKEN AND SEAFOOD

**Preparation time:** 30 minutes
**Total cooking time:** 40 minutes
**Serves 4–6**

★ ★

500 g (1 lb) medium raw prawns
500 g (1 lb) mussels
200 g (6½ oz) squid hoods
¼ teaspoon saffron threads
4 large tomatoes
3 tablespoons oil
2 chorizo sausages, thickly sliced
500 g (1 lb) chicken pieces
300 g (9⅔ oz) pork fillet, thickly sliced
4 cloves garlic, crushed
2 red (Spanish) onions, chopped
¼ teaspoon ground turmeric
2 cups (440 g/14 oz) short-grain rice
1.25 litres chicken stock
125 g (4 oz) green beans, cut into 4 cm (1½ inch) lengths
1 red pepper (capsicum), cut into thin strips
1 cup (155 g/5 oz) peas

1 Peel and devein the prawns, leaving the tails intact. Scrub the mussels thoroughly and remove the beards. Cut the squid hoods into ½ cm (¼ inch) thick slices. Soak the saffron threads in 2 tablespoons boiling water for 15 minutes.

2 Score a cross in the base of each tomato, place in a heatproof bowl, cover with boiling water and leave for 2 minutes. Plunge into cold water and then peel the skin away from the cross. Cut the tomatoes in half horizontally, scoop out the seeds with a teaspoon and chop the flesh.
3 Heat 1 tablespoon oil in a large, heavy-based pan; add the chorizo slices and cook over medium heat for 5 minutes, or until browned. Drain on paper towels. Add the chicken pieces to the pan and cook for 5 minutes, or until golden, turning once. Drain on paper towels. Add the pork to the pan and cook for 3 minutes, or until browned, turning once. Drain on paper towels.
4 Heat the remaining oil in the pan; add the garlic, onion, saffron and soaking liquid and turmeric, and cook over medium heat for 3 minutes or until the onion is golden. Add the tomatoes and cook for 3 minutes or until soft. Add the rice and stir for 5 minutes, or until the rice is translucent. Stir in the stock and bring to the boil; cover and simmer for 10 minutes.
5 Add the chicken pieces to the pan, cover and continue cooking for 20 minutes. Add the pork, prawns, mussels, squid, chorizo and vegetables; cover and cook for 10 minutes or until the liquid is absorbed.

*NUTRITION PER SERVE (6): Protein 55 g; Fat 25 g; Carbohydrate 70 g; Dietary Fibre 5 g; Cholesterol 270 mg; 3115 kJ (740 cal)*

*RICE WITH CHICKEN AND SEAFOOD*

*Drain the browned chorizo slices on paper towels.*

*Cook the pork slices until they are browned, turning once.*

*Below: Rice with Chicken and Seafood*

# COMBINATION NOODLES WITH CHORIZO

•

*Preparation time:* 40 minutes
+ 30 minutes to dry the noodles
*Total cooking time:* 35 minutes
*Serves* 6

500 g (1 lb) thin fresh egg noodles
500 g (1 lb) raw prawns
3 tablespoons oil
4 cloves garlic, crushed
6 spring onions, finely sliced
1 cup (175 g/5²/₃ oz) shredded cooked
    chicken
250 g (8 oz) chorizo sausage, sliced
1 cup (75 g/2¹/₂ oz) shredded cabbage
3 tablespoons soy sauce
3 tablespoons fresh coriander leaves

•

1 Fill a large pan with salted water and bring it to the boil. Cook the noodles for 5 minutes or until tender. Rinse under cold water, drain and spread in a single layer on paper towels. Allow to dry for 30 minutes.
2 Peel and devein the prawns. Dry-fry the heads, tails and shells in a frying pan for about 5 minutes, until they turn bright orange. Add 1 cup (250 ml/8 fl oz) water to the pan, bring to the boil, reduce the heat slightly and cook until the liquid has reduced to about a quarter. Add another ¹/₂ cup (125 ml/4 fl oz) water, bring to the boil, then reduce the heat and simmer for 3 minutes. Strain the liquid and set it aside, discarding all the prawn heads, tails and shells.
3 Heat 1 tablespoon oil in a large wok. When the oil is very hot add a quarter of the noodles and fry until golden all over, turning when necessary. Remove the noodles from the wok and repeat with the remaining noodles, adding more oil when necessary.
4 Add another tablespoon of oil and fry the garlic and spring onion over low heat until soft; remove from the pan. Add the prawns and chicken and fry until golden; remove from the pan. Add the the chorizo and cook until brown. Add the cabbage, soy sauce and prawn cooking liquid, and cook over high heat, stirring all the time until the liquid has reduced by a third.
5 Return the noodles to the wok with the garlic, spring onion, chicken and prawns. Toss well until heated through. Season with salt and black pepper, scatter over the coriander and serve immediately with lemon wedges.

*NUTRITION PER SERVE: Protein 60 g; Fat 20 g;
Carbohydrate 40 g; Dietary Fibre 5 g; Cholesterol 140 mg;
2470 kJ (590 cal)*

---

# BEEF POT ROAST

•

*Preparation time:* 15 minutes
*Total cooking time:* 3 hours 30 minutes
*Serves* 6

✸ ✸

75 g (2¹/₂ oz) pork fat
1.5 kg (3 lb) topside beef
3 medium onions, quartered
4 tomatoes, quartered
¹/₂ cup (125 ml/4 fl oz) white vinegar
2 tablespoons soy sauce
2 bay leaves
3 potatoes, cut into chunks
3 sweet potatoes, cut into chunks
2 tablespoons chopped coriander leaves,
    to serve

•

1 Cut the pork fat into thin strips. Using a sharp knife make deep cuts in the beef. Make these cuts evenly over the beef. Insert a sliver of pork fat into each cut.
2 Place the beef in a large pan which has a tight-fitting lid. Add the onion, tomato, vinegar, soy sauce and bay leaves. Bring the liquid to the boil: reduce the heat to a gentle simmer, cover and cook for 2 hours until the beef is tender. Season well with salt and black pepper. Remove the lid and simmer a further 30 minutes.
3 Add the potato and sweet potato and simmer, uncovered, until tender. Remove the pan from the heat and remove the beef from the pan. Cut the beef into thin slices; drizzle over the gravy and serve with the potato. Scatter over the coriander, to serve.
NOTE: Pork fat is available from butcher shops. If unavailable, lard can be used as a substitute.

*NUTRITION PER SERVE: Protein 20 g; Fat 15 g;
Carbohydrate 65 g; Dietary Fibre 5 g; Cholesterol 95 mg;
1995 kJ (475 cal)*

---

SPANISH INFLUENCE ON THE PHILIPPINES
*Combination noodles and meat is also known as Pancit Guisado. The chorizo in this recipe gives an indication of the long-lasting impact the Spanish made on the people of the Philippines. Many of their traditional dishes, such as paella and empanadas, are popular to this day.*

*Opposite page:
Combination Noodles
with Chorizo (top);
Beef Pot Roast*

## OXTAIL AND VEGETABLE STEW

•

*Preparation time:* 20 minutes
*Total cooking time:* 2 hours 15 minutes
*Serves* 6

★

1.5 kg (3 lb) oxtail, cut into 2 cm
   (3/4 inch) lengths (ask your butcher
   to do this)
1/4 cup (60 g/2 oz) lard
2 tablespoons annatto seeds (see note)
4 cloves garlic, crushed
2 medium onions, finely sliced
1.5 litres water
1 bay leaf
1 tablespoon soy sauce
2 tablespoons fish sauce
2 turnips, chopped
2 cups (250 g/8 oz) sliced green beans
2 slender eggplants (aubergines), sliced
2 large sweet potatoes, chopped
1/2 cup (110 g/3²/3 oz) short- or long-grain
   rice
1/2 cup (80 g/2²/3 oz) unsalted raw peanuts

•

1 Place the oxtail pieces into a large heatproof
bowl, cover with salted boiling water and leave
to stand for 5 minutes; remove and pat dry.
2 Heat the lard in a large frying pan, add the
annatto seeds and cook over medium heat until
the lard turns red. Add the garlic and onion to
the pan and cook for 5 minutes. Remove the
garlic and onion mixture from the pan with a
slotted spoon and drain on paper towels.

*Below: Oxtail and
Vegetable Stew*

3 Heat a large deep pan, add the meat in batches
and cook over medium heat for 5 minutes, or
until brown on both sides. Return all the meat to
the pan and add the onion and garlic mixture,
water, bay leaf, soy sauce and fish sauce. Bring to
the boil, reduce the heat, cover and simmer for
1½ hours. Add the vegetables and simmer,
covered, for 20 minutes, or until tender.
4 Preheat the oven to moderate 180°C (350°F/
Gas 4). Spread the rice on an oven tray and roast
for 15 minutes or until golden. Spread the
peanuts on an oven tray and roast for about
5 minutes, until lightly browned. Remove from
the oven, cool slightly and then process both in a
food processor until the mixture resembles fine
breadcrumbs. Sift the mixture to remove any
large pieces, then add it to the stew and stir until
the sauce thickens.
NOTE: If annatto seeds are unavailable,
substitute 1 tablespoon of paprika combined
with 1/2 teaspoon turmeric. The annatto seeds can
be left in the dish but they are too hard to eat.

NUTRITION PER SERVE: Protein 30 g; Fat 45 g;
Carbohydrate 40 g; Dietary Fibre 10 g; Cholesterol 70 mg;
2815 kJ (670 cal)

•

## FISH WITH GINGER
## AND BLACK PEPPER

•

*Preparation time:* 10 minutes
*Total cooking time:* 20 minutes
*Serves* 4

★

2 whole firm white fish such as snapper or
   bream, each about 500 g (1 lb),
   cleaned and scaled
4 cm (1½ inch) piece fresh ginger, sliced
3 tablespoons oil
4 tablespoons, finely chopped fresh ginger,
   extra
1 teaspoon freshly ground black pepper
1/2 teaspoon salt
1 cup (250 ml/8 fl oz) water
1/2 red (Spanish) onion, finely sliced
1 tablespoon fresh coriander leaves
1 tablespoon finely sliced spring onion

•

1 Preheat the oven to moderate 180°C (350°F/
Gas 4). Wash the fish inside and out and pat dry.
Divide the ginger slices into 2 portions and place
them inside the fish.
2 Heat the oil in a wok; add the chopped ginger
and cook over low heat for 1 to 2 minutes, or
until soft and fragrant. Stir in the black pepper.
3 Place the fish in a baking dish, scatter over the
salt and pour in the water. Place the onion slices

over the fish, cover the pan and bake for approximately 30 minutes or until the fish is cooked. The fish is fully cooked when the flesh flakes apart easily.

4 Carefully lift out the fish and place it on a serving platter. Scatter over the coriander and spring onion. Pour some of the cooking liquid around the fish and serve with steamed rice.

*NUTRITION PER SERVE: Protein 25 g; Fat 20 g; Carbohydrate 2 g; Dietary Fibre 1 g; Cholesterol 90 mg; 1140 kJ (270 cal)*

•

## CHICKEN ADOBO

•

*Preparation time:* 20 minutes
  + 2 hours marinating
*Total cooking time:* 50 minutes
*Serves 6*

★ ★

*6 cloves garlic, crushed*
*1 cup (250 ml/8 fl oz) cider vinegar*
*1½ cups (375 ml/12 fl oz) chicken stock*
*1 bay leaf*
*1 teaspoon coriander seeds*
*1 teaspoon black peppercorns*
*1 teaspoon annatto seeds (see note)*
*3 tablespoons soy sauce*
*1.5 kg (3¼ lb) chicken pieces*
*2 tablespoons oil*

1 Combine the garlic, vinegar, chicken stock, bay leaf, coriander seeds, black peppercorns, annatto seeds and soy sauce in a large bowl. Add the chicken, cover and leave to marinate in the refrigerator for 2 hours.

2 Transfer the chicken mixture to a large heavy-based pan and bring to the boil. Reduce the heat, cover and simmer for 30 minutes. Remove the lid from the pan and continue cooking for 10 minutes, or until the chicken is tender. Remove the chicken from the pan and set aside. Bring the liquid to the boil again and cook over high heat for 10 minutes, or until the liquid has reduced by half.

3 Heat the oil in a wok or large frying pan, add the chicken in batches and cook over medium heat for 5 minutes, or until crisp and brown. Pour the reduced vinegar mixture over the chicken pieces and serve with rice.

NOTE: If annatto seeds are unavailable, substitute ¼ teaspoon paprika combined with a generous pinch of turmeric. The annatto seeds can be left in the dish, but are too hard to eat.

*NUTRITION PER SERVE: Protein 35 g; Fat 15 g; Carbohydrate 1 g; Dietary Fibre 1 g; Cholesterol 115 mg; 1145 kJ (270 cal)*

ANNATTO SEEDS
*Also known as achuete, these small red-brown seeds are used in Filipino cooking for their strong colour. They come from a small flowering tree native to Central and South America which was introduced into the Philippines by Spanish traders. Annatto seeds are also used by the Chinese to colour barbecued pork.*

*Above: Chicken Adobo*

# RICE
As the staple of all Asian cuisines, this grain is of huge importance—in Thailand an invitation to a meal is 'kin khao', literally 'come and eat rice'. Almost all the rice eaten is white rather than brown.

## COOKING METHODS
One cup (200 g/6½ oz) rice makes 3 cups (550 g/1 lb 1⅔oz) cooked rice. Allow 1½–2 cups (280–370 g/9–11¾ oz) cooked rice per person.

## RAPID BOILING
Bring a large pan of water to a fast boil. The quantity of water should be 6 times the quantity of rice. Add the rice and cook, uncovered, for 12–15 minutes, or until the swollen grains are soft and opaque. Drain.

## STEAMING
The most common method of cooking rice throughout Asia, it is easy to obtain good results if the water to rice ratio is correct. A quick and easy method is to place the quantity of rice required in a large pan and add enough water to reach the first joint of your index finger when the tip is on the top of the rice. For a more accurate measure, add 2 cups (500 ml/16 fl oz) water for the first cup (200 g/6½ oz) long-grain rice and 1½ cups (375 ml/12 fl oz) water for each additional cup of rice. For short- or medium-grain rice, add 1½ cups (375 ml/12 fl oz) water for the first cup (200 g/6½ oz) rice and 1 cup (250 ml/8 fl oz) for each additional cup of rice.

**Absorption**: Wash rice in a sieve until the water runs clear; place in a large pan with the water, bring to the boil and boil for 1 minute. Cover with a tight-fitting lid, then reduce the heat to as low as possible and cook for 10–15 minutes, or until all the water has been absorbed. Steam tunnels will form holes on the surface. Turn off the heat and leave the pan, covered, for at least 10 minutes. Fluff the rice with a fork.

**Electric rice cooker**: This appliance steams rice in the same way as the absorption method and is ideal for making large quantities. Wash rice in a sieve until the water runs clear, drain and add to the rice cooker with water. Follow the manufacturer's instructions for cooking times.

## LONG-GRAIN

Cultivated throughout Southeast Asia, this long slender grain is the favoured rice of the Chinese. When cooked the grains separate easily, are non-starchy and are perfect for dishes such as fried rice. Long-grain rice is the most readily available and widely used rice in the Western world.

*NUTRITION PER 100 g: Protein 8 g; Fat 0 g; Carbohydrate 80 g; Dietary Fibre 2 g; Cholesterol 0 mg; 1540 kJ (365 cal)*

## JASMINE

Originating in Thailand, this variety of long-grain rice is now popular throughout Southeast Asia. A lightly fragrant rice which goes well with all kinds of Asian dishes.

*NUTRITION PER 100 g: At present there is no nutritional analysis available for jasmine rice, but it would be similar to long-grain or basmati.*

## BASMATI

This aromatic, narrow, long-grain rice is grown in the foothills of the Himalayas from Bangladesh to India.

It is traditionally used for biryani and pilau dishes which incorporate the delicate flavour and colour of saffron and utilise the firm texture of the cooked basmati rice.

*NUTRITION PER 100 g: Protein 8 g; Fat 0 g; Carbohydrate 80 g; Dietary Fibre 2 g; Cholesterol 0 mg; 1500 kJ (355 cal)*

## SHORT-GRAIN

These small oval grains, which are high in starch, are preferred by the Japanese and Koreans. Best cooked by the absorption method, this rice is sticky and the grains adhere together, making it easier to eat with chopsticks and to prepare sushi.

*NUTRITION PER 100 g: Protein 6 g; Fat 0 g; Carbohydrate 80 g; Dietary Fibre 2 g; Cholesterol 0 mg; 1520 kJ (360 cal)*

## GLUTINOUS

**White glutinous:** This is the staple rice of the Laotians and northern Thais who use it as an accompaniment to savoury dishes. However its main use is for leaf-wrapped snacks or Asian

desserts. The grains are short and turn translucent when cooked. Ill-named because it contains no gluten, it has a high starch content and is commonly called 'sticky rice' or 'sweet rice'.

*NUTRITION PER 100 g: At present there is no nutritional analysis available for white glutinous rice, but it would be similar to black.*

**Black glutinous:** When the layer of bran is left on the rice, it is an unusual dark colour and has a nutty flavour. It combines well with palm sugar, coconut milk and sesame seeds and is a popular dessert rice in Burma, Thailand, Indonesia and the Philippines. For best results, the rice should be soaked overnight.

*NUTRITION PER 100 g: Protein 8 g; Fat 2 g; Carbohydrate 75 g; Dietary Fibre 2 g; Cholesterol 0 mg; 1500 kJ (355 cal)*

*Clockwise from top left: Long-grain rice; jasmine rice; white glutinous rice; basmati rice; short-grain rice (cooked); black glutinous rice; short-grain rice*

2 Brush a small nonstick frying pan or crepe pan with oil, heat over low heat, add 2 tablespoons of the batter and swirl the pan to ensure the base has a very thin covering of batter; pour any excess batter back into the bowl. Cook the crepe for 2 minutes or until lightly golden. Turn and cook the other side for 2 minutes. Repeat with remaining batter.

3 To make Prawn Filling: Peel and devein the prawns, and cut them in half lengthways if large. Heat the oil in a nonstick pan; add the prawns and cook over medium heat for 3 minutes or until they are bright pink. Arrange the prawns, bamboo shoots, bean sprouts, peanuts, lettuce and coriander on a platter.

4 On each crepe place a little shredded lettuce, a few coriander leaves, prawns, bamboo shoots bean sprouts and peanuts; fold in the sides and roll up the crepe to enclose the mixture.

NUTRITION PER SERVE (6): Protein 20 g; Fat 20 g; Carbohydrate 20 g; Dietary Fibre 4 g; Cholesterol 235 mg; 1430 kJ (340 cal)

•

## SOUR BEEF SOUP
•

*Preparation time:* 30 minutes
*Total cooking time:* 2 hours 30 minutes
*Serves* 6

★ ★

500 g (1 lb) chicken bones
500 g (1 lb) lean stewing beef
250 g (8 oz) pork chops, fat removed
2.5 litres water
1 medium onion, finely diced
2 tomatoes, diced
1 teaspoon salt
1 tablespoon dried tamarind pulp
250 g (8 oz) sweet potato,
    cut into chunks
1 large daikon, thinly sliced
2 cups (90 g/3 oz) shredded Chinese
    cabbage
1 tablespoon fish sauce
1 lemon, cut into wedges, to serve

•

1 Place the chicken bones, beef, pork chops and water in a large pan. Stir in the onion, tomato and salt. Bring the pan to the boil, then cover and simmer for 2 hours. Remove the chicken bones, beef and pork. Allow the beef and pork to cool and discard the chicken bones.

2 Pour 2 tablespoons boiling water over the tamarind pulp and soak it for 10 minutes. Stir and press the tamarind pulp with a spoon until it is fully dissolved, then strain it into the soup. Discard any seeds and fibre.

*PRAWN CREPES*

*Drain the bamboo shoots and cut them into matchsticks.*

*Fold in the sides and roll up the crepe to enclose the mixture.*

## PRAWN CREPES
•

*Preparation time:* 40 minutes
    + 20 minutes resting
*Total cooking time:* 20 minutes
*Serves* 4–6

★ ★

5 eggs
1½ cups (375 ml/12 fl oz) water
2 tablespoons oil
½ cup (60 g/2 oz) cornflour
½ cup (60 g/2 oz) plain flour

•

*Prawn Filling*
500 g (1 lb) raw prawns
1 tablespoon oil
300 g (9²⁄₃ oz) bamboo shoots, cut into
    matchsticks
1 cup (90 g/3 oz) bean sprouts, scraggly
    ends removed
½ cup (80 g/2²⁄₃ oz) unsalted roasted
    peanuts, roughly chopped
½ lettuce, shredded
1 cup (30 g/1 oz) fresh coriander leaves

•

1 Beat the eggs, water and oil in a bowl until combined. Whisk in the cornflour and plain flour and beat until smooth. Cover and allow the batter to rest for 20 minutes.

*Above: Prawn Crepes*

3 Dice the beef. Cut the meat from the pork chops, slice it finely and discard the bones. Return the meat to the soup. Add the sweet potato and radish and simmer for 20 minutes. Add the cabbage and fish sauce and serve immediately with the lemon wedges.

*NUTRITION PER SERVE: Protein 25 g; Fat 3 g; Carbohydrate 10 g; Dietary Fibre 2 g; Cholesterol 70 mg; 675 kJ (160 cal)*

### EMPANADAS

*Preparation time:* 30 minutes
   + 30 minutes standing
*Total cooking time:* 40 minutes
*Makes* 24

★ ☆

**Filling**
*1 tablespoon oil*
*4 slices bacon, chopped*
*1 large onion, finely chopped*
*3 cloves garlic, chopped*
*150 g (4³⁄₄ oz) pork and veal mince*
*150 g (4³⁄₄ oz) chicken mince*
*2 tablespoons tomato paste (tomato purée, double concentrate)*
*1 teaspoon soft brown sugar*
*1 tablespoon water*
*2 hard-boiled eggs, chopped*
*4 gherkins, finely chopped, optional*
*¹⁄₂ cup (15 g/¹⁄₂ oz) fresh coriander leaves, chopped*
*1 egg white, beaten*
*oil, for shallow frying*

**Pastry**
*4¹⁄₂ cups (560 g/1 lb 2 oz) plain flour*
*1 cup (250 ml/8 fl oz) water*
*2 eggs, beaten*
*2 teaspoons caster sugar*
*100 g (3¹⁄₃ oz) butter, melted*
*a little extra melted butter for brushing*

1 To make Filling: Heat the oil in a frying pan; add the bacon, onion and garlic and cook over medium heat for 5 minutes, stirring regularly. Add the pork and veal mince and the chicken mince and cook for another 5 minutes or until browned, breaking up any lumps with a fork or wooden spoon.

2 Add the tomato paste, sugar and water to the pan and bring the mixture to the boil, stirring constantly. Reduce the heat and simmer, uncovered, for 20 minutes. Add the eggs, gherkins, if using, and coriander. Set the mixture aside for at least 30 minutes to cool.

3 To make Pastry: Combine the flour, water, egg, sugar and butter in a food processor and process for 20 to 30 seconds or until the mixture comes together. Transfer the pastry to a floured surface and gather together into a ball. Cover with plastic wrap and set aside for 10 minutes.

4 Roll the pastry into a 30 x 20 cm (12 x 8 inch) rectangle. Brush with some extra melted butter and tightly roll up into a long sausage. Cut into 3 cm (1¹⁄₄ inch) slices and cover with a clean tea towel to stop the pastry drying out.

5 Place 1 slice of pastry flat on a lightly floured surface; roll it out to a 12 cm (5 inch) circle. Place 1 heaped tablespoon of filling in the centre and lightly brush the edges with egg white. Bring 1 side over to meet the other and press the edges to seal. Decorate the edge with a fork, if desired. Repeat with the remaining filling and pastry.

6 Heat 2 cm (³⁄₄ inch) of the oil in a large pan; add the empanadas in batches and cook over medium heat for 2 to 3 minutes each side. Drain on paper towels and serve.

*NUTRITION PER EMPANADA: Protein 10 g; Fat 10 g; Carbohydrate 20 g; Dietary Fibre 1 g; Cholesterol 55 mg; 900 kJ (215 cal)*

*Below: Empanadas*

# THAILAND

Every Thai meal is a delicate balancing act of bold flavours. The soups and curries are both tart and creamy sweet, flavoured with sour tamarind, scarlet-hot chillies, tangy lime leaves and handfuls of aromatic basil, coriander and mint. While the cooking of Thailand has borrowed from other countries—stir-fries and steamed dishes from China, spices from India—these influences have been shaped into a cuisine whose tastes and fragrances are uniquely Thai.

TAMARIND PULP

*If tamarind concentrate is not available, soak a piece of tamarind pulp in hot water—3 tablespoons pulp to 1/2 cup (125 ml/4 fl oz) hot water—and work with your fingertips until soft. Strain, using the back of a spoon to force the liquid from the seeds and fibre. The liquid should have the consistency of a light sauce. Any leftover liquid can be frozen in convenient measures and stored in the freezer.*

## TOM YUM GOONG
### (HOT AND SOUR PRAWN SOUP)
•

*Preparation time:* 25 minutes
*Total cooking time:* 45 minutes
*Serves 4–6*

★

500 g (1 lb) raw prawns
1 tablespoon oil
2 litres water
2 tablespoons Red Curry Paste
 (page 112) or ready-made paste
2 tablespoons tamarind concentrate
2 teaspoons ground turmeric
1 teaspoon chopped red chilli, optional
4–8 kaffir lime leaves, whole or shredded
2 tablespoons fish sauce
2 tablespoons lime juice
2 teaspoons soft brown sugar
1/4 cup (7 g/1/4 oz) fresh coriander leaves

•

1 Peel and devein the prawns, leaving the tails intact. Heat the oil in a large pan; add the prawn shells and heads to the pan and cook for 10 minutes over moderately high heat, tossing frequently, until the shells and heads are deep orange.
2 Add 1 cup (250 ml/8 fl oz) of the water and the curry paste to the pan. Boil for 5 minutes, until reduced slightly. Add the remaining water and simmer for 20 minutes. Drain the stock,

*Above: Tom Yum Goong*

discarding the heads and shells.
3 Return the drained stock to the pan. Add the tamarind, turmeric, chilli and lime leaves, bring to the boil and cook for 2 minutes. Add the prawns to the pan and cook for 5 minutes or until the prawns turn pink. Add the fish sauce, lime juice and sugar and stir to combine. Serve immediately, sprinkled with coriander leaves.

NUTRITION PER SERVE (6): Protein 15 g; Fat 10 g; Carbohydrate 5 g; Dietary Fibre 0 g; Cholesterol 160 mg; 615 kJ (145 cal)

•

## GOLDEN PRAWN PUFFS
•

*Preparation time:* 15 minutes
 + 30 minutes resting
*Total cooking time:* 5–10 minutes
*Serves 4–6*

★

750 g (11/2 lb) raw prawns
4 medium red chillies, finely chopped
1/2 cup (15 g/1/2 oz) fresh coriander leaves
2 egg whites
1 tablespoon finely grated fresh ginger
2 cloves garlic, chopped
1 tablespoon fish sauce
1/3 cup (60 g/2 oz) rice flour
 or cornflour
1/2 cup (125 ml/4 fl oz) oil
chilli sauce, to serve

USING DRIED
GALANGAL
*If fresh galangal is not
available, use a similar
amount of dried galangal.
Cover the galangal with
boiling water for
10 minutes; drain. The
soaking water can be
substituted for the stock
in the recipe.*

1 Peel and devein the prawns.
2 Place the prawn meat, chilli, coriander leaves, egg whites, ginger, garlic and fish sauce in a food processor and process for 10 seconds or until the mixture is well combined.
3 Transfer the mixture to a bowl and stir in the flour. Refrigerate the prawn mixture for at least 30 minutes, or until you are ready to fry the puffs.
4 Heat the oil in a heavy-based frying pan. Very gently drop rounded teaspoons of the mixture into the hot oil and cook for 2 minutes, carefully turning them with tongs until golden brown on all sides. Drain the puffs on paper towels and serve immediately with chilli sauce.
NOTE: Do not overprocess or overcook the mixture or it will become tough.

*NUTRITION PER SERVE (6): Protein 10 g; Fat 20 g; Carbohydrate 10 g; Dietary Fibre 1 g; Cholesterol 110 mg; 1140 kJ (270 cal)*

## TOM KHA GAI
### (CHICKEN AND GALANGAL SOUP)
•

*Preparation time:* 20 minutes
*Total cooking time:* 20 minutes
*Serves* 4

5 cm (2 inch) piece fresh galangal
2 cups (500 ml/16 fl oz) coconut milk
1 cup (250 ml/8 fl oz) chicken stock
600 g (1¼ lb) chicken breast fillets, cut
  into thin strips
1–2 teaspoons finely chopped red chilli
2 tablespoons fish sauce
1 teaspoon soft brown sugar
¼ cup (7 g/¼ oz) fresh coriander leaves

1 Cut the galangal into thin slices. Combine the galangal, coconut milk and stock in a medium pan. Bring to the boil, then reduce the heat and simmer over low heat for 10 minutes, stirring occasionally.
2 Add the chicken and chilli to the pan and simmer for 8 minutes. Add the fish sauce and sugar and stir to combine.
3 Add the coriander leaves and serve immediately, garnished with extra sprigs of coriander if you like.

*NUTRITION PER SERVE: Protein 40 g; Fat 30 g; Carbohydrate 5 g; Dietary Fibre 0 g; Cholesterol 80 mg; 1810 kJ (430 cal)*

*Above: Tom Kha Gai*

## RED VEGETABLE CURRY

•

*Preparation time:* 25 minutes
*Total cooking time:* 25–30 minutes
*Serves* 4

★

1 tablespoon oil
1 medium onion, chopped
1–2 tablespoons Red Curry Paste (see
    right) or ready-made paste
1¹/2 cups (375 ml/12 fl oz) coconut milk
1 cup (250 ml/8 fl oz) water
2 medium (350 g/11¹/4 oz) potatoes,
    chopped
200 g (6¹/2 oz) cauliflower florets
6 kaffir lime leaves
150 g (4³/4 oz) snake beans, cut into 3 cm
    (1¹/4 inch) pieces
¹/2 red pepper (capsicum), cut into strips
10 fresh baby corn spears, cut in half
    lengthways
1 tablespoon green peppercorns, roughly
    chopped
¹/4 cup (15 g/¹/2 oz) fresh Thai basil,
    finely chopped
2 tablespoons fish sauce
1 tablespoon lime juice
2 teaspoons soft brown sugar

•

1 Heat the oil in a large wok or frying pan. Cook the onion and curry paste for 4 minutes over medium heat, stirring.
2 Add the coconut milk and water, bring to the boil and simmer, uncovered, for 5 minutes. Add the potato, cauliflower and kaffir lime leaves, and simmer for 7 minutes. Add the snake beans, red pepper, corn and peppercorns and cook for 5 minutes or until the vegetables are tender.
3 Stir in the basil, fish sauce, lime juice and sugar. Serve with steamed rice.

*NUTRITION PER SERVE: Protein 10 g; Fat 30 g; Carbohydrate 25 g; Dietary Fibre 5 g; Cholesterol 5 mg; 1585 kJ (380 cal)*

•

## RED CURRY PASTE

•

*Preparation time:* 20 minutes
*Total cooking time:* 6 minutes
*Makes* approximately 1 cup
    (250 ml/8 fl oz)

★

1 tablespoon coriander seeds
2 teaspoons cumin seeds
1 teaspoon black peppercorns
2 teaspoons shrimp paste
1 teaspoon ground nutmeg
12 dried or fresh red chillies, roughly
    chopped
20 red Asian shallots, chopped
2 tablespoons oil
4 stems lemon grass (white part only),
    finely chopped
12 small cloves garlic, chopped
2 tablespoons fresh coriander roots,
    chopped
2 tablespoons fresh coriander stems,
    chopped
6 kaffir lime leaves, chopped
2 teaspoons grated lime rind
2 teaspoons salt
2 teaspoons ground turmeric
1 teaspoon paprika

•

1 Place the coriander and cumin seeds in a dry frying pan and roast over medium heat for 2 to 3 minutes, shaking the pan constantly.
2 Place the roasted spices and peppercorns in a mortar and pestle and pound until finely ground.
3 Wrap the shrimp paste in a small piece of foil and cook under a hot grill for 3 minutes, turning the package twice.
4 Place the ground spices, shrimp paste, nutmeg and chilli in a food processor and process for 5 seconds. Add the remaining ingredients and process for 20 seconds at a time, scraping down the sides of the processor bowl each time, until a smooth paste is formed.

*NUTRITION PER 100 g: Protein 2 g; Fat 10 g; Carbohydrate 5 g; Dietary Fibre 5 g; Cholesterol 0 mg; 430 kJ (100 cal)*

*Below: Red Vegetable Curry*

# GREEN CHICKEN CURRY

•

*Preparation time*: 20 minutes
*Total cooking time*: 25 minutes
Serves 4

✦

1 tablespoon oil
1 onion, chopped
1–2 tablespoons Green Curry Paste (page
    123) or ready-made paste
1½ cups (375 ml/12 fl oz) coconut milk
½ cup (125 ml/4 fl oz) water
500 g (1 lb) chicken thigh fillets, cut into
    bite-sized pieces
100 g (3⅓ oz) green beans, cut into short
    pieces
6 kaffir lime leaves
1 tablespoon fish sauce
1 tablespoon lime juice
1 teaspoon finely grated lime rind
2 teaspoons soft brown sugar
¼ cup (7 g/¼ oz) fresh coriander leaves

1 Heat the oil in a wok or heavy-based pan. Add the onion and curry paste to the wok and cook for 1 minute, stirring constantly. Add the coconut milk and water to the wok and bring to the boil.
2 Add the chicken pieces, beans and lime leaves to the wok, stirring to combine. Reduce the heat and simmer for 15 to 20 minutes or until the chicken is tender.
3 Add the fish sauce, lime juice, lime rind and sugar to the wok; stir to combine. Sprinkle with fresh coriander leaves just before serving. Serve with steamed rice.
NOTE: Chicken thigh fillets are sweet in flavour and have a good texture for curries, but you can use breast fillets if you prefer. Do not overcook fillets or they will become tough.

NUTRITION PER SERVE: Protein 30 g; Fat 35 g;
Carbohydrate 10 g; Dietary Fibre 1 g; Cholesterol 90 mg;
1910 kJ (455 cal)

*Above: Green
Chicken Curry*

## FRIED CRISPY CHICKEN

•

*Preparation time*: 20 minutes
+ 30 minutes marinating
*Total cooking time*: 30 minutes
*Serves* 4

★

4 chicken marylands (quarters) or
    8 drumsticks
4 cloves garlic, chopped
3 coriander roots, finely chopped
2 teaspoons ground turmeric
1 teaspoon freshly ground pepper
1 teaspoon salt
1 teaspoon caster sugar
2 tablespoons chilli sauce
oil, for deep-frying

•

1 Boil the chicken in water for 15 minutes, or
until cooked through. Cool.
2 Place the garlic, coriander root, turmeric,
pepper, salt, sugar and chilli sauce in a mortar
and pestle or food processor and pound or
process into a smooth paste. Brush over the
chicken, cover and refrigerate for 30 minutes.
3 Heat the oil in a heavy-based pan, add the
chicken and cook until dark brown, turning
frequently. Drain on paper towels. Serve hot or
cold with chilli sauce, if desired.

NUTRITION PER SERVE: Protein 25 g; Fat 15 g;
Carbohydrate 3 g; Dietary Fibre 1 g; Cholesterol 105 mg;
1085 kJ (260 cal)

•

## BRAISED BEEF WITH SPINACH AND LEEKS

•

*Preparation time:* 15 minutes
+ 2 hours marinating
*Total cooking time:* 25 minutes
*Serves* 4

★

400 g (12²/₃ oz) beef fillet
2 tablespoons light soy sauce
2 tablespoons fish sauce
3 tablespoons oil
4 coriander roots, finely chopped
¹/₄ cup (15 g/¹/₂ oz) chopped fresh
    coriander leaves and stems
2 teaspoons cracked black peppercorns
2 cloves garlic, crushed
1 tablespoon soft brown sugar
¹/₂ cup (125 ml/4 fl oz) water
1 leek, sliced
20 spinach leaves, stalks removed
¹/₄ cup (60 ml/2 fl oz) lime juice

1 Slice the beef into 2.5 cm (1 inch) thick steaks.
Place the soy sauce, fish sauce, 1 tablespoon oil,
coriander, peppercorns, garlic and sugar in a
food processor and process until smooth. Pour
the marinade over the beef; cover and refrigerate
for at least 2 hours, or overnight.
2 Drain the beef, reserving the marinade. Heat
1 tablespoon oil in a wok or large frying pan.
Add the steaks and brown well on each side. Add
the marinade and water, reduce the heat and
simmer for 8 minutes. Remove the meat and
keep warm. Simmer the sauce for 10 minutes; set
aside. Slice the beef into bite-sized pieces.
3 Heat the remaining oil in a wok or pan; add
the leek and stir-fry for 2 minutes over medium
heat. Add the spinach and cook for 30 seconds.
4 Arrange the leek and spinach on a serving
plate with the meat. Pour the sauce over the
meat and drizzle over the lime juice. Serve
garnished with chilli slices, if you wish.

NUTRITION PER SERVE: Protein 25 g; Fat 20 g;
Carbohydrate 5 g; Dietary Fibre 2 g; Cholesterol 75 mg;
1290 kJ (305 cal)

•

## GREEN PRAWN CURRY

•

*Preparation time:* 35 minutes
*Total cooking time:* 25 minutes
*Serves* 4

★

500 g (1 lb) raw prawns
1¹/₂ cups (375 ml/12 fl oz) coconut milk
1 cup (250 ml/8 fl oz) water
1–3 tablespoons Green Curry Paste (page
    123) or ready-made paste
6 kaffir lime leaves
100 g (3¹/₃ oz) snake beans, cut into short
    pieces, optional
2 tablespoons fish sauce
2 tablespoons lime juice
2 teaspoons grated lime rind
2 teaspoons soft brown sugar
1 cup (30 g/1 oz) fresh coriander leaves

•

1 Peel and devein the prawns, leaving the tails
intact. Set aside.
2 Heat the coconut milk and water in a wok or
pan over medium heat for 5 minutes. Add the
curry paste, lime leaves and beans; bring to the
boil and simmer for 10 minutes.
3 Add the prawns and simmer for 5 to 6 minutes
or until pink. Add the fish sauce, lime juice and
rind, and sugar. Sprinkle with coriander leaves.

NUTRITION PER SERVE: Protein 15 g; Fat 25 g;
Carbohydrate 5 g; Dietary Fibre 0 g; Cholesterol 125 mg;
1230 kJ (295 cal)

CORIANDER ROOT
*Coriander roots are an
essential ingredient in Thai
cooking, providing the
flavour base, along with
garlic and peppercorns, for
most curry pastes and
soups. When separating
the coriander root from the
plant include about
2 cm (1 inch) of stem.
Wash well and chop finely
before crushing in a
mortar and pestle or food
processor; crushing the
roots helps release the
flavour. Coriander roots
can be frozen.*

*Opposite page: Braised
Beef with Spinach and
Leeks (top); Fried
Crispy Chicken*

1 Heat a wok until hot. Add the whole chillies and roast until just beginning to brown all over. Remove the green chillies, cool and slice.
2 Cut the fish into cubes. Bruise the lemon grass by crushing with the flat side of a knife.
3 Add the lemon grass, coriander roots, lime leaves, ginger, garlic, spring onion, sugar and coconut milk to the wok. Bring to the boil, then simmer for 2 minutes. Add the fish pieces and simmer gently for 2 to 3 minutes, or until the fish is tender. Stir in the coconut cream.
4 Stir through the chopped green chilli, fish sauce, lime juice and salt to taste. Remove the lemon grass and whole chillies to serve.

*NUTRITION PER SERVE: Protein 25 g; Fat 20 g; Carbohydrate 10 g; Dietary Fibre 5 g; Cholesterol 75 mg; 1380 kJ (330 cal)*

## LARB
### (SPICY PORK SALAD)

*Preparation time:* 20 minutes
*Total cooking time*: 8 minutes
*Serves 4–6*

✦

1 tablespoon oil
2 stems lemon grass (white part only), finely sliced
2 fresh green chillies, finely chopped
500 g (1 lb) lean minced pork or beef
1/4 cup (60 ml/2 fl oz) lime juice
2 teaspoons finely grated lime rind
2–6 teaspoons chilli sauce
lettuce leaves, for serving
1/3 cup (10 g/1/3 oz) chopped fresh coriander leaves
1/4 cup (5 g/1/4 oz) chopped fresh mint
1 small red (Spanish) onion, finely sliced
1/3 cup (50 g/12/3 oz) unsalted roasted peanuts, chopped
1/4 cup (25 g/3/4 oz) crisp fried garlic

1 Heat the oil in a wok and stir-fry the lemon grass, chilli and mince over high heat for 6 minutes, until the mince is cooked, breaking up any lumps. Transfer to a bowl; allow to cool.
2 Add the lime juice, rind and chilli sauce to the mince mixture. Arrange the lettuce leaves on a serving plate. Stir most of the coriander, mint, onion, peanuts and fried garlic through the mince, spoon over the lettuce and sprinkle the rest of the coriander, mint, onion, peanuts and garlic over the top.

*NUTRITION PER SERVE (6): Protein 20 g; Fat 15 g; Carbohydrate 3 g; Dietary Fibre 3 g; Cholesterol 45 mg; 965 kJ (230 cal)*

## FISH FILLETS
## IN COCONUT MILK

•

*Preparation time:* 15 minutes
*Total cooking time:* 15 minutes
*Serves 4*

✦

2 long green chillies
2 small red chillies
400 g (122/3 oz) firm white fish fillets
2 stems lemon grass (white part only)
2 coriander roots, finely chopped
4 kaffir lime leaves
2 cm (3/4 inch) piece fresh ginger, grated
2 cloves garlic, crushed
3 spring onions (white part only), finely sliced
1 teaspoon soft brown sugar
1 cup (250 ml/8 fl oz) coconut milk
1/2 cup (125 ml/4 oz) coconut cream
1 tablespoon fish sauce
2–3 tablespoons lime juice
kaffir lime leaves, extra, to garnish

*Above: Fish Fillets in Coconut Milk*

*Fold in the cut corners
of the banana leaf
squares, then staple
them and/or tie around
the edge with string.*

*Fill each cup almost to
the top with the fish
mixture, leaving room
for the cabbage.*

*Sprinkle the shredded
cabbage over each cup
with a little fish sauce.*

## STEAMED FISH
## IN BANANA LEAVES

•

*Preparation time:* 45 minutes
*Total cooking time:* 10 minutes
*Makes* 10

★

2 large banana leaves
350 g (11¼ oz) firm white fish fillets, cut
    into thin strips
1–2 tablespoons Red Curry Paste
    (page 112) or ready-made paste
1 cup (250 ml/8 fl oz) coconut cream
2 cups (150 g/4¾ oz) finely shredded
    cabbage
2 tablespoons fish sauce
2 tablespoons lime juice
1–2 tablespoons sweet chilli sauce
1 fresh red chilli, chopped, optional

1 Cut the banana leaves into squares 10 x 10 cm
(4 x 4 inches) and make a 3 cm (1¼ inch) cut
towards the centre on each corner. Fold in the
corners, then staple and/or tie around with a
piece of string to form a cup. Trim the corners to
neaten, if necessary.

2 Put the fish in a bowl with the curry paste and
coconut cream and stir gently to combine. Place
spoonfuls of the fish mixture in each banana
leaf cup.
3 Line a large steaming basket with extra banana
leaves or cabbage leaves and place the prepared
cups in the basket. Top each piece of fish with
shredded cabbage and a little fish sauce. Place
the basket over a wok of simmering water and
steam, covered, for about 7 minutes. Drizzle lime
juice and sweet chilli sauce over the top and
serve immediately, sprinkled with chilli.
NOTE: The fish can be cooked in foil cups
instead of banana leaves.

*NUTRITION PER BANANA LEAF CUP: Protein 10 g; Fat 10 g;
Carbohydrate 5 g; Dietary Fibre 1 g; Cholesterol 25 mg;
545 kJ (130 cal)*

*Above: Steamed Fish
in Banana Leaves*

## HOT PORK CURRY WITH PUMPKIN

•

*Preparation time:* 20 minutes
*Total cooking time:* 25 minutes
*Serves* 4

★

1 tablespoon oil
1–2 tablespoons Red Curry Paste
   (page 112) or ready-made paste
500 g (1 lb) lean pork, cut into thick
   strips or chunks
1 cup (250 ml/8 fl oz) coconut milk
½ cup (125 ml/4 fl oz) water
350 g (11¼ oz) butternut pumpkin, cut
   into small chunks
6 kaffir lime leaves
¼ cup (60 ml/2 fl oz) coconut cream
1 tablespoon fish sauce
1 teaspoon soft brown sugar
2 red chillies, thinly sliced

•

1 Heat the oil in a wok or heavy-based pan; add the curry paste and stir for 1 minute. Add the pork and stir-fry over moderately high heat until golden brown.
2 Add the coconut milk, water, pumpkin and lime leaves, reduce the heat and simmer for 20 minutes, or until the pork is tender.

*Below: Hot Pork Curry with Pumpkin*

3 Add the coconut cream, fish sauce and sugar to the wok and stir to combine. Scatter the chilli over the top. Garnish with sprigs of basil, if you like, and serve with steamed rice.

*NUTRITION PER SERVE: Protein 35 g; Fat 30 g; Carbohydrate 10 g; Dietary Fibre 0 g; Cholesterol 65 mg; 1860 kJ (445 cal)*

•

## PRAWNS IN LIME COCONUT SAUCE

•

*Preparation time:* 20 minutes
*Total cooking time:* 30 minutes
*Serves* 4

★

¼ cup (15 g/½ oz) shredded coconut
500 g (1 lb) raw prawns
1 teaspoon shrimp paste
1 cup (250 ml/8 fl oz) coconut milk
1 cup (250 ml/8 fl oz) water
2 stems lemon grass (white part only),
   finely chopped
2–4 kaffir lime leaves
2 teaspoons chopped red chilli
2 tablespoons tamarind concentrate
2 teaspoons fish sauce
1 teaspoon soft brown sugar
rind of 2 fresh limes

•

1 Spread the coconut on an oven tray and toast it in a slow 150°C (300°F/Gas 2) oven for 10 minutes, or until it is dark golden, shaking the tray occasionally. Peel and devein the prawns, leaving the tails intact.
2 Place the shrimp paste on a small piece of foil; fold one side over and then fold it into a parcel. Cook the parcel under a hot grill for 2 minutes each side.
3 Combine the coconut milk and water in a wok or frying pan and cook over medium heat until just boiling. Add the lemon grass, lime leaves and chilli; reduce the heat and simmer for 7 minutes. Add the shrimp paste, tamarind, fish sauce and sugar and simmer for 8 minutes.
4 Add the prawns to the sauce and cook for 5 minutes or until they turn pink. Sprinkle with coconut and long, thin shreds of lime rind just before serving with steamed rice.
NOTE: The prawns can be cooked and served in their shells. If so, provide a finger bowl and napkin for each diner.

*NUTRITION PER SERVE: Protein 15 g; Fat 15 g; Carbohydrate 5 g; Dietary Fibre 0 g; Cholesterol 120 mg; 840 kJ (200 cal)*

## CHICKEN AND PEANUT PANANG CURRY

•

*Preparation time:* 25 minutes
*Total cooking time:* 30–40 minutes
*Serves* 4

★

1 tablespoon oil
1 large red (Spanish) onion, chopped
1–2 tablespoons ready-made Panang
   curry paste
1 cup (250 ml/8 fl oz) coconut milk
500 g (1 lb) chicken thigh fillets, cut into
   bite-sized pieces
4 kaffir lime leaves
¼ cup (60 ml/2 fl oz) coconut cream
1 tablespoon fish sauce
1 tablespoon lime juice
2 teaspoons soft brown sugar
½ cup (80 g/2²/₃ oz) unsalted roasted
   peanuts, chopped
½ cup (15 g/½ oz) Thai basil leaves
½ cup (80 g/2²/₃ oz) chopped fresh
   pineapple
1 cucumber, sliced
chilli sauce for serving, optional

1 Heat the oil in a wok or large frying pan; add the onion and curry paste and stir over medium heat for 2 minutes. Add the coconut milk and bring to the boil.
2 Add the chicken and lime leaves to the wok; reduce the heat and cook for 15 minutes. Remove the chicken with a wire mesh strainer or slotted spoon. Simmer the sauce for 5 minutes or until it is reduced and quite thick.
3 Return the chicken to the wok. Add the coconut cream, fish sauce, lime juice and sugar and cook for 5 minutes. Stir in the peanuts, basil and pineapple. Serve with sliced cucumber on the side, some chilli sauce, if desired, as well as steamed rice.
NOTE: Panang curry paste is based on ground nuts (usually peanuts). Panang curry originated in Malaysia but is now also found in Thai and Indonesian cuisines.

*NUTRITION PER SERVE: Protein 35 g; Fat 40 g; Carbohydrate 15 g; Dietary Fibre 5 g; Cholesterol 90 mg; 2330 kJ (555 cal)*

*Above: Chicken and Peanut Panang Curry*

coat the sides. Heat the wok; when it is hot, pour in the egg mixture and swirl it around the wok. Allow the mixture to set on the underneath edges, frequently lifting the edges once set, and tilting the wok a little to let the unset mixture run underneath. Repeat this process until the omelette is nearly all set.

3 Place three-quarters of the prawn mixture in the centre of the omelette and fold in the sides to form a square, overlapping the sides a little, or simply fold the omelette in half.

4 Slide the omelette onto a serving plate and place the remaining prawn mixture on the top. Garnish with the shredded spring onion and coriander, and serve with the chilli sauce and steamed rice.

NOTE: You can also use a mixture of seafood such as prawns and scallops.

*NUTRITION PER SERVE (4): Protein 20 g; Fat 15 g; Carbohydrate 5 g; Dietary Fibre 1 g; Cholesterol 350 mg; 1020 kJ (240 cal)*

*PRAWN OMELETTE*

*Lift the edges of the omelette and tilt the wok so the uncooked mixture runs underneath.*

*Fold the sides of the omelette over the mixture to form a square.*

*Above: Prawn Omelette*

## PRAWN OMELETTE

•

**Preparation time:** 15 minutes
**Total cooking time:** 15 minutes
**Serves 2–4**

★

2 tablespoons oil
3 cloves garlic, chopped
2 stems lemon grass (white part only),
  finely chopped
2 coriander roots, finely chopped
1–2 teaspoons chopped red chilli
500 g (1 lb) small raw prawns, peeled
3 spring onions, chopped
½ teaspoon black pepper
1 tablespoon fish sauce
2 teaspoons soft brown sugar
4 eggs
2 tablespoons water
2 teaspoons fish sauce, extra
shredded spring onion, extra, to garnish
coriander sprigs, to garnish
chilli sauce, to serve

•

1 Heat half the oil in a large wok or heavy-based pan; add the garlic, lemon grass, coriander root and chilli and stir over medium heat for 20 seconds. Add the prawns and stir-fry until prawns change colour. Add the spring onion, pepper, fish sauce and sugar; toss well and remove from the wok.

2 Beat the eggs, water and extra fish sauce in a bowl until the mixture is foamy. Add the remaining oil to the wok and swirl it around to

## CRISP FRIED WHOLE FISH WITH SOUR PEPPER AND CORIANDER SAUCE

•

**Preparation time:** 20 minutes
**Total cooking time:** 15 minutes
**Serves 4**

★

1 whole firm sweet fish such as snapper
  or red emperor, approximately 1 kg
  (2 lb), cleaned and scaled
oil, for deep-frying
4 spring onions, chopped
5 cm (2 inch) piece fresh ginger, grated
2–4 teaspoons fresh green peppercorns,
  crushed
2 teaspoons chopped red chilli
½ cup (125 ml/4 fl oz) coconut milk
1 tablespoon tamarind concentrate
1 tablespoon fish sauce
lettuce leaves, to serve
1 cup (30 g/1 oz) fresh coriander leaves
sweet chilli sauce, to serve

•

1 Cut a shallow, criss-cross pattern on both sides of the fish. Using kitchen scissors or a sharp knife, trim the fins if they are very long.

2 Heat the oil in a large wok or heavy-based, deep frying pan. Place the whole fish in the oil and cook for 4 to 5 minutes on each side, moving it around in the oil to ensure the whole fish is crisp and cooked (including the tail and head). Drain the fish well on paper towels and keep warm.

4 cloves garlic, extra, sliced lengthways
20 leaves spinach, coarsely shredded
$1/2$ teaspoon cracked black pepper
$1/2$ cup (125 ml/4 fl oz) water
1 tablespoon lime juice

•

1 Using a mortar and pestle or a blender, blend the coriander, sugar, turmeric, crushed garlic and 1 tablespoon fish sauce to make a smooth paste.

2 Cut the cauliflower into florets. Cut the spring onions in half lengthways, then cut the white parts into short lengths, reserving some of the green tops for a garnish. Cut the snake beans into short lengths.

3 Heat half the oil in a large pan or wok, add the extra sliced garlic and stir-fry for 30 seconds or until just beginning to brown. Reserve some of the garlic for a garnish.

4 Add the spinach to the pan and stir-fry for another 30 seconds or until just wilted. Add the pepper and the remaining fish sauce and mix well. Arrange on a serving plate; keep warm.

5 Heat the remaining oil in the same pan; add the paste and cook over high heat for 1 minute or until aromatic. Add the cauliflower and stir-fry until well combined. Add the water, bring to the boil, reduce heat and simmer, covered, for 3 minutes. Add the beans, cover and cook for another 3 minutes. Add the spring onion and stir until just wilted. Spoon the vegetables over the spinach, drizzle with lime juice and sprinkle over the reserved fried garlic and spring onion.

*NUTRITION PER SERVE: Protein 5 g; Fat 10 g; Carbohydrate 10 g; Dietary Fibre 5 g; Cholesterol 5 mg; 675 kJ (160 cal)*

3 Drain almost all the oil from the wok. Heat the wok over medium heat, add the spring onion, ginger, peppercorns and chilli and stir-fry for 3 minutes. Add the coconut milk, tamarind and fish sauce and cook for 2 minutes.

4 Place the fish on a bed of lettuce on a serving plate and pour over the sauce. Sprinkle with coriander leaves and serve with chilli sauce.

NOTE: To serve, use tongs or a small spatula to lift pieces of fish away from the bones. Then remove the bones, or turn the fish over, and lift pieces of fish from the underside.

*NUTRITION PER SERVE: Protein 30 g; Fat 25 g; Carbohydrate 0 g; Dietary Fibre 0 g; Cholesterol 80 mg; 1540 kJ (370 cal)*

•

## STIR-FRIED CAULIFLOWER AND SNAKE BEANS

•

**Preparation time:** 15 minutes
**Total cooking time:** 10 minutes
**Serves** 4

★

4 coriander roots, chopped, or
    1 tablespoon chopped leaves and stems
1 teaspoon soft brown sugar
$1/2$ teaspoon ground turmeric
2 cloves garlic, crushed
2 tablespoons fish sauce
400 g ($12^2/3$ oz) cauliflower
6 spring onions
200 g ($6^1/2$ oz) snake beans
2 tablespoons oil

*Above: Crisp Fried Whole Fish with Sour Pepper and Coriander Sauce*
*Below: Stir-Fried Cauliflower and Snake Beans*

## STEAMED FISH CUTLETS WITH GINGER AND CHILLI

*Preparation time:* 15 minutes
*Total cooking time:* 10 minutes
Serves 4

✷

*4 firm white fish cutlets, such as snapper, approximately (200 g/6¹/2 oz) each*
*5 cm (2 inch) piece fresh ginger, cut into fine shreds*
*2 cloves garlic, chopped*
*2 teaspoons chopped red chilli*
*2 tablespoons finely chopped coriander stems*
*3 spring onions, cut into fine shreds each 4 cm (1¹/2 inches) long*
*2 tablespoons lime juice*

1 Line a bamboo steaming basket with banana leaves or baking paper (this is so the fish will not stick or taste of bamboo).
2 Arrange the fish cutlets in the basket and top with the ginger, garlic, chilli and coriander. Cover and steam over a wok or large pan of boiling water for 5 to 6 minutes.
3 Remove the lid and sprinkle the spring onion and lime juice over the fish. Cover and steam for 30 seconds, or until the fish is cooked. Serve immediately with wedges of lime and steamed rice that has been garnished with onions or herbs.

NUTRITION PER SERVE: Protein 40 g; Fat 5 g;
Carbohydrate 0 g; Dietary Fibre 0 g; Cholesterol 120 mg;
850 kJ (205 cal)

## CORIANDER PORK WITH FRESH PINEAPPLE

*Preparation time:* 25 minutes
*Total cooking time:* 10–12 minutes
Serves 4

✷

*400 g (12²/3 oz) pork loin or fillet*
*¹/4 medium pineapple*
*1 tablespoon oil*
*4 cloves garlic, chopped*
*4 spring onions, chopped*
*1 tablespoon fish sauce*
*1 tablespoon lime juice*
*¹/2 cup (15 g/¹/2 oz) fresh coriander leaves*
*¹/4 cup (15 g/¹/2 oz) chopped fresh mint*

1 Partially freeze the pork until it is just firm, then slice it thinly. Trim the skin from the pineapple and cut the flesh into bite-sized pieces.

2 Heat the oil in a wok or heavy-based frying pan. Add the garlic and spring onion and cook for 1 minute. Remove from the wok.
3 Heat the wok to very hot; add the pork in 2 or 3 batches and stir-fry each batch for 3 minutes or until the meat is just cooked. Return the meat, garlic and spring onion to the wok and then add the pineapple pieces, fish sauce and lime juice. Toss well. Just before serving, sprinkle over the coriander leaves and mint and toss lightly. Serve with rice.

NUTRITION PER SERVE: Protein 25 g; Fat 15 g;
Carbohydrate 10 g; Dietary Fibre 5 g; Cholesterol 55 mg;
1105 kJ (265 cal)

## GREEN CURRY PASTE

*Preparation time:* 20 minutes
*Total cooking time:* 6 minutes
*Makes* approximately 1 cup
   (250 ml/8 fl oz)

✷

*1 tablespoon coriander seeds*
*2 teaspoons cumin seeds*
*1 teaspoon black peppercorns*
*2 teaspoons shrimp paste*
*8 large green chillies, roughly chopped*
*20 red Asian shallots*
*5 cm (2 inches) fresh galangal, chopped*
*12 small cloves garlic, chopped*
*1 cup (100 g/3¹/3 oz) chopped fresh coriander leaves, stems and roots*
*6 kaffir lime leaves, chopped*
*3 stems lemon grass (white part only), finely chopped*
*2 teaspoons grated lime rind*
*2 teaspoons salt*
*2 tablespoons oil*

1 Place the coriander and cumin seeds in a dry frying pan and roast over medium heat for 2 to 3 minutes, shaking the pan constantly.
2 Pound the roasted spices and peppercorns in a mortar and pestle until finely ground.
3 Wrap the shrimp paste in a small piece of foil and cook under a hot grill for 3 minutes, turning the package twice.
4 Place the ground spices and shrimp paste in a food processor and process for 5 seconds. Add the remaining ingredients and process for 20 seconds at a time, scraping down the sides of the processor bowl with a spatula each time, until a smooth paste is formed.

NUTRITION PER 100 g: Protein 5 g; Fat 10 g;
Carbohydrate 5 g; Dietary Fibre 5 g; Cholesterol 0 mg;
440 kJ (105 cal)

THAI CURRY PASTES
*Thai curry pastes are traditionally made of fresh herbs that grow in the house gardens or nearby fields, rather than the dry spices (those of the spice trade—cumin, coriander seeds, cardamom, cinnamon and cloves) used in Indian cooking. Throughout Thailand market stalls provide a variety of pastes, each freshly made, for the home cook. The deceptively cool-coloured green curry paste is the most searingly hot; the colour comes from fresh green chilli peppers and fresh coriander leaves. Red curry paste is only marginally milder; here the colour is derived mainly from dried or fresh red chillies.*

*Opposite page:*
*Steamed Fish Cutlets with Ginger and Chilli (top); Coriander Pork with Fresh Pineapple*

## STEAMED MUSSELS WITH LEMON GRASS, BASIL AND WINE

•

*Preparation time:* 30 minutes
*Total cooking time:* 15 minutes
*Serves 4–6*

★

1 kg (2 lb) fresh small black mussels
1 tablespoon oil
1 medium onion, chopped
4 cloves garlic, chopped
2 stems lemon grass (white part only), chopped
1–2 teaspoons chopped red chilli
1 cup (250 ml/8 fl oz) white wine or water
1 tablespoon fish sauce
1 cup (30 g/1 oz) fresh Thai basil, chopped

•

1 Discard any open mussels. Scrub the outside of the mussels with a brush. Remove and discard the beards. Soak the mussels in a bowl of cold water for 10 minutes; drain.
2 Heat the oil in a wok or large pan. Add the onion, garlic, lemon grass and chilli, and cook for 4 minutes over low heat, stirring occasionally. Add the wine and fish sauce and cook for 3 minutes.
3 Add the mussels to the wok and toss well. Cover the wok, increase the heat and cook for 3 to 4 minutes or until the mussels open. (Do not overcook or mussels will become tough.)

Discard any which have not opened after 4 minutes. Add the basil, toss well and serve with steamed rice.

*NUTRITION PER SERVE (6): Protein 15 g; Fat 5 g; Carbohydrate 1 g; Dietary Fibre 1 g; Cholesterol 85 mg; 470 kJ (110 cal)*

•

## MEE GROB
### (FRIED CRISPY NOODLES)

•

*Preparation time:* 30 minutes
*Total cooking time:* 20 minutes
*Serves 4*

★

200 g (6½ oz) raw prawns
100 g (3⅓ oz) dried rice vermicelli
2 cups (500 ml/16 fl oz) oil
100 g (3⅓ oz) fried tofu, cut into matchsticks
2 cloves garlic, finely chopped
4 cm (1½ inch) piece fresh ginger, grated
150 g (4¾ oz) chicken or pork mince, or a combination of both
1 tablespoon white vinegar
2 tablespoons fish sauce
2 tablespoons soft brown sugar
2 tablespoons chilli sauce
1 teaspoon chopped red chilli
2 small knobs pickled garlic, chopped
¼ cup (30 g/1 oz) chopped garlic chives
1 cup (30 g/1 oz) fresh coriander leaves

*Above: Steamed Mussels with Lemon Grass, Basil and Wine*

1 Peel and devein the prawns and finely chop the meat. Set aside.

2 Place the vermicelli in a bowl of hot water for 1 minute, then drain and allow to dry for 20 minutes.

3 Heat the oil in a wok or deep pan; add the tofu in 2 batches and cook for 1 minute or until golden and crisp. Drain.

4 Add the completely dry vermicelli to the wok in several batches; cook for 10 seconds or until puffed and crisp. Remove from the wok immediately to prevent the vermicelli absorbing too much oil. Drain on paper towels; allow to cool.

5 Drain all but 1 tablespoon of the oil from the wok. Reheat the wok over high heat and add the garlic, ginger, mince and prawn meat; stir-fry for 2 minutes or until golden brown. Add the vinegar, fish sauce, sugar, chilli sauce and chilli; stir until boiling.

6 Just before serving, add the noodles and tofu to the wok and toss thoroughly. Quickly toss through the pickled garlic, chives and coriander.

*NUTRITION PER SERVE: Protein 20 g; Fat 5 g; Carbohydrate 35 g; Dietary Fibre 2 g; Cholesterol 120 mg; 1145 kJ (270 cal)*

## PAD THAI
### (THAI FRIED NOODLES)

**Preparation time:** 25 minutes
**Total cooking time:** 10–15 minutes
**Serves** 4

★

*200 g (6½ oz) raw prawns*
*250 g (8 oz) dried rice stick noodles*
*2 tablespoons oil*
*3 cloves garlic, chopped*
*2 teaspoons chopped red chilli*
*150 g (4¾ oz) pork, thinly sliced*
*½ cup (60 g/2 oz) garlic chives, chopped*
*2 tablespoons fish sauce*
*2 tablespoons lime juice*
*2 teaspoons soft brown sugar*
*2 eggs, beaten*
*1 cup (90 g/3 oz) bean sprouts*
*sprigs of fresh coriander*
*¼ cup (40 g/1⅓ oz) unsalted roasted*
*    peanuts, chopped*
*crisp fried onion, soft brown sugar and*
*    unsalted roasted peanuts, to serve*

1 Peel and devein the prawns, and finely chop the meat. Set aside.

2 Soak the noodles in warm water for 10 minute or until they are soft. Drain and set aside.

3 Heat the oil in a wok or large frying pan. When the oil is very hot, add the garlic, chilli and pork, and stir constantly for 2 minutes. Add the prawn meat and cook, stirring constantly, for 3 minutes. Add the garlic chives and drained noodles; cover and cook for another minute.

4 Add the fish sauce, lime juice, sugar and eggs to the wok. Toss well with tongs or 2 wooden spoons until heated through.

5 Sprinkle over the bean sprouts, coriander and peanuts. This dish is traditionally served with crisp fried onion, soft brown sugar and chopped peanuts on the side.

*NUTRITION PER SERVE: Protein 30 g; Fat 25 g; Carbohydrate 55 g; Dietary Fibre 2 g; Cholesterol 235 mg; 2298 kJ (545 cal)*

PICKLED GARLIC
*In China, Korea and Thailand whole garlic heads pickled in a vinegar mixture are often served as a side dish to meat and poultry dishes. They are also added to noodle dishes and sweet and sour sauces, or used as a garnish. The sweet, mild pickled garlic used in Thai dishes is available in jars; the stronger Korean-style is sold sliced and frozen in vacuum packs.*

*Above: Pad Thai*

# CURRY PASTES & POWDERS

The secret to making authentic Asian curries is to grind your own fresh spices into dry powders or wet pastes. Just a few minutes over high heat unlocks the fragrances into the air.

## CEYLON CURRY POWDER

In a small pan, dry-fry 6 tablespoons coriander seeds, 3 tablespoons cumin seeds, 1 teaspoon fennel seeds and ½ teaspoon fenugreek seeds for 8–10 minutes, or until the spices are dark brown, stirring occasionally to prevent the spices from burning. Place the roasted spices with 3 small dried chillies, 3 cloves, ¼ teaspoon cardamom seeds, 1 crushed cinnamon stick and 2 dried curry leaves in a food processor and grind to a fine powder. Cool and transfer to an airtight jar.

*NUTRITION PER 100 g: Protein 5 g; Fat 15 g; Carbohydrate 5 g; Dietary Fibre 3 g; Cholesterol 0 mg; 675 kJ (160 cal)*

## INDONESIAN SAMBAL PASTE

Soak 12 large dried red chillies in hot water for 30 minutes; drain. Place the chillies, 2 roughly chopped large red (Spanish) onions, 6 cloves garlic, 1 teaspoon shrimp paste and 125 ml (4 fl oz) oil in a food processor and mix into a smooth paste, scraping down the sides regularly. Heat a heavy-based pan over low heat and cook the paste for 10 minutes, stirring regularly, until very oily. Stir in ¾ cup (185 ml/6 fl oz) tamarind concentrate, 1 tablespoon grated palm sugar or soft brown sugar, 2 teaspoons salt and 1 teaspoon

ground pepper. Bring to the boil and simmer for 2 minutes. Cool and pour into warm sterilised jars. Store in the fridge for up to 2 weeks or freeze for up to 3 months.

*NUTRITION PER 100 g: Protein 1 g; Fat 15 g; Carbohydrate 5 g; Dietary Fibre 2 g; Cholesterol 0 mg; 735 kJ (175 cal)*

## GARAM MASALA

Put 4 tablespoons coriander seeds, 3 tablespoons cardamom pods, 2 tablespoons cumin seeds, 1 tablespoon whole black peppercorns, 1 teaspoon whole cloves and 3 cinnamon sticks in a pan and dry-fry over moderate heat until fragrant. Open the cardamom pods, retaining the seeds only. Put the fried spices in a food processor or blender with a grated whole fresh nutmeg and process to a powder. Use immediately or store in an airtight jar.

*NUTRITION: Negligible.*

## BALTI MASALA PASTE

Put 4 tablespoons coriander seeds, 2 tablespoons cumin seeds, 2 crumbled cinnamon sticks, 2 teaspoons each of fennel seeds, black mustard seeds and cardamom seeds, 1 teaspoon fenugreek seeds, 6 cloves, 4 bay leaves and 20 curry leaves in a small pan or balti. Dry-fry over moderate heat until the spices just start to become fragrant. Transfer to a mortar and pestle, then allow to cool before grinding to a powder. Add 4 teaspoons each ground turmeric and garlic powder, 2 teaspoons ground ginger, 1½ teaspoons chilli powder and 1 cup (250 ml/8 fl oz) vinegar. Heat 1 cup (250 ml/8 fl oz) oil in the pan, add the paste and stir-fry for 5 minutes. Pour into warm sterilised jars and seal.

*NUTRITION PER 100 g: Protein 1 g; Fat 40 g; Carbohydrate 2 g; Dietary Fibre 0 g; Cholesterol 0 mg; 1470 kJ (350 cal)*

## CHILLI PASTE

Remove the stalks from 200 g (6½ oz) small red chillies. Place in a small pan with 1 cup (250 ml/8 fl oz) water and bring to the boil. Reduce the heat and simmer, partially covered, for 15 minutes, then cool slightly. Transfer the chillies and liquid to a food processor; add 1 teaspoon each of salt and sugar, and 1 tablespoon each of vinegar and oil. Process until finely chopped. Store in a sealed container in the refrigerator for up to 2 weeks.

*NUTRITION PER 100 g: Protein 1 g; Fat 4 g; Carbohydrate 3 g; Dietary Fibre 1 g; Cholesterol 0 mg; 205 kJ (50 cal)*

*From left: Ceylon Curry Powder; Indonesian Sambal Paste; Chilli Paste; Garam Masala; Balti Masala Paste*

*Below: Musaman Beef Curry*

# MUSAMAN CURRY PASTE

•

**Preparation time:** 10 minutes
**Total cooking time:** 3 minutes
**Makes** 1 cup

★

1 tablespoon coriander seeds
1 tablespoon cumin seeds
seeds from 4 cardamom pods
2 teaspoons black peppercorns
1 tablespoon shrimp paste
1 teaspoon nutmeg
1/2 teaspoon ground cloves
15 dried red chillies
10 red Asian shallots, chopped
2 stems lemon grass (white part only), finely chopped
6 small cloves garlic, chopped
1 tablespoon oil

1 Place the coriander, cumin and cardamom seeds in a dry frying pan and roast over medium heat for 2 to 3 minutes, shaking the pan continously.
2 Place the roasted spices and peppercorns in a mortar and pestle and pound until they are finely ground.
3 Place the ground spices and remaining ingredients in a food processor. Process for 20 seconds and scrape down the sides of the bowl with a spatula. Continue processing for 5 seconds at a time, wiping down the sides of the bowl each time, until a smooth paste is formed.

*NUTRITION PER 100 g: Protein 2 g; Fat 5 g; Carbohydrate 5 g; Dietary Fibre 2 g; Cholesterol 3 mg; 305 kJ (75 cal)*

•

# MUSAMAN BEEF CURRY

•

**Preparation time:** 25 minutes
**Total cooking time:** 50 minutes
**Serves** 4

★

1 tablespoon oil
500 g (1 lb) topside steak, cut into large cubes
1–2 tablespoons Musaman Curry Paste (see above)
2 large onions, cut into wedges or thick slices
2 large potatoes, peeled and diced
1 1/2 cups (375 ml/12 fl oz) coconut milk
1 cup (250 ml/8 fl oz) water
2 cardamom pods
2 bay leaves
2 tablespoons tamarind concentrate
2 teaspoons soft brown sugar
1/2 cup (80 g/2 2/3 oz) unsalted roasted peanuts, optional
2 red chillies, finely sliced

•

1 Heat the oil in a wok or large heavy-based pan. Add the meat to the wok in batches and stir-fry each batch over medium heat until it is well browned. Remove the meat from the wok and set aside on paper towels.
2 Add the curry paste to the wok and stir for 1 minute. Add the onion and potatoes and cook, stirring frequently, until golden brown. Remove from the wok and set aside.
3 Add the coconut milk and water. Bring to the boil, stirring; reduce heat and simmer for 15 minutes, uncovered.
4 Return the meat, onions and potatoes to the wok. Add the cardamom, bay leaves, tamarind

and sugar. Stir well and then simmer, uncovered, for 20 minutes or until the meat is tender. Remove the cardamom pods and bay leaves from the mixture. Add the peanuts, if you are using them. When ready to serve, scatter the chilli over the top. Serve with steamed rice.

*NUTRITION PER SERVE: Protein 35 g; Fat 40 g; Carbohydrate 25 g; Dietary Fibre 5 g; Cholesterol 65 mg; 2445 kJ (585 cal)*

•

# CHIANG MAI NOODLES
•

**Preparation time:** 20 minutes
**Total cooking time:** 15 minutes
**Serves 4**

☆

500 g (1 lb) Hokkien noodles
1 tablespoon oil
3 red Asian shallots, chopped
6 cloves garlic, chopped
2 teaspoons finely chopped red chilli, optional
1–2 tablespoons Red Curry Paste (page 112) or ready-made paste
350 g (11¼ oz) lean chicken or pork, finely sliced

1 carrot, cut into fine, thin strips
2 tablespoons fish sauce
2 teaspoons soft brown sugar
3 spring onions, finely sliced
¼ cup (7 g/¼ oz) fresh coriander leaves

•

1 Cook the noodles in a wok or pan of rapidly boiling water for 2 to 3 minutes until they are just tender. Drain and keep warm. Heat the oil in a wok or large frying pan until it is very hot. Add the shallots, garlic, chilli and curry paste; stir-fry for 2 minutes or until fragrant. Add chicken or pork to wok in 2 batches and cook for 3 minutes or until meat changes colour.
2 Return all meat to the wok. Add carrot, fish sauce and sugar; bring to the boil.
3 Divide noodles between serving bowls and mix in portions of the chicken mixture and spring onions. Top with coriander leaves and serve immediately. Delicious with Thai Dipping Sauce (page 169).

*NUTRITION PER SERVE: Protein 35 g; Fat 20 g; Carbohydrate 102 g; Dietary Fibre 10 g; Cholesterol 65 mg; 2905 kJ (690 cal)*

*Above: Chiang Mai Noodles*

NOTE: This dish is quite salty so serve it with a selection of milder flavoured dishes. Barbecued pork can be purchased from a Chinese barbecue shop. Any leftovers freeze well.

NUTRITION PER SERVE: Protein 10 g; Fat 15 g; Carbohydrate 45 g; Dietary Fibre 5 g; Cholesterol 15 mg; 1550 kJ (370 cal)

## PORK BALL CURRY WITH NOODLES

*Preparation time:* 15 minutes
*Total cooking time:* 20 minutes
*Serves* 4

⭐

200 g (6¹/₂ oz) pork mince
3 cloves garlic, chopped
2 stems lemon grass (white part only), finely chopped
3 cm (1¹/₄ inch) piece fresh ginger, grated
1 tablespoon oil
1–2 tablespoons Green Curry Paste (page 123) or ready-made paste
1¹/₂ cups (375 ml/12 fl oz) coconut milk
1 cup (250 ml/8 fl oz) water
2 tablespoons fish sauce
2 teaspoons soft brown sugar
¹/₂ cup (25 g/³/₄ oz) chopped fresh Thai basil
200 g (6¹/₂ oz) Hokkien noodles
3 spring onions, sliced
2 red or green chillies, sliced
fresh coriander leaves, to serve

1 Finely chop the pork mince with a cleaver or large knife. Combine the mince, garlic, lemon grass and ginger in a bowl and mix thoroughly. Form teaspoons of the mixture into small balls.
2 Heat the oil in a wok or frying pan. Add the curry paste and cook over low heat, stirring constantly, for 1 minute or until fragrant. Add the coconut milk and water. Stir until boiling; reduce heat and simmer, uncovered, for 5 minutes. Add the pork balls and simmer gently for 5 minutes or until cooked. Add the fish sauce, sugar and basil.
3 Cook the noodles in boiling water for 4 minutes or until tender; drain. Place the noodles on serving plates, add the pork balls and curry sauce, toss well and serve immediately. Scatter the spring onion, chilli and coriander leaves over the top.
NOTE: Serve this dish as soon as it is cooked as the noodles soak up the sauce on standing.

NUTRITION PER SERVE: Protein 20 g; Fat 40 g; Carbohydrate 45 g; Dietary Fibre 5 g; Cholesterol 35 mg; 2515 kJ (600 cal)

## FRIED NOODLES WITH MUSHROOMS AND BARBECUED PORK

*Preparation time:* 30 minutes
*Total cooking time:* 6 minutes
*Serves* 4

⭐

8 dried Chinese mushrooms
2 tablespoons oil
4 cloves garlic, chopped
4 cm (1¹/₂ inch) piece fresh ginger, grated
1–2 teaspoons chopped red chilli
100 g (3¹/₃ oz) Chinese barbecued pork, cut into small pieces
200 g (6¹/₂ oz) Hokkien noodles
2 teaspoons fish sauce
2 tablespoons lime juice
2 teaspoons soft brown sugar
2 tablespoons crisp fried garlic
2 tablespoons crisp fried onion
chilli flakes, to taste

1 Soak the mushrooms in hot water for 20 minutes. Drain and cut them into quarters.
2 Heat the oil in a large wok or frying pan. Add the garlic, ginger and chilli and stir-fry over high heat for 1 minute. Add the pork to the wok and stir for 1 minute.
3 Add the noodles and mushrooms, and toss well. Sprinkle the fish sauce, lime juice and sugar over the pork and then toss quickly; cover and steam for 30 seconds. Sprinkle the fried garlic, fried onion, and chilli flakes over the top. Garnish with strips of the green section of spring onions, if you like.

*Above: Fried Noodles with Mushrooms and Barbecued Pork*

## VEGETARIAN RICE NOODLES

•

**Preparation time:** 25 minutes
+ 20 minutes soaking
**Total cooking time:** 5 minutes
Serves 4–6

☆

8 dried Chinese mushrooms
100 g (3¹/₃ oz) fried tofu
250 g (8 oz) dried rice vermicelli
2 tablespoons oil
3 cloves garlic, chopped
4 cm (1¹/₂ inch) piece fresh ginger, grated
1 medium carrot, cut into thin shreds
100 g (3¹/₃ oz) green beans, cut into short
    lengths
¹/₂ red pepper (capsicum), cut into fine
    strips
2 tablespoons Golden Mountain sauce
1 tablespoon fish sauce
2 teaspoons soft brown sugar
100 g (3¹/₃ oz) bean sprouts, scraggly
    ends removed
1 cup (75 g/2¹/₂ oz) finely shredded
    cabbage
bean sprouts, extra, to garnish
sweet chilli sauce, to serve

1 Soak the mushrooms in hot water for
20 minutes, then drain and slice. Cut the tofu
into small cubes.
2 Put the vermicelli in a heatproof bowl, cover
with boiling water and soak for 5 minutes until
soft. Drain.
3 Heat a wok or large heavy-based frying pan.
Add the oil and, when very hot, add the garlic,
ginger and tofu; stir-fry for 1 minute. Add the
carrot, beans, red pepper and mushrooms and
stir-fry for 2 minutes. Add the Golden Mountain
sauce, fish sauce and sugar; toss well, cover and
steam for 1 minute.
4 Add the vermicelli, bean sprouts and three-
quarters of the cabbage and toss together. Cover
and steam for 30 seconds. Arrange the vermicelli
on a serving platter, garnish with the extra bean
sprouts and remaining cabbage and serve with
sweet chilli sauce.

NUTRITION PER SERVE (6): Protein 5 g; Fat 10 g;
Carbohydrate 40 g; Dietary Fibre 3 g; Cholesterol 2 mg;
1075 kJ (255 cal)

CRISP FRIED ONION
AND GARLIC
*These tasty garnishes are
available in jars from
Asian food shops, or you
can make your own. Peel
the onion (or use red Asian
shallots if you can get
them) and garlic and cut
into very fine, even slices.
Spread out to dry on a tray
for a few hours before
cooking. Heat oil in a wok
or pan, and deep-fry the
onion and garlic in batches
until it is golden brown
and crisp. Drain well and
spread out on paper towels
to cool. It is best to fry the
onion and garlic separately
as the garlic will not take
as long to cook. If you are
not using it immediately,
store in an airtight
container in the fridge or
freezer. Season with salt
just before use.*

*Above: Vegetarian
Rice Noodles*

1 Slice the chicken into short, thin strips.
2 Place the water, ginger, lemon grass and fish sauce in a frying pan. Bring the mixture to the boil, reduce the heat slightly and simmer for 5 minutes.
3 Add the chicken to the pan and cook in the hot liquid for 5 minutes, stirring occasionally. Drain and allow to cool. Discard liquid.
4 Bring a large pan of water to the boil and cook the broccoli, corn, snow peas, red pepper and spring onion for 2 minutes. Drain and plunge into iced water; drain again.
5 Combine the sweet chilli sauce, honey, lime juice and rind in a small bowl and mix well. Arrange the vegetables and chicken on a serving platter. Pour the sauce over the top and toss gently. Sprinkle over the coriander leaves.
NOTE: To trim snow peas, cut or break both ends off and then pull away any strings from along the sides.

*NUTRITION PER SERVE (6): Protein 20 g; Fat 3 g; Carbohydrate 15 g; Dietary Fibre 5 g; Cholesterol 35 mg; 690 kJ (165 cal)*

## CURRIED RICE NOODLES WITH CHICKEN

*Preparation time*: 25 minutes
*Total cooking time:* 10–15 minutes
*Serves* 4–6

⭐

200 g (6¹/₂ oz) dried rice vermicelli
1¹/₂ tablespoons oil
1 tablespoon Red Curry Paste (page 112)
 or ready-made paste
450 g (14¹/₃ oz) chicken thigh fillets, cut
 into fine strips
1–2 teaspoons chopped red chilli
2 tablespoons fish sauce
2 tablespoons lime juice
100 g (3¹/₃ oz) bean sprouts
¹/₂ cup (80 g/2²/₃ oz) chopped unsalted
 roasted peanuts
¹/₄ cup (20 g/²/₃ oz) crisp fried onion
¹/₄ cup (25 g/³/₄ oz) crisp fried garlic
1 cup (25 g/³/₄ oz) fresh coriander leaves

•

1 Cook the vermicelli in a pot of rapidly boiling water for 2 minutes. Drain and then toss with 2 teaspoons of the oil to prevent the strands from sticking together; set aside.
2 Heat the remaining oil in a wok. Add the curry paste and stir for 1 minute or until fragrant. Add the chicken in batches and stir-fry for 2 minutes or until golden brown. Return all the chicken to the pan.

## CHICKEN AND VEGETABLE SALAD

•

*Preparation time:* 30 minutes
*Total cooking time:* 20 minutes
*Serves* 4–6

⭐

400 g (12²/₃ oz) chicken breast fillets
1 cup (250 ml/8 fl oz) water
3 slices fresh ginger
2 stems lemon grass (white part only),
 roughly chopped
2 tablespoons fish sauce
250 g (8 oz) broccoli, cut into florets
150 g (4³/₄ oz) fresh baby corn
100 g (3¹/₃ oz) snow peas (mange tout),
 trimmed
1 red pepper (capsicum), cut into strips
3 spring onions, cut into strips
¹/₂ cup (125 ml/4 fl oz) sweet chilli sauce
2 tablespoons honey or 2 tablespoons
 grated palm sugar mixed with a little
 warm water
2 tablespoons lime juice
2 teaspoons grated lime rind
¹/₄ cup (7 g/¹/₄ oz) fresh coriander leaves

*Above: Chicken and
Vegetable Salad*

STORING FRESH CORIANDER

*To store a bunch of fresh coriander, stand it, unwashed, in a container of suitable size with the roots in 1 cm (1/2 inch) of water. Enclose the leaves and stems with a large plastic supermarket carrier bag and tie the handles together around the container, then stand the whole thing in the refrigerator. It should keep for up to 2 weeks—break off leaves as you need them. The roots will also freeze well.*

3 Add the chilli, fish sauce and lime juice; bring to the boil and simmer for 1 minute. Add the bean sprouts and vermicelli and toss well. Arrange the mixture on a serving plate and sprinkle with peanuts, onion, garlic and coriander leaves. Serve immediately.

*NUTRITION PER SERVE (6): Protein 15 g; Fat 15 g; Carbohydrate 10 g; Dietary Fibre 2 g; Cholesterol 35 mg; 1040 kJ (245 cal)*

## SPICY ROASTED EGGPLANT (AUBERGINE) WITH TOFU

*Preparation time:* 15 minutes
*Total cooking time:* 10–15 minutes
*Serves* 4

4 small (about 400 g/12²/3 oz) slender eggplants (aubergines)
250 g (8 oz) firm tofu
2–4 small fresh red or green chillies
4 cloves garlic, crushed
4 coriander roots, chopped
1 small onion, chopped
3 teaspoons soft brown sugar
2 tablespoons lime juice
2 tablespoons fish sauce
1 tablespoon oil
1/2 cup (15 g/1/2 oz) fresh Thai basil
2 teaspoons dried shrimp, finely chopped, optional

1 Heat a medium frying pan or wok until hot. Add the eggplant and cook until the skin begins to char, turning to cook all sides. Remove from the heat and cool. Slice the eggplant diagonally into 2 cm (3/4 inch) thick slices. Drain the tofu and cut into 3 cm (1¼ inch) cubes.
2 Using a food processor or blender, blend the chillies, garlic, coriander roots, onion, sugar, lime juice and fish sauce until smooth.
3 Heat the oil in the same pan or wok, add the paste and stir over high heat for 1 minute or until fragrant. Add the eggplant, stir to combine and cook, covered, for 3 minutes or until just tender.
4 Add the tofu and half the basil and gently stir through. Serve garnished with the remaining basil and dried shrimp, if desired.
NOTE: This dish can be eaten hot or as a cold accompaniment. If you prefer a milder, less spicy dish, use only 2 chillies.

*NUTRITION PER SERVE: Protein 10 g; Fat 10 g; Carbohydrate 5 g; Dietary Fibre 5 g; Cholesterol 20 mg; 580 kJ (140 cal)*

*Above: Curried Rice Noodles with Chicken
Below: Spicy Roasted Eggplant with Tofu*

*FRESH SPRING ROLLS*

*Place 2 prawns side by side in the centre of the wrapper and top with the other ingredients.*

*Fold in two sides of the wrapper then roll it up to form a parcel.*

*Below: Fresh Spring Rolls*

# FRESH SPRING ROLLS

•

*Preparation time:* 30 minutes
*Total cooking time:* Nil
*Makes* 8

★

16 cooked prawns
50 g (1²/₃ oz) dried mung bean vermicelli
2 cups (500 ml/16 fl oz) hot water
8 dried rice paper wrappers
16 fresh Thai basil leaves
1 cup (30 g/1 oz) fresh coriander leaves
1 medium carrot, cut into short thin strips
1 tablespoon grated lime rind
2 tablespoons sweet chilli sauce

•

*Dipping Sauce*
¹/₃ cup (80 ml/2³/₄ fl oz) cold water
1 teaspoon sugar
2 tablespoons fish sauce
1 tablespoon white vinegar
1 small red chilli, finely chopped
1 tablespoon chopped fresh coriander leaves and stems

1 Peel and devein the prawns. Soak the vermicelli in the hot water for 10 minutes and then drain. Dip a rice paper wrapper into lukewarm water until it softens and place it on a work surface. Place 2 prawns side by side in the centre of the wrapper and top with 2 basil leaves, 1 tablespoon coriander, a few carrot strips, a little lime rind and a small amount of vermicelli. Spoon a little chilli sauce over the top.
2 Press the filling down to flatten it a little; fold in 2 sides, then roll up the parcel. Lay seam-side down on a serving plate and sprinkle with a little water; cover with plastic wrap. Repeat with the remaining ingredients. Serve with the Dipping Sauce and a little extra sweet chilli sauce.
3 To make Dipping Sauce: Place the cold water in a small bowl; add the sugar and stir until it dissolves. Stir in the fish sauce, vinegar, chilli and coriander leaves and stems.
NOTE: Rice paper wrappers must be kept moist or they become brittle. Continue to sprinkle cold water on them while rolling them up or if they are left for any length of time before serving.

*NUTRITION PER SPRING ROLL WITH SAUCE: Protein 5 g; Fat 0 g; Carbohydrate 5 g; Dietary Fibre 1 g; Cholesterol 40 mg; 260 kJ (60 cal)*

## GREEN PAWPAW AND PEANUT SALAD

•

*Preparation time:* 25 minutes
*Total cooking time:* 5 minutes
*Serves* 4–6

★

50 g (1²/3 oz) dried shrimp
100 g (3¹/3 oz) green beans, cut into short
    pieces
1 medium lettuce
¹/2 medium green pawpaw, peeled and
    grated
¹/4 cup (60 ml/2 fl oz) lime juice
2 tablespoons fish sauce
2 teaspoons soft brown sugar
1–2 teaspoons chopped red chilli
¹/2 cup (80 g/2²/3 oz) unsalted roasted
    peanuts, chopped
1 red chilli, extra, finely chopped

•

1 Pound the dried shrimp in a mortar and pestle, or chop finely.
2 Cook the beans in a pan of boiling water for 2 minutes. Drain and then plunge them into iced water; drain again. Shred the lettuce and arrange it on a serving plate. Top with the shrimp, beans, and pawpaw.
3 Combine the lime juice, fish sauce, sugar and chilli in a small bowl; mix well. Pour over the salad and sprinkle the peanuts and extra chilli over the top.
NOTE: Green pawpaw and dried shrimp are available at Asian food speciality stores—there are no substitutes. When grating pawpaw, lightly oil your hands or wear gloves. Pawpaw can be very sticky and hard to wash off.

*NUTRITION PER SERVE (6): Protein 10 g; Fat 10 g;*
*Carbohydrate 5 g; Dietary Fibre 3 g; Cholesterol 45 mg;*
*550 kJ (130 cal)*

*Above: Green Pawpaw*
*and Peanut Salad*

## SPICY BEEF CURRY

•

*Preparation time*: 20 minutes
*Total cooking time*: 30–35 minutes
*Serves* 4

1 tablespoon oil
1 large onion, chopped
1–2 tablespoons Green Curry Paste
  (page 123) or ready-made paste
500 g (1 lb) round or blade steak, cut
  into thick strips
¾ cup (185 ml/6 fl oz) coconut milk
¼ cup (60 ml/2 fl oz) water
6 kaffir lime leaves
100 g (3⅓ oz) pea eggplants (aubergines)
2 tablespoons fish sauce
1 teaspoon soft brown sugar
2 teaspoons finely grated lime rind
½ cup (15 g/½ oz) fresh coriander leaves
½ cup (30 g/1 oz) shredded fresh basil

*Below: Spicy
Beef Curry*

1 Heat the oil in a wok or large frying pan. Add the onion and curry paste and stir for 2 minutes over medium heat until fragrant.
2 Heat the wok until it is very hot. Add the meat in 2 batches and stir-fry until brown. Return all the meat to the wok. Add the coconut milk, water and lime leaves. Bring to the boil, reduce heat, cover and simmer for 10 minutes. Add the eggplants and simmer, uncovered, for another 10 minutes or until both the meat and eggplants are tender.
3 Add the fish sauce, sugar and lime rind to the wok and mix well. Stir in the coriander and basil. Serve immediately with steamed rice.
NOTE: Use finely sliced slender eggplants if pea eggplants are not available.

*NUTRITION PER SERVE: Protein 30 g; Fat 30g; Carbohydrate 5 g; Dietary Fibre 0 g; Cholesterol 80 mg; 1675 kJ (545 cal)*

•

## SON-IN-LAW EGGS

•

*Preparation time*: 15 minutes
*Total cooking time*: 20 minutes
*Serves* 4

8 eggs
2 tablespoons oil
2 tablespoons grated palm sugar or soft
  brown sugar
1 tablespoon fish sauce
2 tablespoons tamarind concentrate
1 teaspoon chopped red chillies, optional
½ cup (15 g/½ oz) fresh coriander leaves,
  chopped

•

1 Place the eggs in a pan of cold water. Bring the water to the boil and cook the eggs for 7 minutes (begin timing when water boils). Drain and run under cold water until cool. Remove the shells.
2 Heat the oil in a wok or frying pan. Add the eggs to the wok in batches and turn frequently over medium heat. When they are golden brown and blistered, remove the eggs from the wok and keep warm.
3 Remove the excess oil from pan and add the sugar, fish sauce, tamarind and chilli. Bring to the boil and boil rapidly for 2 minutes, or until the mixture resembles a syrup. Serve the eggs with the syrup poured over them and the coriander leaves sprinkled on top.

*NUTRITION PER SERVE: Protein 15 g; Fat 20 g; Carbohydrate 10 g; Dietary Fibre 0 g; Cholesterol 455 mg; 1275 kJ (305 cal)*

## WATERCRESS AND DUCK SALAD WITH LYCHEES

•

*Preparation time:* 25 minutes
*Total cooking time:* 30 minutes
*Serves* 4

★

2 large duck breasts, skin on
1 tablespoon Golden Mountain sauce
½ each red, green and yellow pepper
   (capsicum)
250 g (8 oz) watercress
12 fresh or canned lychees
2 tablespoons pickled shredded ginger
1–2 tablespoons green peppercorns,
   optional
1 tablespoon white vinegar
2 teaspoons soft brown sugar
1–2 teaspoons chopped red chilli
½ cup (15 g/½ oz) fresh coriander leaves

1 Preheat the oven to hot 210°C (415°F/
Gas 6–7). Brush the duck breasts with the
Golden Mountain sauce and place on a rack in a
baking tray. Bake for 30 minutes. Remove from
the oven and allow to cool.
2 Remove the membrane and seeds from the
peppers and slice the flesh into thin strips.
Discard any tough woody stems from the
watercress. Peel the fresh lychees and remove
the seeds or, if you are using canned lychees,
drain them thoroughly.
3 Arrange the pepper strips, watercress, lychees
and ginger on a large serving platter. Slice the
duck into thin pieces and toss gently through the
salad. In a small bowl, mix together the
peppercorns, if using, vinegar, sugar, chilli and
coriander. Serve this on the side for spooning
over the salad.

*NUTRITION PER SERVE: Protein 15 g; Fat 40 g;
Carbohydrate 10 g; Dietary Fibre 2 g; Cholesterol 100 mg;
2035 kJ (485 cal)*

*Above: Watercress
and Duck Salad
with Lychees*

## THAI FISH CAKES

•

*Preparation time:* 25 minutes
*Total cooking time:* 5–10 minutes
*Serves* 4–6

★

450 g (14¹/₃ oz) firm white fish fillets
3 tablespoons cornflour or rice flour
1 tablespoon fish sauce
1 egg, beaten
¹/₂ cup (15 g/¹/₂ oz) fresh coriander leaves
3 teaspoons Red Curry Paste (page 112)
 or ready-made paste
1–2 teaspoons chopped red chilli, optional
100 g (3¹/₃ oz) green beans, very finely
 sliced
2 spring onions, finely chopped
¹/₂ cup (125 ml/4 fl oz) oil
Thai Dipping Sauce (page 169), to serve

•

1 Place the fish in a food processor and process for 20 seconds or until smooth. Add the cornflour, fish sauce, egg, coriander, curry paste and chilli. Process for 10 seconds or until well combined.
2 Transfer the fish mixture to a large bowl. Add the beans and spring onion and mix well. Using wet hands, form 2 rounded tablespoons of the mixture at a time into fairly flat patties.
3 Heat the oil in a heavy-based frying pan over medium heat. Cook 4 fish cakes at a time until they are dark golden brown on both sides. Drain on paper towels and serve immediately with Thai Dipping Sauce.

NOTE: The fish cakes can be prepared ahead up to the end of Step 2 and stored, covered, in the refrigerator for up to 4 hours.

*NUTRITION PER SERVE (6): Protein 20 g; Fat 20 g; Carbohydrate 10 g; Dietary Fibre 1 g; Cholesterol 90 mg; 1260 kJ (300 cal)*

•

## GINGER CHICKEN WITH BLACK FUNGUS

•

*Preparation time:* 25 minutes
 + 15 minutes soaking
*Total cooking time:* 15 minutes
*Serves* 4

★

¹/₄ cup (10 g/¹/₃ oz) dried black fungus
1 tablespoon oil
3 cloves garlic, chopped
6 cm (2¹/₂ inch) piece fresh ginger, cut
 into fine shreds
500 g (1 lb) chicken breast fillets, sliced
4 spring onions, chopped
1 tablespoon Golden Mountain sauce
1 tablespoon fish sauce
2 teaspoons soft brown sugar
¹/₂ red pepper (capsicum), finely sliced
¹/₂ cup (15 g/¹/₂ oz) fresh coriander leaves
¹/₂ cup (25 g/³/₄ oz) chopped fresh Thai
 basil

•

1 Place the fungus in a heatproof bowl, cover with hot water, and leave for 15 minutes until it is soft and swollen; drain and chop roughly.

*Right: Thai Fish Cakes*

# CUCUMBER SALAD WITH PEANUTS AND CHILLI

•

*Preparation time:* 25 minutes
  + 45 minutes marinating
*Total cooking time:* Nil
*Serves 4–6*

★

3 Lebanese cucumbers
2 tablespoons white vinegar
2 teaspoons white sugar
1–2 tablespoons chilli sauce
1/2 red (Spanish) onion, chopped
1/2 cup (15 g/1/2 oz) fresh coriander leaves
1 cup (160 g/51/4 oz) unsalted roasted
  peanuts, chopped
2 tablespoons crisp fried garlic
1/2 teaspoon chopped chilli
1 tablespoon fish sauce

•

2 Heat the oil in a large wok, add the garlic and ginger and stir-fry for 1 minute. Add the chicken in batches, stir-frying over high heat until it changes colour. Return all the chicken to the wok. Add the spring onion and Golden Mountain sauce and stir-fry for 1 minute.
3 Add the fish sauce, sugar and fungus to the wok. Stir thoroughly; cover and steam for 2 minutes. Serve immediately with the red pepper, coriander and basil scattered on top.

*NUTRITION PER SERVE: Protein 30 g; Fat 10 g; Carbohydrate 5 g; Dietary Fibre 2 g; Cholesterol 65 mg; 925 kJ (220 cal)*

1 Peel the cucumbers and slice in half lengthways. Remove the seeds with a teaspoon and slice thinly.
2 Combine the vinegar and sugar in a small bowl, and stir until the sugar dissolves. Transfer to a large bowl and toss with the cucumber, chilli sauce, onion and coriander. Allow to marinate for 45 minutes.
3 Just before serving, add peanuts, garlic, chilli and fish sauce; toss lightly.

*NUTRITION PER SERVE (6): Protein 10 g; Fat 15 g; Carbohydrate 10 g; Dietary Fibre 5 g; Cholesterol 2 mg; 845 kJ (200 cal)*

*Above: Ginger Chicken with Black Fungus Left: Cucumber Salad with Peanuts and Chilli*

## GREEN VEGETABLE CURRY WITH SWEET POTATO AND EGGPLANT (AUBERGINE)

•

*Preparation time:* 25 minutes
*Total cooking time:* 30 minutes
*Serves 4–6*

★

1 tablespoon oil
1 medium onion, chopped
1–2 tablespoons Green Curry Paste
   (page 123) or ready-made paste
1¹/2 cups (375 ml/12 fl oz) coconut milk
1 cup (250 ml/8 fl oz) water
1 medium (300 g/9²/3 oz) sweet potato,
   cut into cubes
1 medium (200 g/6¹/2 oz) eggplant
   (aubergine), quartered and sliced
6 kaffir lime leaves
2 tablespoons fish sauce
2 tablespoons lime juice
2 teaspoons lime rind
2 teaspoons soft brown sugar
fresh coriander leaves, to garnish

*Below: Green Vegetable Curry with Sweet Potato and Eggplant*

1 Heat the oil in a large wok or frying pan. Add the onion and curry paste and stir for 3 minutes over medium heat.
2 Add the coconut milk and water to the wok. Bring to the boil, reduce heat and simmer, uncovered, for 5 minutes.
3 Add the sweet potato to the wok; cook for 6 minutes. Add the eggplant and lime leaves; cook for 10 minutes, or until the vegetables are very tender, stirring occasionally.
4 Add the fish sauce, lime juice, lime rind and sugar; toss. Sprinkle over some fresh coriander leaves. Garnish the curry with extra kaffir lime leaves, if you wish. Serve with steamed rice.
NOTE: Traditional Thai pea eggplants can be used instead of the sliced eggplant. Add them to the curry about 6 minutes before serving.

NUTRITION PER SERVE (6): *Protein 5 g; Fat 20 g; Carbohydrate 15 g; Dietary Fibre 0 g; Cholesterol 5 mg; 1080 kJ (255 cal)*

•

## FRIED RICE WITH CORIANDER AND BASIL

•

*Preparation time:* 20 minutes
   + overnight standing
*Total cooking time:* 20 minutes
*Serves 4*

★

100 g (3¹/3 oz) pork loin
300 g (9²/3 oz) chicken thigh fillets
2 tablespoons oil
3 cm (1¹/4 inch) piece pork fat, chopped
4 cloves garlic, chopped
4 cm (1¹/2 inch) piece fresh ginger, grated
2 teaspoons chopped red chilli
2¹/2 cups (500 g/1 lb) jasmine rice, cooked
   and cooled (see note)
1 tablespoon fish sauce
2 teaspoons Golden Mountain sauce
2 spring onions, chopped
1 cup (30 g/1 oz) fresh Thai basil,
   chopped
¹/2 cup (15 g/¹/2 oz) fresh coriander leaves,
   chopped

•

1 Dice the pork and the chicken.
2 Heat the oil in a wok or large heavy-based frying pan. When the oil is very hot, add the pork fat, garlic, ginger and chilli; stir for 2 minutes.
3 Add the diced chicken and pork to the wok and stir-fry for 3 minutes or until the meat changes colour. Break up any lumps in the rice and add it to the wok; toss well using 2 wooden spoons. When the rice has warmed, add the fish

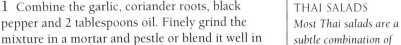

sauce and Golden Mountain sauce and toss through with the spring onion, basil and most of the coriander, reserving some for garnish. Serve immediately, garnished with the remaining coriander leaves.
NOTE: If possible, cook the rice a day ahead and refrigerate it overnight before making the fried rice so the finished dish is not gluggy.

NUTRITION PER SERVE: *Protein 25 g; Fat 22 g; Carbohydrate 100 g; Dietary Fibre 5 g; Cholesterol 60 mg; 2940 kJ (700 cal)*

## THAI BEEF SALAD

*Preparation time:* 35 minutes
*Total cooking time:* 10 minutes
*Serves 4*

⭐

3 cloves garlic, finely chopped
4 coriander roots, finely chopped
1/2 teaspoon freshly ground black pepper
3 tablespoons oil
400 g (12 2/3 oz) rump or sirloin steak
1 small soft-leaf lettuce
200 g (6 1/2 oz) cherry tomatoes
1 medium Lebanese cucumber
4 spring onions
1/2 cup (15 g/1/2 oz) fresh coriander leaves

**Dressing**
2 tablespoons fish sauce
2 tablespoons lime juice
1 tablespoon soy sauce
2 teaspoons chopped fresh red chilli
2 teaspoons soft brown sugar

1 Combine the garlic, coriander roots, black pepper and 2 tablespoons oil. Finely grind the mixture in a mortar and pestle or blend it well in a food processor or blender. Spread the mixture evenly over the steak.
2 Heat the remaining oil in a heavy-based frying pan or wok over high heat. Add the steak to the pan and cook for about 4 minutes each side, turning the steak once only during the cooking time. Remove the steak from the pan and allow to cool.
3 Wash the lettuce and separate the leaves, cut the tomatoes in half, cut the cucumber into chunks and chop the spring onions.
4 To make Dressing: Combine the fish sauce, lime juice, soy sauce, chilli and brown sugar in a small bowl, stirring until the sugar has dissolved.
5 Cut the cooled steak into thin strips. Place the prepared lettuce on a serving plate and arrange the tomatoes, cucumber, spring onion and strips of steak over the top. Drizzle over the Dressing and scatter over the coriander leaves. Serve immediately.

NUTRITION PER SERVE: *Protein 25 g; Fat 20 g; Carbohydrate 5 g; Dietary Fibre 2 g; Cholesterol 70 mg; 1300 kJ (310 cal)*

**THAI SALADS**
*Most Thai salads are a subtle combination of apparently opposing tastes and textures—crisp raw vegetables and chilli-hot meat or seafood—and are made with a range of ingredients, from rose petals to squid. Raw or rare beef salads are a traditional feature of north-eastern Thailand.*

*Above: Fried Rice wih Coriander and Basil
Below: Thai Beef Salad*

# LAOS & CAMBODIA

The cuisine of these two neighbours owes much to the influence of the country that they both border, Thailand, and the abundance of fresh fish caught in the Mekong River in landlocked Laos or the Gulf of Thailand in Cambodia. The fish are cooked simply with aromatic herbs or citrus marinades, while other soups, meat and vegetable dishes may be flavoured with garlic, ginger, peppers, galangal and lime leaves and scattered with bunches of fresh basil, coriander and mint.

lemon grass, chilli and onion and stir over medium heat for 5 minutes or until the onion is golden.

3 Add the tomatoes to the pan and cook for 3 minutes. Stir in the fish stock, water, lime leaves, pineapple, tamarind, palm sugar, lime juice and fish sauce; cover, bring to the boil, reduce heat and simmer for 15 minutes.

4 Add the fish fillets, prawns and coriander to the pan, and simmer for 10 minutes or until the seafood is tender. Serve immediately.

*NUTRITION PER SERVE: Protein 25 g; Fat 5 g; Carbohydrate 10 g; Dietary Fibre 3 g; Cholesterol 130 mg; 835 kJ (200 cal)*

## LAOTIAN FISH BALLS

•

***Preparation time:*** 30 minutes
***Total cooking time:*** 10 minutes
***Makes*** 24 balls

★

*500 g (1 lb) white fish fillets*
*2 tablespoons fish sauce*
*3 red chillies, seeded and finely chopped*
*1 1/2 teaspoons finely chopped lemon grass (white part only)*
*4 cloves garlic, crushed*
*3 spring onions, finely chopped*
*2 tablespoons chopped fresh coriander leaves*
*1 egg, beaten*
*2 tablespoons rice flour*
*oil, for deep-frying*
*2 tablespoons chopped fresh coriander leaves, extra*
*1 lemon, cut into wedges, to serve*

•

1 Finely chop the fish fillets. (You can chop the fish in a food processor but be careful not to overwork it.) Place the fish and the fish sauce in a bowl and mix to combine. Add the chilli, lemon grass, garlic, spring onion and coriander and mix well. Add the egg and rice flour and mix until thoroughly combined.

2 With slightly damp hands, make small balls from the mixture, each with a diameter of approximately 3 cm (1 1/4 inches).

3 Heat the oil in a deep-sided frying pan or deep fryer; add the fish balls in 2 batches and fry over medium heat until golden. Remove from the oil and drain on paper towels. Sprinkle the extra coriander over the fish balls and serve immediately with the lemon wedges.

*NUTRITION PER FISH BALL: Protein 5 g; Fat 5 g; Carbohydrate 1 g; Dietary Fibre 0 g; Cholesterol 20 mg; 305 kJ (75 cal)*

## SEAFOOD SOUP

•

***Preparation time:*** 30 minutes
***Total cooking time:*** 40 minutes
***Serves*** 6

★

*500 g (1 lb) firm white fish fillets*
*500 g (1 lb) raw prawns*
*1 tablespoon oil*
*5 cm (2 inch) piece fresh ginger, grated*
*3 tablespoons finely chopped lemon grass (white part only)*
*3 small red chillies, finely chopped*
*2 medium onions, chopped*
*4 medium tomatoes, peeled, seeded and chopped*
*3 cups (750 ml/24 fl oz) fish stock*
*3 cups (750 ml/24 fl oz) water*
*4 kaffir lime leaves, finely shredded*
*1 cup (160 g/5 1/4 oz) chopped fresh pineapple*
*1 tablespoon tamarind concentrate*
*1 tablespoon grated palm sugar or soft brown sugar*
*2 tablespoons lime juice*
*1 tablespoon fish sauce*
*2 tablespoons chopped fresh coriander leaves*

•

1 Cut the fish fillets into 2 cm (3/4 inch) cubes. Peel and devein the prawns.

*Above: Seafood Soup*

2 Heat the oil in a large pan; add the ginger,

## CHICKEN AND PUMPKIN STEW

•

*Preparation time:* 20 minutes
*Total cooking time:* 50 minutes
*Serves* 6

✷ ✷

½ cup (110 g/3²/3 oz) short-grain rice
2 tablespoons oil
1 kg (2 lb) chicken pieces
3 cloves garlic, crushed
3 tablespoons finely chopped lemon grass
  (white part only)
2 teaspoons grated fresh turmeric or
  1 teaspoon ground turmeric
2 tablespoons grated fresh galangal
6 kaffir lime leaves, finely shredded
6 spring onions, chopped
4 cups (1 litre) chicken stock
500 g (1 lb) pumpkin, cubed
1 small green pawpaw, peeled and
  chopped
125 g (4 oz) snake beans, cut into short
  lengths

1 Preheat the oven to moderate 180°C
(350°F/Gas 4). Spread the rice on a baking tray
and roast it for 15 minutes or until golden.
Remove the rice from the oven, allow it to cool
slightly and then process it in a food processor
until finely ground.
2 Heat the oil in a large pan; add the chicken
pieces in batches and cook for 5 minutes, or
until brown. Drain on paper towels.
3 Add the garlic, lemon grass, turmeric,
galangal, lime leaves and spring onion to the
pan; cook over medium heat for 3 minutes or
until the spring onion is golden. Return the
chicken to the pan; add the stock, cover and
simmer for 20 minutes.
4 Add the pumpkin and pawpaw, and simmer,
covered, for 10 minutes. Add the beans and
simmer, covered, for another 10 minutes, or
until the chicken is tender. Stir in the ground
rice, bring to the boil, reduce heat and simmer,
uncovered, for 5 minutes or until the mixture
thickens slightly.
NOTE: Green pawpaw is available at Asian
grocery stores. If it is not available, green mango
can be substituted.

*NUTRITION PER SERVE: Protein 25 g; Fat 20 g;
Carbohydrate 25 g; Dietary Fibre 3 g; Cholesterol 85 mg;
1615 kJ (385 cal)*

*Above: Chicken and
Pumpkin Stew*

## STEAMED SPICY CHICKEN

***Preparation time:*** 40 minutes
***Total cooking time:*** 30 minutes
Serves 4

★ ★

### Spice Paste
*7 dried chillies, seeded*
*1/2 teaspoon salt*
*4 stems lemon grass (white part only),*
  *finely chopped*
*1 slice fresh galangal, finely chopped*
*1 slice fresh turmeric, finely chopped*
*6 cm (21/2 inch) strip kaffir lime rind,*
  *chopped*
*1 teaspoon shrimp paste*
*4 cloves garlic, chopped*
*4 red Asian shallots, chopped*

*1/2 cup (125 ml/4 fl oz) coconut cream*
*2 teaspoons grated palm sugar or soft*
  *brown sugar*
*1 tablespoon fish sauce*
*2 kaffir lime leaves, shredded*
*500 g (1 lb) chicken breast fillet, cut into*
  *5 cm (2 inch) strips*
*4 cups (180 g/53/4 oz) shredded silverbeet*
  *(Swiss chard) or spinach*

•

1 To make Spice Paste: Soak the chillies in hot water for 30 minutes or until soft; drain. Place the softened chillies and salt in a food processor and process until a smooth paste is formed. Add all the other paste ingredients one at a time while continuing to run the processor.
2 Combine the coconut cream, palm sugar, fish sauce and lime leaves in a large bowl. Add the Spice Paste and stir together until well combined. Stir in the chicken strips.
3 Select a round heatproof serving dish which will fit into a large, deep pan. Put the silverbeet onto the serving dish. Spoon the spicy chicken mixture over the silverbeet.
4 Place a saucer or rack on the base of the pan and pour in enough boiling water to cover it. Place the dish on top of the saucer or rack, cover the pan with a tight-fitting lid and steam over medium heat for about 30 minutes or until the chicken is cooked. Check from time to time that there is enough water in the pan. Serve with rice.

NUTRITION PER SERVE: *Protein 30 g; Fat 10 g; Carbohydrate 5 g; Dietary Fibre 3 g; Cholesterol 65 mg; 1010 kJ (240 cal)*

## FISH AND NOODLE SOUP

•

***Preparation time:*** 15 minutes
***Total cooking time:*** 20 minutes
Serves 4

★

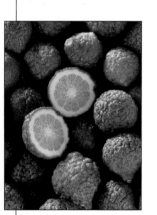

*200 g (61/2 oz) dried rice vermicelli*
*1 tablespoon oil*
*2.5 cm (1 inch) piece fresh ginger, grated*
*3 small red chillies, finely chopped*
*4 spring onions, chopped*
*31/2 cups (875 ml/28 fl oz) coconut milk*
*2 tablespoons fish sauce*
*2 tablespoons tomato paste (tomato purée,*
  *double concentrate)*
*500 g (1 lb) firm white fish fillets, cubed*
*2 ham steaks, diced*
*150 g (5 oz) snake beans, chopped*
*180 g (6 oz) bean sprouts, trimmed*
*1 cup (20 g/2/3 oz) fresh mint*
*1/2 cup (80 g/22/3 oz) unsalted roasted*
  *peanuts*

•

1 Soak the vermicelli in boiling water for 5 minutes; drain well. Heat the oil in a large, heavy-based pan and cook the ginger, chilli and spring onion and for 3 minutes, or until golden.
2 Stir in the coconut milk, fish sauce and tomato paste, cover and simmer for 10 minutes. Add the fish, ham and snake beans and simmer for 10 minutes, or until the fish is tender.
3 Divide the vermicelli among four bowls and top with bean sprouts and mint. Spoon the soup into the bowls and sprinkle with peanuts.

*Above: Fish and*
*Noodle Soup*

NUTRITION PER SERVE: *Protein 50 g; Fat 65 g; Carbohydrate 60 g; Dietary Fibre 5 g; Cholesterol 105 mg; 4260 kJ (1015 cal)*

# PRAWNS STEAMED IN BANANA LEAVES

•

*Preparation time:* 25 minutes
+ 2 hours marinating
*Total cooking time:* 10 minutes
*Serves* 4

★ ★

1 kg (2 lb) raw prawns
8 small banana leaves
1 tablespoon sesame seeds
2.5 cm (1 inch) piece fresh ginger, grated
2 small red chillies, finely chopped
4 spring onions, finely chopped
2 stems lemon grass (white part only),
  finely chopped
2 teaspoons soft brown sugar
1 tablespoon fish sauce
2 tablespoons lime juice
2 tablespoons chopped fresh coriander
  leaves

•

1 Peel and devein the prawns. Put the banana leaves in a large heatproof bowl, cover with boiling water and leave them to soak for 3 minutes, or until softened. Drain and pat dry. Cut the banana leaves into squares, about 18 cm (7 inches). Toast the sesame seeds in a dry pan over medium heat for 3 to 4 minutes, shaking the pan gently, until the seeds are golden brown. Remove from the pan at once to prevent the seeds burning.
2 Place the ginger, chilli, spring onion and lemon grass in a food processor, and process in short bursts until a paste is formed. Transfer the paste to a bowl; stir in the sugar, fish sauce, lime juice, sesame seeds and coriander and mix well. Add the prawns and toss to coat. Cover and marinate for 2 hours in the refrigerator.
3 Divide the mixture into eight, and place a portion on each banana leaf. Fold the leaf to enclose the mixture, and then secure the parcels with a wooden skewer.
4 Cook the parcels in a bamboo steamer over simmering water for 8 to 10 minutes or until the prawn filling is cooked.
NOTE: Banana leaves are available from Asian food stores and speciality fruit and vegetable shops. Alternatively, you may have a friend with a banana tree.

*NUTRITION PER SERVE: Protein 25 g; Fat 4 g;
Carbohydrate 4 g; Dietary Fibre 1 g; Cholesterol 240 mg;
590 kJ (140 cal)*

*PRAWNS STEAMED IN
BANANA LEAVES*

*Cut the banana leaves
into squares.*

*Fold the leaf to enclose
the filling, then secure
the parcel with a
wooden skewer.*

*Above: Prawns
Steamed in
Banana Leaves*

# COLD DRINKS These delicious drinks are

made from fresh fruit juices and chilled milk or yoghurt. Mix up a jug as a

perfect cooler for a tropically hot afternoon.

### GINGERED WATERMELON JUICE

Remove skin and seeds from 500 g (1 lb) watermelon and roughly chop. Place in a blender or food processor with 2 teaspoons grated fresh ginger. Process for 2 minutes. Add 6 ice cubes and process a 1 more minute or until the ice is crushed. Serve garnished with a thin wedge of watermelon. Makes 2½ cups (600 ml/20 fl oz).

*NUTRITION PER 100 ml: Protein 0 g; Fat 0 g; Carbohydrate 3 g; Dietary Fibre 0 g; Cholesterol 0 mg; 60 kJ (15 cal)*

### LASSI

Place ¾ cup (185 g/6 oz) yoghurt, 2 cups (250 ml/8 fl oz) water and ¼ teaspoon salt into a blender or food processor. Blend for 1–2 minutes, until smooth and frothy. Serve with ice cubes. Makes 3 cups (750 ml/24 fl oz). Variations: For Mint Lassi, add 8–10 fresh mint leaves before blending. For Sweet Lassi, add 4 teaspoons sugar and ¼ teaspoon rose water before blending and omit the salt.

*NUTRITION PER 100 ml: Protein 2 g; Fat 1 g; Carbohydrate 2 g; Dietary Fibre 0 g; Cholesterol 7 mg; 130 kJ (30 cal)*

### MINTY MELON JUICE

Roughly chop 1 peeled and cored green apple and ½ small honeydew melon. Place in a blender or food processor with 1 cup (250 ml/8 fl oz) orange juice and 8 fresh mint leaves. Process for 1–2 minutes until smooth. Add ¾ cup (100 g/3⅓ oz) ice cubes and process for 1 minute. Pour into 4 large glasses and garnish with fresh mint leaves. Makes 1.25 litres.

*NUTRITION PER 100 ml: Protein 1 g; Fat 0 g; Carbohydrate 10 g; Dietary Fibre 1 g; Cholesterol 0 mg; 155 kJ (35 cal)*

## MANGO FRAPPE

Peel and roughly chop 2 or 3 fresh mangoes. Place ¾ cup (100 g/3⅓ oz) ice cubes in a blender or food processor and process in short bursts for 5 minutes, or until the ice is roughly chopped. Add the mango and process until smooth. Add a little water to thin if you wish. Makes 2½ cups (600 ml/20 fl oz). Variations: Fresh pineapple, guava, carambola or melons can be used to make other tropical frappés.

*NUTRITION PER 100 ml: Protein 1 g;*
*Fat 0 g; Carbohydrate 10 g; Dietary Fibre 1 g;*
*Cholesterol 0 mg; 210 kJ (50 cal)*

## LIME SODA

Place 1 cup (250 g/8 oz) sugar and 2½ cups (600 ml/20 fl oz) water in a large pan. Dissolve sugar over low heat, stirring occasionally. Bring to the boil and cook, uncovered, for 5 minutes. Add 1½ cups (375 ml/12 fl oz) fresh lime juice and boil for

5 minutes more. Cool then chill for 1 hour. Makes 2¼ cups (560 ml/18 fl oz) syrup. Dilute about 2–3 tablespoons per glass with soda or sparkling mineral water.

*NUTRITION PER 50 ml: Protein 0 g;*
*Fat 0 g; Carbohydrate 10 g; Dietary Fibre 0 g;*
*Cholesterol 0 mg; 180 kJ (45 cal)*

## TROPICAL THICKSHAKE

Put ½ cup (80 g/2⅔ oz) chopped fresh pineapple, ½ cup (110 g/3⅔ oz) chopped papaya, 2 chopped bananas, ½ cup (125 ml/4 fl oz) coconut milk and 1 cup (250 ml/8 fl oz) orange juice in a food processor or blender. Blend for 1–2 minutes, or until the fruit is puréed. Add ¾ cup (100 g/3⅓ oz) ice cubes and process in bursts for 5 minutes, or until the ice is crushed. Garnish with banana slices. Makes 1 litre.

*NUTRITION PER 100 ml: Protein 9 g;*
*Fat 27 g; Carbohydrate 100 g; Dietary Fibre 13 g;*
*Cholesterol 0 mg; 2840 kJ (680 cal)*

## FRAGRANT MILK SHERBET

Place ¾ cup (100 g/3⅓ oz) ice cubes in a blender or food processor and process in bursts for 5 minutes, or until the ice is crushed. Place the ice in 4 tall glasses. Place ½ cup (75 g/2½ oz) shelled pistachio nuts, ¼ cup (60 g/2 oz) caster sugar, ½ teaspoon ground cardamom and ½ teaspoon ground cinnamon in the blender. Process for 2 minutes until smooth. Add 1.25 litres milk, process until frothy and pour over the ice. Sprinkle 1 teaspoon roughly chopped shelled pistachios over each sherbet. Makes 1.5 litres.

*NUTRITION PER 100 ml: Protein 4 g;*
*Fat 6 g; Carbohydrate 8 g; Dietary Fibre 0 g;*
*Cholesterol 10 mg; 430 kJ (100 cal)*

*From left: Gingered Watermelon Juice;*
*Mint Lassi; Minty Melon Juice;*
*Mango Frappé; Lime Soda; Tropical*
*Thickshake; Fragrant Milk Sherbet*

3 Add the lemon juice, lemon grass, fish sauce, onion, coriander and mint and mix until well combined. Cover and leave in the refrigerator for 2 hours to marinate.

4 Stir in the chopped cucumber. Serve the salad on a bed of shredded cabbage, garnished with extra mint leaves if you like.

NOTE: If you prefer your steak more well done, increase the char-grilling time.

*NUTRITION PER SERVE: Protein 45 g; Fat 10 g; Carbohydrate 105 g; Dietary Fibre 2 g; Cholesterol 4 mg; 1130 kJ (270 cal)*

## CHICKEN MINCE WITH HERBS AND SPICES

*Preparation time:* 30 minutes
*Total cooking time:* 20 minutes
*Serves 4–6*

★

1/4 cup (55 g/1³/4 oz) short-grain rice
1 kg (2 lb) chicken thigh fillets
2 tablespoons peanut oil
4 cloves garlic, crushed
2 tablespoons grated fresh galangal
2 small red chillies
4 spring onions, finely chopped
1/4 cup (60 ml/2 fl oz) fish sauce
1 tablespoon shrimp paste
3 tablespoons chopped fresh Vietnamese mint
2 tablespoons chopped fresh basil
4 tablespoons lime juice

---

### CONTAINERS FOR MARINATING

*As a marinade usually contains an acid, such as vinegar, rice wine, lime juice or lemon juice, always use a non-metallic container to marinate food as acid will react with metal. A dish of glass or glazed china is best. Use a wooden spoon to stir or turn the food.*

## LAOTIAN BEEF SALAD

*Preparation time:* 15 minutes
  + 2 hours marinating
*Total cooking time:* 10 minutes
*Serves 4*

★

500 g (1 lb) rump steak
4 tablespoons water
3 tablespoons lemon juice
2 tablespoons finely chopped lemon grass
  (white part only)
1 tablespoon fish sauce
1 medium onion, finely sliced
2 tablespoons chopped fresh coriander
  leaves
1 tablespoon chopped fresh mint
2 Lebanese cucumbers, chopped
1/2 small Chinese cabbage, shredded

1 Char-grill the steak for 3 minutes on each side or until cooked to medium-rare. Remove, cover and set aside for 5 minutes. Use a sharp knife to cut the steak into 5 mm (1/4 inch) thick slices.

2 Heat the water in a wok, add the sliced beef and cook over medium heat for 2 minutes. Do not overcook. Transfer the beef and liquid to a non-metallic bowl.

*Above: Laotian
Beef Salad
Right: Chicken Mince
with Herbs and Spices*

1 Preheat the oven to moderate 180°C (350°F/Gas 4). Spread the rice on an oven tray and roast it for 15 minutes or until golden. Cool slightly, then transfer the rice to a food processor and process until finely ground. Set aside.
2 Place the chicken fillets in a food processor and process until finely minced.
3 Heat the oil in a wok or frying pan; add the garlic, galangal, chilli and spring onion and cook over medium heat for 3 minutes. Add the minced chicken to the wok and stir for 5 minutes, or until the mince is browned, breaking up any large lumps with a wooden spoon. Stir in the fish sauce and shrimp paste and bring to the boil, then reduce the heat and simmer for 5 minutes.
4 Remove the wok from the heat, stir in the rice, mint, basil and lime juice, and mix to combine.

NUTRITION PER SERVE (6): Protein 40 g; Fat 15 g; Carbohydrate 10 g; Dietary Fibre 1 g; Cholesterol 125 mg; 1315 kJ (315 cal)

•

## LAOTIAN DRIED BEEF WITH GREEN PAWPAW SALAD

•

**Preparation time:** 30 minutes
+ 4 hours marinating
**Total cooking time:** 5 hours
**Serves** 6

★

1 kg (2 lb) piece of topside steak, partially frozen
2 teaspoons salt
1/4 teaspoon chilli powder
1 teaspoon ground black pepper
1 tablespoon soft brown sugar
4 cloves garlic, crushed
2 teaspoons sesame oil
1 tablespoon peanut oil

•

**Green Pawpaw Salad**
1 small green pawpaw, peeled and seeded
1 carrot
2 cloves garlic, crushed
6 cm (2 1/2 inch) piece fresh ginger, grated
2 small red chillies
2 tablespoons fish sauce
4 kaffir lime leaves, finely shredded
1 tablespoon lime juice
2 teaspoons soft brown sugar
1 teaspoon sesame oil
1 cup (30 g/1 oz) fresh coriander leaves
1 cup (160 g/5 1/4 oz) unsalted roasted peanuts

1 Preheat the oven to very slow 120°C (250°F/Gas 1–2).
2 Trim any excess fat from the steak. Cut the steak into 2.5 mm (1/8 inch) thick slices, then into strips. Mix the salt, chilli powder, pepper, sugar, garlic, sesame oil and peanut oil in a bowl. Add the steak and, using your fingertips, toss it in the oil mixture until coated. Cover and marinate for 4 hours in the refrigerator.
3 Place the meat on a rack in a large baking dish and bake for 5 hours, or until it has dried out.
4 Cook the beef under a hot grill for 3 minutes, then serve with Green Pawpaw Salad.
5 To make Green Pawpaw Salad: Cut the pawpaw and carrot into shreds, using a citrus zester if you have one. Combine the pawpaw and carrot in a bowl with the remaining ingredients and toss lightly.
NOTE: The dried beef will keep for 3 weeks in an airtight container or can be frozen for up to 6 months.

NUTRITION PER SERVE: Protein 45 g; Fat 30 g; Carbohydrate 15 g; Dietary Fibre 5 g; Cholesterol 95 mg; 2020 kJ (480 cal)

*LAOTIAN DRIED BEEF WITH GREEN PAWPAW SALAD*

Place the meat strips on a rack in a baking dish.

Shred the green pawpaw with a citrus zester, if you have one.

Above: Laotian Dried Beef with Green Pawpaw Salad

## SPICY ROAST CHICKEN

•

*Preparation time:* 15 minutes
*Total cooking time:* 50 minutes
*Serves* 6

★

1 tablespoon peanut oil
2 medium onions, chopped
250 g (8 oz) pork mince
1/2 cup (80 g/2²/₃ oz) unsalted roasted
   peanuts, roughly chopped
3 tablespoons lime juice
1 tablespoon chopped fresh mint
2 tablespoons chopped fresh coriander
   leaves
3 small dried red chillies
1 teaspoon fennel seeds
1 teaspoon cumin seeds
1 teaspoon coriander seeds
1/8 teaspoon salt
1 x 1.5 kg (3¹/₄ lb) chicken
2 cloves garlic, crushed
1 teaspoon oil, extra
1/2 cup (125 ml/4 fl oz) coconut milk

•

1 Preheat the oven to moderate 180°C (350°F/
Gas 4).
2 Heat the oil in a wok; add the onion and cook
over medium heat for 3 minutes or until golden.
Add the mince and cook for 10 minutes or until
the pork is brown. Remove the wok from the
heat; stir in the peanuts, lime juice, mint and
coriander and allow the mixture to cool slightly.

*Below: Spicy
Roast Chicken*

3 Place the chillies, fennel, cumin and coriander
seeds, and salt in a food processor or mortar and
pestle and process until a powder is formed.
4 Remove any excess fat from the chicken; rub
the skin and inside cavity with the garlic. Stuff the
chicken with the pork mince mixture. Secure the
opening with a wooden skewer and tie the legs
together with kitchen string. Brush the outside
of the chicken lightly with the oil. Rub the skin
of the chicken with the chilli spice mixture.
Place the chicken on a rack in a baking dish and
bake for 20 minutes. Remove the chicken from
the oven and baste it with the coconut milk and
pan juices. Bake it for another 40 minutes,
basting frequently until the chicken is tender.
Remove the skewer and string before serving.

*NUTRITION PER SERVE: Protein 35 g; Fat 20 g;
Carbohydrate 5 g; Dietary Fibre 0 g; Cholesterol 95 mg;
1455 kJ (345 cal)*

•

## STIR-FRIED PORK WITH
## ASPARAGUS AND TOFU

•

*Preparation time:* 20 minutes
*Total cooking time:* 10 minutes
*Serves* 4

★

1 bunch (155 g/5 oz) asparagus spears
150 g (4³/₄ oz) firm tofu
1 tablespoon oil
2 cloves garlic, crushed
400 g (12²/₃ oz) pork mince
1 red chilli, seeded and finely sliced,
   optional
3 tablespoons garlic chives, finely chopped
3 teaspoons oyster sauce
3 teaspoons fish sauce
1 teaspoon sugar

•

1 Trim the asparagus and cut it into bite-sized
pieces. Place the asparagus in a heatproof bowl,
cover it with boiling water and stand for
3 minutes; drain. Cut the tofu into bite-sized
pieces.
2 Place a wok over high heat; when it is very
hot, add the oil and swirl it around. Add the
garlic, pork and chilli, if using, and quickly
brown the meat while tossing. When the meat
has browned, add the asparagus and tofu and
combine well.
3 Add the garlic chives, oyster sauce, fish sauce
and sugar and stir through the pork mixture.
Serve immediately with rice.

*NUTRITION PER SERVE: Protein 25 g; Fat 10 g;
Carbohydrate 4 g; Dietary Fibre 1 g; Cholesterol 50 mg;
830 kJ (195 cal)*

## SPICY FRIED FISH

•

**Preparation time:** 20 minutes
**Total cooking time:** 20 minutes
**Serves 6**

★ ★

1 teaspoon sesame oil
2 cloves garlic, crushed
2.5 cm (1 inch) piece fresh ginger, grated
1 medium onion, sliced
4 spring onions, cut into short lengths
1 tablespoon fish sauce
2 tablespoons light soy sauce
1 tablespoon soft brown sugar
1 cup (250 ml/8 fl oz) water
1 cup (125 g/4 oz) plain flour
1 teaspoon ground cumin
1 teaspoon ground coriander
1 teaspoon ground paprika
750 g (1½ lb) firm white fish fillets
2 egg whites, lightly beaten
oil, for deep-frying
1 tablespoon cornflour
1 tablespoon water, extra

1 Heat the sesame oil in a small pan: add the garlic, ginger, onion and spring onion, and cook over medium heat for 3 minutes or until the onion is golden. Stir in the fish sauce, soy sauce, sugar and water. Set aside while preparing and cooking the fish.

2 Mix the flour, cumin, coriander and paprika in a medium-sized bowl. Cut the fish fillets into 2 cm (¾ inch) cubes. Dip the cubes in the egg whites and dust lightly with the spiced flour, shaking off any excess. Heat the oil in a deep pan or wok; add the fish pieces in batches and deep-fry over high heat for 3 to 4 minutes or until golden and cooked through. Drain on paper towels, and keep warm.

3 Dissolve the cornflour in the water; add it to the sauce mixture, stirring constantly until the mixture boils and thickens. Serve the fried fish pieces topped with the hot sauce. Garnish with sliced spring onions.

*NUTRITION PER SERVE: Protein 30 g; Fat 5 g; Carbohydrate 20 g; Dietary Fibre 2 g; Cholesterol 140 mg; 1070 kJ (255 cal)*

*Above: Spicy Fried Fish*

## GRILLED PORK

•

*Preparation time:* 10 minutes
+ 4 hours marinating
*Total cooking time:* 15 minutes
*Serves* 4

★

*1 kg (2 lb) pork chops*
*8 cloves garlic, crushed*
*2 tablespoons fish sauce*
*1 tablespoon soy sauce*
*2 tablespoons oyster sauce*
*½ teaspoon ground black pepper*
*2 tablespoons finely chopped spring onion*

•

1 Place the pork chops in a large glass bowl and add the garlic, fish sauce, soy sauce, oyster sauce and black pepper. Stir well so that all the meat is covered with the marinade; cover and marinate for 4 hours in the refrigerator.
2 Preheat the grill to hot; grill the pork on all sides until browned and cooked through. If the meat starts to burn, move it further away from the grill element. Alternatively you can cook the meat on a hot barbecue grill.
3 Arrange the pork on a serving platter and scatter over the spring onion.

NUTRITION PER SERVE: Protein 60 g; Fat 5 g; Carbohydrate 4 g; Dietary Fibre 1 g; Cholesterol 130 mg; 1265 kJ (300 cal)

*Above: Grilled Pork*

## SPICY EGGPLANT (AUBERGINE) AND FISH PUREE IN SALAD LEAVES

•

*Preparation time:* 45 minutes
*Total cooking time:* 1 hour
*Serves* 6

★

*1 large eggplant (aubergine),*
*approximately 800 g (1 lb 10 oz)*
*12 cloves garlic, unpeeled*
*4 red Asian shallots, unpeeled*
*600 g (1¼ lb) white fish fillets*
*100 g (3⅓ oz) dried mung bean vermicelli*
*2 tablespoons fish sauce*
*3 red chillies, seeded and finely chopped*
*2 tablespoons fresh mint, roughly chopped*
*2 tablespoons fresh coriander leaves,*
*roughly chopped*
*1 mignonette lettuce*
*1 butter lettuce*
*50 g (1⅔ oz) fresh coriander sprigs*

*Sauce*
*3 tablespoons fish sauce*
*3 tablespoons lime juice*
*1 teaspoon caster sugar*
*1 red chilli, seeded and finely sliced*

1 Preheat the oven to moderate 180°C (350°F/ Gas 4). Place the eggplant on a baking tray and bake for 50 minutes, or until soft and tender. Add the garlic and shallots to the baking tray after 15 minutes of cooking. Allow to cool.

2 Brush the fish fillets with oil and cook them under a hot grill until cooked through. Allow the fish to cool, then break it into pieces.

3 Place the vermicelli in boiling water and cook for 1 to 2 minutes or until tender. Drain, cool and chop roughly.

4 Cut the eggplant in half, scoop out the soft flesh and place it in a food processor. Squeeze 6 of the soft garlic cloves and all the shallots from their skins into the food processor. Add the fish, fish sauce, chilli, mint and coriander, and process until a fine-textured purée is formed. Transfer the purée to a bowl, season to taste with salt, and stir in the vermicelli.

5 To make Sauce: Place the fish sauce, lime juice, sugar and chilli in a food processor. Squeeze the remaining cloves of garlic into the food processor and process until a smooth sauce is formed. Heat the sauce in a small pan, stirring to dissolve the sugar, and then allow it to cool to room temperature.

6 To serve, place the bowl containing the purée onto a platter and surround it with the lettuce leaves and coriander sprigs. Place the Sauce in a separate bowl. The diners help themselves—each takes a lettuce leaf and places a sprig of coriander on top of it. They then place a spoonful of purée and a teaspoon of the Sauce on the leaves and roll them up to eat.

*NUTRITION PER SERVE: Protein 25 g; Fat 4 g; Carbohydrate 20 g; Dietary Fibre 5 g; Cholesterol 70 mg; 935 kJ (220 cal)*

# GRILLED SKEWERED BEEF

·

***Preparation time:*** 15 minutes +
  4 hours marinating
***Total cooking time:*** 8 minutes
***Serves*** 4

✴

*500 g (1 lb) sirloin steak*
*2 teaspoons chilli flakes*
*4 stems lemon grass (white part only),*
  *finely chopped*
*2 slices fresh galangal, finely chopped*
*2 slices fresh turmeric, finely chopped*
*4 cloves garlic, crushed*
*4 teaspoons grated palm sugar or soft*
  *brown sugar*
*½ cup (125 ml/4 fl oz) oyster sauce*
*1 teaspoon salt*
*2 tablespoons oil*

·

1 Cut the steak into long thin strips. Place the strips of meat in a glass bowl.

2 Pound the chilli, lemon grass, galangal, turmeric and garlic in a mortar and pestle. Add the palm sugar, oyster sauce, salt and oil and combine well.

3 Spoon the marinade over the meat and mix well. Cover with plastic wrap and refrigerate for 4 hours. Thread the meat onto wooden skewers which have been soaked in water for 30 minutes.

4 Preheat the grill to hot; grill the skewered beef on both sides until browned. Alternatively you can cook the meat on a hot barbecue grill.

*NUTRITION PER SERVE: Protein 30 g; Fat 20 g; Carbohydrate 15 g; Dietary Fibre 1 g; Cholesterol 60 mg; 1365 kJ (325 cal)*

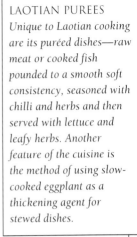

## LAOTIAN PUREES
*Unique to Laotian cooking are its puréed dishes—raw meat or cooked fish pounded to a smooth soft consistency, seasoned with chilli and herbs and then served with lettuce and leafy herbs. Another feature of the cuisine is the method of using slow-cooked eggplant as a thickening agent for stewed dishes.*

*Left: Grilled Skewered Beef*

# VIETNAM

The lush greenness of Vietnam produces a wide range of vegetables and herbs that impart a fresh taste and fragrance to its cooking. Bunches of coriander and mint are scattered over steaming bowls of pho, a soupy noodle and meat dish which can be bought on every street corner. The basic flavour of many Vietnamese dishes comes from nuoc mam, a fish sauce that is added to soups and stir-fries, or used in marinades with lemon grass, lemon juice and chillies to give a tangy, pungent flavour to meat and fish.

*Above: Stir-fried Chicken with Lemon Grass, Ginger and Chilli*

## STIR-FRIED CHICKEN WITH LEMON GRASS, GINGER AND CHILLI

•

***Preparation time:*** 30 minutes
***Total cooking time:*** 20 minutes
***Serves*** 4

☆

2 tablespoons oil
2 medium brown onions, roughly chopped
4 cloves garlic, finely chopped
5 cm (2 inch) piece fresh ginger, finely grated
3 stems lemon grass (white part only), very finely sliced
2 teaspoons chopped green chilli
500 g (1 lb) chicken thigh fillets, thinly sliced
2 teaspoons sugar
1 tablespoon fish sauce
finely chopped fresh coriander leaves and Vietnamese mint, to garnish

•

1 Heat the oil in a heavy-based frying pan or wok; add the onion, garlic, ginger, lemon grass and chilli, and stir for 3 to 5 minutes over medium heat until the mixture is lightly golden. Take care not to burn the mixture or it will become bitter.
2 Increase heat to high; when the pan is very hot, add the chicken and toss well. Sprinkle the sugar over the chicken and cook for about 5 minutes, tossing regularly until the chicken is just cooked.

3 Add the fish sauce, cook for another 2 minutes and serve immediately, garnished with the coriander and mint.

*NUTRITION PER SERVE: Protein 30 g; Fat 15 g; Carbohydrate 5 g; Dietary Fibre 0 g; Cholesterol 90 mg; 1135 kJ (270 cal)*

•

## CRAB, PRAWN AND POTATO FRITTERS

•

***Preparation time:*** 25 minutes
***Total cooking time:*** 20 minutes
***Makes*** 18 fritters

☆

200 g (6½ oz) raw prawns
200 g (6½ oz) can crab meat
200 g (6½ oz) potatoes
½ cup (60 g/2 oz)) self-raising flour
1 cup (250 ml/8 fl oz) coconut milk
2 teaspoons fish sauce
½ teaspoon salt
½ teaspoon freshly ground black pepper
1 teaspoon sugar
oil, for shallow frying
lettuce leaves, to serve
fresh chopped mint leaves, to garnish
Vietnamese Dipping Sauce (page 169), to serve

•

1 Peel and devein the prawns; finely chop the meat. Drain the crab meat. Finely grate the potatoes, squeezing out as much water as possible.

When water is added to the caramel sauce, hard lumps will form.

Toss the unpeeled prawns in the pan until they turn pink.

Add the lime juice, sugar, salt and remaining spring onion to the pan.

2 Place the prawn meat, crab meat, potato, flour, coconut milk, fish sauce, salt, pepper and sugar in a large bowl and combine well.

3 Heat the oil in a frying pan or wok until hot; cook tablespoons of the mixture, about 3 at a time, tossing gently until golden brown. Drain the fritters on paper towels.

4 Arrange the fritters on a bed of lettuce leaves and garnish with mint leaves. Serve with Vietnamese Dipping Sauce.

NOTE: Grate the potatoes just before cooking to stop them going brown.

NUTRITION PER FRITTER: Protein 5 g; Fat 5 g; Carbohydrate 5 g; Dietary Fibre 0 g; Cholesterol 25 mg; 425 kJ (100 cal)

•

## CARAMELISED PRAWNS
•

**Preparation time:** 25 minutes
**Total cooking time:** 5 minutes
**Serves** 4

✷ ✷

500 g (1 lb) medium raw prawns
6 spring onions
1 tablespoon oil
3 cloves garlic, finely chopped
2 tablespoons caramel sauce (see note)
1 tablespoon fish sauce
1 tablespoon lime juice
1 tablespoon soft brown sugar
1/2 teaspoon salt
1/4 red pepper (capsicum), cut into fine
 strips

1 Remove the prawn heads and, using a fine needle, devein prawns, leaving the tails, shells and legs intact. Rinse the prawns under running water and pat dry with paper towels.

2 Finely chop half the spring onions. Cut the rest into 4 cm (1½ inch) long pieces and then finely shred the pieces into thin strips.

3 Heat the oil in a heavy-based frying pan; add the garlic, chopped spring onion and prawns, and cook over medium heat for about 3 minutes, tossing the prawns until they turn pink. Drizzle the caramel sauce and fish sauce over the top and cook for 1 minute. Add the lime juice, sugar, salt and remaining spring onion. Toss well and serve immediately, garnished with the red pepper. If the prawn shells are tender, they can be eaten, but supply finger bowls and napkins at the table so your diners can peel the prawns if they prefer.

NOTE: To make the caramel sauce, combine 4 tablespoons of sugar with 3 tablespoons of water in a small pan. Stir over low heat, without boiling, until the sugar has dissolved. Bring the syrup to the boil, reduce the heat and simmer gently for about 5 minutes, until the syrup turns dark golden. Take care not to burn it. Remove the pan from the heat and add 4 tablespoons of water—it will spit and sizzle, and the caramel will form hard lumps. Return the pan to the heat and cook, stirring, until the lumps become liquid again. The sauce can be stored in the refrigerator for up to 1 week.

NUTRITION PER SERVE: Protein 15 g; Fat 5 g; Carbohydrate 20 g; Dietary Fibre 0 g; Cholesterol 95 mg; 790 kJ (190 cal)

Above: Caramelised Prawns

## BARBECUED WHOLE FISH

•

*Preparation time:* 20 minutes
+ 20 minutes marinating
*Total cooking time:* 25 minutes
*Serves* 4–6

★

750 g (1¹/2 lb) *small snapper or bream,
    cleaned and scaled*
2 teaspoons green peppercorns, finely
    crushed
2 teaspoons chopped red chilli
3 teaspoons fish sauce
1 tablespoon oil
2 medium onions, finely sliced
4 cm (1¹/2 inch) piece fresh ginger, cut into
    very thin slices
3 cloves garlic, cut into very thin slices
2 teaspoons sugar
4 spring onions, cut into 4 cm (1¹/2 inch)
    pieces, then finely shredded
*Lemon and Garlic Dipping Sauce*
    (page 169), to serve

*Above: Barbecued
Whole Fish*

1 Wash the fish inside and out and pat dry with
paper towels. Cut 2 diagonal slashes into the
thickest part of the fish on both sides.
2 Place the peppercorns, chilli and fish sauce in
a food processor or mortar and pestle, and
process or grind until a paste is formed. Brush
the paste lightly over the fish, cover and
refrigerate for 20 minutes.
3 Heat the barbecue until very hot; lightly brush
it with oil. Cook the fish for 8 minutes on each
side, or until the flesh flakes easily when tested.
4 While the fish is cooking, heat the oil in a
frying pan; add the onion and cook over medium
heat, stirring, until golden. Add the ginger, garlic
and sugar and cook for 3 minutes.
5 Place the fish on a serving plate, top with the
onion mixture, sprinkle over the spring onion
and serve immediately with Lemon and Garlic
Dipping Sauce and steamed rice.

*NUTRITION PER SERVE (6): Protein 25 g; Fat 5 g;
Carbohydrate 5 g; Dietary Fibre 0 g; Cholesterol 80 mg;
780 kJ (185 cal)*

## BEEF PHO
### (BEEF SOUP)

•

*Preparation time:* 45 minutes
*Total cooking time:* 5 hours
*Serves* 4

★ ★

1 kg (2 lb) beef shin bones
350 g (11¼ oz) gravy beef
5 cm (2 inch) piece fresh ginger, thinly
    sliced
1 teaspoon salt
2.5 litres water
6 black peppercorns
1 cinnamon stick
4 cloves
6 coriander seeds
2 tablespoons fish sauce
400 g (12⅔ oz) thick fresh rice noodles
150 g (4¾ oz) rump steak, thinly sliced
3 spring onions, finely chopped
1 medium onion, very thinly sliced

•

**Toppings**
chopped red chilli, bean sprouts, fresh
    purple basil leaves, chopped spring
    onion, thin lime wedges, fresh
    coriander leaves
chilli sauce and hoisin sauce, optional

•

1 Place the bones, gravy beef, ginger, salt and water in a large pan. Bring to the boil, reduce the heat to low and simmer very gently, uncovered, for 3½ hours. Skim off any scum that forms on the surface. Add the peppercorns, cinnamon, cloves, coriander seeds and fish sauce, and cook for another 40 minutes. Remove the gravy beef and set it aside to cool. Drain the stock, reserving all the liquid and discarding the bones and spices; return the liquid to the pan. When the gravy beef is cool enough to handle, cut it against the grain into very fine slices. Set aside.
2 Close to serving time, plunge the noodles into a pan of boiling water and cook them for about 10 seconds only, otherwise they will soften and fall apart. Drain the noodles well and divide them among large individual soup bowls.
3 Arrange the toppings on a platter in the centre of the table.
4 Bring the beef stock to a rapid boil. Place some slices of the cooked meat as well as a few slices of the raw steak into each bowl of noodles. Ladle the boiling stock over the top, sprinkle over the spring onion and onion slices and serve. Each diner chooses their own toppings and can also add sauces such as sweet chilli sauce and hoisin sauce to their dish.
NOTE: The success of this dish depends on the full-flavoured stock, for which there is no quick substitute. Even though it takes a long time to cook, it is well worth the effort. The stock can be made in advance and frozen, making it easy to put the dish together when required.

*NUTRITION PER SERVE: Protein 40 g; Fat 10 g;
Carbohydrate 5 g; Dietary Fibre 0 g; Cholesterol 105 mg;
1145 kJ (270 cal)*

PHO
*Pho, the famous noodle soup of Hanoi and considered by some to be Vietnam's national dish, is a common breakfast or snack. Steaming bowls of soup, often topped with chopped cooked chicken instead of the more expensive rare beef, are sold from numerous food stalls and small restaurants in city streets.*

*Left: Beef Pho*

1 Slice the chicken into long, thin strips. Combine the chicken, celery, carrot, cabbage, onion, coriander and mint in a large bowl.
2 To make Dressing: Place all the ingredients in a small bowl. Whisk until the sugar is dissolved and the ingredients are well combined.
3 To make Topping: Heat the oil in a wok; add the garlic and cook over moderate heat, stirring, until pale golden. Stir in the peanuts and sugar.
4 Pour the Dressing over the chicken mixture and toss to combine. Place the chicken salad on a serving plate, and sprinkle over the Topping just before serving.

*NUTRITION PER SERVE: Protein 25 g; Fat 20 g; Carbohydrate 25 g; Dietary Fibre 5 g; Cholesterol 70 mg; 1590 kJ (380 cal)*

## EGGPLANT (AUBERGINE) SLICES IN BLACK BEAN SAUCE

*Preparation time:* 20 minutes
*Total cooking time:* 35 minutes
*Serves* 4

✴

*500 g (1 lb) medium eggplant (aubergine)*
*1/3 cup (80 ml/2¾ fl oz) oil*
*4 cloves garlic, finely chopped*
*4 cm (1½ inch) piece fresh ginger, grated*
*2 medium onions, finely chopped*
*1/3 cup (80 ml/2¾ fl oz) chicken stock*
*2 teaspoons canned black beans, rinsed*
*    well, roughly chopped*
*2 tablespoons oyster sauce*
*1 tablespoon soy sauce*
*2 teaspoons fish sauce*
*4 spring onions, sliced into long*
*    diagonal strips*

•

1 Slice the eggplant into long slices and lightly brush each side with oil.
2 Heat a frying pan over moderately low heat; add the eggplant, 4 to 5 slices at a time, and cook until golden on both sides; remove from the pan. Do not hurry this process as cooking the eggplant slowly allows the natural sugars to caramelise and produces a wonderful flavour. If the eggplant begins to burn, reduce the heat and sprinkle it with a little water.
3 Increase the heat to moderately high and add any remaining oil, the garlic, ginger, onion and about 1 tablespoon of the chicken stock; cover and cook for 3 minutes. Add the remaining stock, black beans, oyster sauce, soy sauce and fish sauce. Bring to the boil and cook for 2 minutes. Return the eggplant to the pan and simmer for 2 minutes or until it is heated

## VIETNAMESE CHICKEN SALAD

•

*Preparation time:* 40 minutes
*Total cooking time:* 5 minutes
*Serves* 4

★

*600 g (1¼ lb) chicken thigh fillets, cooked*
*1 cup (125 g/4 oz) thinly sliced celery*
*2 medium carrots, cut into thin 5 cm*
*    (2 inch) lengths*
*1 cup (75 g/2½ oz) finely shredded*
*    cabbage*
*1 small onion, sliced*
*3 tablespoons fresh coriander leaves*
*3 tablespoons fresh mint, finely shredded*

•

*Dressing*
*3 tablespoons caster sugar*
*2 tablespoons water*
*1 tablespoon fish sauce*
*1 teaspoon crushed garlic*
*2 tablespoons white vinegar*
*1 red chilli, seeded and finely chopped*

•

*Topping*
*2 tablespoons peanut oil*
*1½ teaspoons chopped garlic*
*1/3 cup (50 g/1⅔ oz) unsalted roasted*
*    peanuts, finely chopped*
*1 tablespoon soft brown sugar or*
*    2 teaspoons caster sugar*

*Above: Vietnamese Chicken Salad*

CRAB MEAT
*Fresh crab meat is always best, but it is expensive and not always easily available. Canned crab meat has a slightly different flavour and texture to fresh—salt will have been added. After draining, use a knife or your finger to check for pieces of membrane or shell, and remove. Note that when drained, the crab meat is only about half the weight shown on the can.*

through. Scatter over the spring onion and serve. NOTE: Always rinse black beans very well before using, as they are extremely salty. They will keep indefinitely if refrigerated after opening.

*NUTRITION PER SERVE: Protein 5 g; Fat 20 g; Carbohydrate 10 g; Dietary Fibre 5 g; Cholesterol 0 mg; 985 kJ (235 cal)*

## VERMICELLI AND CRAB MEAT STIR-FRY

**Preparation time:** 20 minutes
  + 20 minutes soaking
**Total cooking time:** 15 minutes
Serves 4

✬

*200 g (6¹/₂ oz) dried mung bean vermicelli*
*2 tablespoons oil*
*10 red Asian shallots, very finely sliced*
*3 cloves garlic, finely chopped*
*2 stems lemon grass (white part only), very finely sliced*
*1 red pepper (capsicum), cut into thin 4 cm (1¹/₂ inch) matchsticks*
*170 g (5¹/₂ oz) can crab meat, well drained*
*2 tablespoons fish sauce*
*2 tablespoons lime juice*
*2 teaspoons sugar*
*3 spring onions, cut into very fine diagonal slices*

1 Soak the noodles in hot water for 20 minutes or until softened; drain. Using scissors, cut the noodles into short lengths for easy eating.
2 Heat the oil in a wok or heavy-based pan; add the shallots, garlic and lemon grass and stir-fry over high heat for 2 minutes. Add the red pepper and cook for 30 seconds, tossing well. Add the vermicelli and toss. Cover and steam for 1 minute, or until the vermicelli is heated through.
3 Add the crab meat, fish sauce, lime juice and sugar and toss well, using 2 wooden spoons. Season with salt and pepper to taste, sprinkle with the spring onion and serve.

*NUTRITION PER SERVE: Protein 15 g; Fat 10 g; Carbohydrate 45 g; Dietary Fibre 5 g; Cholesterol 40 mg; 1410 kJ (335 cal)*

*Above: Eggplant Slices in Black Bean Sauce Below: Vermicelli and Crab Meat Stir-fry*

## PORK AND LETTUCE PARCELS

•

*Preparation time:* 1 hour
*Total cooking time:* 55 minutes
*Serves 4–6*

★

500 g (1 lb) pork loin
5 cm (2 inch) piece fresh ginger, thinly
    sliced
1 tablespoon fish sauce
20 spring onions (choose thin ones)
2 soft-leaf lettuces
1 Lebanese cucumber, thinly sliced
3 tablespoons fresh mint
3 tablespoons fresh coriander leaves
2 green chillies, seeded and very finely
    sliced, optional
2 teaspoons sugar
Lemon and Garlic Dipping Sauce
    (page 169), to serve

•

1 Place the pork, ginger and fish sauce in a large
pan and cover with cold water. Bring to the boil,
reduce the heat and simmer, covered, for about
45 minutes or until the pork is tender. Remove
the pork and allow to cool; discard the liquid.
2 Trim both ends from all the spring onions so
that you have long stems of equal length. Bring a
large pot of water to the boil and blanch the
spring onions 2 to 3 at a time for about

*Below: Pork and
Lettuce Parcels*

2 minutes, or until softened. Remove the spring
onions from the hot water with tongs and place
them in a bowl of iced water. Drain them and lay
them flat and straight on a tray to be used later.
3 Separate the lettuce into leaves. If the leaves
have a firm section at the base, trim this away
(or making a neat parcel will be difficult).
4 When the pork is cool enough to handle, cut it
into thin slices and finely shred each slice.
Spread out a lettuce leaf, place about
1 tablespoon of the shredded pork in the centre
of the leaf. Top with a few slices of cucumber, a
few mint and coriander leaves, a little chilli, if
using, and a light sprinkling of sugar. Fold a
section of the lettuce over the filling, bring in the
sides to meet each other and carefully roll up the
parcel. Tie one of the spring onions around the
parcel; trim off the excess or tie it into a bow.
Repeat with the remaining ingredients. Arrange
the parcels on a serving platter and serve with
Lemon and Garlic Dipping Sauce.

NUTRITION PER SERVE (6): Protein 20 g; Fat 10 g;
Carbohydrate 5 g; Dietary Fibre 5 g; Cholesterol 50 mg;
755 kJ (180 cal)

•

## SEARED PORK SKEWERS

•

*Preparation time:* 15 minutes
    + 20 minutes marinating
*Total cooking time:* 8 minutes
*Serves 4*

★

500 g (1 lb) pork fillet, cut into 2 cm
    (3/4 inch) cubes
5 cm (2 inch) piece fresh ginger, grated
2 cloves garlic, finely chopped
2 tablespoons fish sauce
1 tablespoon dry sherry
1/2 teaspoon salt
1/2 teaspoon pepper
2 teaspoons oil
fresh mint, to garnish
Vietnamese Dipping Sauce (page 169),
    to serve

•

1 Soak 8 wooden skewers in water while you are
preparing the recipe.
2 Place the pork in a bowl with the ginger,
garlic, fish sauce, sherry, salt and pepper and
marinate it for 20 minutes. Drain the pork and
reserve the marinade. Dry the skewers with
paper towels and thread the meat onto them.
3 Brush a heavy-based pan with oil and heat
until extremely hot. Cook the skewers of pork,
3 at a time, for about 3 to 4 minutes; turn the
skewers regularly until the pork becomes a dark

golden brown and sprinkle over a little of the marinade. Do not overcook the pork or it will become very dry.

4 Garnish with the mint and serve with Vietnamese Dipping Sauce and steamed rice or cooked rice noodles.

NUTRITION PER SERVE: Protein 30 g; Fat 15 g; Carbohydrate 0 g; Dietary Fibre 0 g; Cholesterol 70 mg; 1025 kJ (245 cal)

•

### WARM BEEF AND WATERCRESS SALAD
•

**Preparation time:** 25 minutes
    + 30 minutes marinating
**Total cooking time:** 10 minutes
**Serves** 4

350 g (11¼ oz) fillet steak, partially
    frozen (see Note)
1 tablespoon green peppercorns, roughly
    chopped
4 cloves garlic, crushed
3 stems lemon grass (white part only),
    very finely sliced
3 tablespoons oil
¼ teaspoon salt

¼ teaspoon freshly ground black pepper
250 g (8 oz) watercress
125 g (4 oz) cherry tomatoes, halved
4 spring onions, chopped
2 tablespoons lime juice

•

1 Cut the steak into thin slices. Place the steak, peppercorns, garlic, lemon grass, 2 tablespoons oil, salt and pepper in a bowl. Mix well, cover and marinate in the refrigerator for 30 minutes.

2 Remove the watercress sprigs from the tough stems, break them into small pieces, and wash and drain them well. Arrange the watercress on a serving platter and place the tomatoes on top, around the outside edge.

3 Heat the remaining oil in a wok or heavy-based frying pan until very hot and lightly smoking. Add the beef mixture and stir-fry it quickly until the meat is just cooked. Add the spring onion and toss through. Remove the beef mixture from the pan, pile it up in the centre of the watercress and sprinkle lime juice over the top. Serve immediately.

NOTE: If time allows, partially freezing the meat for about 30 minutes makes it firm and therefore easier to slice very finely.

NUTRITION PER SERVE: Protein 20 g; Fat 20 g; Carbohydrate 0 g; Dietary Fibre 5 g; Cholesterol 60 mg; 1135 kJ (270 cal)

*Above: Warm Beef
and Watercress Salad*

cook over medium heat for about 8 minutes, turning regularly, until browned. (The darker the browning at this stage, the better the colour when finished.) Between each batch, wipe out the pan with crumpled paper towels to remove excess oil.

4 Wipe the pan with paper towels again and return all the duck to the pan. Add the mushrooms, soy sauce, wine, sugar and orange peel. Bring the mixture to the boil; reduce the heat, cover and simmer gently for 35 minutes or until the duck is tender.

5 Carefully skim off any surface oil. Season with salt and pepper to taste, and stand for 10 minutes, covered, before serving. Remove the duck from the sauce and discard the orange peel. Pick off small sprigs of the watercress and arrange them on one side of a large serving platter. Carefully place the duck segments on the other side of the plate—try not to place the duck on the watercress as it will become soggy. Carefully spoon a little of the sauce over the duck and serve.

NOTE: Braising the duck over low heat produces tender, melt-in-the-mouth meat and a delicious sauce. If the heat is too high, the duck will dry out and lose its flavour.

*NUTRITION PER SERVE: Protein 20 g; Fat 55 g; Carbohydrate 5 g; Dietary Fibre 0 g; Cholesterol 130 mg; 2450 kJ (585 cal)*

## BRAISED DUCK WITH MUSHROOMS

•

*Preparation time:* 20 minutes
+ 20 minutes soaking
*Total cooking time:* 1 hour 10 minutes
*Serves* 6

✩ ✩

1 cup (15 g/½ oz) dried Chinese
  mushrooms
1 x 1.5 kg (3 lb) duck
2 teaspoons oil
2 tablespoons soy sauce
2 tablespoons Chinese rice wine
2 teaspoons sugar
2 wide strips fresh orange peel
125 g (4 oz) watercress

•

1 Soak the mushrooms in hot water for 20 minutes. Drain well and slice.
2 Using a large heavy knife or cleaver, chop the duck into small pieces, cutting through the bone. Arrange the pieces on a rack and pour boiling water over them—the water will plump up the skin and help keep the duck succulent. Drain and pat dry with paper towels.
3 Brush the base of a heavy-based frying pan with the oil; add the duck in 2 or 3 batches and

*Above: Braised Duck with Mushrooms*

## VIETNAMESE COLESLAW

•

*Preparation time:* 35 minutes
+ 20 minutes standing
*Total cooking time:* 10 minutes
*Serves* 4

✩

500 g (1 lb) chicken breast fillets
350 g (11¼ oz) Chinese cabbage, finely
  shredded
3 sticks celery, finely sliced
1 medium carrot, cut into fine matchsticks
1½ tablespoons oil
2 tablespoons shredded Vietnamese mint
1 tablespoon chopped garlic chives
1 tablespoon crisp fried onion

•

*Dressing*
4 tablespoons rice vinegar
2 tablespoons caster sugar
1 tablespoon fish sauce
1 tablespoon lime juice
½ teaspoon salt
½ teaspoon freshly ground black pepper
1 medium onion, finely sliced

1 Place the chicken in a frying pan with enough water to just cover it. Poach the chicken over low heat for 8 to 10 minutes or until it is cooked—do not let the water boil; it should just simmer gently. Drain and cool. When the chicken is cool enough to touch, shred it into fine pieces using your fingertips.

2 To make Dressing: Place the vinegar, sugar, fish sauce, lime juice, salt, pepper and onion in a small bowl and toss well to combine. Let stand for at least 20 minutes so the onion absorbs the flavours.

3 Place the chicken, cabbage, celery, carrot, oil and Dressing in a bowl and toss well. Arrange the salad on a serving plate, scatter over the mint, chives and crisp fried onion, and serve immediately.

*NUTRITION PER SERVE: Protein 35 g; Fat 15 g; Carbohydrate 15 g; Dietary Fibre 5 g; Cholesterol 70 mg; 1442 kJ (345 cal)*

## VIETNAMESE LETTUCE-WRAPPED SPRING ROLLS

**Preparation time:** 50 minutes
**Total cooking time:** 20 minutes
**Makes** 20

✷ ✷

*50 g (1²⁄₃ oz) dried mung bean vermicelli*
*2 tablespoons black fungus*
*500 g (1 lb) prawns*
*20 rice paper wrappers*
*150 g (4³⁄₄ oz) pork mince*
*4 spring onions, chopped*
*¹⁄₂ cup (45 g/1¹⁄₂ oz) bean sprouts, roughly chopped*
*1 teaspoon sugar*
*1 egg, beaten*
*oil, for deep-frying*
*20 lettuce leaves*
*1 cup (90 g/3 oz) bean sprouts, extra, scraggly ends removed*
*1 cup (20 g/²⁄₃ oz) fresh mint*
*Vietnamese Dipping Sauce (page 169), to serve*

1 Place the vermicelli and fungus in separate heatproof bowls. Cover with hot water and soak for 10 minutes, or until soft. Drain both, and chop the fungus roughly. Peel and devein the prawns; finely chop the prawn meat.

2 Using a pastry brush, brush both sides of each rice paper wrapper liberally with water. Allow to stand for 2 minutes or until they become soft and pliable; stack the wrappers on a plate. Sprinkle over a little extra water and cover the plate with plastic wrap to keep the wrappers moist until needed.

3 Combine the vermicelli, fungus, prawn meat, pork mince, spring onion, bean sprouts, sugar, and salt and pepper to taste in a bowl; stir well. Place 1 tablespoon of the filling along the base of a wrapper. Fold in the sides, roll the wrapper up tightly, and brush the seam with egg. Repeat with the remaining wrappers and filling.

4 Press the rolls with paper towels to remove any excess water. Heat 4 to 5 cm oil in a pan until moderately hot; add the spring rolls in batches and cook for 2 to 3 minutes or until dark golden brown. Drain on paper towels.

5 Place a spring roll in each lettuce leaf, top with 1 tablespoon bean sprouts and 2 mint leaves, and roll up to form a neat parcel. Serve with Vietnamese Dipping Sauce.

*NUTRITION PER SPRING ROLL: Protein 10 g; Fat 2 g; Carbohydrate 10 g; Dietary Fibre 1 g; Cholesterol 65 mg; 385 kJ (90 cal)*

*Above: Vietnamese Lettuce-Wrapped Spring Rolls*

# DIPPING SAUCES
A small bowl of one of these delicious sauces will enhance the flavour of dishes ranging from spring rolls, satays and fritters, to noodles and fish dishes.

## SWEET CHILLI SAUCE
Remove the seeds from 6 large red chillies and soak for 15 minutes in hot water. Process with 1 tablespoon chopped red chilli, 1/4 cup (60 ml/ 2 fl oz) white vinegar, 1 cup (250 g/ 8 oz) caster sugar, 1 teaspoon salt and 4 chopped cloves garlic until smooth. Transfer to a pan and cook for 15 minutes over medium heat, stirring frequently until thickened. Cool. Stir in 2 teaspoons fish sauce.

*NUTRITION PER 100 g: Protein 1 g;*
*Fat 0 g; Carbohydrate 55 g; Dietary Fibre 1 g;*
*Cholesterol 0 mg; 910 kJ (215 cal)*

## SESAME SEED SAUCE
Toast 100 g (3 1/3 oz) Japanese white sesame seeds in a dry pan over medium heat for 3–4 minutes, shaking the pan gently, until seeds are golden brown; remove from the pan at once to prevent burning. Grind the seeds in a mortar and pestle until a paste is formed. Add 2 teaspoons oil, if necessary, to assist in forming a paste. Mix the paste with 1/2 cup (125 ml/4 fl oz) Japanese soy sauce, 2 tablespoons mirin, 3 teaspoons caster sugar, 1/2 teaspoon instant dashi granules and 1/2 cup (125 ml/4 fl oz) warm water. Store, covered, in the refrigerator and use within 2 days of preparation.

*NUTRITION PER 100 g: Protein 2 g;*
*Fat 4 g; Carbohydrate 1 g; Dietary Fibre 1 g;*
*Cholesterol 0 mg; 220 kJ (50 cal)*

## SOY AND GINGER SAUCE
In a bowl combine 1 tablespoon grated fresh ginger, 2 teaspoons sugar and 1 cup (250 ml/8 fl oz) soy sauce. Mix well and serve immediately.

*NUTRITION PER 100 g: Protein 5 g;*
*Fat 0 g; Carbohydrate 5 g; Dietary Fibre 0 g;*
*Cholesterol 0 mg; 210 kJ (50 cal)*

## PEANUT SATAY SAUCE

Place 1 cup (160 g/5¼ oz) unsalted roasted peanuts in a food processor and process until finely chopped. Heat 2 tablespoons oil in a medium pan. Add 1 chopped onion and cook over medium heat for 5 minutes or until softened. Add 2 crushed cloves garlic, 2 teaspoons grated fresh ginger, ½ teaspoon chilli powder, 2 teaspoons curry powder and 1 teaspoon ground cumin, and cook, stirring, for 2 minutes. Add 1⅔ cups (410 ml/13 fl oz) coconut milk, 3 tablespoons soft brown sugar and chopped peanuts. Reduce heat and cook for 5 minutes or until the sauce thickens. Add 1 tablespoon lemon juice, season and serve. (For a smoother sauce, process in a food processor for 30 seconds.)

*NUTRITION PER 100 g: Protein 5 g;*
*Fat 15 g; Carbohydrate 10 g; Dietary Fibre 2 g;*
*Cholesterol 0 mg; 830 kJ (200 cal)*

## LEMON AND GARLIC DIPPING SAUCE

In a small bowl, stir ¼ cup (60 ml/ 2 fl oz) lemon juice, 2 tablespoons fish sauce and 1 tablespoon sugar until the sugar has dissolved. Stir in 2 chopped small red chillies and 3 finely chopped cloves garlic.

*NUTRITION PER 100 g: Protein 2 g;*
*Fat 0 g; Carbohydrate 15 g; Dietary Fibre 2 g;*
*Cholesterol 0 mg; 325 kJ (80 cal)*

## VIETNAMESE DIPPING SAUCE

In a bowl, mix together 2 tablespoons fish sauce, 2 tablespoons cold water, 2 tablespoons chopped fresh coriander leaves, 1 teaspoon chopped red chilli and 1 teaspoon soft brown sugar and serve.

*NUTRITION PER 100 g: Protein 3 g;*
*Fat 0 g; Carbohydrate 5 g; Dietary Fibre 1 g;*
*Cholesterol 0 mg; 170 kJ (40 cal)*

## THAI DIPPING SAUCE

In a small pan, combine ½ cup (125 g/ 4 oz) sugar, ½ cup (125 ml/4 fl oz) water, ¼ cup (60 ml/2 fl oz) white vinegar, 1 tablespoon fish sauce and 1 small chopped red chilli. Bring to the boil and simmer, uncovered, for 5 minutes or until slightly thickened. Remove from heat and cool slightly. Stir in ¼ small, peeled, seeded and finely chopped cucumber, ¼ small finely chopped carrot, and 1 tablespoon chopped roasted peanuts.

*NUTRITION PER 100 g: Protein 1 g;*
*Fat 2 g; Carbohydrate 30 g; Dietary Fibre 1 g;*
*Cholesterol 0 mg; 550 kJ (130 cal)*

*From left: Vietnamese Dipping Sauce;*
*Sesame Seed Sauce; Thai Dipping Sauce;*
*Soy and Ginger Sauce; Peanut Satay*
*Sauce; Sweet Chilli Sauce; Lemon and*
*Garlic Dipping Sauce*

noodles as they need to form a solid pancake. Run an egg slice underneath to loosen the base then turn it over with 2 egg slices and cook the other side. Be patient because if the pancake is moved before it sets it will break up. Transfer to a plate, cover and keep warm.

3 Heat a heavy-based pan or wok. Sprinkle the sugar and fish sauce over the beef mixture. Add the beef mixture in 2 batches, and toss it over high heat for 2 to 3 minutes. Place the stock and cornflour in a bowl and stir until a smooth paste forms. Add the cornflour mixture to the meat and toss for 1 minute. Do not overcook the meat or it will become tough.

4 Place the pancake on a large serving plate, cut it into serving wedges and place the beef mixture on top, piling it up in the centre. Garnish with the spring onion and serve immediately.

*NUTRITION PER SERVE (6): Protein 15 g; Fat 15 g; Carbohydrate 20 g; Dietary Fibre 2 g; Cholesterol 45 mg; 1210 kJ (290 cal)*

## GREEN PAWPAW, CHICKEN AND FRESH HERB SALAD

•

*Preparation time:* 40 minutes
*Total cooking time:* 10 minutes
Serves 4

★

350 g (11¼ oz) chicken breast fillets
1 large green pawpaw
1 cup (20 g/⅔ oz) Vietnamese mint
½ cup (15 g/½ oz) fresh coriander leaves
2 red chillies, seeded and finely sliced
2 tablespoons fish sauce
1 tablespoon rice vinegar
1 tablespoon lime juice
2 teaspoons sugar
2 tablespoons finely chopped unsalted
    roasted peanuts

•

1 Place the chicken in a frying pan with enough water to just cover it. Simmer gently for 8 to 10 minutes or until cooked. Remove from the liquid, cool completely, then slice finely.
2 Peel the pawpaw, then grate the flesh into long shreds. Mix gently with the mint, coriander, chilli, fish sauce, vinegar, lime juice and sugar.
3 Arrange the pawpaw mixture on a serving plate and top with the chicken. Scatter with peanuts and serve immediately.
NOTE: Green pawpaw is under-ripe pawpaw, used for tartness and texture.

*NUTRITION PER SERVE: Protein 25 g; Fat 5 g; Carbohydrate 10 g; Dietary Fibre 5 g; Cholesterol 50 mg; 802 kJ (190 cal)*

## FRIED RICE NOODLE PANCAKE WITH GARLIC BEEF

•

*Preparation time:* 20 minutes
    + 30 minutes marinating
*Total cooking time:* 30 minutes
Serves 4–6

★ ★

350 g (11¼ oz) fillet steak, thinly sliced
1 red pepper (capsicum), cut into short,
    thin strips
6 cloves garlic, finely chopped
¼ teaspoon pepper
4 tablespoons oil
400 g (12⅔ oz) thick fresh rice noodles
1 tablespoon sugar
2 tablespoons fish sauce
½ cup (125 ml/4 fl oz) beef stock
2 teaspoons cornflour
4 spring onions, cut into long thin
    diagonal slices

•

1 Place the steak, red pepper, garlic, pepper and half the oil in a large bowl; mix well to combine and marinate for 30 minutes.
2 Gently separate the noodles. Heat the remaining oil in a heavy-based pan over medium heat, swirling the oil to coat the pan well. Add the noodles and press them down firmly with an egg slice to form a large flat pancake the size of the pan. Cook the noodles for 10 to 15 minutes, pressing down occasionally, until the base is very crisp and golden. Do not disturb or lift the

### MUNG BEAN VERMICELLI

*Mung bean vermicelli, made by extruding a paste of mung bean flour and water, readily absorb the flavours of other foods and are popular throughout China, Southeast Asia and Japan. For vegetarians, the boiled noodles can be mixed with herbs, spices and flavourings to take the place of meat or prawns in stuffings or salads. In Indonesia, Malaysia and Singapore they are used as an ingredient in some sweet drinks and desserts.*

*Above: Fried Rice Noodle Pancake with Garlic Beef*

## CHICKEN WITH PINEAPPLE AND CASHEWS

•

*Preparation time:* 35 minutes
*Total cooking time:* 20 minutes
*Serves* 4

★

2 tablespoons shredded coconut
½ cup (80 g/2²/3 oz) raw cashews
2 tablespoons oil
1 large onion, cut into large chunks
4 cloves garlic, finely chopped
2 teaspoons chopped red chilli
350 g (11¼ oz) chicken thigh fillets,
    chopped
½ red pepper (capsicum), chopped
½ green pepper (capsicum), chopped
2 tablespoons oyster sauce
1 tablespoon fish sauce
1 teaspoon sugar
2 cups (320 g/10¼ oz) chopped fresh
    pineapple
3 spring onions, chopped

•

1 Preheat the oven to slow 150°C (300°F/Gas 2).
Spread the coconut on an oven tray and toast in
the oven for 10 minutes or until dark golden,

shaking the tray occasionally. Remove the
coconut from the tray immediately, to prevent
burning, and set aside.
2 Increase the heat to moderate 180°C (350°F/
Gas 4). Roast the cashews on an oven tray in the
oven for about 15 minutes, until deep golden.
Remove the cashews from the tray and set aside
to cool.
3 Heat the oil in a wok or large, deep frying pan;
add the onion, garlic and chilli and stir-fry over
medium heat for 2 minutes, then remove from
the pan. Increase the heat to high; add the
chicken and red and green pepper, in 2 batches,
and stir-fry until the chicken is light brown.
Return the onion mixture to the wok; add the
oyster sauce, fish sauce, sugar and pineapple and
toss for 2 minutes. Toss the cashews through.
4 Arrange the chicken mixture on a serving
plate, scatter the toasted coconut and spring
onion over the top, and serve immediately.

NUTRITION PER SERVE: Protein 25 g; Fat 25 g;
Carbohydrate 20 g; Dietary Fibre 5 g; Cholesterol 65 mg;
1705 kJ (405 cal)

*Below: Chicken
with Pineapple
and Cashews*

# VIETNAMESE FRIED RICE

•

*Preparation time:* 30 minutes
*Total cooking time:* 35 minutes
*Serves* 4

★

3 eggs
1/4 teaspoon salt
1/2 cup (125 ml/4 fl oz) oil
1 large onion, finely chopped
6 spring onions, chopped
4 cloves garlic, finely chopped
5 cm (2 inch) piece fresh ginger, finely
    grated
2 small red chillies, seeded and finely
    chopped
250 g (8 oz) pork loin, finely chopped
125 g (4 oz) dried Chinese pork sausage,
    thinly sliced (see note)
100 g (3 1/3 oz) green beans, chopped
100 g (3 1/3 oz) carrots, cut into small
    cubes
1/2 large red pepper (capsicum), cut into
    small cubes
1 cup (200 g/6 1/2 oz) long-grain rice,
    steamed and cooled
3 tablespoons fish sauce
2 tablespoons soy sauce
2 teaspoons sugar
1/4 teaspoon salt, extra, or to taste
fresh coriander leaves, to garnish

1 Whisk the eggs and salt in a bowl until frothy. Heat 1 tablespoon of the oil in a wok and swirl it around to coat the sides. Pour in the egg and cook it gently over medium heat, stirring regularly for 2 to 3 minutes, or until the egg is just cooked. Remove the scrambled egg from the wok and set it aside.

2 Add 1 more tablespoon of oil to the wok and, when hot, add the onion, spring onion, garlic, ginger and chilli and cook for 7 minutes, stirring regularly, or until the onion is soft and golden; remove the onion mixture from the wok. Add another tablespoon of oil and, when hot, add the pork and sausage and stir-fry for 3 to 4 minutes or until cooked; remove the meat from the wok.

3 Add the remaining oil to the wok and swirl it to coat the sides; add the beans, carrot and red pepper, and stir-fry over high heat for 1 minute. Add the rice to the wok, toss it well to coat it with the vegetables and oil, and stir-fry for 2 minutes. Return the onion mixture and the meat mixture to the wok and add the fish sauce, soy sauce, sugar and salt; toss well for about 30 seconds until heated. Lightly toss in the scrambled egg and serve immediately, sprinkled with coriander leaves.

NOTE: These spicy, dried sausages (lup chiang) are available from Asian food stores. They will keep for up to 3 months in the refrigerator.

*NUTRITION PER SERVE: Protein 35 g; Fat 48 g; Carbohydrate 25 g; Dietary Fibre 5 g; Cholesterol 235 mg; 2780 kJ (660 cal)*

---

## RICE FOR FRIED RICE

*To avoid gluggy fried rice, the cooked rice used should be cold and firm. Cook the day before and refrigerate, or use leftover cooked rice. If this is not possible, use slightly less water than usual when steaming, and as soon as the rice is cooked, spread it over a baking tray or similar surface to hasten the cooling process.*

*Below: Vietnamese
Fried Rice*

---

•

# NORTH VIETNAMESE
# BRAISED PORK

•

*Preparation time:* 35 minutes
  + 1 hour marinating
*Total cooking time:* 1 hour 40 minutes
*Serves* 4

★ ★

4 cm (1 1/2 inch) piece fresh galangal
3 cm (1 1/4 inch) piece fresh turmeric
10 peppercorns
1 teaspoon shrimp paste
4 cloves garlic
1 teaspoon sugar
1 tablespoon fish sauce
500 g (1 lb) piece pork shoulder (with fat
    and skin on)
2 tablespoons oil
1 medium onion, chopped
1 cup (250 ml/8 fl oz) water
1 teaspoon vinegar

1 Thinly slice the galangal and turmeric, then pound them in a mortar and pestle with the peppercorns. Remove the galangal mixture from the mortar and pestle; add the shrimp paste and garlic, and pound. Place all the pounded ingredients in a large bowl with the sugar and fish sauce and set aside.

2 Place the pork (skin-side up) on a foil-lined grill tray, and cook under a hot grill until well browned and the crackling is blistering. Turn the pork over and grill the flesh side until it browns. When cool enough to touch, cut the pork into large bite-sized pieces. Combine the pork with the spice paste mixture, and marinate for 1 hour. Drain the pork and reserve the marinade. Lightly pat the meat dry with paper towels (so the meat browns well and does not stew).

3 Heat the oil in a heavy-based pan; add the pork and onion in 3 batches, and cook over high heat until well browned. Drain any excess oil from the pan. Add the marinade, water and vinegar, and bring to the boil; cover and simmer for 1 hour or until the pork is tender. Uncover and cook for about 10 minutes, until the sauce thickens. Season well with salt and pepper and serve with steamed rice.

NUTRITION PER SERVE: Protein 30 g; Fat 10 g; Carbohydrate 5 g; Dietary Fibre 0 g; Cholesterol 65 mg; 1005 kJ (240 cal)

•

# CHICKEN CURRY

•

*Preparation time:* 30 minutes
*Total cooking time:* 55 minutes
*Serves* 4

★ ★

1.5 kg (3¼ lb) chicken pieces, such as
    thighs, drumsticks and wings
2 tablespoons oil
4 cloves garlic, finely chopped
5 cm (2 inch) piece fresh ginger, finely
    chopped
2 stems lemon grass (white part only),
    finely chopped
2 teaspoons chilli flakes
2 tablespoons curry powder (see note)
2 medium brown onions, chopped
2 teaspoons sugar
1 teaspoon salt
1½ cups (375 ml/12 fl oz) coconut milk
½ cup (125 ml/4 fl oz) water

•

*Garnishes*
garlic chives, thickly chopped
fresh coriander leaves
unsalted roasted peanuts

1 Using a large heavy knife or cleaver, chop each piece of chicken into 2 pieces, chopping straight through the bone. Wash the chicken and pat dry with paper towels.

2 Heat the oil in a large pan; add the garlic, ginger, lemon grass, chilli and curry powder, and cook over medium heat for 3 minutes, stirring regularly. Add the chicken, onion, sugar and salt, and toss gently. Cover and cook for 8 minutes, until the onion has softened, and then toss well to coat the chicken pieces evenly with the curry mixture. Cover and cook for 15 minutes over low heat—the chicken will braise gently, producing its own liquid.

3 Add the coconut milk and water to the pan and bring it to the boil, stirring occasionally. Reduce the heat and simmer, uncovered, for 30 minutes or until chicken is very tender. Serve garnished with the chives, coriander and peanuts.

NOTE: Use a mild Asian curry powder labelled 'for chicken', available from Asian food stores. A standard supermarket curry powder is not suitable for this recipe.

NUTRITION PER SERVE: Protein 60 g; Fat 45 g; Carbohydrate 10 g; Dietary Fibre 5 g; Cholesterol 175 mg; 2920 kJ (700 cal)

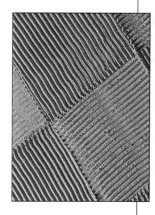

*Above: Chicken Curry*

1 Peel and devein the prawns. Top and tail the beans and cut them into 2 cm (³/4 inch) pieces.
2 Heat the oil in a large heavy-based wok, add the onion, garlic, lemon grass and chilli and stir-fry over moderately high heat for 4 minutes, or until the onion is soft and golden.
3 Add the beans to the wok and stir-fry for 2 to 3 minutes or until they become bright green. Add the prawns and sugar and toss gently for 2 minutes. Add the fish sauce and vinegar, toss well and serve immediately, sprinkled with the garlic chives.
NOTE: The equivalent weight of green beans may be used if snake beans are unavailable.

*NUTRITION PER SERVE: Protein 15 g; Fat 10 g; Carbohydrate 10 g; Dietary Fibre 5 g; Cholesterol 145 mg; 850 kJ (200 cal)*

## SWEET BRAISED PUMPKIN

*Preparation time:* 20 minutes
*Total cooking time:* 15 minutes
Serves 4

☆

750 g (1¹/2 lb) pumpkin
1¹/2 tablespoons oil
3 cloves garlic, finely chopped
4 cm (1¹/2 inch) piece fresh ginger, grated
6 red Asian shallots, chopped
1 tablespoon soft brown sugar
¹/2 cup (125 ml/4 fl oz) chicken stock
2 tablespoons fish sauce
1 tablespoon lime juice

1 Peel the pumpkin and cut it into large chunks.
2 Heat the oil in a heavy-based frying pan; add the garlic, ginger and shallots and cook over medium heat for 3 minutes, stirring regularly.
3 Add the pumpkin and sprinkle with the sugar. Cook for 7 to 8 minutes, turning the pieces regularly, until the pumpkin is golden and just tender.
4 Add the chicken stock and fish sauce, bring to the boil, then reduce the heat and simmer until all the liquid has evaporated, turning the pumpkin over regularly. Sprinkle with the lime juice, season to taste with salt and pepper, and serve. Delicious as an accompaniment to meat dishes such as curries, or on its own with plenty of steamed rice.
NOTE: The sweeter pumpkins, such as butternut and Japanese pumpkin, will produce a dish with a delicious flavour and soft texture.

*NUTRITION PER SERVE: Protein 5 g; Fat 8 g; Carbohydrate 20 g; Dietary Fibre 3 g; Cholesterol 0 mg; 700 kJ (165 cal)*

### CHILLI PRAWN AND SNAKE BEAN STIR-FRY

•

*Preparation time:* 35 minutes
*Total cooking time:* 15 minutes
Serves 4

☆

300 g (9²/3 oz) medium raw prawns
250 g (8 oz) snake beans
2 tablespoons oil
2 medium onions, very finely sliced
5 cloves garlic, finely chopped
2 stems lemon grass (white part only), very finely sliced
3 red chillies, seeded and very finely sliced
2 teaspoons sugar
1 tablespoon fish sauce
1 tablespoon rice vinegar
chopped garlic chives, to garnish

*Above: Chilli Prawn and Snake Bean Stir-fry (top); Sweet Braised Pumpkin*

## VIETNAMESE PANCAKES IN LETTUCE PARCELS

•

*Preparation time:* 20 minutes
+ 45 minutes standing
*Total cooking time:* about 30 minutes
*Makes* 10

★★★

*1 cup (175 g/5²/₃ oz) rice flour*
*2 teaspoons cornflour*
*¹/₂ teaspoon curry powder (see note)*
*¹/₂ teaspoon ground turmeric*
*1 cup (250 ml/8 fl oz) coconut milk*
*¹/₂ cup (125 ml/4 fl oz) water*
*¹/₄ cup (60 ml/2 fl oz) coconut cream*
*2 teaspoons oil*
*150 g (4³/₄ oz) pork ribs, boned and thinly sliced*
*300 g (9²/₃ oz) raw prawns, peeled, deveined and the meat finely chopped*
*4 spring onions, chopped*
*150 g (4³/₄ oz) bean sprouts, scraggly ends removed*
*10 large lettuce leaves*
*1 cup (20 g/²/₃ oz) fresh mint*

•

*Dipping Sauce*
*2 tablespoons fish sauce*
*2 tablespoons lime juice*
*1–2 teaspoons chopped fresh chilli*
*¹/₂ teaspoon sugar*

•

1 Place the rice flour, cornflour, curry powder, turmeric, coconut milk, water and coconut cream in a food processor, and process for 30 seconds or until smooth. Cover and set aside for 45 minutes so the batter thickens.
2 Heat 1 teaspoon oil in a heavy-based frying pan; cook the pork in batches over moderately high heat for 1 to 2 minutes or until browned.
3 Stir the batter well. Heat the remaining oil and add 2 tablespoons batter to the pan, swirling it to form a small round pancake. Cook the pancake for 30 seconds or until it begins to crisp on the underside. Place 2 pieces of pork, 1 tablespoon prawn meat, 1 tablespoon spring onion and 1 tablespoon bean sprouts in the centre of the pancake. Cover the pan and cook for 1 to 2 minutes, or until the prawns become pink and the vegetables soften. (The base of the pancake will be very crisp, the top side will be set but soft.) Place the pancake on a platter and repeat with the remaining ingredients.
4 Place each cooked pancake inside a lettuce leaf and top with 2 mint leaves. Fold the lettuce to form a parcel. Serve with the Dipping Sauce.
5 To make Dipping Sauce: Combine the fish sauce, lime juice, chilli and sugar in a bowl and whisk until well blended.
NOTE: Use a mild Asian curry powder labelled 'for meat', available from Asian food stores. A standard supermarket curry powder is not suitable for this recipe.

*NUTRITION PER PARCEL WITH SAUCE: Protein 10 g; Fat 10 g; Carbohydrate 15 g; Dietary Fibre 2 g; Cholesterol 60 mg; 770 kJ (185 cal)*

### CHOPPING PORK MINCE
*For some dishes, such as meatballs, you need a really finely chopped mince, which will hold together well and keep it shape during cooking. If you have bought mince from your butcher, chopping at home will give it this finer texture.*

*Left: Vietnamese Pancakes in Lettuce Parcels*

## SPICY GRILLED FISH PIECES

•

*Preparation time:* 15 minutes
+ 15 minutes marinating
*Total cooking time:* 6 minutes
Serves 4

★

3 cloves garlic
4 red Asian shallots
3 stems lemon grass (white part only),
    finely sliced
1 teaspoon ground turmeric
1 teaspoon galangal powder
2 red chillies
¼ teaspoon salt
¼ teaspoon pepper
2 tablespoons oil
500 g (1 lb) boneless white fish fillets
1 tablespoon fish sauce
fresh coriander leaves or watercress,
    to garnish

•

1 Place the garlic, shallots, lemon grass, turmeric, galangal powder, chillies, salt and pepper in a food processor and process until a paste is formed, adding the oil to help the grinding.
2 Cut the fish into large bite-sized pieces. Place the fish in a bowl with the spice paste, toss well and cover and refrigerate for 15 minutes.
3 Place the fish on a foil-lined grill tray and cook under a hot grill for 3 to 4 minutes, turning the pieces over so the fish browns on all sides.

*Above: Spicy Grilled Fish Pieces*

4 Arrange the fish on a serving plate and sprinkle over the fish sauce. Serve immediately with rice.

NUTRITION PER SERVE: Protein 25 g; Fat 15 g; Carbohydrate 0 g; Dietary Fibre 0 g; Cholesterol 90 mg; 980 kJ (235 cal)

•

## VERMICELLI WITH STIR-FRIED SQUID AND TOMATOES

•

*Preparation time:* 20 minutes
+ 15 minutes marinating
*Total cooking time:* 20 minutes
Serves 4

★

100 g (3⅓ oz) dried mung bean
    vermicelli
350 g (11¼ oz) squid hoods, cut into rings
2 tablespoons fish sauce
2 tablespoons oil
3 cloves garlic, finely chopped
3 stems lemon grass (white part only),
    finely sliced
2 teaspoons sugar
¼ teaspoon salt
¼ teaspoon pepper
1 red (Spanish) onion, finely sliced
2 ripe tomatoes, diced
2 tablespoons lime juice
2 tablespoons chopped garlic chives

1 Soak the vermicelli in hot water for 5 to 10 minutes or until softened; drain.

2 Place the squid in a bowl with 1 tablespoon fish sauce, 1 tablespoon oil, half the garlic, half the lemon grass, and the sugar, salt and pepper. Mix well to combine and marinate for 15 minutes.

3 Heat a wok until it is extremely hot; add the squid in 2 batches, stir-fry until it just changes colour, and remove it from the wok. Reheat the wok until hot; add the remaining oil, garlic, lemon grass and onion, and stir-fry for 1 minute. Add the tomato and toss well. Add the vermicelli and return the squid (with any juices) to the pan, and toss well. Add the lime juice, chives and remaining fish sauce, and serve immediately.

NUTRITION PER SERVE: Protein 20 g; Fat 10 g; Carbohydrate 25 g; Dietary Fibre 2 g; Cholesterol 180 mg; 1210 kJ (290 cal)

# VIETNAMESE PORK AND PRAWN SALAD

**Preparation time:** 30 minutes
+ 1 hour marinating
**Total cooking time:** 6 minutes
**Serves** 6–8

★

250 g (8 oz) pork fillet
300 g (9²/3 oz) raw prawns
1/4 cup (60 ml/2 fl oz) white vinegar
1/2 cup (125 ml/4 fl oz) water
1 tablespoon sugar
1 carrot, cut into matchsticks
1 Lebanese cucumber, cut into matchsticks
1 red pepper (capsicum), cut into matchsticks
1 Chinese cabbage, finely shredded
1 tablespoon oil
100 g (3¹/3 oz) unsalted roasted peanuts, roughly chopped

**Dressing**
2 red Asian shallots, finely chopped
1 clove garlic, crushed
1 tablespoon fish sauce
1 tablespoon lime juice
1 teaspoon brown sugar
1 teaspoon sesame oil
1 tablespoon chopped Vietnamese mint

1 Cut the pork into thin strips. Peel and devein the prawns, leaving the tails intact.

2 Place the vinegar, water and sugar into a bowl and mix to combine. Add the carrot, cucumber, red pepper and Chinese cabbage and toss to coat in the marinade. Cover and refrigerate for 1 hour.

3 Heat the oil in a wok; stir-fry the pork in 2 batches over high heat for 3 minutes or until browned. Remove the pork from the wok. Add the prawns and stir-fry over high heat for 3 minutes or until bright pink.

4 Remove the vegetables from the marinade and drain thoroughly. Combine the vegetables with the pork, prawns and peanuts and toss well. Pour the Dressing over the salad and toss to coat.

5 To make Dressing: Combine the shallots, garlic, fish sauce, lime juice, brown sugar and sesame oil. Add the Vietnamese mint and mix together well.

NUTRITION PER SERVE (8): Protein 20 g; Fat 10 g; Carbohydrate 5 g; Dietary Fibre 2 g; Cholesterol 90 mg; 820 kJ (195 cal)

Above: Vietnamese Pork and Prawn Salad

## PORK BALL SOUP WITH NOODLES

•

*Preparation time:* 25 minutes
*Total cooking time:* 30 minutes
Serves 4

⭐

250 g (8 oz) pork bones
5 cm (2 inch) piece fresh ginger, thinly
    sliced
1 teaspoon salt
1 teaspoon pepper
4 cups (1 litre) water
6 spring onions, chopped
300 g (9²/3 oz) Shanghai noodles
250 g (8 oz) pork mince
2 tablespoons fish sauce
150 g (4³/4 oz) fresh pineapple, cut into
    small chunks
100 g (3¹/3 oz) bean sprouts, scraggly ends
    removed
2 tablespoons shredded fresh mint

•

1 Place the pork bones, ginger, salt, pepper and water in a pan, and bring it to the boil. Skim off any scum, add the spring onion and simmer for 20 minutes. Remove and discard the bones and set the stock aside.
2 Cook the noodles in a pan of boiling water for 5 minutes. Drain and rinse in cold water.
3 Chop the mince very finely with a cleaver or

*Below: Pork Ball Soup
with Noodles*

large knife for 3 minutes or until the meat feels very soft and spongy. Wet your hands and roll 2 teaspoons of mince at a time into small balls.
4 Return the stock to the heat and bring it to the boil. Add the pork balls and cook for 4 minutes. Add the fish sauce and pineapple.
5 Place the noodles in individual soup bowls and ladle the hot stock over them, making sure each bowl has pork balls and pineapple. Scatter the bean sprouts and mint over the soup, and serve immediately.

NUTRITION PER SERVE: Protein 25 g; Fat 10 g; Carbohydrate 60 g; Dietary Fibre 5 g; Cholesterol 40 mg; 1825 kJ (435 cal)

•

## PEPPERY PORK WITH VEGETABLES
•

*Preparation time:* 40 minutes +
    20 minutes marinating
*Total cooking time:* 20 minutes
Serves 4

⭐ ⭐

2 teaspoons black peppercorns
350 g (11¹/4 oz ) pork loin
1 tablespoon fish sauce
4 cloves garlic, very finely sliced
¹/4 teaspoon salt
4 spring onions, finely chopped
3 tablespoons oil
8 red Asian shallots, finely sliced
200 g (6¹/2 oz) baby corn, cut in half
    lengthways
100 g (3¹/3 oz) green beans, cut into short
    lengths
1 tablespoon water
1 teaspoon sugar
150 g (4³/4 oz) broccoli, cut into small
    florets
200 g (6¹/2 oz) bean sprouts, scraggly ends
    removed

•

1 Dry-fry the peppercorns in a hot frying pan for 2 minutes, shaking the pan constantly. Place the peppercorns in a mortar and pestle and pound until roughly ground.
2 Cut the pork into thin pieces. Place the pork, pepper, fish sauce, garlic, salt, spring onion and half the oil in a bowl. Mix well to combine and refrigerate, covered, for 20 minutes.
3 Heat a wok to extremely hot and stir-fry the pork in 3 batches for about 1¹/2 minutes, or until just golden brown, reheating the wok between batches.
4 Heat the remaining oil in the wok; add the shallots, corn and beans and stir-fry over medium heat for 1 minute. Sprinkle over the

water and sugar; cover and steam for 1 minute. Add the broccoli and steam for 1 minute more. Return the pork and any juices to the wok, add the bean sprouts and stir-fry for 30 seconds. Serve with steamed rice.

NUTRITION PER SERVE: Protein 25 g; Fat 20 g; Carbohydrate 5 g; Dietary Fibre 5 g; Cholesterol 50 mg; 1330 kJ (315 cal)

### BEEF FONDUE WITH RICE PAPER WRAPPERS AND SALAD

**Preparation time:** 20 minutes
**Total cooking time:** about 30 minutes
**Serves** 4

☆ ☆

1 red (Spanish) onion, finely sliced
3/4 cup (185 ml/6 fl oz) rice vinegar
3 red chillies, finely chopped
2 tablespoons fish sauce
2 tablespoons lime juice
6 cloves garlic, finely chopped
2 tablespoons sugar
500 g (1 lb) beef fillet
1/2 teaspoon freshly ground black pepper
4 cups (1 litre) water
410 g (13 oz) can chopped tomatoes
12 rice paper wrappers (plus a few extras to allow for breakages)
75 g (2 1/2 oz) lettuce leaves, shredded
1/2 cup (10 g/1/3 oz) fresh mint
1 small Lebanese cucumber, sliced

1 Place the onion and 3 tablespoons of the vinegar in a small bowl; mix to combine and set aside. To make a dipping sauce, place the chilli, fish sauce, lime juice, half the garlic and half the sugar in a small bowl; mix to combine and set aside for the flavours to mingle. Cut the beef into thin slices, season well with the pepper and set aside.
2 Place the water in a large pan and bring it to the boil. Add the tomato and the remaining garlic, sugar and vinegar, and simmer for 20 minutes.
3 Using a pastry brush, brush both sides of each rice paper wrapper liberally with water. Allow to stand for 2 minutes or until they become soft and pliable. Stack the wrappers on a plate. Sprinkle over a little extra water and cover the plate with plastic wrap to keep the wrappers moist until needed.
4 Place the tomato mixture in a food processor and process until smooth. Return the tomato stock to the pan and reheat to simmering point. Add the beef in batches to the simmering stock, and cook it quickly, just until it changes colour, then place it in a serving bowl.
5 To serve, place the rice paper wrappers, lettuce, mint and cucumber on a serving platter in separate piles. Each diner takes a wrapper, places a few slices of beef on it along with a little of the lettuce, cucumber, mint and the marinated onion, then rolls it up and dips it in the dipping sauce to eat.

NUTRITION PER SERVE: Protein 35 g; Fat 10 g; Carbohydrate 40 g; Dietary Fibre 5 g; Cholesterol 90 mg; 1585kJ (380 cal)

Above: Beef Fondue with Rice Paper Wrappers and Salad

4 Pile the meat into the centre of a serving plate, decorate with the lettuce, cucumber and onion, and serve immediately.

NOTE: The term 'shaking beef' comes from the French 'sauté'.

*NUTRITION PER SERVE: Protein 30 g; Fat 20 g; Carbohydrate 5 g; Dietary Fibre 2 g; Cholesterol 90 mg; 1180 kJ (280 cal)*

## PRAWN BALLS ON SKEWERS

*Preparation time:* 50 minutes
  + 1 hour refrigeration
*Total cooking time:* 20 minutes
*Makes* about 10

✹ ✹

1 kg (2 lb) raw prawns
50 g (1²⁄₃ oz) pork fat, chopped
5 cm (2 inch) piece fresh ginger, grated
4 cloves garlic, finely chopped
1 tablespoon cornflour
1 tablespoon sugar
1 teaspoon salt
12 sugar cane sticks (see note)
2 tablespoons oil

**To serve**
24 rice paper wrappers, each about 15 cm
  (6 inches) round
10 soft-leaf lettuce leaves
1 cup (90 g/3 oz) bean sprouts, scraggly
  ends removed
1 cup (20 g/²⁄₃ oz) fresh mint
¹⁄₃ cup (50 g/1²⁄₃ oz) finely chopped
  unsalted roasted peanuts
Sweet Chilli Sauce (page 168), to serve

1 Peel and devein the prawns; roughly chop the meat. Place the prawn meat on paper towels and pat dry. Place the prawn meat and pork fat in a food processor and process in short bursts until finely chopped.
2 Combine the prawn mixture, ginger, garlic, cornflour, sugar and salt in a mixing bowl. Knead the mixture very well with your fingertips for 2 minutes. This will make the mixture easier to place around the sugar cane and also create a smooth texture.
3 Using wet hands, roll about 2 tablespoons of the mixture into a rough ball shape. Wrap the ball around the middle of a sugar cane stick, leaving about 4 cm (1¹⁄₂ inches) at the end of the stick, and gently press the mixture onto the stick. Place the stick on a sheet of baking or greaseproof paper and repeat with the remaining prawn mixture and sugar cane sticks. Refrigerate

## SHAKING BEEF

*Preparation time:* 30 minutes
  + 1 hour marinating
*Total cooking time:* 15 minutes
*Serves* 4

✹ ✹

500 g (1 lb) fillet steak
4 cloves garlic, finely chopped
2 tablespoons oil
1 tablespoon fish sauce
1 teaspoon sugar
¹⁄₂ teaspoon salt
¹⁄₂ teaspoon freshly ground black pepper
1 mignonette lettuce
1 small Lebanese cucumber
¹⁄₂ red (Spanish) onion

1 Cut the steak into bite-sized cubes. Place it in a bowl with the garlic, oil, fish sauce, sugar, salt and pepper, and mix well to combine. Cover and marinate for 1 hour in the refrigerator.
2 Wash the lettuce and separate the leaves. Cut the cucumber and onion into very thin slices.
3 Heat a heavy-based wok until very hot; add the beef in 3 batches and toss, by shaking the wok and turning the meat with tongs, until brown and seared on the outside but still very pink in the centre.

*Above: Shaking Beef*

the sticks while preparing the serving accompaniments.

4 Using a pastry brush, brush both sides of each rice paper wrapper liberally with water. Allow to stand for 2 minutes or until they become soft and pliable. Stack the wrappers on a plate. Sprinkle over a little extra water and cover the plate with plastic wrap to keep the wrappers moist until needed. Arrange the lettuce leaves, bean sprouts and mint in separate piles on a serving plate.

5 Lightly brush a grill tray with the oil, and heat. Cook the prawn skewers for about 7 minutes under a moderate heat, turning them regularly until the prawn meat is cooked and golden brown. Alternatively the skewers can be cooked on a barbecue.

6 To serve, each diner takes 1 prawn skewer, removes the meat from the skewer and slices it into thin slices. They then place the prawn meat in a rice paper wrapper, top it with a few bean sprouts and a little mint, and wrap the bundle neatly in a lettuce leaf. Serve with Sweet Chilli Sauce.

NOTE: Sugar cane is available frozen or canned from Asian food stores. It is not edible as it is too fibrous, but it is sweet and it keeps the prawn meat moist and succulent. Pork fat, available from butchers, is an essential ingredient which adds moistness and flavour.

*NUTRITION PER SKEWER: Protein 10 g; Fat 10 g; Carbohydrate 5 g; Dietary Fibre 2 g; Cholesterol 100 mg; 685 kJ (165 cal)*

# FRIED CHICKEN PIECES

•

**Preparation time:** 10 minutes
**Total cooking time:** 30 minutes
**Serves** 4

★

1½ kg (3 lb) chicken pieces
2 teaspoons salt
1 teaspoon fresh ground black pepper
1 teaspoon five spice powder
oil, for deep-frying
1 tablespoon fish sauce
1 tablespoon lime juice
red chopped chilli, to serve

•

1 Place the chicken pieces in a medium pan, cover with cold water and bring to the boil. Skim any scum from the surface. Add the salt, pepper and five spice powder and simmer for 15 minutes or until the chicken is tender. Drain the chicken and pat it dry with paper towels.

2 Heat the oil in a deep pan; add the chicken pieces, about 3 at a time, and fry until golden and very crisp. Drain on paper towels.

3 Place the chicken on a serving plate, and sprinkle over the fish sauce, lime juice and chilli.

*NUTRITION PER SERVE: Protein 50 g; Fat 45 g; Carbohydrate 0 g; Dietary Fibre 0 g; Cholesterol 200 mg; 2515 kJ (600 cal)*

## VIETNAMESE INFLUENCES

*Vietnamese cuisine, while distinctive, has elements in common with both Chinese and Thai cooking. The use of chopsticks and soup bowls, and ingredients such as soy sauce, bean curd, bean sprouts and egg noodles are from China. From Thailand come fishy and sour flavours, a number of herbs and the use of sugar as a flavouring, though Vietnamese food is usually sweeter and not as hot as Thai food. Legacies of French colonial times are to be found in the making of sausages from meat and fish, and baguettes which, with a spicy filling, have became a favoured lunchtime snack.*

*Above: Fried Chicken Pieces*

# KOREA

Caught between Japan and China, Korean food is a wonderful combination of the two, mixed with its own distinctive elements. The food has a warming robustness that defies the winter ice and snow, most notably in its national dish, kim chi, a spicy pickle served at every meal. Korean meals are made up of many small, tempting dishes, flavoured with soy sauce, ginger, bean paste and toasted sesame seeds, while the centrepiece may be a steaming hotpot or thinly sliced meat, grilled at the table.

4 Combine the steak, soy sauce, garlic, spring onions and half the sesame seeds, mixing well. Marinate for 2 hours.
5 Combine the oils and brush them onto a cast-iron grill-plate, heavy-based frying pan or barbecue plate. Heat to very hot and cook the meat in 3 batches, searing each side for about 1 minute (don't overcook the steak or it will become chewy). Re-brush the grill with oil and allow it to reheat to very hot between batches. Sprinkle the extra crushed sesame seeds over the steak and serve with Kim Chi (see opposite).

*NUTRITION PER SERVE (6): Protein 20 g; Fat 15 g; Carbohydrate 1 g; Dietary Fibre 1 g; Cholesterol 40 mg; 930 kJ (220 cal)*

## EGG STRIP BUNDLES

*Preparation time*: 25 minutes
*Total cooking time*: 15 minutes
Serves 4

✲ ✲

*1 tablespoon white sesame seeds*
*10 spring onions*
*5 eggs*
*¼ teaspoon salt*
*¼ teaspoon white pepper*
*3 teaspoons oil*
*2 tablespoons rice vinegar*
*2 tablespoons Japanese soy sauce*

1 Toast the sesame seeds in a dry pan over medium heat for 3 to 4 minutes, shaking the pan gently, until the seeds are golden brown; remove from the pan at once to prevent burning.
2 Trim the white ends from the spring onions and discard; take off the outside layer and discard. Make a bunch of the green stems, then trim them all to the same size, cutting off the skinny tip. Plunge 2 spring onions at a time into a large pot of boiling water and cook for about 30 seconds or until softened; remove with tongs and place in iced water. Repeat for all the spring onions. Drain well and dry lightly on paper towels. Cut each spring onion in half lengthways using a small sharp knife.
3 Beat the eggs with the salt and pepper until they are foamy.
4 Brush a medium-sized frying pan with the oil, and place it over medium heat. Pour in half the eggs, cover and cook for 2 minutes. Run a spatula around the edge of the omelette to loosen it, then turn the omelette over and cook it for a further 2 minutes. Remove the omelette from the pan, and cook the remaining egg mixture. Trim the curved edges from the

## BARBECUED BEEF

*Preparation time*: 15 minutes
+ 30 minutes freezing
+ 2 hours marinating
*Total cooking time*: 15 minutes
Serves 4–6

✲

*500 g (1 lb) scotch fillet or sirloin steak*
*¼ cup (40 g/1⅓ oz) white sesame seeds*
*½ cup (125 ml/4 fl oz) soy sauce*
*2 cloves garlic, finely chopped*
*3 spring onions, finely chopped*
*1 tablespoon sesame oil*
*1 tablespoon oil*

1 Freeze the steak for 30 minutes.
2 Toast the sesame seeds in a dry pan over medium heat for 3 to 4 minutes, shaking the pan gently, until the seeds are golden brown; remove from the pan at once to prevent burning. Crush the seeds in a food mill or with a mortar and pestle.
3 Slice the steak into thin strips, cutting across the natural grain of the meat.

*Above: Barbecued Beef*

*Layer cabbage pieces in a bowl, sprinkling lightly with salt between each layer and on top.*

*Fit a plate snugly on top of the cabbage and weigh it down with cans or a small brick.*

*After rinsing, squeeze as much excess water from the cabbage as you can.*

omelettes to make a square shape. Cut thin strips of omelette about 7 cm (2¾ inches) long and 5 mm (1¼ inch) wide.

5 Gather together 8 strips of egg, carefully wrap one piece of spring onion 4 or so times around the middle of the bundle, tucking in the ends. Repeat with the remaining egg strips and arrange the bundles on a serving platter. Combine the vinegar, Japanese soy sauce and sesame seeds, drizzle over the bundles and serve.

*NUTRITION PER SERVE: Protein 10 g; Fat 10 g; Carbohydrate 2 g; Dietary Fibre 1 g; Cholesterol 235 mg; 640 kJ (150 cal)*

•

# KIM CHI

•

***Preparation time:*** *9 days*
***Total cooking time:*** *Nil*
***Makes*** *about 3 cups*

★

*1 large Chinese cabbage*
*½ cup (160 g/5¼ oz) sea salt*
*½ teaspoon cayenne pepper*
*5 spring onions, finely chopped*
*2 cloves garlic, finely chopped*
*5 cm (2 inch) piece fresh ginger, grated*
*3 teaspoons to 3 tablespoons chopped*
   *fresh chilli (see note)*
*1 tablespoon caster sugar*
*2½ cups (600 ml/20 fl oz) cold water*

1 Cut the cabbage in half, then into large bite-sized pieces. Place a layer of cabbage in a large bowl and sprinkle with a little salt. Continue with layers of cabbage and salt, finishing with a salt layer. Cover with a dinner plate that will fit as snugly as possible over the top of the cabbage. Weigh down the plate with cans or a small brick and leave the bowl in a cool place for 5 days.

2 Remove the weights and plate, pour off any liquid, then rinse the cabbage well under cold running water. Squeeze out any excess water and combine the cabbage with the cayenne pepper, spring onion, garlic, ginger, chilli and sugar. Mix well to combine before spooning the cabbage into a large sterilised jar. Pour the water over the top and seal with a tight-fitting lid. Refrigerate for 3 to 4 days before eating.

NOTE: Kim Chi is an accompaniment eaten with Korean main meals and with steamed rice. For an authentic flavour, use 3 tablespoons of chilli. Bottled chopped chilli can be used instead of fresh chilli.

*NUTRITION PER SERVE (6): Protein 1 g; Fat 0 g; Carbohydrate 5 g; Dietary Fibre 1 g; Cholesterol 0 mg; 90 kJ (20 cal)*

*Above: Kim Chi*

# FRIED NOODLES

•

*Preparation time:* 30 minutes
*Total cooking time:* 25 minutes
*Serves* 4

☆

¼ cup (40 g/1⅓ oz) white sesame
   seeds
2 tablespoons oil
2 teaspoons sesame oil
4 spring onions, chopped
2 cloves garlic, finely chopped
2 teaspoons finely chopped red chilli
300 g (9⅔ oz) raw prawns, peeled and
   deveined
150 g (4¾ oz) firm tofu, diced
100 g (3⅓ oz) button mushrooms, thinly
   sliced
1 red pepper (capsicum), cut into thin
   strips
2 tablespoons water
2 tablespoons soy sauce
2 teaspoons sugar
300 g (9⅔ oz) Hokkien noodles

*Above: Fried Noodles*

1 Toast the sesame seeds in a dry pan over medium heat for 3 to 4 minutes, shaking the pan gently, until the seeds are golden brown; remove the seeds from the pan at once to prevent burning. Crush the seeds in a food mill or with a mortar and pestle.

2 Combine the oils in a small bowl and pour about half into a wok or a large heavy-based frying pan. Heat over moderately high heat. Stir-fry the onion, garlic, chilli and prawns for 2 minutes; remove from pan and set aside. Stir-fry the tofu, tossing it occasionally until it is lightly golden; remove from the pan and set aside. Add the remaining oil to the pan and add the mushrooms and red pepper; stir-fry for 3 minutes or until just crisp.

3 Add the water, soy sauce, sugar and noodles to the pan. Toss gently to separate and coat the noodles in liquid. Cover and steam for 5 minutes; toss well. Add the prawns and tofu; toss for 3 minutes over medium heat. Sprinkle with crushed sesame seeds and serve.

*NUTRITION PER SERVE: Protein 20 g; Fat 20 g;
Carbohydrate 25 g; Dietary Fibre 4 g; Cholesterol 95 mg;
1530 kJ (365 cal)*

## COOKED VEGETABLE SALAD

•

*Preparation time:* 45 minutes
 + 20 minutes standing
*Total cooking time:* 15 minutes
*Serves* 4

★

1 small turnip, peeled, cut into fine strips
2 teaspoons salt
½ cup (80 g/2⅔ oz) pine nuts
2 tablespoons sesame oil
1 tablespoon oil
2 cloves garlic, finely chopped
1 large onion, thinly sliced into rings
2 sticks celery, sliced
200 g (6½ oz) button mushrooms, sliced
1 large carrot, cut into fine strips
½ red pepper (capsicum), cut into fine
 strips
4 spring onions, chopped

•

*Dressing*
¼ cup (60 ml/2 fl oz) soy sauce
1 tablespoon white vinegar
3 cm (1¼ inch) piece fresh ginger,
 very finely sliced and cut into
 fine strips
1–2 teaspoons soft brown sugar

•

1 Place the turnip on a plate lined with a paper towel. Sprinkle with salt, and then set it aside for at least 20 minutes. Rinse the turnip under cold water and pat dry with paper towels.

2 Toast the pine nuts in a dry pan over medium heat for 3 to 4 minutes, shaking the pan gently, until the seeds are golden brown; remove from the pan at once to prevent burning and set aside.
3 Heat the combined oils in a large frying pan or wok. Stir-fry the turnip, garlic and onion for 3 minutes over medium heat until lightly golden. Add the celery, mushrooms, carrot, red pepper and spring onion and toss well; cover and steam for 1 minute. Remove the vegetables from the wok and set aside to cool.
4 To make Dressing: Combine the soy sauce, vinegar, ginger and sugar in a bowl.
5 Pour the dressing over the cooled vegetables and toss. Arrange them on a serving plate and sprinkle over the pine nuts. Serve with steamed rice, if you like.

*NUTRITION PER SERVE: Protein 5 g; Fat 30 g;*
*Carbohydrate 10 g; Dietary Fibre 5 g; Cholesterol 0 mg;*
*1375 kJ (325 cal)*

•

## GRILLED FISH

•

*Preparation time:* 20 minutes
 + 15 minutes marinating
*Total cooking time:* 6 minutes
*Serves* 4

★

4 firm white fish fillets, such as deep sea
 perch or ling, (about 600 g/1¼ lb total)
3 cloves garlic, finely chopped
3 cm (1¼ inch) piece fresh ginger, grated
2 teaspoons Korean chilli powder
 (see note)
2 teaspoons sugar
1½ tablespoons Japanese soy sauce
1 tablespoon rice vinegar

•

1 Pat the fish dry with paper towels and place it in a shallow dish.
2 Combine the garlic, ginger, chilli, sugar, soy sauce and vinegar. Spoon over the fish and let marinate for 15 minutes.
3 Arrange the fillets on a foil-lined grill tray and cook under a medium heat for about 5 minutes, or until the fish is cooked through. Do not turn the fish over during the cooking. Serve with plenty of steamed rice.
NOTE: Korean chilli powder is available from Asian speciality stores or may be replaced with 1 teaspoon each of cayenne pepper and sweet paprika for each teaspoon of chilli powder.

*NUTRITION PER SERVE: Protein 30 g; Fat 3 g;*
*Carbohydrate 3 g; Dietary Fibre 0 g; Cholesterol 90 mg;*
*655 kJ (155 cal)*

KIM CHI
*Pickled vegetables are a popular year-round accompaniment to meals in Korea. Most common is pickled cabbage leaves, traditionally harvested in late autumn and prepared for use through winter. Salted cabbage leaves, alternated with layers of a strongly flavoured mixture of finely sliced vegetables, garlic, red chilli and sometimes salted shrimp, are packed into large ceramic jars. The necks are covered with plastic, fitted with a lid, then topped with a stone to stop the fermenting mixture oozing out. The jars are buried so they do not freeze in the winter. The tartly spicy relish is a source of valuable minerals and vitamin C and replaces fresh vegetables in the barren winter months.*

*Left: Cooked*
*Vegetable Salad*

# PICKLES & CHUTNEYS Just a

spoonful of these spicy relishes will lift an Indian dish, while the pickled

vegetables and ginger are traditional in Japanese and Korean meals.

## LIME OIL PICKLE

Cut 12 limes into 8 thin wedges each, sprinkle with salt and set aside. In a medium pan, dry roast 3 teaspoons mustard seeds and 2 teaspoons each ground turmeric, cumin seeds, fennel seeds and fenugreek seeds for 1–2 minutes. Remove and grind to a fine powder in a mortar and pestle. Over low heat, fry 5 chopped green chillies, 4 sliced cloves garlic and 2 teaspoons grated fresh ginger in 1 tablespoon oil until golden brown. Add 2 cups (500 ml/ 16 fl oz) oil, 1 tablespoon sugar, the lime wedges

and spices; simmer over low heat for 10 minutes, stirring occasionally. Spoon into warm sterilised jars and seal. Store in the refrigerator.

*NUTRITION PER 100 g: Protein 1 g;*
*Fat 40 g; Carbohydrate 2 g; Dietary Fibre 1 g;*
*Cholesterol 0 mg; 1565 kJ (370 cal)*

## SWEET MANGO CHUTNEY

Peel 3 large green mangoes, remove stones, chop into large slices, and sprinkle with salt. Seed 2 red chillies; chop finely. Blend ½ teaspoon garam masala with 1½ cups (330 g/10½ oz)

raw sugar and place in a large pan with 1 cup (250 ml/8 fl oz) white vinegar; bring to the boil. Reduce heat and simmer for 5 minutes. Add mango, chilli, 1 tablespoon finely grated fresh ginger and ½ cup (95 g/ 3¼ oz) finely chopped dates. Simmer for 1 hour or until the mango is tender. Pour into warm sterilised jars and seal. Store in the refrigerator.

*NUTRITION PER 100 g: Protein 1 g;*
*Fat 0 g; Carbohydrate 30 g; Dietary Fibre 1 g;*
*Cholesterol 0 mg; 520 kJ (125 cal)*

## PICKLED VEGETABLES

Put ⅓ cup (80 ml/2¾ fl oz) rice (or white) vinegar, 2 teaspoons salt and 1 teaspoon sugar into a large non-metallic bowl. Pour over 2 cups (500 ml/16 fl oz) boiling water, mix well and allow to cool until lukewarm. Cut 250 g (8 oz) cabbage into 4 cm (1½ inch) strips, 1 small Lebanese cucumber and 2 medium carrots into matchsticks and 1 medium white onion into thick rings, and add to the warm pickling mixture. Put a flat plate on top of the vegetables. Place a small bowl filled with water on top of the plate to weigh it down and submerge the vegetables. Leave for 3 days. Place into sterilised jars, seal and store in the refrigerator for up to 1 month.

*NUTRITION PER 100 g: Protein 1 g;*
*Fat 0 g; Carbohydrate 2 g; Dietary Fibre 2 g;*
*Cholesterol 0 mg; 55 kJ (15 cal)*

## EGGPLANT (AUBERGINE) PICKLE

Cut 1 kg (2 lb) slender eggplants (aubergines) lengthways and sprinkle lightly with salt. In a food processor, place 6 cloves garlic, 2.5 cm (1 inch) piece roughly chopped fresh ginger, 4 teaspoons garam masala, 1 teaspoon ground turmeric, 1 teaspoon chilli powder and 1 tablespoon oil; process until a paste forms. Rinse salt off eggplant and pat dry. Heat ⅓ cup (80 ml/2¾ fl oz) oil in a large pan and fry eggplant for 5 minutes or until golden brown. Add paste and fry for 2 minutes. Stir in 1⅔ cups (410 ml/ 13 fl oz) oil and cook, uncovered, for 10–15 minutes, stirring occasionally. Spoon into warm sterilised jars and seal. Store in a cool, dark place for up to 2 months.

*NUTRITION PER 100 g: Protein 1 g;*
*Fat 30 g; Carbohydrate 2 g; Dietary Fibre 2 g;*
*Cholesterol 0 mg; 1235 kJ (295 cal)*

## PICKLED GINGER

Cut 125 g (4 oz) fresh ginger into 2.5 cm (1 inch) pieces. Sprinkle with 2 teaspoons salt, cover and refrigerate for 1 week. With a very sharp knife, cut into paper-thin slices across the grain. Over low heat dissolve 2 tablespoons sugar in ½ cup (125 ml/4 fl oz) rice vinegar and 2 tablespoons water. Bring to the boil and simmer for 1 minute. Place ginger in sterilised jars, cover with the marinade, seal and refrigerate for 1 week before using. The ginger will turn pale pink or it can be coloured using 1 teaspoon grenadine. Store in the refrigerator for up to 3 months.

*NUTRITION PER 100 G: Protein 0 g;*
*Fat 0 g; Carbohydrate 15 g; Dietary Fibre 1 g;*
*Cholesterol 0 mg; 260 kJ (60 cal)*

*From left: Lime Oil Pickle; Sweet Mango Chutney; Pickled Vegetables; Eggplant Pickle; Pickled Ginger*

4 Add the soy sauce, sugar and spinach, and toss lightly. Cover and cook for 2 minutes or until the spinach is just soft. Return the pork to the pan, add the sesame seeds, toss well and serve immediately.

NUTRITION PER SERVE: Protein 20 g; Fat 25 g; Carbohydrate 4 g; Dietary Fibre 3 g; Cholesterol 35 mg; 1265 kJ (300 cal)

## SHREDDED POTATO PANCAKES

**Preparation time:** 25 minutes
**Total cooking time:** 30 minutes
**Makes** about 18

**Dipping Sauce**
2 teaspoons white sesame seeds
2 cloves garlic, finely chopped
2 spring onions, very finely sliced
1/4 cup (60 ml/2 fl oz) soy sauce
1 tablespoon white wine
1 tablespoon sesame oil
2 teaspoons caster sugar
1 teaspoon chopped red chilli

500 g (1 lb) potatoes
1 large onion, very finely chopped
2 eggs, beaten
2 tablespoons cornflour
1/4 cup (60 ml/2 fl oz) oil

1 To make Dipping Sauce: Toast the sesame seeds in a dry pan over medium heat for 3 to 4 minutes, shaking the pan gently, until they are golden brown; remove from the pan at once to prevent burning and cool for 5 minutes. Combine with the garlic, spring onion, soy

## PORK WITH SPINACH

**Preparation time:** 20 minutes
**Total cooking time:** 15 minutes
**Serves** 4

1 tablespoon white sesame seeds
400 g (12²/₃ oz) spinach
2 cloves garlic, very finely sliced
3 spring onions, chopped
1/2 teaspoon cayenne pepper
300 g (9²/₃ oz) pork loin, cut into thick strips
2 tablespoons oil
2 teaspoons sesame oil
2 tablespoons Japanese soy sauce
2 teaspoons sugar

1 Toast the sesame seeds in a dry pan over medium heat for 3 to 4 minutes, shaking the pan gently, until the seeds are golden brown; remove from the pan at once to prevent burning.
2 Trim the ends from the spinach, roughly chop the leaves and wash to remove all grit.
3 Combine the garlic, spring onion, cayenne pepper and pork, mixing well. Heat the oils in a heavy-based frying pan and stir-fry the pork quickly in 3 batches over very high heat until golden. Remove the meat and set aside.

*Above: Pork with Spinach; Right: Shredded Potato Pancakes*

sauce, white wine, sesame oil, sugar and chilli. Mix well and then place in a serving bowl.

2 Peel the potatoes and grate them on the coarse side of a grater. Place the potatoes in a large bowl with the onion, eggs and cornflour, and season with salt and pepper to taste. Stir very well, making certain that the cornflour is mixed in thoroughly.

3 Heat the oil in a large heavy-based frying pan (an electric frying pan is good for this). Drop about 1 rounded tablespoon of mixture onto the hot surface and spread it out gently with the back of a spoon so the pancake is about 6 cm (2½ inches) in size. Cook for 2 to 3 minutes or until golden brown. Turn it over with an egg slice and cook another 2 minutes on the other side. Cook 4 to 5 pancakes, or as many as you can fit in the pan at one time. Do not have the pan too hot or the pancakes will burn and not cook through. Keep the cooked pancakes warm in a very slow 120°C (250°F/Gas 1–2) oven while cooking the remaining pancakes.

4 Serve with the sauce as a snack or with rice and Kim Chi (page 185) as part of a meal. NOTE: Have all the ingredients ready before the potatoes are grated as they discolour quickly.

*NUTRITION PER PANCAKE: Protein 2 g; Fat 5 g; Carbohydrate 5 g; Dietary Fibre 1 g; Cholesterol 20 mg; 325 kJ (75 cal)*

•

## MEAT DUMPLING SOUP

•

***Preparation time**: 45 minutes*
***Total cooking time**: 35 minutes*
***Serves** 4–6*

☆ ☆

*1 tablespoon white sesame seeds*
*2 tablespoons oil*
*2 cloves garlic, finely chopped*
*150 g (4¾ oz) lean pork mince*
*200 g (6½ oz) lean beef mince*
*⅓ cup (80 ml/2¾ fl oz) water*
*200 g (6½ oz) Chinese cabbage, finely shredded*
*100 g (3⅓ oz) bean sprouts, chopped, scraggly ends removed*
*100 g (3⅓ oz) mushrooms, finely chopped*
*3 spring onions, finely chopped*
*150 g (4¾ oz) gow gee wrappers*

•

*Soup*
*2.5 litres beef stock*
*2 tablespoons soy sauce*
*3 cm (1¼ inch) piece fresh ginger, very finely sliced*
*4 spring onions, chopped*

1 Toast the sesame seeds in a dry pan over medium heat for 3 to 4 minutes, shaking the pan gently, until the seeds are golden brown; remove from the pan at once to prevent burning. Crush the seeds in a food mill or with a mortar and pestle.

2 Heat the oil in a pan. Cook the garlic and mince over medium heat until the meat changes colour, breaking up any lumps with a fork. Add the water, cabbage, sprouts and mushrooms. Cook, stirring occasionally, for 5 to 6 minutes or until the water evaporates and the vegetables soften. Add the spring onion, crushed seeds and season with salt and pepper to taste; set aside.

3 Work with one gow gee wrapper at a time and keep the extra wrappers covered with a damp tea towel. Place 1 teaspoon of filling on a wrapper, just off-centre, and gently smooth out the filling a little. Brush the edges of the wrapper with a little water and fold it over the filling to form a semicircle. Press the edges together to seal. Repeat with the extra wrappers and filling.

4 To make Soup: Combine the stock, soy sauce, ginger and half the spring onion in a large pan; bring to the boil and simmer for 15 minutes.

5 Drop the dumplings into the soup and cook gently for 5 minutes, or until they change colour and look plump. Garnish with the remaining spring onion and serve immediately.

*NUTRITION PER SERVE (6): Protein 15 g; Fat 15 g; Carbohydrate 10 g; Dietary Fibre 2 g; Cholesterol 35 mg; 925 kJ (220 cal)*

*MEAT DUMPLING SOUP*

*Place 1 teaspoon filling onto the gow gee wrapper, just off-centre.*

*Fold the wrapper over the filling to form a semicircle, then press the edges together.*

*Above: Meat Dumpling Soup*

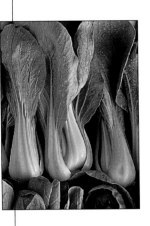

## POTATO NOODLES WITH VEGETABLES

•

*Preparation time:* 25 minutes
+ 10 minutes soaking
*Total cooking time:* 25 minutes
*Serves 4*

★

300 g (9²/₃ oz) dried potato starch noodles
  (see note)
4 tablespoons dried black fungus
¹/₄ cup (60 ml/2 fl oz) sesame oil
2 tablespoons vegetable oil
3 cloves garlic, finely chopped
4 cm (1¹/₂ inch) piece fresh ginger, grated
2 spring onions, finely chopped
2 carrots, cut into 4 cm (1¹/₂ inch)
  matchsticks
2 spring onions, extra, cut into 4 cm
  (1¹/₂ inch) pieces
500 g (1 lb) baby bok choy or 250 g
  (8 oz) spinach, roughly chopped
¹/₄ cup (60 ml/2 fl oz) Japanese soy sauce
2 tablespoons mirin
1 teaspoon sugar
2 tablespoons sesame and seaweed
  sprinkle

•

*Above: Potato Noodles
with Vegetables*

1 Cook the noodles in a large pot of boiling water for about 5 minutes, or until they are translucent. Drain and rinse thoroughly under cold running water until the noodles are cold (this will also remove any excess starch). Use scissors to roughly chop the noodles into shorter lengths—this will make them easy to eat with chopsticks. Pour hot water over the black fungus and soak for about 10 minutes.
2 Heat 1 tablespoon of the sesame oil with the vegetable oil in a large heavy-based pan or wok. Cook the garlic, ginger and spring onion for 3 minutes over medium heat, stirring regularly. Add the carrots and stir-fry for 1 minute. Add the drained cooled noodles, extra spring onion, bok choy, remaining sesame oil, soy sauce, mirin and sugar. Toss well to coat the noodles with the sauce. Cover and cook over low heat for 2 minutes. Add the fungus, then cover and cook for 2 minutes further. Scatter over the sesame and seaweed sprinkle and serve immediately.
NOTE: Potato starch noodles are also known as Korean pasta and are available from Asian food stores.

*NUTRITION PER SERVE: Protein 10 g; Fat 30 g;
Carbohydrate 20 g; Dietary Fibre 10 g; Cholesterol 0 mg;
1515 kJ (360 cal)*

## SPARERIBS WITH SESAME SEEDS

•

*Preparation time:* 30 minutes
*Total cooking time:* 1 hour
*Serves 4–6*

☆

1 tablespoon white sesame seeds
1 kg (2 lb) pork spareribs, cut into 3 cm
   (1¼ inch) pieces
2 tablespoons oil
2 spring onions, finely chopped
4 cm (1½ inch) piece fresh ginger, grated
3 cloves garlic, finely chopped
2 tablespoons caster sugar
2 tablespoons sake
1 tablespoon soy sauce
2 teaspoons sesame oil
1¼ cups (315 ml/10 fl oz) hot water
2 teaspoons cornflour

•

1 Toast the sesame seeds in a dry pan over medium heat for 3 to 4 minutes, shaking the pan gently, until the seeds are golden brown.

Remove the seeds from the pan immediately, to prevent them burning. Crush the seeds in a food mill or with a mortar and pestle.
2 Trim the pork of excess fat. Heat the oil in a heavy-based frying pan. Brown the spareribs over high heat, turning regularly, until dark golden brown. Drain any excess oil from the pan. Add half the sesame seeds, spring onion, ginger, garlic, sugar, sake, soy sauce, sesame oil and water; stir well to evenly coat the ribs. Bring to the boil over medium heat, then cover and simmer 45 to 50 minutes, stirring occasionally.
3 Combine the cornflour with a little cold water and mix to a smooth paste. Add to the pan, stirring constantly, until the mixture boils and thickens. Sprinkle with the remaining sesame seeds. Serve with steamed rice and Kim Chi (page 185), if you like.
NOTE: Make sure the rib pieces can be held easily with chopsticks—if necessary, cut them into smaller pieces.

*NUTRITION PER SERVE (6): Protein 25 g; Fat 55 g;
Carbohydrate 10 g; Dietary Fibre 1 g; Cholesterol 165 mg;
2805 kJ (665 cal)*

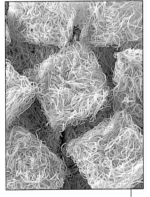

*Above: Spareribs
with Sesame Seeds*

*SPLIT PEA AND RICE PANCAKES WITH VEGETABLES*

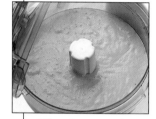

*When the peas and rice are cool, purée them in a food processor*

*Using a sharp knife, cut the vegetables into matchsticks.*

*When the base is cooked, gently lift and turn the pancakes and cook them for another 2 minutes.*

*Above: Split Pea and Rice Pancakes with Vegetables*

## SPLIT PEA AND RICE PANCAKES WITH VEGETABLES

*Preparation time:* 30 minutes
*Total cooking time:* 50 minutes
*Makes* about 15

★ ★

200 g (6¹/2 oz) dried split green peas
100 g (3¹/3 oz) short-grain rice
¹/2 cup (60 g/2 oz) plain flour
2 eggs, beaten
1 cup (250 ml/8 fl oz) water
1 medium carrot
¹/2 green pepper (capsicum)
¹/2 red pepper (capsicum)
6 spring onions
3 cm (1¹/4 inch) piece fresh ginger
2 cloves garlic
2 teaspoons soy sauce
2 tablespoons oil
1 tablespoon sesame oil
finely sliced spring onions, to garnish
sweet chilli sauce, to serve

•

1 Wash the peas and rice in a colander under cold running water until the water runs clear. Place in a pan, cover with cold water and bring to the boil. Cook for 25 minutes, adding more water if necessary, or until the peas are very soft. Cool, then purée in a food processor. Add the flour, eggs and most of the water and pulse until a smooth batter forms, adding more water until the mixture is of a thick pouring consistency. (You may need a little extra water.)
2 Cut the carrot, peppers and spring onions into fine matchsticks about 3 cm (1¹/4 inches) long. Finely grate the ginger and chop the garlic. Pour the batter into a bowl and stir in the vegetables, ginger, garlic and soy sauce.
3 Heat a heavy-based pan over medium heat and, when hot, brush with a little oil and sesame oil. Pour in 2 tablespoons of batter and cook for 3 to 5 minutes. When the base is cooked, gently run a spatula around the bottom of the pancake to release it from the pan. Turn the pancake over and cook the other side for 2 minutes. Cover the pan for about 30 seconds to ensure the pancake is cooked, then place it on a plate. Keep it warm in a very slow oven while the other pancakes cook.
4 Scatter the spring onion over the pancakes and serve with sweet chilli sauce.

NUTRITION PER PANCAKE: Protein 5 g; Fat 5 g;
Carbohydrate 15 g; Dietary Fibre 2 g; Cholesterol 25 mg;
565 kJ (135 cal)

# VERMICELLI WITH STIR-FRIED BEEF AND VEGETABLES

•

*Preparation time:* 40 minutes
 + 30 minutes soaking and marinating
*Total cooking time:* 25 minutes
*Serves* 4

✫ ✫

8 dried Chinese mushrooms
150 g (4¾ oz) dried mung bean vermicelli
1 tablespoon white sesame seeds
150 g (4¾ oz) sirloin steak, partially
 frozen
4 cloves garlic, finely chopped
2 tablespoons soy sauce
2 tablespoons water
2 teaspoons sesame oil
1–2 teaspoons fresh chopped red chilli
1 large carrot
½ medium red pepper (capsicum)
75 g (2½ oz) asparagus spears
2 tablespoons oil
6 spring onions, thinly sliced
soy sauce and sesame oil, extra, to serve

•

1 Soak the mushrooms in warm water for 20 to 30 minutes, or until soft. Soak the vermicelli for 10 minutes.
2 Toast the sesame seeds in a dry pan over medium heat for 3 to 4 minutes, shaking the pan gently, until the seeds are golden brown; remove from the pan at once to prevent burning.
3 Slice the steak into very thin strips. Combine the steak, garlic, soy sauce, water, sesame oil and chilli; marinate for 15 minutes. Cut the carrot, red pepper and asparagus into thin strips about 4 cm (1½ inches) long. Drain the vermicelli and mushrooms, reserving 2 tablespoons of the mushroom liquid. Finely slice the mushrooms and discard the hard stem. Mix the mushrooms with the meat; drain off any liquid and set aside.
4 Heat a wok or large heavy-based frying pan over medium heat until very hot. Add a little oil; stir-fry the meat and mushroom mixture in 2 batches. Sear the meat quickly, but do not overcook it; remove from pan. Add a little oil; stir-fry the vegetables for 2 minutes, then cover with a lid and steam for 1 minute, or until just softened. Add the vermicelli, reserved liquid and spring onion; toss well. Return the meat to the pan, cover and steam for 1 minute.
5 Divide the vermicelli among four serving bowls, sprinkle with the sesame seeds and serve with extra soy sauce and sesame oil.

*NUTRITION PER SERVE: Protein 15 g; Fat 15 g;*
*Carbohydrate 35 g; Dietary Fibre 3 g; Cholesterol 20 mg;*
*1440 kJ (340 cal)*

# CHICKEN STEW

•

*Preparation time:* 30 minutes
*Total cooking time:* 50 minutes
*Serves* 4

✫

1 x 1.6 kg (3½ lb) chicken
6 cloves garlic, finely chopped
4 spring onions, chopped
1 teaspoon Korean chilli powder (see note
 page 187)
2 tablespoons Japanese soy sauce
2 tablespoons sesame oil
1 tablespoon rice vinegar
2 zucchini (courgettes), thickly sliced

•

1 Using a cleaver or large cook's knife, cut the chicken into quarters, then into small eating pieces, chopping straight through the bone.
2 Combine the chicken, garlic, spring onion, chilli powder, soy sauce, sesame oil, vinegar and zucchini in a heavy-based pan or flameproof casserole dish. Toss the chicken well to coat it in the sauce. Cover and cook over a low heat for 45 to 50 minutes or until the chicken is very tender. The chicken should come off the bone easily, so it can be eaten with chopsticks.

*NUTRITION PER SERVE: Protein 35 g; Fat 15 g;*
*Carbohydrate 2 g; Dietary Fibre 2 g; Cholesterol 115 mg;*
*1280 kJ (305 cal)*

*Above: Chicken Stew*

# JAPAN

Japanese food is a treat for the eye as well as the palate. Meals are beautifully presented and only the freshest of ingredients are used. Japanese food contains few spices; instead chefs concentrate on bringing out the natural taste of the individidual ingredients in a dish. The characteristic flavour of Japanese food comes from dashi, a stock made from dried fish and dried kelp; the rice wines mirin and sake; and miso, tofu and Japanese soy sauce, all products of soy beans.

SUSHI

*Pat a quarter of the rice over about half of the nori sheet along one long side, leaving a small border.*

*Roll the nori up firmly from the bottom, enclosing the rice and other ingredients.*

*Use a sharp knife to cut the roll into 2.5 cm (1 inch) slices.*

## SUSHI

•

*Preparation time:* 45 minutes
*Total cooking time:* 10 minutes
*Makes* about 30

★ ★ ★

*1 cup (220 g/7 oz) short-grain rice*
*2 cups (500 ml/16 fl oz) water*
*2 tablespoons rice vinegar*
*1 tablespoon caster sugar*
*1 teaspoon salt*
*125 g (4 oz) very fresh salmon, tuna or*
*  trout*
*1 small Lebanese cucumber, peeled*
*1/2 small avocado, optional*
*4 sheets nori*
*wasabi, to taste*
*3 tablespoons pickled ginger (page 189)*
*Japanese soy sauce, for dipping*
*wasabi, extra*

•

1 Wash the rice under cold running water until the water runs clear; drain thoroughly. Place the rice in a pan with the water and bring to the boil. Reduce the heat and simmer for 4 to 5 minutes, or until all the water has been absorbed. Reduce the heat to very low, cover and cook for another 4 to 5 minutes. Remove the pan from the heat and leave, covered, for about 10 minutes.
2 Add the combined vinegar, sugar and salt to the rice, tossing with a wooden spoon until the rice is cool.

3 Cut the fish into thin strips. Cut the cucumber and avocado into matchsticks about 5 cm (2 inches) in length.
4 Place a sheet of nori on a piece of greaseproof paper or on a sushi mat on a flat surface, with the longest sides at the top and bottom; pat a quarter of the rice over about half of the nori sheet along one long side, leaving a 2 cm (3/4 inch) space around the sides. Spread a very small amount of wasabi down the centre of the rice. Arrange a quarter of the pieces of fish, cucumber, avocado, if using, and ginger along the top of the wasabi stripe.
5 Using the paper or mat as a guide, roll the nori up firmly from the bottom, enclosing the rice around the centred ingredients. Press the nori edges together to seal the roll. Using a sharp flat-bladed or electric knife, cut the roll into 2.5 cm (1 inch) rounds. Repeat with the remaining ingredients. Serve the Sushi on individual small plates with small bowls of soy sauce and extra wasabi to be mixed to taste to make a dipping sauce.
NOTE: Make sure the fish for Sushi is extremely fresh. Sushi can be made up to 4 hours in advance and kept, covered, in the refrigerator. Slice the rolls just before serving. Sushi mats, available from Asian food stores, make the rolling of the Sushi much easier.

*NUTRITION PER PIECE: Protein 2 g; Fat 1 g; Carbohydrate 10 g; Dietary Fibre 0 g; Cholesterol 2 mg; 235 kJ (55 cal)*

*Above: Sushi*

## STEAMED SAKE CHICKEN

•

*Preparation time:* 25 minutes
+ 30 minutes marinating
*Total cooking time:* 15–20 minutes
*Serves* 4

★

*500 g (1 lb) chicken breast fillets with
  skin on*
*1 teaspoon salt*
*1/3 cup (80 ml/2¾ fl oz) sake*
*2 tablespoons lemon juice*
*4 cm (1½ inches) fresh ginger, cut into
  very fine matchsticks*

•

*Sauce*
*2 tablespoons Japanese soy sauce*
*1 tablespoon mirin*
*1 teaspoon sesame oil*
*1 spring onion, sliced*

•

*Garnish*
*2 spring onions*
*½ small red pepper (capsicum)*

•

1 Use a fork to prick the skin on the chicken in
several places. Place chicken, skin-side up, in a
shallow dish; sprinkle with the salt. Combine
sake, lemon juice and ginger in a bowl; pour
over chicken, cover and and marinate in the
refrigerator for 30 to 40 minutes.
2 To make Sauce: Combine the soy sauce, mirin,
sesame oil and spring onion in a small bowl.
3 To make Garnish: Peel the outside layer from
the spring onions, then cut finely into diagonal
pieces. Lay the red pepper flat on a board, skin-
side down. Holding a knife in a horizontal
position, cut just under the membrane surface to
remove the top layer; discard top layer. Cut the
pepper into very fine 3 cm (1¼ inch) strips.
4 Line the base of a bamboo or metal steamer
with baking paper. Arrange the chicken, skin-
side up, in the steamer. Fill a wok or frying pan
with 2 cups water; sit the steamer in the pan.
Cover, cook over gently boiling water for 15 to
20 minutes, or until chicken is cooked.
5 Cut the chicken into bite-sized pieces (remove
skin if you prefer); arrange in the centre of a
serving plate and drizzle over the Sauce. Arrange
pepper strips in a bundle on the side of the
serving dish, scatter spring onion over chicken.
Serve warm or cold, with rice if desired.

*NUTRITION PER SERVE: Protein 25 g; Fat 15 g;
Carbohydrate 5 g; Dietary Fibre 1 g; Cholesterol 75 mg;
1085 kJ (260 cal)*

## SASHIMI

•

*Preparation time:* 30 minutes
*Total cooking time:* Nil
*Serves* 4

★ ★

*500 g (1 lb) very fresh fish, such as tuna,
  salmon, kingfish, ocean trout, snapper,
  whiting, bream or jewfish*
*1 carrot*
*1 daikon*
*Japanese soy sauce, to serve*
*wasabi, to serve*

•

1 Use a very sharp, flat-bladed knife to remove
any skin from the fish. Place the fish in the
freezer and chill it until it is just firm enough to
be cut thinly and evenly into slices, about 5 mm
(¼ inch) in width. Try to make each cut one
motion in one direction, taking care not to saw
the fish.
2 Use a zester to scrape the carrot and daikon
into long fine strips or cut them into fine
julienne strips.
3 Arrange the sashimi pieces on a platter.
Garnish with the carrot and daikon and serve
with the soy sauce and wasabi.
NOTE: It is crucial that the fish used for making
Sashimi is very fresh.

*NUTRITION PER SERVE: Protein 30 g; Fat 5 g;
Carbohydrate 2 g; Dietary Fibre 1 g; Cholesterol 55 mg;
740 kJ (175 cal)*

### SASHIMI AND SUSHI
*The fortuitous discovery
that fresh fish fillets stored
on rice sprinkled with rice
vinegar not only remained
fresh but took on a
pleasing flavour is said to
have been made in the
huts of humble Japanese
fishermen. Today specialist
sushi bars are devoted
to the dish; sashimi,
accompanied by sake, is
traditionally served as first
course, and an array of
sushi with various
toppings follow. The chefs
who slice the fish and
prepare the delicacies are
highly skilled masters of
their art.*

*Above: Sashimi*

## SUNOMONO
### (PRAWN AND CUCUMBER SALAD)

•

*Preparation time:* 20 minutes
+ 1 hour marinating
*Total cooking time:* 5 minutes
*Serves* 4

✮✮

1 Lebanese cucumber
375 g (12 oz) raw prawns
¼ cup (60 ml/2 fl oz) rice vinegar
1 tablespoon caster sugar
1 tablespoon Japanese soy sauce
1 teaspoon finely grated fresh ginger
1 tablespoon Japanese white sesame seeds

•

1 Peel the cucumber with a vegetable peeler, halve it lengthways and remove any seeds with a teaspoon. Cut the cucumber into thin slices, sprinkle thoroughly with salt and set aside for 5 minutes. Rinse to remove salt, and pat dry with paper towels.

2 Place the prawns in a pan of lightly salted boiling water and simmer for 2 minutes, or until just cooked. Drain the prawns and plunge them into cold water. When the prawns are cool, peel and devein them, leaving the tails intact.

3 Place the vinegar, sugar, soy sauce and ginger in a large bowl and stir until the sugar dissolves. Add the prawns and cucumber, cover and marinate in the refrigerator for 1 hour.

4 Toast the sesame seeds in a dry pan over medium heat for 3 to 4 minutes, shaking the pan gently, until the seeds are golden brown; remove the seeds from the pan at once to prevent burning.

5 Drain the prawns and cucumber from the marinade. Arrange on serving plates, sprinkle with the sesame seeds and serve.

*NUTRITION PER SERVE: Protein 15 g; Fat 5 g; Carbohydrate 5 g; Dietary Fibre 1 g; Cholesterol 180 mg; 525 kJ (125 cal)*

*Above: Sunomono*

## RICE BALLS

•

**Preparation time:** 40 minutes
**Total cooking time:** 20 minutes
**Serves** 4–6

⋆ ⋆

1¼ cups (275 g/9 oz) short-grain rice
1⅓ cups (350 ml/11 fl oz) water
2 teaspoons black sesame seeds
50 g (1⅔ oz) smoked salmon, chopped
2 tablespoons finely chopped pickled
 ginger (page 189)
2 spring onions, finely chopped

•

1 Wash the rice thoroughly in a sieve under
running water until the water runs clear. Place
the rice in a heavy-based pan with the water and
bring it to the boil. Reduce the heat to very low,
cover and cook for 15 minutes. Remove the pan
from heat and stand, with the lid on, for
20 minutes.
2 Dry-roast the sesame seeds in a frying pan
over low heat, constantly shaking the pan, for
1 to 2 minutes, or until the seeds begin to pop.
3 Combine the salmon, ginger and spring onion
in a small bowl. Using wet hands, form ⅓ cup
(60 g/2 oz) rice into a ball; push 2 teaspoons of
the salmon mixture into the centre of the rice
and re-form the ball around it. Repeat with the
remaining rice and salmon, keeping your hands
wet to prevent the rice from becoming sticky.
4 Arrange the balls on a serving platter and
sprinkle with the sesame seeds.

NUTRITION PER SERVE (6): Protein 5 g; Fat 2 g;
Carbohydrate 40 g; Dietary Fibre 1 g; Cholesterol 5 mg;
770 kJ (185 cal)

## TOFU MISO SOUP

•

**Preparation time:** 15 minutes
**Total cooking time:** 7 minutes
**Serves** 4

⋆

250 g (8 oz) firm tofu
1 spring onion
4 cups (1 litre) water
½ cup (80 g/2⅔ oz) dashi granules
100 g (3⅓ oz) miso
1 tablespoon mirin

•

1 Use a sharp knife to cut the tofu into 1 cm
(½ inch) cubes. Slice the spring onion
diagonally into 1 cm (½ inch) lengths.
2 Using a wooden spoon, combine the water and
dashi granules in a small pan, then bring the
mixture to the boil.
3 Reduce the heat to medium, add the miso and
mirin and stir to combine, being careful the
mixture does not boil (overheating will result in
the loss of miso flavour). Add the tofu cubes to
the hot stock and heat, without boiling, over
medium heat for 5 minutes, until the tofu is
warmed through. Serve in individual soup
bowls, garnished with the spring onion.

NUTRITION PER SERVE: Protein 5 g; Fat 5 g;
Carbohydrate 1 g; Dietary Fibre 0 g; Cholesterol 0 mg;
260 kJ (60 cal)

MAKING DASHI
STOCK FROM
GRANULES
Dashi, Japanese soup
stock, can be made from
granules (dashi-no-moto)
which are dissolved in hot
water. The strength of the
granules varies according
to the brand, so follow the
instructions. However,
as a general rule use
½ cup (80 g/2⅔ oz) of
granules to 1 litre of
water. This can be
strengthened or diluted
to taste.

Above: Tofu
Miso Soup
Left: Rice Balls

# TEPPAN YAKI
## (GRILLED STEAK AND VEGETABLES)

•

*Preparation time*: 45 minutes
*Total cooking time*: 25 minutes
*Serves* 4

★ ★

350 g (11¼ oz) scotch fillet, partially
    frozen
4 small slender eggplants (aubergines)
100 g (3⅓ oz) fresh shiitake mushrooms
100 g (3⅓ oz) small green beans
6 baby yellow or green squash
1 red or green pepper (capsicum), seeded
6 spring onions, outside layer removed
200 g (6½ oz) can bamboo shoots,
    drained
¼ cup (60 ml/2 fl oz) oil
Soy and Ginger Sauce (page 168) or
    Sesame Seed Sauce (page 168), to serve

•

1 Slice the steak into very thin pieces. Place the meat slices in a single layer on a large serving platter and season thoroughly with plenty of salt and freshly ground pepper. Set aside.

2 Trim the ends from the eggplants and cut the flesh into long, very thin diagonal slices. Trim any hard stems from the mushrooms. Top and tail the beans. If the beans are longer than about 7 cm (2¾ inches), cut them in half. Quarter, halve or leave the squash whole, depending on the size. Cut the pepper into thin strips and slice the spring onions into lengths about 7 cm (2¾ inches) long, discarding the tops. Arrange all the vegetables in separate bundles on a plate.

3 When the diners are seated, heat an electric grill or electric frying pan until very hot, and then lightly brush it with the oil. Quickly fry about a quarter of the meat, searing on both sides, and then push it over to the edge of the pan. Add about a quarter of the vegetables and quickly stir-fry, adding a little more oil as needed. Serve a small portion of the meat and vegetables to the diners, who dip the food into a sauce of their choice. Repeat the process with the remaining meat and vegetables, cooking in batches as extra helpings are required. Serve with steamed rice.

NUTRITION PER SERVE: Protein 25 g; Fat 20 g; Carbohydrate 20 g; Dietary Fibre 10 g; Cholesterol 60 mg; 1440 kJ (345 cal)

## TEPPAN YAKI

*In restaurants specialising in teppan yaki, or Japanese barbecue-style cooking, diners sit around a bench which has a hotplate at its centre. As with all Japanese food, presentation plays a major role in the enjoyment of the meal. Food is skilfully sliced, seasoned and swiftly cooked in front of the diners, then served to each of them on an individual griddle. At home an electric frying pan can be used.*

*Right: Teppan Yaki*

## SHABU-SHABU
### (BRAISED BEEF AND VEGETABLE STEAMBOAT)

•

*Preparation time:* 50 minutes +
    30 minutes refrigeration
*Total cooking time:* 30 minutes
*Serves* 4

★ ★

*750 g (1½ lb) scotch fillet, partially
    frozen*
*15 spring onions*
*3 carrots*
*400 g (12²/₃ oz) button mushrooms*
*½ Chinese cabbage*
*150 g (4¾ oz) firm tofu*
*Sesame Seed Sauce (page 168) or ready-
    made shabu-shabu sauce, to serve*
*1 cup (220 g/7 oz) short-grain rice,
    cooked*
*8 cups (2 litres) chicken stock*

•

1 Cut the steak into very thin slices and set aside. Cut the firm section of the spring onions into 4 cm (1½ inch) lengths and discard the dark green tops. Slice the carrots very thinly. Slice the the mushrooms. Chop the cabbage into bite-sized pieces, discarding any tough parts. Cut the tofu into bite-sized cubes.

2 Arrange the prepared vegetables, tofu and meat in separate piles on a serving platter; cover with plastic wrap and refrigerate until about 30 minutes before cooking time.
3 Set the table with individual place settings, each with a serving bowl, a bowl of Sesame Seed Sauce, a bowl of rice, chopsticks, soup spoons (if desired) and napkins. Position the serving platter and cooking vessel (see note) so they are within easy reach of each diner.
4 When all the diners are seated, pour the stock into the cooking vessel, cover and bring to a simmer. Each diner then picks up an ingredient or two with their chopsticks, and places it in the simmering stock for about a minute, or until just cooked. (Do not overcook—the vegetables should be just tender and the steak still pink in the centre.) The food is then dipped into the Sesame Seed Sauce and eaten with the rice. The remaining stock can be served as soup at the end of the meal.
NOTE: Dashi, made from dashi granules, can be substituted for the chicken stock.
  Use an electric wok, a frying pan or casserole on a burner, or a steamboat to cook this dish.

*NUTRITION PER SERVE: Protein 50 g; Fat 15 g;
Carbohydrate 25 g; Dietary Fibre 5 g; Cholesterol 130 mg;
1775 kJ (425 cal)*

*Above: Shabu-Shabu*

## SAVOURY EGG CUSTARD

•

*Preparation time:* 20 minutes
*Total cooking time:* 20 minutes
*Serves* 6

★

200 g (6½ oz) chicken breast fillets, cut
    into bite-sized pieces
2 teaspoons sake
2 teaspoons Japanese soy sauce
2 leeks, sliced
1 small carrot, sliced
200 g (6½ oz) spinach, chopped

•

*Custard*
4 cups (1 litre) boiling water
½ cup (80 g/2⅔ oz) dashi granules
2 tablespoons Japanese soy sauce
6 eggs

•

1 Place the chicken pieces into 6 heatproof
bowls. Combine the sake and soy sauce, and
pour the mixture over the chicken.
2 Divide the vegetables between the 6 bowls.
3 To make Custard: Combine the water and
dashi granules in a heatproof bowl and stir to
dissolve; cool completely. Combine the dashi,
soy sauce and eggs, and strain equal amounts
into the 6 bowls.
4 Cover the bowls with foil, place them in a
steamer, and cook on high for 20 to 30 minutes.
Test the custard by inserting a fine skewer into
the centre; it is cooked when the skewer comes
out with no moisture clinging to it. Serve
immediately.

*NUTRITION PER SERVE: Protein 15 g; Fat 5 g;
Carbohydrate 2 g; Dietary Fibre 2 g; Cholesterol 240 mg;
595 kJ (140 cal)*

## PRAWN AND VEGETABLE TEMPURA

•

*Preparation time:* 40 minutes
*Total cooking time:* 15 minutes
*Serves* 4

★ ★

20 large raw prawns
plain or tempura flour, for coating
1¾ cups (215 g/6¾ oz) tempura flour
1¾ cups (440 ml/14 fl oz) iced water
2 egg yolks
oil, for deep frying
1 large zucchini (courgette), cut into
    strips
1 red pepper (capsicum), cut into strips
1 onion, cut into rings
Japanese soy sauce, to serve

•

1 Peel and devein the prawns, leaving the tails
intact. Cut 4 incisions in the under-section of
each prawn and straighten them out.
2 Coat the prawns lightly with flour, leaving the
tail uncoated, and shake off the excess. In a
bowl, gently mix the tempura flour, water and
egg yolks and use at once (the batter will be
lumpy—don't overmix).
3 Heat the oil in a deep pan or wok to
moderately hot. Working with a few at a time,
dip each prawn into the batter, still leaving the
tail uncoated. Fry briefly in the hot oil until
lightly golden; remove from the pan and drain
well on paper towels. Repeat this process with
the vegetable pieces, doing about 2 to 3 pieces at
a time. Serve immediately with soy sauce. Add
strips of fresh ginger to the soy sauce if you like.
NOTE: Tempura flour is available from
speciality Asian shops, and makes the lightest
tempura batter. Plain flour can be used but the
batter will be slightly heavier.

*NUTRITION PER SERVE: Protein 30 g; Fat 25 g;
Carbohydrate 50 g; Dietary Fibre 5 g; Cholesterol 231 mg;
2190 kJ (520 cal)*

TEMPURA
*There are several methods
of Japanese-style deep-
frying, the best known of
which is tempura—batter
coated deep-frying. There
are tempura bars and
restaurants throughout
Japan where these dishes
are cooked to perfection.
The oil should be very
light (polyunsaturated
vegetable oil is best) and
perfectly clean. A few
drops of sesame oil can be
added for flavour.*

*Opposite page: Prawn
and Vegetable
Tempura*

toss until the chicken pieces are evenly coated with the marinade. Set aside for 15 minutes, then drain off any excess marinade.

3 Mix the nori with the cornflour. Using your fingertips, lightly coat each piece of chicken in the cornflour mixture.

4 Heat the oil in a pan until moderately hot; add the chicken, 6 to 7 pieces at a time, and fry until golden, turning regularly. Drain on paper towels. Serve with steamed rice, pickled ginger and sliced cucumber. Garnish with extra strips of nori, if desired.

*NUTRITION PER SERVE: Protein 25 g; Fat 20 g; Carbohydrate 10 g; Dietary Fibre 0 g; Cholesterol 50 mg; 1370 kJ (325 cal)*

## MUSHROOMS IN SPRING ONION DRESSING

*Preparation time:* 15 minutes
+ 15 minutes marinating
*Total cooking time:* Nil
*Serves* 4

☆

2 cm (¾ inch) piece fresh ginger
500 g (1 lb) button mushrooms
6 spring onions
¼ cup (60 ml/2 fl oz) Japanese rice
    vinegar
¼ cup (60 ml/2 fl oz) Japanese soy sauce
2 tablespoons mirin

1 Cut the ginger into very thin slices, place into a bowl and cover with iced water. Set aside.
2 Wipe the mushrooms with damp paper towels and trim the stalks. Slice the spring onions finely, including most of the green tops. Combine the mushrooms and spring onion in a bowl.
3 Place the vinegar, soy sauce, mirin and salt to taste in a small bowl and mix to combine. Pour the marinade over the mushroom mixture, toss to coat and leave to marinate for 15 minutes.
4 Remove the mushrooms and spring onion from the marinade with a slotted spoon, draining excess liquid. Arrange the mushroom mixture on a platter. Drain the ginger and scatter the slices over the mushrooms.

*NUTRITION PER SERVE: Protein 5 g; Fat 0 g; Carbohydrate 5 g; Dietary Fibre 5 g; Cholesterol 0 mg; 165 kJ (40 cal)*

## DEEP-FRIED CHICKEN WITH SEAWEED

*Preparation time:* 25 minutes
+ 15 minutes marinating
*Total cooking time:* 20 minutes
*Serves* 4

☆

400 g (12⅔ oz) chicken breast fillets
¼ cup (60 ml/2 fl oz) Japanese soy sauce
¼ cup (60 ml/2 fl oz) mirin
4 cm (1½ inch) piece fresh ginger, very
    finely grated
1 sheet nori, finely chopped or crumbled
    into very small pieces
⅓ cup (40 g/1⅓ oz) cornflour
oil, for deep-frying
pickled ginger (page 189) and thin
    cucumber slices, to serve

1 Carefully trim any sinew from the chicken. Cut the chicken into bite-sized pieces and discard any thin ends so that the pieces will be even in size. Place the chicken pieces in a bowl.
2 Combine the soy sauce, mirin and ginger in a small jug and pour the mixture over the chicken;

*Above: Deep-fried Chicken with Seaweed*

# SUKIYAKI
## (BEEF AND VEGETABLE HOTPOT)

•

*Preparation time:* 1 hour
*Total cooking time:* 15 minutes
*Serves* 6

★★★

500 g (1 lb) scotch fillet, partially frozen
3 small white onions
5 spring onions
1 large carrot
400 g (12²/₃ oz) small button mushrooms
½ small Chinese cabbage
2 cups (180 g/5¾ oz) bean sprouts
225 g (7¼ oz) can bamboo shoots,
    drained
100 g (3¹/₃ oz) firm tofu
100 g (3¹/₃ oz) fresh shirataki noodles
6 eggs
¼ cup (60 ml/2 fl oz) oil

•

*Sauce*
¹/₃ cup (80 ml/2¾ fl oz) Japanese soy
    sauce
¼ cup (60 ml/2 fl oz) beef stock
¼ cup (60 ml/2 fl oz) sake
¼ cup (60 ml/2 fl oz) mirin
2 tablespoons caster sugar

•

1 Using an extremely sharp knife, slice the partially frozen fillet as thinly as possible, then arrange the slices on a large tray or platter, leaving room for the vegetables, tofu and noodles. Cover the fillet slices and refrigerate the platter while preparing the remaining ingredients.
2 Cut each of the white onions into 6 wedges. Slice the firm section of the spring onions into 4 cm (1½ inch) lengths and discard the dark green tops. Cut the carrot into 4 cm (1½ inch) long thin matchsticks. Trim the stalks and cut the mushrooms in half. Cut the cabbage into bite-sized pieces, discarding any tough parts. Trim the scraggly ends from the bean sprouts. Trim the bamboo shoots into evenly sized pieces, similar to the other vegetables. Cut the tofu into 2 cm (¾ inch) cubes. Arrange the vegetables and tofu on the platter with the meat.
3 Cook the noodles for about 3 minutes or until just soft; do not overcook them or they will fall apart. Drain thoroughly and, if you like, use scissors to cut the cooked noodles into shorter lengths that can be picked up easily with chopsticks. Arrange the noodles on the platter with the meat and vegetables.

4 To make Sauce: Place the soy sauce, beef stock, sake, mirin and sugar in a small bowl and mix until the sugar dissolves.
5 Set the table with individual place settings, each with a serving bowl, a bowl of rice (see note), a bowl to break an egg into, chopsticks and napkins. Place an electric frying pan on the table so it is within easy reach of each diner.
6 When all the diners are seated, heat the frying pan and brush it lightly with oil. When the pan is very hot, take about a third of each of the vegetables and cook them quickly for about 2 minutes, tossing constantly. Push the vegetables to the side of the pan. Add about a third of the meat in one layer and sear the slices for 30 seconds on each side, taking care not to overcook them. Drizzle a little of the Sauce over the meat. Add some of the noodles and tofu to the pan and gently toss with the other ingredients.
7 Each diner breaks an egg into a bowl and whisks it with chopsticks. Mouthfuls of Sukiyaki are then selected from the hot pan, dipped into the egg and eaten. When the diners are ready for more, the pan is reheated and the cooking process repeated.
NOTE: Some people prefer to have Sukiyaki on rice but it is not traditionally served with rice.

*NUTRITION PER SERVE: Protein 35 g; Fat 20 g; Carbohydrate 25 g; Dietary Fibre 5 g; Cholesterol 280 mg; 1865 kJ (445 cal)*

## SUKIYAKI

*Buddhist prohibitions against eating flesh meant that red meat was not part of the Japanese diet until the mid-nineteenth century when, weakened by foreign influence, the taboo was abandoned. The beef dish sukiyaki dates from this time. A feature of the dish is the thin, translucent, jelly-like noodles (called shirataki noodles) which are made from the starchy root of a plant known in Japan as devil's tongue. Shirataki noodles are also available dried.*

*Below: Sukiyaki*

## STEAK IN ROASTED SESAME SEED MARINADE

•

*Preparation time:* 25 minutes
+ 30 minutes marinating
*Total cooking time:* 12 minutes
*Serves 4*

★★

2 tablespoons white Japanese sesame seeds
1 clove garlic, crushed
3 cm (1¼ inch) piece fresh ginger, grated
2 tablespoons Japanese soy sauce
1 tablespoon sake
1 teaspoon caster sugar
500 g (1 lb) scotch fillet, cut into 4 steaks
3 spring onions, to garnish
1 tablespoon oil

•

*Dipping Sauce*
4 cm (1½ inch) piece fresh ginger
½ teaspoon shichimi togarashi
½ cup (125 ml/4 fl oz) Japanese soy sauce
2 teaspoons dashi granules
2 tablespoons water

•

1 Roast the sesame seeds in a dry frying pan over moderately low heat for 2 minutes, shaking the pan constantly, until the seeds begin to pop. Crush the roasted seeds in a mortar and pestle.
2 Place the crushed sesame seeds, garlic, ginger, soy sauce, sake and sugar in a bowl and whisk until the sugar has dissolved. Place the steaks in a shallow dish; spoon the marinade over the top and marinate for 30 minutes.
3 To make Dipping Sauce: Cut the ginger lengthways into very fine strips about 4 cm (1½ inches) long. Place the ginger, shichimi togarashi, soy sauce, dashi and water in a small bowl and whisk lightly until well combined.

4 Cut the spring onions lengthways into very fine strips about 4 cm (1½ inches) long. Place the strips in a bowl of iced water and leave until they are crisp and curled; drain.
5 Lightly brush the oil over the steaks and then grill or fry them for about 4 to 6 minutes on each side—don't overcook or the steaks will become very tough. Set the steaks aside for 5 minutes before cutting them into diagonal slices. Arrange the slices on serving plates and then drizzle over a little of the Dipping Sauce. Garnish with the spring onion curls and serve with steamed rice and the remaining Dipping Sauce.

NUTRITION PER SERVE WITH SAUCE: Protein 30 g; Fat 20 g; Carbohydrate 5 g; Dietary Fibre 2 g; Cholesterol 85 mg; 1265 kJ (300 cal)

•

## TONKATSU
### (CRUMBED FRIED PORK)

•

*Preparation time:* 35 minutes + 2 hours refrigeration
*Total cooking time:* 12 minutes
*Serves 4*

★★

500 g (1 lb) pork loin
½ cup (60 g/2 oz) plain flour
6 egg yolks, beaten with 2 tablespoons water
2 cups (120 g/4 oz) Japanese dried breadcrumbs
2 spring onions
pickled ginger (page 189) and pickled daikon
1 sheet nori
oil, for shallow frying
2 cups (90 g/3 oz) finely shredded Chinese cabbage
1 cup (250 ml/8 fl oz) Tonkatsu sauce

1 Trim the pork of any sinew and cut it into 8 thin slices. Sprinkle the slices with a good pinch of salt and pepper and lightly coat with flour. Shake off excess flour.
2 Dip each steak into the egg mixture and then into the breadcrumbs; press the crumbs on with your fingertips to ensure an even coating. Place the steaks in a single layer on a plate and refrigerate, uncovered, for at least 2 hours.
3 Meanwhile prepare the garnishes. Peel away the outside layers of the spring onions, slice the stems very finely and place them in a bowl of cold water until serving time. Slice the ginger and daikon. Using a sharp knife, shred the nori very finely and then break it into strips about 4 cm (1½ inches) long.

*Below: Steak in Roasted Sesame Seed Marinade*

1 Add the noodles to a large pan of boiling water. When the water returns to the boil, pour in 1 cup (250 ml/8 fl oz) cold water. Bring the water back to the boil and cook the noodles for about 2 to 3 minutes or until just tender—take care not to overcook them. Drain the noodles in a colander and then cool them under cold running water. Drain thoroughly and set aside.

2 Cut the ginger and carrot into fine matchsticks about 4 cm (1½ inches) long. Slice the spring onions very finely. Bring a small pan of water to the boil, then add the ginger, carrot and spring onion. Blanch for about 30 seconds, drain and place in a bowl of iced water to cool. Drain again when the vegetables are cool.

3 To make Dipping Sauce: Combine the water, dashi granules, soy sauce, mirin and a good pinch each of salt and pepper in a small pan. Bring the sauce to the boil, then cool completely. When ready to serve, pour the sauce into 4 small, wide dipping bowls.

4 Gently toss the cooled noodles and vegetables to combine. Arrange in 4 individual serving bowls, and sit the serving bowls onto plates.

5 Toast the nori by holding it over low heat and moving it back and forward for about 15 seconds. Cut it into thin strips with scissors, and scatter the strips over the noodles. Place a little pickled ginger and shredded daikon on the side of each plate. Serve the noodles with the Dipping Sauce. The noodles should be dipped into the sauce before being eaten.

*NUTRITION PER SERVE: Protein 10 g; Fat 2 g;
Carbohydrate 55 g; Dietary Fibre 1 g; Cholesterol 0 mg;
1185 kJ (280 cal)*

4 Heat 1 cm (½ inch) oil in a heavy-based frying pan; add the steaks 2 or 3 at a time and cook over medium heat until golden brown on both sides, then drain on paper towels.

5 Carefully slice each steak into 1 cm (½ inch) strips and then reassemble the strips into the original steak shape. Top each of the steaks with a small bundle of the nori strips. Serve with the drained spring onion, ginger, daikon, cabbage, Tonkatsu sauce and steamed rice.

NOTE: Tonkatsu is barbecue-style sauce made with tomatoes, Japanese soy sauce, Worcestershire sauce and mustard.

*NUTRITION PER SERVE: Protein 35 g; Fat 20 g;
Carbohydrate 35 g; Dietary Fibre 2 g; Cholesterol 335 mg;
1860 kJ (440 cal)*

## CHILLED SOBA NOODLES

*Preparation time:* 25 minutes
*Total cooking time:* 15 minutes
Serves 4

✩

*250 g (8 oz) dried soba (buckwheat)
  noodles
4 cm (1½ inch) piece fresh ginger
1 medium carrot
4 spring onions, outside layer removed*

*Dipping Sauce*
*1½ cups (375 ml/12 fl oz) water
3 tablespoons dashi granules
½ cup (125 ml/4 fl oz) Japanese soy sauce
⅓ cup (80 ml/2¾ fl oz) mirin*

*Garnishes*
*1 sheet nori
pickled ginger (page 189)
thinly sliced pickled daikon*

*Above: Tonkatsu
Below: Chilled
Soba Noodles*

# TEAS It was China which first introduced tea to the rest of the world. Whether it be black or green, plain or highly spiced, tea is an important part of the meal in most Asian countries.

## BLACK TEA

Mainly produced in India, China and Sri Lanka, black tea leaves undergo fermentation which gives them their characteristic full, aromatic flavour and rich colour and strength.

● ASSAM: Grown in north-east India, this classic tea has a strong, full-flavoured malty taste and is ideal for drinking with milk.

● DARJEELING: Grown in the foothills of the Himalayas, this prized tea has a subtle 'muscatel' flavour and a light reddish-brown colour.

● CEYLON: Produced in the high-altitude areas of Sri Lanka and widely known for its excellent quality, this tea has a strong rich flavour.

● LAPSANG SOUCHONG: A famous tea from China and Taiwan, this is rich and full-bodied, with a distinctive smoky, tarry taste due to the unique smoking process it undergoes. Well suited for lemon tea.

● YUNNAN: Often used in blended teas, this Chinese tea produces a sweet light golden liquid, considered to have health-giving properties.

## OOLONG TEA

Semi-fermented oolong teas are stronger than green teas and milder than black. They are often scented with jasmine, gardenia or rose petals and are then known as pouchong. Oolong tea originated in China, but the highest grade is now produced in Taiwan.

● FORMOSA: These Taiwanese leaves produce a dark tea with a natural fruity flavour.

## GREEN TEA

A favourite in the East, green tea is served with meals in many Asian restaurants and is believed to aid digestion. It is always made weak: only 1 teaspoon of tea for the whole pot. Sugar and milk are never added.

● GUNPOWDER: A high quality, small Chinese leaf which yields a very pale green, fruity and slightly bitter tea.

● JASMINE: This Chinese green tea is scented with jasmine petals and traditionally served with yum cha.

● SENCHA: A Japanese tea with a delicate, light flavour and colour.

● GENMAI-CHA: This blend of rolled Japanese green tea leaves and toasted, puffed rice is a nutty-flavoured tea.

## BLENDED TEA

Blended teas are a combination of 15–20 leaves from different areas. They were introduced to provide tea that was unaffected by fluctuations in price and availability.

● ENGLISH BREAKFAST: A mix of a number of strong Indian leaves and Ceylon tea which produces a full-flavoured, fragrant tea.

● IRISH BREAKFAST: A strong, fragrant tea which is a combination of Assam and Ceylon leaves.

● RUSSIAN CARAVAN: Originally transported from India to Russia by camels, this tea is a blend of Keemun, Assam and Chinese green leaves.

● EARL GREY: Scented with oil of bergamot, this blend of Keemun and Darjeeling leaves produces a pale tea with a citrus flavour.

## BREWING THE PERFECT CUP OF TEA

1 Bring cold water to the boil rapidly to prevent the water being de-aerated.

2 Use a china or glazed earthenware teapot that will retain the heat, and warm it by swirling a little hot water around the sides and emptying it out.

3 Measure the tea carefully: 1 heaped teaspoon leaves for each cup and 1 for the pot.

4 Follow the old adage 'bring your teapot to the kettle, not the kettle to the teapot' to ensure the water is still on the boil when it is poured onto the tea leaves. This will agitate the leaves and release the full flavour of the tea.

5 Put the lid on the pot and leave for 5 minutes to infuse the leaves.

6 If using, add milk to the cup before the tea. The scalding tea will slightly cook the milk and blend the flavours.

7 Stir the pot and pour tea through a strainer into each cup. Add sugar to taste and a slice of lemon if desired.

*Above: The selection of teas from Asia is colourful and fragrant, vast and varied.*

## UDON NOODLE SOUP

•

*Preparation time*: 20 minutes
*Total cooking time*: 16 minutes
*Serves* 4

★

400 g (12²/₃ oz) dried udon noodles
4 cups (1 litre) water
3 teaspoons dashi granules
2 medium leeks (white and pale green
  parts), well washed and cut into very
  thin slices
200 g (6¹/₂ oz) pork loin, cut into thin
  strips
¹/₂ cup (125 ml/4 fl oz) Japanese soy sauce
2 tablespoons mirin
4 spring onions, very finely chopped
shimichi togarashi, to serve

•

1  Cook the noodles in a large pan of rapidly
boiling water for 5 minutes, or until tender.
Drain and cover to keep warm.
2  Combine the water and dashi in a large pan
and bring to the boil. Add the leeks, reduce heat
and simmer for 5 minutes. Add the pork, soy
sauce, mirin and spring onion; simmer for
2 minutes or until the pork is cooked.

*Above: Udon
Noodle Soup*

3  Divide the noodles among 4 serving bowls
and ladle the soup over the top. Garnish with the
spring onion and sprinkle the shimichi togarashi
over the top.

*NUTRITION PER SERVE: Protein 25 g; Fat 5 g;
Carbohydrate 75 g; Dietary Fibre 10 g; Cholesterol 26 mg;
1880 kJ (445 cal)*

•

## EGGS SCRAMBLED
## WITH PRAWNS AND PEAS

•

*Preparation time*: 10 minutes
  + 15 minutes soaking
*Total cooking time*: 7 minutes
*Serves* 4

★

¹/₄ cup (10 g/¹/₃ oz) dried shiitake
  mushrooms
250 g (8 oz) raw prawns
4 eggs
1 teaspoon dashi granules
2 teaspoons Japanese soy sauce
2 teaspoons sake
2 teaspoons oil
100 g (3¹/₃ oz) frozen peas
3 spring onions, finely chopped

1 Soak the mushrooms in hot water for
15 minutes; drain and slice. Peel and devein the
prawns and pat dry with paper towels.
2 Place the eggs, dashi, soy sauce and sake in a
bowl and beat until well combined.
3 Heat the oil in a frying pan; add the prawns
and stir-fry over medium heat for 2 minutes or
until just cooked. Add the peas, cover and steam
for 2 minutes.
4 Pour in the egg mixture; cook over low heat
until lightly set, stirring gently occasionally so
the egg sets in large curds. Sprinkle over the
spring onions and serve immediately with
steamed rice.

*NUTRITION PER SERVE: Protein 15 g; Fat 10 g;
Carbohydrate 5 g; Dietary Fibre 2 g; Cholesterol 285 mg;
635 kJ (150 cal)*

•

# CHICKEN DOMBURI
•

**Preparation time:** 35 minutes
**Total cooking time:** 30 minutes
**Serves** 4

★ ★

*2 cups (440 g/14 oz) short-grain rice*
*2¹/₂ cups (600 ml/20 fl oz) water*
*2 tablespoons oil*
*200 g (6¹/₂ oz) chicken breast fillet, cut
 into thin strips*
*2 medium onions, thinly sliced*
*4 tablespoons water, extra*
*4 tablespoons Japanese soy sauce*
*2 tablespoons mirin*
*1 teaspoon dashi granules*
*5 eggs, lightly beaten*
*2 sheets nori*
*2 spring onions, sliced*

•

1 Wash the rice in a colander under cold
running water until the water runs clear. Place
the rice in a medium heavy-based pan, add the
water and bring to the boil over high heat. Cover
the pan with a tight-fitting lid, reduce the heat to
as low as possible (otherwise the rice in the
bottom of the pan will burn) and cook for
15 minutes. Turn heat to very high for
15 to 20 seconds and remove the pan from heat.
Set the pan aside for 12 minutes, without lifting
the lid (don't allow steam to escape).
2 Heat the oil in a frying pan over high heat,
and stir-fry the chicken until golden and tender;
set aside. Reheat the pan, add the onion and
cook, stirring occasionally, for 3 minutes or until
beginning to soften. Add the extra water, soy
sauce, mirin and dashi granules. Stir to dissolve

the dashi and bring the stock to the boil. Cook
for 3 minutes or until onion is tender.
3 Return the chicken to the pan and pour in the
eggs, stirring gently to just break up the eggs.
Cover and simmer over very low heat for 2 to
3 minutes or until the eggs are just set. Remove
the pan from the heat.
4 Toast the nori by holding it over low heat and
moving it back and forward for about
15 seconds; crumble it into small pieces.
5 Transfer the rice to an earthenware dish,
carefully spoon over the chicken and egg
mixture and sprinkle over the nori. Garnish with
the spring onion.
NOTE: Domburi is actually an earthenware dish,
but the food served in the dish has also taken on
the name.

*NUTRITION PER SERVE: Protein 30 g; Fat 20 g;
Carbohydrate 95 g; Dietary Fibre 3 g; Cholesterol 305 mg;
2770 kJ (660 cal)*

A NOISY AFFAIR
*While etiquette dictates
that Japanese mealtimes
should be silent affairs,
an exception is made for
noodles, which may be
eaten with gusto and much
lip-smacking. Some say
this allows an intake of air
to cool the noodles, but
chilled noodles, a favourite
summer dish in Japan, are
eaten with the same
enthusiastic slurping.*

*Above: Chicken
Domburi*

# FRIED PORK AND NOODLES

•

*Preparation time:* 25 minutes
*Total cooking time:* 15 minutes
*Serves* 4

★ ★

1 sheet nori
1 tablespoon oil
150 g (4¾ oz) pork loin, cut into small
    strips
5 spring onions, cut into short lengths
1 medium carrot, cut into thin strips
200 g (6½ oz) Chinese cabbage, shredded
500 g (1 lb) Hokkien noodles, gently
    pulled apart to separate
2 tablespoons water
2 tablespoons Japanese soy sauce
1 tablespoon Worcestershire sauce
1 tablespoon mirin
2 teaspoons caster sugar
1 cup (90 g/3 oz) bean sprouts, scraggly
    ends removed

1 Toast the nori by holding it over low heat and moving it back and forward for about 15 seconds; cut it into fine shreds.
2 Heat the oil in a large deep pan or wok; add the pork, spring onion and carrot and stir-fry over medium heat for 1 to 2 minutes, or until the pork just changes colour. Take care not to overcook the mixture or the pork will toughen and the vegetables will become limp.
3 Add the cabbage, noodles, water, soy sauce, Worcestershire sauce, mirin and sugar to the

pan; cover and cook for 1 minute. Add the bean sprouts and toss to coat the vegetables and noodles with the sauce. Serve immediately, sprinkled with the shredded nori.

NUTRITION PER SERVE: Protein 25 g; Fat 15 g; Carbohydrate 100 g; Dietary Fibre 10 g; Cholesterol 20 mg; 2505 kJ (615 cal)

•

# GLAZED PRAWNS WITH EGG

*Preparation time:* 35 minutes
*Total cooking time:* 10 minutes
*Serves* 4

★ ★

12 raw prawns
¼ cup (30 g/1 oz) cornflour
1 teaspoon dashi granules
2 tablespoons water
3 tablespoons sake
½ teaspoon sugar
½ teaspoon salt
3 egg yolks, lightly beaten

•

1 Peel and devein the prawns, leaving the tails intact. Bring a large pan of water to the boil. Coat each prawn lightly in the cornflour, shaking off any excess. Drop the prawns 2 or 3 at a time into the boiling water and cook for about 7 seconds only. Remove the prawns and rinse them under cold running water.
2 Combine the dashi, water, sake, sugar and salt in a frying pan, and bring it to the boil, stirring. Add the prawns, coating them in the sauce. Pour

## WASABI PASTE

*Wasabi is the very hot green paste served as a condiment with some Japanese dishes. To make your own, blend 1 tablespoon wasabi powder and 1 tablespoon water in a small bowl. Cover and allow to stand for 5 minutes for the flavour to develop. Use immediately, as it will lose its heat on standing.*

*Right: Fried Pork and Noodles*

the beaten egg over the prawns, cover and simmer over very low heat for 3 minutes. Serve at once with steamed vegetables and rice.
NOTE: Dusting the raw prawns in cornflour, quickly blanching and then rinsing gives them are very crisp texture and it is an essential step in this style of recipe—omitting it will result in the prawn 'weeping' as it cooks in the stock.

*NUTRITION PER SERVE: Protein 10 g; Fat 5 g; Carbohydrate 10 g; Dietary Fibre 0 g; Cholesterol 195 mg; 480 kJ (115 cal)*

•
## SALTED GRILLED FISH
•

**Preparation time:** 25 minutes
**Total cooking time:** 20 minutes
**Serves** 4

✫✫

*400 g (12²/₃ oz) small whole bream, whiting or snapper, cleaned and scaled with eyes removed (see note)*
*¹/₂ lemon, cut into thin slices*
*5 cm (2 inch) piece fresh ginger*
*1 tablespoon mirin*
*2 tablespoons Japanese soy sauce*
*3 teaspoons salt*

•

*Garnishes*
*1 large carrot*
*¹/₄ daikon*
*5 cm (2 inch) piece fresh ginger, very finely sliced*

1 Rinse the fish under cold water and pat dry with paper towels. Place the lemon slices inside the fish. Finely grate the ginger over a plate using the smallest side of a metal grater or, alternatively, use a Japanese wooden or ceramic ginger grater. Use your hands to squeeze out as much juice as possible from the pulp. Reserve the juice and discard the dry pulp.
2 Place the ginger juice, mirin and soy sauce in a small bowl and mix to combine. Lightly brush some of the mixture over the fish and sprinkle both sides of each fish with about ¹/₄ teaspoon salt. Sprinkle a thicker coating of salt onto the fins and tail (this will help stop them burning).
3 Line a grill tray with aluminium foil and place it on the level furthest away from heat—if the fish is too close to the heat it will cook too quickly and perhaps burn. Cook the fish until golden brown on both sides and the flesh flakes easily when tested with a fork—this will take about 6 to 8 minutes, depending on the thickness and variety of the fish.
4 Finely grate the carrot and daikon in longish strips using the thick side of a cheese grater. Arrange the strips on a serving platter with the sliced ginger. Place the fish on the platter, garnish with some of the ginger slices, and serve immediately with steamed rice.
NOTE: As the eyes of fish are unappealing when cooked, ask the fishmonger to remove them when scaling and cleaning.

*NUTRITION PER SERVE: Protein 20 g; Fat 5 g; Carbohydrate 1 g; Dietary Fibre 0 g; Cholesterol 75 mg; 570 kJ (135 cal)*

*Above: Salted Grilled Fish*

# MARINATED SALMON STRIPS

*Preparation time:* 15 minutes
+ 1 hour marinating
*Total cooking time:* Nil
*Serves* 4

⭐

2 salmon fillets, each about 400 g
(12²/3 oz), skinned
4 cm (1¹/2 inch) piece fresh ginger, grated
2 cloves garlic, finely chopped, optional
3 spring onions, finely chopped
1 teaspoon sugar
1 teaspoon salt
2 tablespoons Japanese soy sauce
¹/2 cup (125 ml/4 fl oz) sake
pickled ginger (page 189) and pickled
cucumber, to garnish

1 Cut the salmon into thin strips, and arrange them in a single layer in a large deep dish.
2 Place the ginger, garlic, spring onion, sugar, salt, soy sauce and sake in a small bowl and stir to combine. Pour the marinade over the salmon, cover and refrigerate for 1 hour.
3 Arrange the salmon, strip by strip, on a serving plate. Garnish with the pickled ginger and cucumber, and serve chilled.

NUTRITION PER SERVE: Protein 20 g; Fat 10 g; Carbohydrate 5 g; Dietary Fibre 1 g; Cholesterol 70 mg; 905 kJ (215 cal)

# HAND-SHAPED TUNA SUSHI

**Preparation time:** 20 minutes
**Total cooking time:** 30 minutes
+ 10 minutes cooling
**Makes** about 30

⭐ ⭐

1 cup (220 g/7 oz) short-grain rice
2 cups (500 ml/16 fl oz) water
2 tablespoons rice vinegar
1 tablespoon caster sugar
1 teaspoon salt
300 g (9²/3 oz) very fresh tuna
wasabi, to taste
wasabi, extra, and Japanese soy sauce,
to serve

1 Wash the rice under cold running water until the water runs clear; drain thoroughly. Place the rice and water in a medium pan and bring it to the boil. Reduce the heat; simmer, uncovered, for 4 to 5 minutes or until the water is absorbed. Reduce the heat to very low. Cover and cook for

another 4 to 5 minutes. Remove the pan from the heat and let stand, covered, for 10 minutes.
2 Add the combined vinegar, sugar and salt to the rice, tossing with a wooden spoon until the rice is cool.
3 Cut the tuna into thin strips about 5 cm (2 inches) long. Place a little wasabi on each.
4 Using your hands, roll a tablespoon of rice into a ball. Place the rice ball onto a strip of fish and then gently mould the tuna around the rice. Flatten the ball slightly to elongate. Repeat with the remaining ingredients. Serve with the soy sauce and wasabi.

NUTRITION PER ROLL: Protein 5 g; Fat 0 g; Carbohydrate 5 g; Dietary Fibre 0 g; Cholesterol 5 mg; 175 kJ (40 cal)

# INARI SUSHI

*Preparation time:* 10 minutes
*Total cooking time:* 40 minutes
+ 15 minutes cooling
*Makes* 6

⭐ ⭐

1 cup (220 g/7 oz) short-grain rice
2 cups (500 ml/16 fl oz) water
2 tablespoons Japanese white sesame seeds
2 tablespoons rice vinegar
1 tablespoon caster sugar
1 teaspoon mirin
1 teaspoon salt
6 inari pouches (see note)

1 Wash the rice under cold running water until the water runs clear; drain thoroughly. Place the rice and water in a medium pan, and bring to the boil. Reduce the heat and simmer, uncovered, for 4 to 5 minutes or until the water is absorbed. Cover, reduce the heat to very low and cook for another 4 to 5 minutes. Remove the pan from the heat and let stand, covered, for 10 minutes.
2 Toast the sesame seeds in a dry pan over medium heat for 3 to 4 minutes, shaking the pan gently, until the seeds are golden brown; remove seeds from the pan at once to prevent burning.
3 Add the combined vinegar, sugar, mirin and salt to the rice, tossing with a wooden spoon until the rice is cool.
4 Gently separate the inari pockets and open them up. Place a ball of the rice mixture inside. Sprinkle the rice with the toasted sesame seeds and press the inari closed with your fingers. Serve on a plate, cut-side down.
NOTE: Inari are small 'pouches' made from bean curd and are available from Japanese food shops.

NUTRITION PER PIECE: Protein 5 g; Fat 5 g; Carbohydrate 35 g; Dietary Fibre 2 g; Cholesterol 0 mg; 905 kJ (215 cal)

MARINATED
SALMON STRIPS

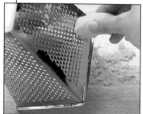

*Grate the piece of fresh ginger.*

*Use a sharp knife to cut the salmon into thin strips.*

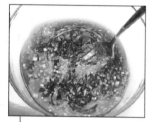

*Place all the ingredients for the marinade in a small bowl and stir together well.*

*Opposite page: Inari Sushi (top); Marinated Salmon Strips (centre); Hand-shaped Tuna Sushi*

## TERIYAKI CHICKEN

•

*Preparation time*: 15 minutes
*Total cooking time*: 40 minutes
*Serves* 6

½ cup (125 ml/4 fl oz) Japanese soy sauce
2 tablespoons mirin
1 tablespoon sugar
2 tablespoons oil
12 chicken drumsticks

•

1 Place the soy sauce, mirin and sugar in a small pan and stir over low heat until the sugar dissolves. Bring to the boil, reduce the heat and simmer, uncovered, for 2 minutes.
2 Heat the oil in a large heavy-based frying pan; add the chicken drumsticks in batches and cook over high heat until browned on both sides.
3 Return all the chicken to the pan, add the sauce, cover and cook for 20 minutes or until the chicken is tender. Serve with rice.

*Below: Teriyaki Chicken*

NUTRITION PER SERVE: Protein 30 g; Fat 20 g; Carbohydrate 5 g; Dietary Fibre 0 g; Cholesterol 125 mg; 1345 kJ (320 cal)

## GRILLED FISH STEAKS

•

*Preparation time*: 15 minutes
 + 15 minutes marinating
*Total cooking time*: 10 minutes
*Serves* 4

★ ★

5 cm (2 inch) piece fresh ginger
3 tablespoons Japanese soy sauce
1 tablespoon mirin
3 spring onions, very finely chopped
3 teaspoons sugar
4 small fish cutlets, each about 150 g
 (4¾ oz), such as tuna, blue eye cod,
 jewfish
slices of cucumber, to garnish
pickled ginger (page 189), to garnish

•

1 Finely grate the ginger. Squeeze the ginger firmly with your fingertips to remove all the juice; reserve the juice and discard the dry pulp. Place the ginger juice, soy sauce, mirin, spring onion and sugar in a small bowl and stir until the sugar dissolves.
2 Place the fish in a shallow dish. Pour the

marinade over the fish and marinate for
15 minutes. Drain the fish, reserving the
marinade, and place it on a foil-lined grill tray.
3 Cook the fish under medium heat for about
3 minutes each side, carefully turning the fish
over with egg slices.
4 Pour the reserved marinade into a small pan
and boil it over high heat for 2 minutes until
thickened. Drizzle the marinade over the fish,
garnish with cucumber and pickled ginger, and
serve with steamed rice.

*NUTRITION PER SERVE: Protein 20 g; Fat 5 g;
Carbohydrate 5 g; Dietary Fibre 0 g; Cholesterol 40 mg;
585 kJ (140 cal)*

•
## EGGPLANT (AUBERGINE) KEBABS
## WITH MISO
•

***Preparation time:*** 10 minutes
+ 15 minutes standing
***Total cooking time:*** 15 minutes
***Makes*** 10 kebabs

★

*2 medium eggplants (aubergines)
2 tablespoons Japanese white sesame seeds
1/2 cup (140 g/4²/3 oz) red miso
2 tablespoons mirin
2 tablespoons sake
3 tablespoons oil*

1 Soak 10 wooden skewers in water while
preparing the recipe. Cut the eggplants into 2 cm
(3/4 inch) cubes. Place in a colander and sprinkle
generously with salt. Set aside for 15 minutes, or
until the moisture has been drawn out of the
eggplant (this removes the bitterness). Rinse
thoroughly and pat dry with paper towels.
2 Drain the skewers and dry with paper towel.
Thread the eggplant cubes onto the skewers.
3 Toast the sesame seeds in a dry pan over
medium heat for 3 to 4 minutes, shaking the pan
gently, until the seeds are golden brown.
Remove the seeds from the pan at once to
prevent burning.
4 Combine the miso, mirin and sake in a small
pan. Bring to the boil, then reduce the heat and
simmer for 5 minutes.
5 Heat the oil on a flat barbecue plate and cook
the eggplant skewers for 5 minutes, turning
frequently until golden brown. Spread the miso
topping over the skewers, and sprinkle with the
sesame seeds. Serve with rice.

*NUTRITION PER SERVE: Protein 5 g; Fat 20 g;
Carbohydrate 5 g; Dietary Fibre 5 g; Cholesterol 0 mg;
1005 kJ (240 cal)*

*Above: Grilled
Fish Steaks*

219

formed (the mixture will become damp as oil is released from the seeds).

3 Combine the sesame seed paste with the ginger, soy sauce, mirin and sugar. Pour the sauce over the beans, scatter over the extra sesame seeds and serve.

NOTE: The beans can be marinated in the sauce overnight if desired. Japanese sesame seeds are plump and large, with a fuller flavour than other sesame seeds.

NUTRITION PER SERVE: Protein 5 g; Fat 5 g; Carbohydrate 10 g; Dietary Fibre 5 g; Cholesterol 0 mg; 570 kJ (135 cal)

•

# YAKITORI
## (SKEWERED CHICKEN)

•

**Preparation time:** 20 minutes
**Total cooking time:** 10 minutes
**Makes** 25 skewers

✦

1 kg (2 lb) chicken thigh fillets
6 spring onions
½ cup (125 ml/4 fl oz) sake
¾ cup (185 ml/6 fl oz) soy sauce (see note)
½ cup (125 ml/4 fl oz) mirin
2 tablespoons sugar

•

1 Soak 25 wooden skewers in water while you are preparing the recipe. Cut the chicken fillets into bite-sized pieces. Trim the spring onions, then cut diagonally into 2 cm (¾ inch) lengths.

2 Combine the sake, soy sauce, mirin and sugar in a small pan. Bring to the boil, then remove from the heat and set aside.

3 Drain the skewers and dry with paper towels. Thread the chicken and spring onion pieces alternately onto the skewers. Place the skewers on a foil-lined tray and cook under a preheated moderate grill, turning and brushing frequently with the sauce, for 7 to 8 minutes, or until the chicken is cooked through. Yakitori is traditionally served as a snack with beer.

NOTE: For this dish, it is best to use a darker soy sauce rather than the lighter Japanese one.

NUTRITION PER SKEWER: Protein 10 g; Fat 2 g; Carbohydrate 2 g; Dietary Fibre 0 g; Cholesterol 30 mg; 270 kJ (65 cal)

# GREEN BEANS IN ROASTED
## SESAME SEED SAUCE

•

**Preparation time:** 15 minutes
**Total cooking time:** 8 minutes
**Serves** 4 as a starter or side dish

✦ ✦

500 g (1 lb) slender green beans, trimmed
2 tablespoons Japanese white sesame seeds
6 cm (2½ inch) piece fresh ginger
1 tablespoon Japanese soy sauce
1 tablespoon mirin
3 teaspoons sugar
1 teaspoon Japanese white sesame seeds, extra

•

1 Cook the beans in a large pan of boiling water for 2 minutes; drain, plunge into iced water to stop the cooking, drain again and set aside.

2 Toast the sesame seeds in a dry frying pan, over a medium heat, for about 5 minutes shaking the pan constantly until golden brown. Pound the seeds in a mortar and pestle until a paste is

*Above: Green Beans in Roasted Sesame Seed Sauce*

## SALMON NABE

•

*Preparation time:* 20 minutes
*Total cooking time:* 40 minutes
*Serves* 3–4

✷ ✷

12 dried shiitake mushrooms
250 g (8 oz) firm tofu
½ Chinese cabbage
4 salmon cutlets
2 x 5 cm (2 inch) pieces canned bamboo
   shoot
2 litres dashi
⅓ cup (80 ml/2¾ fl oz) Japanese soy
   sauce
¼ cup (60 ml/2 fl oz) mirin or sake
pinch of salt
Sesame Seed Sauce (page 168), to serve

•

1 Soak the mushrooms in warm water for
15 minutes, then drain. Cut the tofu into
12 squares. Coarsely shred the cabbage into 5 cm
(2 inch) wide pieces.

2 Place the mushrooms, tofu, cabbage, salmon,
bamboo shoot, dashi, soy sauce, mirin and salt in
a large pan and bring to the boil. Reduce the
heat, cover and simmer over medium heat for
15 minutes. Turn the salmon pieces over and
simmer for a further 15 minutes, or until tender.
3 Pour the Salmon Nabe into a warmed serving
bowl and serve with the Sesame Seed Sauce.
NOTE: This dish is traditionally cooked in a clay
pot over a burner and served in the same pot.
Diners dip the fish and vegetable pieces into the
accompanying sauce and the broth is served in
small bowls at the end of the meal.

*NUTRITION PER SERVE (4): Protein 30 g; Fat 20 g;
Carbohydrate 10 g; Dietary Fibre 1 g; Cholesterol 90 mg;
1330 kJ (315 cal)*

*Above: Salmon Nabe*

## NOODLE-COATED PRAWNS

•

*Preparation time:* 20 minutes
*Total cooking time:* 15 minutes
*Serves* 2

✶✶

6 large raw prawns
¼ sheet nori
100 g (3⅓ oz) somen noodles
oil, for deep-frying
Soy and Ginger Sauce (page 168),
   to serve

•

**Batter**
1 cup (125 g/4 oz) plain flour
1 egg yolk
1 cup (250 ml/8 fl oz) iced water

•

1 Peel and devein the prawns. Make a shallow incision in the underside of the prawns and then open up the cut to straighten the prawns out. Cut the nori into strips about 7 cm (2¾ inches) long and 1.5 cm (⅝ inch) wide.
2 To make Batter: Place the flour, egg yolk and water in a bowl and whisk until just combined.
3 Break the noodles so that they are the same length as the prawns, not including the tails. Place the noodles on a board. Dip each prawn into the batter, then lay it on the noodles and gather up to cover the prawns all around; press so they stick to the prawn. Wrap a strip of nori

*Above: Noodle-Coated Prawns*

around the centre of the prawn, dampen the ends with a little water and press to seal.
4 Heat the oil in a large pan or wok to moderately hot. Cook the prawn bundles in 2 batches, until the noodles are golden brown. Serve immediately with Soy and Ginger Sauce.

*NUTRITION PER SERVE: Protein 30 g; Fat 5 g; Carbohydrate 110 g; Dietary Fibre 2 g; Cholesterol 175 mg; 2465 kJ (590 cal)*

•

## SMALL SKEWERS OF BEEF, PEPPER (CAPSICUM) AND SPRING ONION

•

*Preparation time:* 40 minutes
   + 20 minutes marinating
*Total cooking time:* 20 minutes
*Makes* 12

✶✶

3 tablespoons Japanese soy sauce
2 tablespoons mirin
2 teaspoons sesame oil
1 teaspoon sugar
2 tablespoons Japanese white sesame seeds
350 g (11¼ oz) scotch fillet
1 green pepper (capsicum)
6 spring onions
oil, for shallow-frying
2 eggs, beaten
½ cup (60 g/2 oz) plain flour

1 Place the soy sauce, mirin, sesame oil, sugar and half the sesame seeds in a large bowl. Cut the meat into bite-sized cubes, add it to the marinade, toss to combine, and marinate for 20 minutes. Soak 12 small wooden skewers in water for 15 minutes.

2 Cut the green pepper into small bite-sized pieces. Cut the firm part of the spring onion into short lengths, discarding the soft dark green tops.

3 Drain the meat and gently pat it dry with paper towels. Thread a piece of meat, green pepper and spring onion onto each skewer, repeating this pattern twice.

4 Heat 1 cm (½ inch) oil in a frying pan until moderately hot. Roll each skewer in the egg, then lightly coat it in the flour. Add the skewers to the pan in 2 or 3 batches, and fry until golden brown, turning each skewer regularly. Sprinkle over the remaining seame seeds and serve immediately.

NUTRITION PER SKEWER: Protein 10 g; Fat 10 g; Carbohydrate 5 g; Dietary Fibre 1 g; Cholesterol 55 mg; 560 kJ (135 cal)

•

## RICE WITH CHICKEN AND MUSHROOMS
•

*Preparation time:* 15 minutes
*Total cooking time:* 40 minutes
*Serves 4–6*

★

*500 g (1 lb ) short-grain rice*
*2½ cups (600 ml/20 fl oz) water*
*8 dried shiitake mushrooms*
*2 tablespoons Japanese soy sauce*
*2 tablespoons sake*
*2 teaspoons sugar*
*600 g (1¼ lb) chicken breast fillets, cut*
*    into strips*
*200 g (6½ oz) frozen peas*
*2 eggs, lightly beaten*

•

1 Wash the rice thoroughly in a sieve under running water until the water runs clear. Place the rice in a heavy-based pan with the water and bring it to the boil. Reduce the heat to very low, cover and cook for 15 minutes. Remove the pan from the heat and stand, with the lid on, for 20 minutes.

2 Soak the mushrooms in hot water for about 15 minutes, until soft. Drain well and slice into thin strips, discarding the hard stem.

3 Combine the soy sauce, sake and sugar in a frying pan. Cook over low heat stirring until the sugar dissolves. Add the mushrooms, chicken

and peas. Cover and cook for 5 minutes until the chicken is cooked. Set aside and cover to keep warm.

4 Heat a nonstick pan; pour in the eggs and cook over medium heat, swirling the pan gently until the egg sets. Turn the omelette over and cook the other side. Remove the omelette from the pan and cut it into thin strips.

5 Arrange the rice in individual serving bowls, spoon over the chicken mixture with a little of the soy liquid and scatter over the egg strips. Serve immediately.

NUTRITION PER SERVE (6): Protein 35 g; Fat 5 g; Carbohydrate 70 g; Dietary Fibre 5 g; Cholesterol 125 mg; 1967 kJ (470 cal)

*Above: Rice with Chicken and Mushrooms*

# INDIA & PAKISTAN

At the heart of Indian and Pakistani cooking are its spices which are ground up to produce masalas, aromatic blends created freshly for each different dish. The variety of food reflects the religious, cultural and geographic diversity of the sub-continent itself. In Pakistan and the north of India, the cooking is meat-based: curries, tikkas and koftas mopped up with fresh breads. The dishes of the south are predominantly vegetarian, spicy-hot and bursting with colour. Special dishes are prepared for religious or cultural events, from a festive pan of biryani, flavoured with fragrant saffron, to coconut sweets, served up at weddings and other celebrations.

3 Heat the oil in a large pan; add the onion and cook over medium heat until just soft. Add the spice paste and stir for 1 minute. Add the meat and cook, stirring, until it is coated with the spice paste. Add the tomato paste and stock. Simmer, covered, for 1 hour 30 minutes, or until the meat is tender.

NUTRITION PER SERVE: *Protein 55 g; Fat 15 g; Carbohydrate 5 g; Dietary Fibre 0 g; Cholesterol 185 mg; 1620 kJ (385 cal)*

## HOT LENTIL SOUP

**Preparation time**: 15 minutes
**Total cooking time**: 45 minutes
**Serves** 6

*1/2 cup (95 g/3 1/4 oz) brown lentils (see note)*
*2 tablespoons ghee or oil*
*1 medium onion, finely chopped*
*1/2 teaspoon grated fresh ginger*
*1 large potato, cut into small cubes*
*2 large tomatoes, chopped*
*2 teaspoons ground coriander*
*1 teaspoon ground cumin*
*1/2 teaspoon ground turmeric*
*1/2 teaspoon chilli flakes*
*2 tablespoons desiccated coconut*
*4 cups (1 litre) water*
*1–2 teaspoons tamarind concentrate*
*150 g (4 3/4 oz) finely shredded cabbage*
*1 tablespoon chopped fresh coriander leaves or mint, to garnish*

1 Place the lentils in a medium pan, cover with water, bring to the boil and simmer, uncovered, for about 20 minutes or until tender. Drain well.
2 Heat the ghee in a large pan; add the onion and ginger and cook over medium heat until deep brown. Add the potato and tomato, and cook for 5 minutes, then add the coriander, cumin, turmeric, chilli and coconut and cook for another 2 to 3 minutes.
3 Add the drained lentils and the water and bring to the boil. Simmer until the lentils and potato begin to break up. Add the tamarind and cabbage. Cook until the cabbage is soft. Season with black pepper to taste. Serve with chopped coriander or mint as a garnish, if desired, and chapattis.
NOTE: Red or yellow lentils, which require less cooking time, can be used instead of brown.

NUTRITION PER SERVE: *Protein 10 g; Fat 10 g; Carbohydrate 15 g; Dietary Fibre 5 g; Cholesterol 20 mg; 800 kJ (190 cal)*

## MADRAS CURRY

**Preparation time**: 20 minutes
**Total cooking time**: 1 hour 30 minutes
**Serves** 4

*1 kg (2 lb) skirt or chuck steak*
*1/4 cup (25 g/3/4 oz) ground coriander*
*6 teaspoons ground cumin*
*1 teaspoon brown mustard seeds*
*1/2 teaspoon cracked black peppercorns*
*1 teaspoon chilli powder*
*1 teaspoon ground turmeric*
*1 teaspoon salt*
*2 teaspoons crushed garlic*
*2 teaspoons grated fresh ginger*
*2–3 tablespoons white vinegar*
*1 tablespoon oil or ghee*
*1 medium onion, chopped*
*1/4 cup (60 g/2 oz) tomato paste (tomato purée, double concentrate)*
*1 cup (250 ml/8 fl oz) beef stock*

1 Trim the excess fat and sinew from the meat, and cut it into 2.5 cm (1 inch) cubes.
2 Place the coriander, cumin, mustard seeds, peppercorns, chilli powder, turmeric, salt, garlic and ginger in a small bowl; stir to combine. Add the vinegar and mix to a smooth paste.

*Above: Madras Curry*

## DRY POTATO AND PEA CURRY

•

*Preparation time*: 15 minutes
*Total cooking time*: 20–25 minutes
*Serves* 4

☆

750 g (1¹/2 lb) potatoes
2 teaspoons brown mustard seeds
2 tablespoons ghee or oil
2 medium onions, sliced
2 cloves garlic, crushed
2 teaspoons grated fresh ginger
1 teaspoon ground turmeric
¹/2 teaspoon chilli powder
1 teaspoon ground cumin
1 teaspoon garam masala
¹/2 cup (125 ml/4 fl oz) water
²/3 cup (100 g/3¹/3 oz) peas
2 tablespoons chopped fresh mint

1 Peel the potatoes and cut them into small cubes.
2 Place the mustard seeds in a large dry pan and cook over medium heat until the seeds start to pop. Add the ghee, onion, garlic and ginger, and cook, stirring, until the onion is soft.
3 Add the turmeric, chilli powder, cumin, garam masala and potato; stir until the potato is coated. Add the water, cover and simmer for about 15 to 20 minutes, or until the potato is just tender, stirring occasionally.
4 Add the peas and stir until combined; season with salt and pepper to taste. Simmer, covered, for a further 3 to 5 minutes, or until the potato is cooked through and the liquid is absorbed. Stir in the mint and serve with rice.

*NUTRITION PER SERVE: Protein 10 g; Fat 10 g; Carbohydrate 30 g; Dietary Fibre 5 g; Cholesterol 30 mg; 1095 kJ (260 cal)*

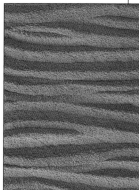

*Above: Dry Potato and Pea Curry*

## PRAWNS IN COCONUT MILK

·

*Preparation time*: 10 minutes
*Total cooking time*: 25 minutes
*Serves* 4–6

★

750 g (1½ lb) raw prawns
1 tablespoon ghee or oil
2 onions, sliced
2 cloves garlic, crushed
2 red chillies, seeded and chopped
1 teaspoon ground turmeric
8 curry leaves
2 cups (500 ml/16 fl oz) coconut milk
½–1 teaspoon salt

·

1 Peel and devein the prawns. Heat the ghee or oil in a medium pan. Add the onion and cook until soft. Add the garlic, chilli, turmeric and curry leaves. Stir over medium heat for 1 minute.
2 Add the coconut milk and salt. Simmer, uncovered, over low heat for 10 minutes.
3 Add the prawns and stir gently. Simmer for 12 minutes, or until the prawns are tender. Fresh curry leaves sprinkled on top make a perfect garnish, if necessary.

*NUTRITION PER SERVE (6): Protein 15 g; Fat 20 g; Carbohydrate 5 g; Dietary Fibre 0 g; Cholesterol 105 mg; 1065 kJ (255 cal)*

## BOMBAY CURRY

·

*Preparation time*: 20 minutes
*Total cooking time*: 1 hour 15 minutes
   to 1 hour 45 minutes
*Serves* 4–6

★

1 tablespoon ghee or oil
2 medium onions, chopped
2 cloves garlic, crushed
2 green chillies, chopped
1 tablespoon grated fresh ginger
1½ teaspoons ground turmeric
1 teaspoon ground cumin
1 tablespoon ground coriander
½–1 teaspoon chilli powder
1 kg (2 lb) beef or lamb, cut into
   bite-sized cubes
1 teaspoon salt
410 g (13 oz) can crushed tomatoes
1 cup (250 ml/8 fl oz) coconut
   milk
fresh coriander leaves, to garnish

·

1 Heat the ghee in a large pan; add the onion and cook over medium heat, stirring, until just soft. Add the garlic, chilli, ginger, turmeric, cumin, coriander and chilli powder. Stir until just heated through.
2 Add the meat and cook, stirring, over high heat until the meat is well coated with the spice mixture and browned all over. Stir in the salt and undrained tomatoes and simmer, covered, for 1 to 1½ hours, or until the meat is tender.
3 Add the coconut milk and stir; simmer, uncovered, for another 5 minutes or until the sauce has thickened slightly. Serve garnished with coriander leaves, if desired.
NOTE: Raw, unsalted cashew nuts make a delicious garnish for this dish. Scatter them on top of the curry before serving.

*NUTRITION PER SERVE (6): Protein 37 g; Fat 25 g; Carbohydrate 5 g; Dietary Fibre 0 g; Cholesterol 100 mg; 1640 kJ (390 cal)*

·

## SAFFRON CHICKEN PILAU

·

*Preparation time*: 25 minutes
*Total cooking time*: 30 minutes
*Serves* 6

★

2 cups (400 g/12⅔ oz) long-grain rice
4 tablespoons ghee
½ teaspoon powdered saffron
1 cinnamon stick, broken
3 cloves
2 cardamom pods, lightly crushed
3 cups (750 ml/24 fl oz) water
2 tablespoons sultanas
2 tablespoons blanched almonds
300 g (9⅔ oz) skinless chicken breast
   fillet, diced

·

1 Place the rice and half the ghee in a large, heavy-based pan and stir until the rice grains are well coated with ghee. Add the saffron, cinnamon, cloves, cardamom pods and water. Cover and bring to the boil, then reduce the heat to as low as possible and cook without removing the lid for 20 minutes.
2 Heat the remaining ghee in a frying pan, add the sultanas, almonds and chicken and cook over medium heat for about 5 minutes, or until the chicken is cooked through. Season with salt to taste.
3 Stir the chicken mixture into the rice and leave to stand for 5 minutes before serving.

*NUTRITION PER SERVE: Protein 20 g; Fat 20 g; Carbohydrate 60 g; Dietary Fibre 0 g; Cholesterol 65 mg; 1960 kJ (465 cal)*

### GHEE

*Ghee is clarified butter or pure butter fat. It gives a rich buttery taste to food and, because it has no milk solids, won't burn at high temperatures. Butter or a bland oil can be substituted for ghee. Alternatively, a mixture of half ghee and half extra light olive oil (which has little taste) has both the rich flavour of ghee and the health benefits of olive oil.*

*Opposite page: Prawns in Coconut Milk (top); Bombay Curry*

2 Place the onion, garlic, ginger, coriander and cumin seeds, extra lemon juice and salt in a food processor and process until a smooth paste is formed. Combine the spice paste with the paprika, chilli powder and yoghurt, and mix together until smooth. Add enough drops of food colouring to make the mixture a deep red colour.

3 Place the chicken pieces in a large shallow dish, and spread liberally with the spicy yoghurt mixture. Cover with plastic wrap and refrigerate. Marinate the chicken for at least 4 hours or overnight.

4 Preheat the oven to moderate 180°C (350°F/Gas 4). Place the chicken pieces on a wire rack over a large baking dish. Bake for 45 minutes, or until the chicken pieces are tender and cooked through. Serve with rice.

*NUTRITION PER SERVE (6): Protein 20 g; Fat 5 g; Carbohydrate 5 g; Dietary Fibre 0 g; Cholesterol 70 mg; 645 kJ (155 cal)*

## ONION BHAJI

*Preparation time*: 20 minutes
*Total cooking time*: 15 minutes
*Makes* 25–30

⭐ ⭐

*³/4 cup (80 g/2²/3 oz) besan (chickpea flour)*
*¹/2 cup (60 g/2 oz) plain flour*
*1¹/2 teaspoons bicarbonate of soda*
*1 teaspoon chilli powder*
*1 egg, lightly beaten*
*1¹/4 cups (315 ml/10 fl oz) water*
*4 large onions, halved and thinly sliced*
*4 cloves garlic, chopped*
*oil, for shallow-frying*

1 Sift the flours, bicarbonate of soda and chilli powder into a bowl. Make a well in the centre, add the combined egg and water and stir to make a smooth creamy batter, adding a little more water if necessary. Add the onion and garlic and mix well.

2 Heat the oil, about 1 cm (¹/2 inch) deep, in a wide flat pan. Drop in tablespoons of the mixture and press into patties. Fry the bhaji on both sides until golden brown and cooked through; drain on paper towels. Serve hot with chilli sauce or mango chutney.

NOTE: Use sweet paprika instead of chilli powder for a milder taste.

*NUTRITION PER BHAJI: Protein 1 g; Fat 2 g; Carbohydrate 5 g; Dietary Fibre 1 g; Cholesterol 5 mg; 160 kJ (40 cal)*

TANDOORI CHICKEN

*Brush the skinned chicken thighs with lemon juice.*

*Add several drops of red food colouring to the spice and yoghurt mixture.*

*Above: Tandoori Chicken*

## TANDOORI CHICKEN

*Preparation time*: 25 minutes
 + 4 hours 30 minutes marinating
*Total cooking time*: 45 minutes
*Serves* 4–6

⭐

*6 chicken thighs*
*¹/4 cup (60 ml/2 fl oz) lemon juice*
*¹/2 small onion, chopped*
*4 cloves garlic*
*1 tablespoon grated fresh ginger*
*3 teaspoons coriander seeds*
*1 tablespoon cumin seeds*
*1 tablespoon lemon juice, extra*
*1 teaspoon salt*
*¹/4 teaspoon paprika*
*pinch chilli powder*
*1 cup (250 g/8 oz) yoghurt*
*red food colouring*

1 Remove the skin from the chicken pieces and brush the flesh with lemon juice; cover and marinate in the refrigerator for 30 minutes.

## PORK VINDALOO

•

**Preparation time**: 20 minutes
**Total cooking time**: 1 hour 45 minutes
**Serves** 4

★

**Vindaloo Paste**
2 tablespoons grated fresh ginger
4 cloves garlic, chopped
3 red chillies, chopped
2 teaspoons ground turmeric
2 teaspoons ground cardamom
4 whole cloves
6 peppercorns
1 teaspoon ground cinnamon
1 tablespoon ground coriander
1 tablespoon cumin seeds
1/2 cup (125 ml/4 fl oz) lemon juice

•

1 kg (2 lb) pork fillets
1/4 cup (60 ml/2 fl oz) oil
2 teaspoons brown mustard seeds
2 1/2 cups (600 ml/20 fl oz) water

1 To make Vindaloo Paste: Place the ginger, garlic, chilli, turmeric, cardamom, cloves, peppercorns, cinnamon, coriander, cumin seeds and lemon juice in a food processor. Process for 20 seconds or until all the ingredients are combined and the mixture is quite smooth.
2 Trim the pork of excess fat and sinew and cut it into cubes.
3 Heat the oil in a heavy-based pan; add the meat in small batches, and cook quickly over medium heat until browned.
4 Return all the meat to the pan. Add the Vindaloo Paste and mustard seeds, and cook, stirring, for 2 minutes. Add the water and bring to the boil. Reduce heat and simmer, covered, for 1 1/2 hours or until the meat is tender. Serve with rice and pappadums.
NOTE: The Vindaloo Paste can be made ahead of time and stored in an airtight container in the refrigerator. Ready-made vindaloo paste is available from supermarkets.

NUTRITION PER SERVE: Protein 55 g; Fat 35 g; Carbohydrate 0 g; Dietary Fibre 0 g; Cholesterol 130 mg; 2270 kJ (540 cal)

THE TANDOOR OVEN
*Tandoori is the name given to food traditionally threaded onto spits and cooked in a tandoor or clay oven. Barrel-shaped and often as high as a man, the ovens are usually set into the ground with a small circular opening at the top. Long spits, laden with marinated meats, are lowered in over the white-hot coals.*

*Below: Pork Vindaloo*

## ROGAN JOSH

•

*Preparation time*: 25 minutes
*Total cooking time*: 1 to 1½ hours
*Serves* 4–6

✫

1 kg (2 lb) lamb
1 tablespoon ghee or oil
2 medium onions, chopped
½ cup (125 g/4 oz) yoghurt
1 teaspoon chilli powder
1 tablespoon ground coriander
2 teaspoons ground cumin
1 teaspoon ground cardamom
½ teaspoon ground cloves
1 teaspoon ground turmeric
3 cloves garlic, crushed
1 tablespoon grated fresh ginger
1 teaspoon salt
410 g (13 oz) can chopped tomatoes
¼ cup (30 g/1 oz) slivered almonds
3 teaspoons garam masala
chopped coriander leaves, to garnish

•

1 Cut the lamb into 2.5 cm (1 inch) cubes.
2 Heat the ghee in a large pan; add the onion and cook, stirring, until soft. Add the yoghurt, chilli powder, coriander, cumin, cardamom, cloves, turmeric, garlic and ginger. Combine well. Add the salt and undrained tomatoes, and simmer, uncovered, for 5 minutes.
3 Add the lamb and stir until coated. Cover and cook over low heat for 1 to 1½ hours, or until the lamb is tender, stirring occasionally. Uncover and simmer until the liquid is thick.

4 Meanwhile toast the almonds in a dry pan over medium heat for 3 to 4 minutes, shaking the pan gently, until the nuts are golden brown; remove from the pan at once to prevent burning.
5 Sprinkle the lamb with the garam masala and mix through. Serve with the almonds sprinkled over and garnished with coriander leaves.

NUTRITION PER SERVE (6): *Protein 40 g; Fat 20 g; Carbohydrate 5 g; Dietary Fibre 0 g; Cholesterol 130 mg; 1545 kJ (365 cal)*

•

## CHICKEN TIKKA

•

*Preparation time*: 30 minutes
+ 4 hours marinating
*Total cooking time*: 10–15 minutes
*Makes* 12

✫

750 g (1½ lb) chicken thigh fillets
¼ medium onion, chopped
2 cloves garlic, crushed
1 tablespoon grated fresh ginger
2 tablespoons lemon juice
3 teaspoons ground coriander
3 teaspoons ground cumin
3 teaspoons garam masala
⅓ cup (90 g/3 oz) yoghurt
1 teaspoon salt

•

1 Cut the chicken into 3 cm (1¼ inch) cubes. Soak 12 wooden skewers in water.
2 Place the onion, garlic, ginger, lemon juice and spices in a food processor and process until finely chopped. Add the yoghurt and salt and

*Above: Rogan Josh*

process briefly to combine.

3 Thread the chicken pieces onto the skewers. Place the skewers in a large baking dish; coat the chicken with the spice mixture, and marinate for at least 4 hours or overnight, covered, in the refrigerator.

4 Cook the chicken on a hot barbecue grill or in a large, well-greased frying pan over high heat for about 5 minutes each side, or until golden brown and cooked through.

*NUTRITION PER SKEWER: Protein 15 g; Fat 7 g; Carbohydrate 2 g; Dietary Fibre 0 g; Cholesterol 40 mg; 555 kJ (130 cal)*

•

# LENTIL BHUJA CASSEROLE
•

**Preparation time**: 40 minutes
+ overnight soaking
+ 30 minutes refrigeration
**Total cooking time**: 1 hour 10 minutes
*Serves 4–6*

✷ ✷

2 cups (370 g/11¾ oz) green lentils
1 large onion
1 large potato
1 teaspoon ground cumin
1 teaspoon ground coriander
1 teaspoon ground turmeric
¾ cup (90 g/3 oz) plain flour
oil, for shallow frying
2 tablespoons oil, extra
2 cloves garlic, crushed
1 tablespoon grated fresh ginger

1 cup (250 ml/8 fl oz) tomato purée (passata)
2 cups (500 ml/16 fl oz) vegetable stock
1 cup (250 ml/8 fl oz) cream
200 g (6½ oz) green beans, topped and tailed
2 carrots, sliced

•

1 Cover the lentils with cold water and soak overnight. Drain well.

2 Grate the onion and potato and drain the excess liquid. Combine the lentils, onion, potato, cumin, coriander, turmeric and flour in a bowl, and mix well. Roll the mixture into walnut-sized balls and place them on a foil-lined tray. Cover and refrigerate for 30 minutes.

3 Heat the oil, about 2 cm (¾ inch) deep, in a frying pan; add the lentil balls in small batches and fry over high heat for 5 minutes or until golden brown. Drain on paper towels.

4 Heat the extra oil in a large pan; add the garlic and ginger, and cook, stirring, over medium heat for 1 minute. Stir in the tomato purée, stock and cream. Bring to the boil, reduce the heat and simmer, uncovered, for 10 minutes. Add the lentil balls, beans and carrot, cover and simmer for 35 minutes, stirring occasionally. Serve with pitta bread.

NOTE: Make sure your hands are dry when shaping the lentil mixture into balls. The lentil balls can be made a day ahead and stored in an airtight container in the refrigerator.

*NUTRITION PER SERVE (6): Protein 20 g; Fat 35 g; Carbohydrate 45 g; Dietary Fibre 10 g; Cholesterol 60 mg; 2325 kJ (555 cal)*

*LENTIL BHUJA CASSEROLE*

*Roll the lentil mixture into walnut-sized balls.*

*Fry the lentil balls over high heat until they are golden brown.*

*Add the lentil balls, beans and carrot to the curry sauce.*

*Left: Lentil Bhuja Casserole*

# VEGETABLE KORMA

•

*Preparation time*: 20 minutes
*Total cooking time*: 50 minutes
*Serves* 4–6

★

2 tablespoons oil
2 tablespoons ready-made green masala
    paste
1 teaspoon chilli powder
1 tablespoon grated fresh ginger
1 medium onion, chopped
300 g (9²/₃ oz) cauliflower, cut into florets
300 g (9²/₃ oz) pumpkin, cut into large
    pieces
3 slender eggplants (aubergines), cut into
    large pieces
2 carrots, cut into large pieces
3 tomatoes, peeled, seeded and chopped
1¹/₂ cups (375 ml/12 fl oz) vegetable stock
125 g (4 oz) green beans, chopped

•

1 Heat the oil in a large heavy-based pan; add
the masala paste and cook over medium heat for
2 minutes or until the oil begins to separate from
the paste.

2 Add the chilli powder, ginger and onion, and
cook for 3 minutes or until the onion softens.
3 Add the cauliflower, pumpkin, eggplant and
carrot and stir to coat in the paste mixture. Stir
in the tomatoes and stock and bring to the boil,
then reduce the heat and simmer, uncovered, for
30 minutes.
4 Add the beans and cook for 10 minutes or
until the vegetables are tender. Serve with rice.
NOTE: To make a Balti Vegetable Korma,
replace the green masala paste with Balti Masala
Paste (page 127).

*NUTRITION PER SERVE (6): Protein 5 g; Fat 10 g;
Carbohydrate 10 g; Dietary Fibre 5 g; Cholesterol 0 mg;
490 kJ (115 cal)*

•

# CHICKPEA CURRY

•

*Preparation time*: 20 minutes
*Total cooking time*: 30 minutes
*Serves* 4–6

★

2 x 400 g (12²/₃ oz) cans chickpeas
3 tablespoons ghee, oil or butter
2 medium onions, finely chopped
1 teaspoon grated fresh ginger
¹/₂ teaspoon crushed garlic
1–2 green chillies, seeded and finely
    chopped
¹/₂ teaspoon ground turmeric
2 large well-ripened tomatoes, seeded and
    chopped
1 tablespoon ground coriander
2 teaspoons garam masala
2 tablespoons lemon juice
2–3 tablespoons fresh chopped coriander
    leaves

•

1 Drain the chickpeas, reserving the liquid.
2 Heat the ghee in a large pan; add the onion,
ginger, garlic, chilli and turmeric and cook over
medium heat until the onion is soft and golden.
3 Add the tomato and cook until soft. Add the
coriander and chickpeas, and cook for
10 minutes. Add 1 cup of the reserved liquid and
cook for a further 10 minutes.
4 Add the garam masala, lemon juice and
coriander, and cook gently for 2 to 3 minutes,
adding more liquid, if needed, to make a sauce.
Pour the chickpeas into a serving dish and serve
with rice.

*NUTRITION PER SERVE (6): Protein 30 g; Fat 20 g;
Carbohydrate 70 g; Dietary Fibre 20 g; Cholesterol 30 mg;
2260 kJ (540 cal)*

*Below: Vegetable
Korma*

Mix the mince with the other ingredients until well combined.

Cook the meatballs in two batches until browned all over.

Mix together the yoghurt and coconut milk and stir in.

# LAMB KOFTA

•

**Preparation time**: 25 minutes
**Total cooking time**: 50 minutes
**Serves 4–6**

★

1 kg (2 lb) lamb mince
1 medium onion, finely chopped
2 green chillies, finely chopped
3 teaspoons grated fresh ginger
3 cloves garlic, crushed
1 teaspoon ground cardamom
1 egg
1/3 cup (25 g/3/4 oz) fresh breadcrumbs
2 tablespoons ghee or oil

•

**Sauce**
1 tablespoon ghee or oil
1 medium onion, sliced
1 green chilli, finely chopped
3 teaspoons grated fresh ginger
2 cloves garlic, crushed
1 teaspoon ground turmeric
3 teaspoons ground coriander
2 teaspoons ground cumin
1 teaspoon chilli powder
2 tablespoons white vinegar
1 1/3 cups (350 ml/11 fl oz) water
3/4 cup (185 g/6 oz) yoghurt
1 1/4 cups (315 ml/10 fl oz) coconut milk

1 Line an oven tray with baking paper. Place the mince in a large mixing bowl. Add the onion, chilli, ginger, garlic, cardamom, egg and breadcrumbs, and season well with salt and pepper; mix until combined. Roll level tablespoons of the mixture into balls, and place them on the prepared tray.

2 Heat the ghee in a frying pan; add the meatballs in 2 batches and cook over medium heat until browned all over. Transfer the meatballs to a large bowl.

3 To make Sauce: Heat the ghee in the pan; add the onion, chilli, ginger, garlic and turmeric, and cook, stirring, over low heat until the onion is soft. Add the coriander, cumin, chilli powder, vinegar, meatballs and water, and stir gently. Cover and simmer for 30 minutes.

4 Stir in the combined yoghurt and coconut milk and simmer for another 10 minutes with the pan partially covered. Serve with rice.

NUTRITION PER SERVE (6): Protein 40 g; Fat 45 g; Carbohydrate 10 g; Dietary Fibre 0 g; Cholesterol 180 mg; 2450 kJ (585 cal)

*Above: Lamb Kofta*

# RAITAS & RELISHES Add interest to

your curries with one of these spicy relishes, then cool down with a chilled

vegetable or herb yoghurt raita. All these serve four, as an accompaniment.

### CUCUMBER RAITA
Mix 2 peeled, finely chopped
Lebanese cucumbers with 1 cup
(250 g /8 oz) yoghurt. Fry 1 teaspoon
each ground cumin and mustard
seeds in a dry pan for 1 minute until
fragrant. Add to the yoghurt mixture
with 1/2 teaspoon grated fresh ginger.
Season well with salt and pepper and
garnish with paprika. Serve chilled.

*NUTRITION PER 100 g: Protein 5 g;
Fat 2 g; Carbohydrate 5 g; Dietary Fibre 0 g;
Cholesterol 10 mg; 190 kJ (45 cal)*

### CARROT RAITA
Place 1/4 cup (35 g/1 1/4 oz) chopped
pistachio nuts, 1/3 cup (40 g/1 1/3 oz)
sultanas and 1/3 cup (80 ml/2 3/4 fl oz)
boiling water in a small bowl. Soak
for 30 minutes, then drain and pat
dry with paper towels. In another
bowl, place 2 grated carrots, 3/4 cup
(185 g/6 oz) yoghurt, 1 teaspoon
crushed cardamom seeds, 1 teaspoon
ground cumin and 1/4 teaspoon chilli
powder and mix well. Chill for
30 minutes. Stir the pistachio nut

mixture into the yoghurt mixture,
keeping a couple of tablespoons aside
to garnish. Serve chilled.

*NUTRITION PER 100 g: Protein 5 g;
Fat 5 g; Carbohydrate 10 g; Dietary Fibre 2 g;
Cholesterol 5 mg; 485 kJ (115 cal)*

### CORIANDER CHUTNEY
Wash, dry and roughly chop 1 bunch
(90 g/3 oz) coriander, including the
roots. Place in a food processor with
1/4 cup (25 g/3/4 oz) desiccated
coconut, 1 tablespoon soft brown

sugar, 1 teaspoon salt, 1 tablespoon grated fresh ginger, 1 small chopped onion, 2 tablespoons lemon juice and 1–2 small green seeded chillies. Process for about 1 minute, or until finely chopped. Serve chilled.

*NUTRITION PER 100 g: Protein 2 g; Fat 5 g; Carbohydrate 10 g; Dietary Fibre 5 g; Cholesterol 0 mg; 380 kJ (90 cal)*

## FRESH MINT RELISH

Finely chop 50 g (1²/₃oz) fresh mint, 2 spring onions and 1 green chilli. Mix with 1 crushed clove garlic, 1 teaspoon caster sugar, ¹/₂ teaspoon salt and 2 tablespoons lemon juice. Cover and chill for at least 1 hour. Garnish with fine slices of lemon and spring onion and serve.

*NUTRITION PER 100 g: Protein 2 g; Fat 0 g; Carbohydrate 10 g; Dietary Fibre 5 g; Cholesterol 0 mg; 180 kJ (45 cal)*

## FRESH TOMATO RELISH

Mix together 2 diced tomatoes, 3 finely sliced spring onions, 2 tablespoons finely chopped fresh coriander leaves, 1 finely sliced green chilli, 1 tablespoon lemon juice and 1 teaspoon soft brown sugar. Season with salt and pepper. Serve chilled.

*NUTRITION PER 100 g: Protein 1 g; Fat 0 g; Carbohydrate 5 g; Dietary Fibre 1 g; Cholesterol 0 mg; 85 kJ (20 cal)*

## COCONUT BANANAS

Peel 2 large bananas and cut into thick slices. Dip into ¹/₃ cup (80 ml/2³/₄ fl oz) lemon juice, then toss in enough desiccated coconut to coat each piece. Serve at room temperature.

*NUTRITION PER 100 g: Protein 2 g; Fat 5 g; Carbohydrate 15 g; Dietary Fibre 5 g; Cholesterol 0 mg; 465 kJ (110 cal)*

## YOGHURT AND MINT RAITA

Combine 1 cup (250 ml/8 fl oz) yoghurt, ¹/₃ cup (20 g/²/₃ oz) chopped fresh mint and a pinch of cayenne pepper and mix well. Serve chilled.

*NUTRITION PER 100 g: Protein 5 g; Fat 5 g; Carbohydrate 5 g; Dietary Fibre 0 g; Cholesterol 15 mg; 285 kJ (70 cal)*

*Clockwise from top left: Fresh Coriander Chutney; Carrot Raita; Fresh Tomato Relish; Yoghurt and Mint Raita; Coconut Bananas; Fresh Mint Relish; Cucumber Raita*

## BALTI DISHES

*Balti is a type of curry originating in a region of north-eastern Pakistan formerly known as Baltistan, and cooked in a traditional two-handled, cast iron balti pan, karahi, which is similar to a wok. (Any lidded, heavy-based saucepan is a suitable replacement.) Traditional balti recipes are based on meat with subtle aromatic spices and only a small amount of chilli. The curry is slightly oily, contains fresh garlic, ginger and coriander, and is spiced with fennel, black mustard seeds, cloves, cardamom, coriander seeds, cumin, cassia bark and garam masala.*

*Above: Mulligatawny*

## MULLIGATAWNY

•

**Preparation time**: 40 minutes
**Total cooking time**: 1 hour 20 minutes
**Serves** 6

☆

1 kg (2 lb) chicken pieces
2 tablespoons plain flour
2 teaspoons Madras curry powder
1 teaspoon ground turmeric
½ teaspoon ground ginger
60 g (2 oz) butter
6 whole cloves
12 black peppercorns
1 large apple, peeled and chopped
6 cups (1.5 litres) chicken stock
2 tablespoons lemon juice
½ cup (125 ml/4 fl oz) cream

•

1 Trim the chicken of excess fat and sinew. Combine the flour, curry powder, turmeric and ginger, and rub the mixture into the chicken.
2 Heat the butter in a large pan; add the chicken and cook it on all sides over medium heat until lightly browned. Tie the cloves and peppercorns in a small piece of muslin, and add to the pan with the apple and stock. Bring to the boil, then reduce heat slightly and simmer, covered, for 1 hour.
3 Remove the chicken from the pan and discard the muslin bag. Remove the meat from the bones and finely chop. Discard the skin and bones. Skim the fat from the soup.
4 Return the chicken meat to the pan. Stir in the lemon juice and cream, and heat gently. (Do not allow the soup to boil or it will curdle.)

NUTRITION PER SERVE: Protein 30 g; Fat 25 g; Carbohydrate 10 g; Dietary Fibre 0 g; Cholesterol 140 mg; 1495 kJ (355 cal)

•

## BALTI LAMB

•

**Preparation time**: 15 minutes
**Total cooking time**:1 hour 30 minutes
**Serves** 4

☆ ☆

1 kg (2 lb) lamb leg steaks
1½ cups (375ml/12 fl oz) boiling water
1 tablespoon Balti Masala Paste (page 127)
2 tablespoons ghee or oil
3 cloves garlic, crushed
1 tablespoon garam masala
1 large onion, finely chopped
4 tablespoons Balti Masala Paste, extra
2 tablespoons chopped fresh coriander leaves
1 cup (250 ml/8 fl oz) water
fresh coriander leaves, extra, to garnish

1 Preheat the oven to moderately hot 190°C (375°F/Gas 5).

2 Cut the meat into 3 cm (1¼ inch) cubes.

3 Place the meat, boiling water and masala paste in a large casserole dish. Cover and cook for 30 to 40 minutes, or until slightly undercooked. Drain and reserve the stock.

4 Heat the ghee in a balti pan or wok; stir-fry the garlic and garam masala for 1 minute. Add the onion and cook over medium heat until the onion is soft and golden brown. Increase the heat, add the extra masala paste and the lamb. Stir-fry for 5 minutes to brown the meat.

5 Slowly add the reserved stock and simmer over low heat, stirring for 15 minutes.

6 Add the coriander leaves and water. Simmer for 15 minutes or until the meat is tender and the sauce has thickened slightly. Season to taste. Garnish with coriander leaves and serve with roti or naan bread.

*NUTRITION PER SERVE: Protein 55 g; Fat 30 g; Carbohydrate 5 g; Dietary Fibre 0 g; Cholesterol 190 mg; 2130 kJ (510 cal)*

•

## LAMB KORMA

•

**Preparation time**: 30 minutes
 + 1 hour marinating
**Total cooking time**: 1 hour
*Serves 4–6*

☆

2 kg (4 lb) leg of lamb, boned
1 medium onion, chopped
2 teaspoons grated fresh ginger
3 cloves garlic
1 tablespoon coriander seeds
2 teaspoons ground cumin
1 teaspoon cardamom pods
½ teaspoon salt
large pinch cayenne pepper
2 tablespoons ghee or oil
1 medium onion, extra, sliced
2 tablespoons tomato paste (tomato purée, double concentrate)
½ cup (125 g/4 oz) yoghurt

•

1 Remove all excess fat, skin and sinew from the lamb. Cut the meat into 3 cm (1¼ inch) cubes and place it in a large bowl.

2 Place the onion, ginger, garlic, coriander seeds, cumin, cardamom pods, salt and cayenne pepper in a food processor and process until the mixture forms a smooth paste. Add the spice mixture to the lamb and mix well to coat. Set aside for 1 hour.

3 Heat the ghee in a large pan; add the extra onion and cook, stirring, over moderately low heat until the onion is soft. Add the lamb mixture and cook for 8 to 10 minutes, stirring constantly, until the lamb cubes are browned all over. Add the tomato paste and 2 tablespoons of the yoghurt, and stir until combined. Simmer, uncovered, until the liquid has been absorbed.

4 Add the remaining yoghurt, 2 tablespoons at a time, stirring until the mixture is nearly dry between each addition.

5 Cover the pan and simmer over low heat for 30 minutes, or until the meat is tender, stirring occasionally. Add a little water if the mixture becomes too dry. Serve with rice.

*NUTRITION PER SERVE (6): Protein 53 g; Fat 20 g; Carbohydrate 5 g; Dietary Fibre 1 g; Cholesterol 175 mg; 1645 kJ (390 cal)*

*Below: Lamb Korma*

## FRIED FISH WITH MILD CURRY AND CORIANDER

•

*Preparation time*: 15 minutes
*Total cooking time*: 10 minutes
*Serves* 4

★

2 tablespoons ghee or oil
4 firm white fish fillets, 125 g (4 oz) each
1 medium onion, finely chopped
1 teaspoon finely chopped garlic
1 teaspoon ground coriander
2 teaspoons ground cumin
1/2 teaspoon ground turmeric
1/2 teaspoon chilli flakes
1 tablespoon tomato paste (tomato purée, double concentrate)
1/2 cup (125 ml/4 fl oz) water
chopped coriander leaves, to serve

•

1 Melt the ghee in a large pan and cook the fish over medium heat for 1 minute on each side. Transfer the fish to a plate.
2 Add the onion and garlic to the pan and cook until soft and golden. Add the coriander, cumin, turmeric and chilli and stir-fry for 30 seconds.
3 Add the tomato paste and water and simmer for 2 minutes. Add the fish and cook for 1 minute on each side. Sprinkle with coriander and serve with rice.

*NUTRITION PER SERVE: Protein 30 g; Fat 10 g; Carbohydrate 0 g; Dietary Fibre 0 g; Cholesterol 110 mg; 905 kJ (215 cal)*

## BEEF VINDALOO

•

*Preparation time*: 20 minutes
*Total cooking time*: 1 hour 45 minutes
*Serves* 4

★

1 kg (2 lb) chuck, blade or skirt steak
1/2 teaspoon ground cumin
1 tablespoon coriander seeds
1/2 teaspoon cardamom seeds
1 teaspoon ground fenugreek
2 teaspoons chilli powder
1 teaspoon ground turmeric
1 teaspoon mustard powder
2 tablespoons ghee or oil
3 medium onions, sliced
3 teaspoons grated fresh ginger
3 cloves garlic, crushed
1 cinnamon stick
1/3 cup (80 ml/2¾ fl oz) brown vinegar
1/2 cup (125 ml/4 fl oz) beef stock
1 teaspoon sugar

•

1 Cut the steak into 3 cm (1¼ inch) cubes.
2 Place the cumin, coriander and cardamom seeds, fenugreek, chilli powder, turmeric and mustard powder in a food processor and process until finely ground.
3 Heat the ghee in a large pan; add the meat in 2 batches and cook over medium heat until browned all over. Transfer the meat to a bowl.
4 Add the onion, ginger, garlic and cinnamon to the pan, and stir over low heat until the onion is

## SERVING AN INDIAN MEAL

*All Indian meals are served with either rice or bread or both. Rice is the major part of the meal and is placed in the centre of the plate with small portions of curries and various raitas arranged around it. Bread is used to sop up the curries and sop up the juices.*

*with
and
r*

1 Peel the eggs and coat them with the turmeric.
2 Melt the ghee in a large pan and cook the eggs over moderate heat for 2 minutes until they are light brown, stirring constantly. Set aside.
3 Add the bay leaf, onion and garlic to the pan and cook over moderately high heat, stirring frequently, until the mixture is well reduced and pale gold. Lower the heat if the mixture is browning too quickly. Add the coriander, garam masala and chilli powder, if using, and cook until fragrant.
4 Add the tomato, tomato paste and water; cover and simmer for 5 minutes. Return the eggs to the pan with the ricotta, salt, yoghurt and peas, and cook for 5 minutes. Remove the bay leaf, sprinkle with coriander and serve immediately.
NOTE: Baked ricotta is available from delicatessens and some supermarkets, but it is easy enough to prepare your own. Preheat the oven to warm 160°C (315°F/Gas 2–3). Slice 500 g (1 lb) fresh ricotta (not cottage cheese or blended ricotta) into 3 cm (1¼ inch) thick slices. Place the ricotta on a lightly greased baking tray and bake for 25 minutes.

*NUTRITION PER SERVE: Protein 15 g; Fat 20 g; Carbohydrate 5 g; Dietary Fibre 5 g; Cholesterol 302 mg; 1075 kJ (255 cal)*

## GARAM MASALA

*Although one of the best known Indian spice mixtures, garam masala does not contain turmeric, the ingredient that gives many curries their characteristic yellow colour. Garam masala was popularised in northern India during the Moghul reign of the seventeenth and eighteenth centuries; curries there are usually brown or pale in colour. (See recipe on page 127.)*

soft. Add the spices and meat and stir until the meat is well coated. Add the vinegar, stock, sugar, and salt and pepper to taste. Cover and cook over low heat for 1½ hours, or until the meat is tender. Remove the cinnamon stick before serving.

*NUTRITION PER SERVE: Protein 50 g; Fat 20 g; Carbohydrate 5 g; Dietary Fibre 0 g; Cholesterol 190 mg; 1720 kJ (410 cal)*

*Above: Beef Vindaloo*
*Below: Pea, Egg and Ricotta Curry*

# PEA, EGG AND RICOTTA CURRY

**Preparation time**: 15 minutes
**Total cooking time**: 30 minutes
**Serves 4**

4 hard-boiled eggs
½ teaspoon ground turmeric
3 tablespoons ghee or oil
1 bay leaf
2 small onions, finely chopped
1 teaspoon finely chopped garlic
1½ teaspoons ground coriander
1½ teaspoons garam masala
½ teaspoon chilli powder, optional
½ cup (125 g/4 oz) chopped, canned, peeled tomatoes
1 tablespoon tomato paste (tomato purée, double concentrate)
½ cup (125 ml/4 fl oz) water
125 g (4 oz) baked ricotta, cut in 1 cm (½ inch) cubes
¼ teaspoon salt
1 tablespoon yoghurt
½ cup (80 g/2⅔ oz) frozen peas
2 tablespoons finely chopped fresh coriander leaves

## BALTI CHICKEN

•

*Preparation time*: 10 minutes
*Total cooking time*: 50 minutes
*Serves 4*

★

1 kg (2 lb) chicken thigh fillets
2 tablespoons ghee or oil
2 cloves garlic, crushed
1 cinnamon stick
½ teaspoon cardamom seeds
1 tablespoon garam masala
1 teaspoon sesame seeds
1 teaspoon poppy seeds
½ teaspoon fennel seeds
2 medium onions, finely sliced
3 tablespoons Balti Masala Paste (page 127)
1 cup (250 ml/8 fl oz) chicken stock
1 cup (250 ml/8 fl oz) cream
1 tablespoon fresh coriander leaves

*Above: Balti Chicken*

1 Cut the chicken into 3 cm (1¼ inch) cubes.
2 Heat the ghee in a balti pan or wok; stir-fry the garlic, cinnamon stick, cardamom seeds and garam masala over medium heat for 1 minute. Add the sesame, poppy and fennel seeds, and fry for a further 30 seconds. Reduce the heat, add the onion and cook for 10 minutes or until the onion is soft and golden brown.
3 Add the masala paste and chicken and cook, stirring occasionally, for 5 minutes.
4 Reduce the heat and add the stock. Cover and simmer for 20 minutes. Add the cream and cook for a further 10 minutes, stirring occasionally.
5 Stir in the coriander leaves, and season with salt and pepper to taste. Serve with roti or naan bread.

NUTRITION PER SERVE: Protein 35 g; Fat 50 g; Carbohydrate 5 g; Dietary Fibre 0 g; Cholesterol 230 mg; 2570 kJ (615 cal)

# SAMOSAS

•

**Preparation time**: 30 minutes
**Total cooking time**: 25 minutes
**Makes** about 24

⭐

2 medium potatoes, cut into chunks
1/2 cup (80 g/2²/3 oz) frozen peas
1/4 cup (35 g/1¹/4 oz) currants
2 tablespoons chopped fresh coriander
    leaves
2 tablespoons lemon juice
1 tablespoon soy sauce
1 teaspoon ground cumin
1 teaspoon ground chilli powder
1/2 teaspoon chopped fresh chilli
1/4 teaspoon ground cinnamon
1 packet (1 kg/2 lb) ready-rolled frozen
    puff pastry, thawed
oil, for shallow-frying

•

**Mint Yoghurt Sauce**
1/2 cup (125 g/4 oz) yoghurt
1/2 cup (125 ml/4 fl oz) buttermilk
1/4 cup (15 g/¹/2 oz) finely chopped
    fresh mint
1/2 teaspoon ground cumin

1 Cook the potatoes in a large pan of boiling water until tender. Cool and chop finely. Mix together the potato, peas, currants, coriander, lemon juice, soy sauce, cumin, chilli powder, chilli and cinnamon.

2 Cut the pastry into rounds using a 10 cm (4 cm) cutter. Place 1 tablespoon of the mixture on one half of each round. Fold the pastry over the filling to make a semicircle. Press the edges together firmly with a fork.

3 Heat the oil, about 2 cm (¾ inch) deep, in a frying pan; cook the samosas two at a time, for about 2 minutes on each side or until golden brown and puffed. Drain on paper towels and serve with Mint Yoghurt Sauce.

4 To make Mint Yoghurt Sauce: Combine the yoghurt, buttermilk, mint and cumin and stir until smooth.

NUTRITION PER SAMOSA WITH SAUCE: Protein 5 g;
Fat 10 g; Carbohydrate 15 g; Dietary Fibre 1 g; Cholesterol
10 mg; 635 kJ (150 cal)

SAMOSAS

Mix together the
vegetables, currants,
spices, lemon juice and
soy sauce.

Fold the pastry over
the filling to make a
semi-circle and press
the edges together with
a fork.

Cook the samosas two
at a time until golden
brown and puffed.

*Above: Samosas*

243

## ROSE WATER
*Used as a flavouring in Indian drinks, desserts and some savoury dishes, rose water is the diluted essence extracted from rose petals. It is a thin, pale pink liquid and not to be confused with rose essence which is 40 times stronger.*

## CHICKEN MASALA

•

*Preparation time*: 25 minutes
  + 4 hours marinating
*Total cooking time*: 45 minutes
*Serves 4–6*

★

6 chicken thigh cutlets
2 teaspoons ground fenugreek
2 cloves garlic, crushed
1 teaspoon grated fresh ginger
1/2 cup (10 g/1/3 oz) fresh mint
1/4 cup (60 ml/2 fl oz) vinegar
1/2 cup (15 g/1/2 oz) fresh coriander leaves
1 teaspoon salt
2 teaspoons ground turmeric
1/2 teaspoon ground cloves
1/2 teaspoon ground cardamom

*Below: Chicken Masala*

1 Trim the chicken of any excess fat and sinew; cut a few slits in each cutlet.
2 Place the fenugreek, garlic, ginger, mint, vinegar, coriander, salt, turmeric, cloves and cardamom in a food processor and process until a smooth paste is formed.
3 Place the chicken in a shallow non-metallic baking dish and rub it all over with the spice paste. Cover and marinate for at least 4 hours or overnight in the refrigerator.
4 Preheat the oven to moderate 180°C (350°F/ Gas 4). Bake the chicken for 45 minutes. Serve with rice.

*NUTRITION PER SERVE (6): Protein 20 g; Fat 3 g; Carbohydrate 0 g; Dietary Fibre 0 g; Cholesterol 55 mg; 420 kJ (100 cal)*

•

## LAMB BIRYANI

•

*Preparation time*: 50 minutes
  + 1 hour marinating
*Total cooking time*: 1 hour 45 minutes
*Serves 6–8*

★ ★

1 kg (2 lb) diced lamb
1 medium onion, chopped
4 cloves garlic, crushed
4 cm (11/2 inch) piece fresh ginger, chopped
2 green chillies, seeded and chopped
2 tablespoons ground coriander
2 cups (500 g/1 lb) yoghurt
2 tablespoons ghee or oil
2 medium onions, extra, finely sliced
2 tablespoons blanched almonds
2 tablespoons sultanas
500 g (1 lb) basmati rice
5 cardamom pods
1 cinnamon stick
2 tablespoons rose water
6 tablespoons ghee
1 teaspoon salt
4 cups (1 litre) chicken stock
1/2 teaspoon saffron threads
2 tablespoons hot milk
4 hard-boiled eggs, sliced

•

1 Place the lamb, chopped onion, garlic, ginger, chilli, coriander and yoghurt in a bowl and mix to combine. Cover andleave in the fridge to marinate for 1 hour.
2 Heat the ghee in a frying pan; add the extra onion and cook over medium heat for 15 minutes or until the onion is slightly crisp and golden brown. Remove the onion from the pan and drain on paper towels. Add the almonds

and sultanas to the pan and cook for 3 minutes, or until the sultanas are plump. Remove from the pan and set aside.

3 Wash the rice under cold water and drain for 15 minutes. Place the rice in a large pan and add the cardamom, cinnamon, rose water and 2 tablespoons of the ghee. Cook over medium heat for 3 minutes, or until the rice is translucent. Add the salt and chicken stock and bring to the boil, then reduce the heat, cover and simmer for 15 minutes.

4 Soak the saffron in the hot milk for 5 minutes, pour over the cooked rice and mix thoroughly to combine.

5 Preheat the oven to hot 220°C (425°F/Gas 7). Layer a large lightly greased casserole dish with half the rice, the lamb, the egg, half the fried onions, almonds and sultanas, and the other half of the rice to finish. Dot with the remaining ghee. Cover and bake in the oven for 50 minutes, or until the meat is tender. Garnish with the remaining fried onions, the almonds and sultanas.

*NUTRITION PER SERVE (8): Protein 40 g; Fat 35 g; Carbohydrate 60 g; Dietary Fibre 5 g; Cholesterol 275 mg; 2980 kJ (710 cal)*

## SWEET VEGETABLE CURRY

**Preparation time**: 20 minutes
**Total cooking time**: 40 minutes
**Serves** 4

★

2 medium carrots
1 medium parsnip
1 medium potato
2 tablespoons oil
2 medium onions, chopped
1 teaspoon ground cardamom
1/4 teaspoon ground cloves
1 1/2 teaspoons cumin seeds
1 teaspoon ground coriander
1 teaspoon ground turmeric
1 teaspoon brown mustard seeds
1/2 teaspoon chilli powder
2 teaspoons grated fresh ginger
1 1/3 cups (350 ml/11 fl oz) vegetable stock
3/4 cup (185 ml/6 fl oz) apricot nectar
2 tablespoons fruit chutney
1 medium green pepper (capsicum), cut into 2 cm (3/4 inch) squares
200 g (6 1/2 oz) small button mushrooms
300 g (9 2/3 oz) cauliflower, cut into small florets
1/4 cup (45 g/1 1/2 oz) ground almonds

1 Cut the carrots, parsnip and potato into 2 cm (3/4 inch) pieces.

2 Heat the oil in a large heavy-based pan; add the onion and cook over medium heat for 4 minutes, or until just soft. Add the cardamom, cloves, cumin seeds, coriander, turmeric, mustard seeds, chilli powder and ginger, and cook, stirring, for 1 minute or until aromatic.

3 Add the carrot, parsnip, potato, stock, nectar and chutney. Cook, covered, over medium heat for 25 minutes, stirring occasionally.

4 Stir in the green pepper, mushrooms and cauliflower. Simmer for 10 minutes more or until the vegetables are tender. Stir in the ground almonds and serve with rice.

NOTE: Any vegetables can be used in this curry. For example, broccoli, zucchini (courgette), red pepper (capsicum) or orange sweet potato would be suitable.

*NUTRITION PER SERVE: Protein 10 g; Fat 15 g; Carbohydrate 25 g; Dietary Fibre 10 g; Cholesterol 0 mg; 1245 kJ (295 cal)*

---

### BIRYANI
*There are many kinds of biryani, which is rice fried in ghee and spices, and layered with spiced meat, poultry or seafood. They differ from other rice dishes, such as pilaus, in three main ways: biryanis are always flavoured and coloured with saffron or turmeric, large amounts of ghee are used, and there is always a large proportion of meat or fish to rice, sometimes twice as much.*

*Above: Sweet Vegetable Curry*

4 Add the lamb to the pan in batches and cook over high heat until browned. Remove from the pan and cover loosely with foil.

5 Add the onion paste to the pan; cook for 5 minutes, or until the ghee starts to separate from the onion. Reduce the heat to low, return the meat to the pan with the cardamom, cover and cook for 1 hour or until the meat is tender.

6 Add the fried onion and sprinkle the garam masala over the lamb; cover and continue cooking for 15 minutes. Serve with rice and naan bread.

*NUTRITION PER SERVE (6): Protein 40 g; Fat 25 g; Carbohydrate 10 g; Dietary Fibre 5 g; Cholesterol 150 mg; 1770 kJ (420 cal)*

## SAAG PANIR
### (CHEESE IN SPINACH SAUCE)

*Preparation time*: 20 minutes
  + 3 hours standing
*Total cooking time*: 30 minutes
*Serves 4*

★★

2 litres milk
4 tablespoons lemon juice
2 tablespoons yoghurt
500 g (1 lb) spinach
2 cloves garlic
2 cm (3/4 inch) piece fresh ginger, grated
2 green chillies, chopped
1 medium onion, chopped
2 tablespoons ghee or oil
1 teaspoon salt
1 teaspoon ground cumin
1/2 teaspoon nutmeg
3 tablespoons yoghurt
1 cup (250 ml/8 fl oz) water
1/2 cup (125 ml/4 fl oz) cream

1 Heat the milk in a large pan until just boiling; reduce the heat, add the lemon juice and yoghurt, and stir until the mixture begins to curdle. Remove the pan from the heat and allow the milk mixture to stand for 5 minutes or until curds start to form.

2 Line a colander with muslin. Pour the curd mixture into the colander and leave until most of the liquid has drained away. Gather up the corners of the muslin, hold them together and squeeze as much moisture as possible from the curd. Return the muslin-wrapped curd to the colander and leave in a cool place for 3 hours until the curd is very firm and all the whey has drained away. Cut the cheese into 4 cm (1½ inch) cubes.

## LAMB DOPIAZA

*Preparation time*: 20 minutes
*Total cooking time*: 2 hours
*Serves 4–6*

★★

1 kg (2 lb) onions
5 cloves garlic
5 cm (2 inch) piece fresh ginger, grated
2 red chillies
1 teaspoon paprika
4 tablespoons chopped fresh coriander
  leaves
2 tablespoons ground coriander
2 teaspoons black cumin seeds
4 tablespoons yoghurt
4 tablespoons ghee or oil
1 kg (2 lb) diced lamb
6 cardamom pods, lightly crushed
1 teaspoon garam masala

1 Slice half the onions and set aside; roughly chop the remaining onions.

2 Place the chopped onion, garlic, ginger, chilli, paprika, fresh and ground coriander, cumin seeds and yoghurt in a food processor and process until a smooth paste is formed.

3 Heat the ghee in a large pan; add the sliced onion and cook over medium heat for 10 minutes or until golden brown. Remove the onion from the pan using a slotted spoon and drain on paper towels.

*Above: Lamb Dopiaza*

3 Steam the spinach over simmering water until tender. Squeeze out any excess moisture and chop finely.

4 Place the garlic, ginger, chilli and onion in a food processor and process until very finely chopped.

5 Heat the ghee in a wok; add the paste and cook over medium heat for 5 minutes or until the ghee begins to separate from the paste. Add the salt, cumin, nutmeg, yoghurt and water, and simmer for 5 minutes. Transfer the mixture to a food processor, add the steamed spinach and process until smooth. Return the mixture to the wok, add the chopped cheese and cream, and cook for 10 minutes or until the sauce is heated through. Serve with rice.

NUTRITION PER SERVE: Protein 25 g; Fat 40 g; Carbohydrate 30 g; Dietary Fibre 5 g; Cholesterol 135 mg; 2450 kJ (585 cal)

### BUTTER CHICKEN

**Preparation time**: 30 minutes
+ 4 hours marinating
**Total cooking time**: 30 minutes
**Serves** 4

★ ★

1 kg (2 lb) chicken thigh fillets
1 teaspoon salt
1/4 cup (60 ml/2 fl oz) lemon juice
1 cup (8 fl oz) yoghurt
1 medium onion, chopped
2 cloves garlic, crushed
3 cm (1 1/4 inch) piece fresh ginger, grated
1 green chilli, chopped
2 teaspoons garam masala
2 teaspoons yellow food colouring
1 teaspoon red food colouring
1/2 cup (125 ml/4 fl oz) tomato purée
   (passata)
1/2 cup (125 ml/4 fl oz) water
2 cm (3/4 inch) piece fresh ginger, extra,
   finely grated
1 cup (250 ml/8 fl oz) cream
1 teaspoon garam masala, extra
2 teaspoons sugar
1/4 teaspoon chilli powder
1 tablespoon lemon juice
1 teaspoon ground cumin
100 g (3 1/3 oz) butter

1 Cut the chicken into strips 2 cm (3/4 inch) thick. Sprinkle with the salt and lemon juice.

2 Place the yoghurt, onion, garlic, ginger, chilli and garam masala in a food processor and process until smooth.

3 Combine the food colourings in a small bowl, brush over the chicken and turn to coat. Add the yoghurt mixture and toss to combine. Cover and refrigerate for 4 hours. Remove the chicken from the marinade and allow to drain for 5 minutes.

4 Preheat the oven to hot 220°C (425°F/Gas 7). Bake the chicken in a shallow baking dish for 15 minutes, or until tender. Drain off any excess juice, cover loosely with foil and keep warm.

5 Combine the tomato purée and water in a large jug. Add the ginger, cream, extra garam masala, sugar, chilli powder, lemon juice and cumin and stir to combine.

6 Melt the butter in a large pan over medium heat. Stir in the tomato mixture and bring to the boil. Cook for 2 minutes, then reduce the heat and add the chicken pieces. Stir to coat the chicken in the sauce and simmer for 2 minutes longer or until heated through. Serve with rice.

NUTRITION PER SERVE: Protein 60 g; Fat 60 g; Carbohydrate 10 g; Dietary Fibre 0 g; Cholesterol 330 mg; 3400 kJ (810 cal)

### GHEE

Ghee is clarified butter or pure butter fat. It gives a rich buttery taste to food and, because it has no milk solids, won't burn at high temperatures. Butter or a bland oil can be substituted for ghee. Alternatively, a mixture of half ghee and half extra light olive oil (which has little taste) has both the rich flavour of ghee and the health benefits of olive oil.

*Below: Butter Chicken*

# BREADS
One of the surprises of northern Indian cuisine is the beautiful breads. From paper-thin parathas to puffed-up naan, they are traditionally cooked in a clay oven and torn apart to mop up curries.

## PARATHAS
Place 2¼ cups (280 g/9 oz) atta flour and a pinch of salt in a large bowl. Rub in 40 g (1⅓ oz) ghee with your fingertips until fine and crumbly. Make a well in the centre and gradually add ¾ cup (185 ml/6 fl oz) cold water to form a firm dough. Turn onto a well-floured surface and knead until smooth. Cover with plastic wrap and set aside for 40 minutes. Divide into 10 portions. Roll each on a floured surface to a

13 cm (5 inch) circle. Brush lightly with melted ghee or oil. Cut through each round to the centre and roll tightly to form a cone shape, then press down on the pointed top. Re-roll into a 13 cm (5 inches) circle again. Cook one at a time in hot oil or ghee in a frying pan until puffed and lightly browned on both sides. Drain on paper towels. Makes 10.

*NUTRITION PER PARATHA: Protein 3 g; Fat 15 g; Carbohydrate 20 g; Dietary Fibre 1 g; Cholesterol 10 mg; 900 kJ (215 cal)*

## NAAN
Preheat the oven to moderately hot, 200°C (400°F/Gas 6). Sift together 500 g (1 lb) plain flour, 1 teaspoon baking powder, ½ teaspoon bicarbonate of soda and 1 teaspoon salt. Add 1 beaten egg, 1 tablespoon melted ghee or butter, ½ cup (125 g/ 4 oz) yoghurt and gradually add 1 cup (250 ml/8 fl oz) milk or enough to form a soft dough. Cover with a damp cloth and leave in a warm place for 2 hours. Knead on a well-floured

surface for 2–3 minutes, or until smooth. Divide into 8 portions and roll each one into an oval 15 cm (6 inches) long. Brush with water and place, wet-side-down, on greased baking trays. Brush with melted ghee or butter and bake for 8–10 minutes, or until golden brown. Makes 8.

*NUTRITION PER NAAN: Protein 10 g; Fat 5 g; Carbohydrate 50 g; Dietary Fibre 2 g; Cholesterol 35 mg; 1185 kJ (280 cal)*

## PURIS

Sift together 2½ cups (375 g/12 oz) wholemeal flour and a pinch of salt. With your fingertips, rub in 1 tablespoon ghee or oil. Gradually add 1 cup (250 ml/8 oz) water to form a firm dough. Knead on a lightly floured surface until smooth. Cover with plastic wrap and set aside for 50 minutes. Divide into 18 portions and roll each into a 14 cm (5½ inch) circle. Heat 3 cm (1¼ inches) oil in a deep frying pan until moderately hot; fry one at a time, spooning oil over until they puff up and swell. Cook on each side until golden brown. Drain on paper towels. Serve immediately. Makes 18.

*NUTRITION PER PURI: Protein 3 g; Fat 5 g; Carbohydrate 10 g; Dietary Fibre 2 g; Cholesterol 3 mg; 460 kJ (110 cal)*

## CHAPATTIS

Place 2¼ cups (280 g/9 oz) atta flour and a pinch of salt in a large bowl. Gradually add 1 cup (250 ml/8 fl oz) water, or enough to form a firm dough. Knead on a lightly floured surface until smooth. Cover with plastic wrap and set aside for 50 minutes. Divide into 14 portions and roll into 14 cm (5½ inch) circles. Brush a heated frying pan with a little melted ghee or oil. Cook over medium heat, flattening the surface, until both sides are golden brown and bubbles appear. Makes 14.

*NUTRITION PER CHAPATTI: Protein 2 g; Fat 0 g; Carbohydrate 15 g; Dietary Fibre 1 g; Cholesterol 0 mg; 285 kJ (65 cal)*

## POPPADOMS

Poppadoms are thin wafers made of lentil, rice or potato flour. Use tongs to slide them one at a time into 2 cm (¾ inch) very hot oil—they should puff at once. Turn over, remove quickly and drain on paper towels.

*NUTRITION PER POPPADOM: Protein 2 g; Fat 2 g; Carbohydrate 4 g; Dietary Fibre 1 g; Cholesterol 0 mg; 155 kJ (35 cal)*

*From left: Parathas; Naan; Puris; Chapattis; Poppadoms*

## DHAL

•

**Preparation time:** 15 minutes
**Total cooking time:** 1 hour
**Serves** 4–6

★

200 g (6½ oz) red lentils
4 cups (1 litre) water
4 cm (1½ inch) piece fresh ginger, cut
  into 3 slices
½ teaspoon ground turmeric
½ teaspoon salt
3 tablespoons ghee or oil
2 cloves garlic, crushed
1 medium onion, finely chopped
pinch of asafoetida, optional
1 teaspoon cumin seeds
1 teaspoon ground coriander
¼ teaspoon chilli powder
1 tablespoon chopped fresh coriander
  leaves

•

1 Place the lentils and water in a medium pan, and bring to the boil. Reduce heat to low, add the ginger and turmeric, and simmer, covered, for 1 hour or until the lentils are tender. Stir every 5 minutes during the last 30 minutes to prevent the lentils sticking to the pan. Remove the ginger and stir in the salt.

2 Heat the ghee in a frying pan; add the garlic and onion, and cook over medium heat for 3 minutes or until the onion is golden. Add the asafoetida, if using, cumin seeds, coriander and chilli powder, and cook for 2 minutes.

3 Add the onion mixture to the lentils and stir gently to combine. Serve sprinkled with fresh coriander.

*NUTRITION PER SERVE (6): Protein 10 g; Fat 10 g; Carbohydrate 15 g; Dietary Fibre 5 g; Cholesterol 30 mg; 810 kJ (190 cal)*

•

## INDIAN PRAWN FRITTERS

•

**Preparation time:** 25 minutes
  + 30 minutes standing
**Total cooking time:** 20 minutes
**Makes** 15

★

350 g (11¼ oz) raw prawns
1 medium onion, roughly chopped
2 cloves garlic, chopped
4 cm (1½ inch) piece fresh ginger, grated
1–2 tablespoons ready-made curry paste
2 tablespoons lemon juice
½ cup (15 g/½ oz) fresh coriander leaves
1 teaspoon ground turmeric
½ teaspoon salt
¼ teaspoon cracked black pepper
½ cup (55 g/1¾ oz) besan (chickpea
  flour)
oil, for shallow frying

•

1 Peel and devein the prawns. Place the prawns, onion, garlic, ginger, curry paste, lemon juice, coriander, turmeric, salt and pepper in a food processor and process for 20 to 30 seconds or until well combined. Cover and refrigerate for 30 minutes.

2 Roll tablespoons of the prawn mixture into round patties and lightly coat in besan. Heat the oil, about 2 cm (¾ inch) deep, in a frying pan; add the fritters in batches, and cook over medium heat for 3 minutes or until golden brown. Drain on paper towels and serve with yoghurt and lemon wedges, if desired.

NOTE: Use any Indian curry paste of your choice. Pastes suitable for prawns are rogan josh, balti, tikka masala, vindaloo and tandoori.

*NUTRITION PER FRITTER: Protein 5 g; Fat 5 g; Carbohydrate 0 g; Dietary Fibre 0 g; Cholesterol 15 mg; 350 kJ (85 cal)*

*Below: Dhal*

## INDIAN FRIED FISH

•

*Preparation time*: 15 minutes
*Total cooking time*: 20 minutes
*Serves 4*

⭐

500 g (1 lb) *firm white fish fillets*
¾ cup (80 g/2²/₃ oz) *besan (chickpea
  flour)*
1 *teaspoon salt*
1 *teaspoon garam masala*
¼ *teaspoon chilli powder*
¼ *teaspoon ground turmeric*
¼ *teaspoon freshly ground black pepper*
2 *tablespoons chopped fresh coriander
  leaves*
2 *eggs, lightly beaten*
*oil, for shallow-frying*

1 Wash the fish fillets, pat them dry, and cut
them in half lengthways.
2 Sift the besan, salt, garam masala, chilli
powder, turmeric and black pepper into a bowl.
Add the coriander and stir to combine, then
spread the mixture out on a plate.
3 Dip each fish fillet into the egg, then into the
spiced flour, shaking off any excess.
4 Heat 2 cm (¾ inch) oil in a frying pan; fry the
coated fish fillets in batches over high heat for
5 minutes or until crisp and golden. Serve with
rice and raitas (see pages 236 to 237).

NUTRITION PER SERVE: *Protein 35 g; Fat 25 g;
Carbohydrate 10 g; Dietary Fibre 5 g; Cholesterol 200 mg;
1730 kJ (415 cal)*

*Above: Indian
Fried Fish*

*Opposite: Hyderabadi
Fish (top); Goan
Spiced Mussels*

## CAULIFLOWER, TOMATO AND GREEN PEA CURRY

*Preparation time*: 25 minutes
*Total cooking time*: 20 minutes
*Serves 4–6*

✮

1 small cauliflower, cut into small florets
1½ cups (240 g/7½ oz) green peas
4 tablespoons ghee or oil
1 medium onion, thinly sliced
1 teaspoon crushed garlic
1 teaspoon grated fresh ginger
¾ teaspoon ground turmeric
1 tablespoon ground coriander
1 tablespoon ready-made vindaloo paste
2 teaspoons sugar
2 cardamom pods, lightly crushed
¾ cup (185 g/6 oz) yoghurt
2 large tomatoes, cut into thin wedges

1 Steam the cauliflower and peas until tender.
2 Heat the ghee in a large pan and cook the onion, garlic and ginger over medium heat until soft and golden. Add the turmeric, coriander, vindaloo paste, sugar, cardamom pods and yoghurt and cook for 3 to 4 minutes. Add the tomato and cook for 3 to 4 minutes.
3 Add the cauliflower and peas and simmer for 3 for 4 minutes. Serve with rice.

*NUTRITION PER SERVE (6): Protein 10 g; Fat 15 g; Carbohydrate 10 g; Dietary Fibre 5 g; Cholesterol 45 mg; 965 kJ (230 cal)*

## HYDERABADI FISH

*Preparation time*: 20 minutes
*Total cooking time*: 40 minutes
*Serves 4*

✮

3 tablespoons desiccated coconut
2 tablespoons cumin seeds
3 tablespoons sesame seeds
1 tablespoon fenugreek seeds
2 medium onions, finely chopped
3 tablespoons oil
500 g (1 lb) firm white fish fillets, cut into 5 cm (2 inch) pieces
1 tablespoon ground coriander
1 teaspoon ground ginger
1 teaspoon chilli powder
1 teaspoon ground turmeric
1 tomato, chopped
1 tablespoon tamarind concentrate
¼ cup (60 ml/2 fl oz) water

1 Dry-fry the coconut, cumin, sesame seeds, fenugreek seeds and onion in a frying pan for 10 minutes or until fragrant.
2 Transfer the mixture to a mortar and pestle or food processor; process until a paste is formed.
3 Heat the oil in a large deep frying pan; add the fish and cook over medium heat for 5 minutes.
4 Add the coconut mixture and the remaining ingredients and stir gently to combine. Cover and simmer for 5 to 10 minutes or until the fish is tender. Serve with rice.

*NUTRITION PER SERVE: Protein 30 g; Fat 30 g; Carbohydrate 5 g; Dietary Fibre 5 g; Cholesterol 90 mg; 1600 kJ (380 cal)*

## GOAN SPICED MUSSELS

*Preparation time*: 20 minutes
*Total cooking time*: 20 minutes
*Serves 4*

✮

1 kg (2 lb) black mussels
3 tablespoons ghee or oil
5 cloves garlic, crushed
5 cm (2 inch) piece fresh ginger, grated
2 medium onions, finely chopped
3 red chillies, finely chopped
2 teaspoons ground cumin
2 teaspoons ground coriander
4 tomatoes, peeled, seeded and chopped
2 cups (500 ml/16 fl oz) fish stock
1 cup (50 g/1⅔ oz) chopped fresh coriander leaves
2 tablespoons lemon juice

1 Remove the beards from the mussels and scrub them under cold water to remove any excess grit. Discard any which are already open.
2 Heat the ghee in a wok, add the garlic, ginger and onion and cook over medium heat for 5 minutes, or until the onion is soft and golden. Add the chilli, cumin, coriander and tomato, and cook for 5 minutes.
3 Add the mussels and fish stock and bring to the boil. Reduce the heat and simmer for 5 minutes. Discard any mussels that have not opened after this time.
4 Remove the wok from the heat, stir through the chopped coriander and lemon juice, and serve with rice.

*NUTRITION PER SERVE: Protein 25 g; Fat 20 g; Carbohydrate 5 g; Dietary Fibre 4 g; Cholesterol 165 mg; 1210 kJ (290 cal)*

creamy batter, adding a little more water if necessary. Add the vegetables and mix in evenly.
4 Heat about 2 cm (¾ inch) oil in a frying pan; place tablespoons of the mixture in the oil, about 8 at a time, and fry over moderately high heat until golden; drain on paper towels. Serve hot with sweet mango chutney or tamarind sauce.

*NUTRITION PER PAKORA: Protein 2 g; Fat 2 g; Carbohydrate 5 g; Dietary Fibre 1 g; Cholesterol 0 mg; 195 kJ (45 cal)*

## BATTERED CHICKEN

**Preparation time**: 30 minutes
  + 3 hours marinating
**Total cooking time**: 30 minutes
**Serves** 6

✴ ✴

6 small chicken thighs, about 150 g
  (4¾ oz) each
6 cloves garlic, crushed
5 cm (2 inch) piece fresh ginger,
  finely grated
½ teaspoon salt
½ teaspoon freshly ground black pepper
3 tablespoons lime juice
½ cup (125 g/4 oz) yoghurt

**Batter**
¾ cup (80 g/2⅔ oz) besan (chickpea
  flour)
1 teaspoon baking powder
1 teaspoon garam masala
¼ teaspoon ground turmeric
2 eggs, lightly beaten
2 tablespoons yoghurt
¼ cup (60 ml/2 fl oz) water
oil, for deep-frying

1 Remove the skin from the chicken and cut 3 deep incisions in each thigh.
2 Combine the garlic, ginger, salt, pepper, lime juice and yoghurt in a large bowl. Add the chicken thighs and toss to coat thoroughly. Cover and refrigerate for 3 hours.
3 To make Batter: Sift the besan, baking powder, garam masala and turmeric into a bowl. Make a well in the centre, add the combined eggs, yoghurt and water, and stir until smooth.
4 Heat the oil in a wok or large pan. Dip each chicken thigh into the batter and deep-fry in batches for 8 to 10 minutes or until the chicken is crisp and tender. Serve with mango chutney.

*NUTRITION PER SERVE: Protein 15 g; Fat 10 g; Carbohydrate 5 g; Dietary Fibre 0 g; Cholesterol 0 mg; 690 kJ (165 cal)*

## VEGETABLE PAKORAS

**Preparation time**: 30 minutes
**Total cooking time**: 20 minutes
**Makes** about 40

✴ ✴

1 large potato
1 small cauliflower
1 small red pepper (capsicum)
1 medium onion
2 cabbage or 5 spinach leaves
1½ cups (165 g/5½ oz) besan (chickpea
  flour)
3 tablespoons plain flour
2 teaspoons garam masala
2 teaspoons ground coriander
1 teaspoon bicarbonate of soda
1 teaspoon chilli powder
1½ cups (375 ml/12 fl oz) water
1 tablespoon lemon juice
½ cup frozen corn kernels, thawed
oil, for shallow-frying

1 Boil the potato until just tender, then peel and chop finely.
2 Finely chop the cauliflower, red pepper and onion. Shred the cabbage or spinach leaves.
3 Sift the flours, garam masala, coriander, bicarbonate of soda and chilli powder into a bowl. Make a well in the centre, add the water and lemon juice, and stir to make a smooth

*Above: Vegetable Pakoras*

# SPICED ROAST LEG OF LAMB

•

*Preparation time*: 35 minutes
*Total cooking time*: 2 hours
*Serves* 6

★ ★

2 kg (4¹/2 lb) leg of lamb
1 tablespoon lemon juice
freshly ground black pepper
1 whole head garlic, unpeeled
2 tablespoons ghee or oil
1¹/2 tablespoons ground coriander
2 teaspoons ground cumin
2 cinnamon sticks
2 cloves
4 bay leaves
1 teaspoon chilli powder
4 cardamom pods, lightly crushed
1¹/2 cups (375 ml/12 fl oz) water
¹/2 cup (125 g/4 oz) yoghurt

•

1 Preheat the oven to moderate 180°C (350°F/
Gas 4).

2 Trim the excess fat from the lamb. Rub it all
over with lemon juice and pepper, and place it in
a roasting pan with the whole garlic and ghee.
Bake for about 50 minutes, or until the garlic
cloves are soft.
3 Squeeze the soft cooked garlic pulp from the
skins. Spread the garlic pulp evenly over the
lamb and sprinkle over the coriander and cumin.
Add the cinnamon sticks, cloves, bay leaves,
chilli powder and cardamom pods to the pan.
4 Roast the lamb for a further 50 minutes, or
until cooked, basting it occasionally with the pan
juices. Remove the lamb and set aside for 10 to
15 minutes before carving.
5 Add the water to the baking pan and stir to
combine the juices. Place the pan on the stove
top; cook over high heat until the liquid reduces
and thickens. Remove the whole spices, and
season with salt and pepper to taste. Stir in the
yoghurt and heat through. Spoon the sauce over
the carved roast.

*NUTRITION PER SERVE: Protein 53 g; Fat 20 g;
Carbohydrate 0 g; Dietary Fibre 0 g; Cholesterol 180 mg;
1665 kJ (395 cal)*

*Above: Spiced Roast
Leg of Lamb*

## SPICY TOMATO AND PEA SOUP

•

*Preparation time*: 15 minutes
*Total cooking time*: 20–25 minutes
*Serves* 6

★

5 large very ripe tomatoes, chopped
2 cups (500 ml/16 fl oz) water
2 tablespoons ghee or butter
1 large onion, thinly sliced
1 clove garlic, crushed
2 teaspoons ground coriander
2 teaspoons ground cumin
1/2 teaspoon fennel seeds
2 bay leaves
1 green chilli, seeded and sliced
1 1/2 cups (375 ml/12 fl oz) coconut cream
1 1/2 cups (240 g/7 1/2 oz) frozen peas
1 tablespoon sugar
1 tablespoon chopped fresh mint

•

1 Simmer the tomato in the water until very
tender, then blend the tomato and water in a
food processor.
2 Heat the ghee in a large pan; add the onion
and garlic and cook over medium heat until
very soft. Add the coriander, cumin, fennel
seeds, bay leaves and chilli, and cook, stirring,
for 1 minute.
3 Add the coconut cream and the puréed tomatoes,

and bring to the boil. Reduce the heat, add the
peas and cook until tender. Remove the bay leaves,
add the sugar and mint, and season with freshly
ground pepper to taste. Serve with hot toasted
chapattis (see page 249) brushed with ghee.

NUTRITION PER SERVE: Protein 5 g; Fat 20 g;
Carbohydrate 15 g; Dietary Fibre 5 g; Cholesterol 20 mg;
1110 kJ (265 cal)

•

## SPICED FISH FILLETS
## WITH YOGHURT

•

*Preparation time*: 10 minutes +
  20 minutes marinating
*Total cooking time*: 6 minutes
*Serves* 4

★

4 white fish fillets, about 180 g
  (5 3/4 oz) each
3 tablespoons yoghurt
1 1/2 teaspoons garam masala
1 clove garlic, crushed
1/2 teaspoon salt
1/2 teaspoon chilli flakes

•

1 Place the fish in a large dish. Combine the
yoghurt, garam masala, garlic, salt and chilli. Spread
the yoghurt mixture over the fish fillets, cover and
leave to marinate for 20 minutes in a cool place.

*Above: Spicy Tomato
and Pea Soup*

2 Place the fish on a lightly oiled grill tray. Cook under high heat for 2 to 3 minutes each side. The fish should only take a few minutes; it is ready when it can be flaked easily with the point of a knife. Serve with rice.

*NUTRITION PER SERVE: Protein 10 g; Fat 0 g; Carbohydrate 0 g; Dietary Fibre 0 g; Cholesterol 35 mg; 255 kJ (60 cal)*

•
## SAFFRON YOGHURT CHICKEN
•

**Preparation time**: 30 minutes
**Total cooking time**: 1 hour 15 minutes
**Serves 4–6**

★

1 x 1.5 kg (3 lb) chicken
1/2 teaspoon saffron threads
2 tablespoons hot milk
3 cloves garlic, crushed
3 cm (1 1/4 inch) piece fresh ginger,
    finely grated
1/2 teaspoon ground turmeric
1/2 teaspoon ground cumin
1/4 teaspoon ground cardamom
1/4 teaspoon ground cloves
1/4 teaspoon ground cinnamon
1/4 teaspoon ground mace
4 tablespoons yoghurt
1 tablespoon ghee or oil

1 Preheat the oven to moderate 180°C (350°F/ Gas 4).
2 Wash the chicken and pat dry. Remove any excess fat from inside the cavity.
3 Soak the saffron threads in the hot milk for 10 minutes, then squeeze the saffron to release the flavour and colour into the milk.
4 Transfer the saffron milk to a larger bowl; add the remaining ingredients and mix to combine.
5 Carefully lift the skin on the breast side of the chicken by working your fingers between the skin and the flesh. Pat half the spice mixture over the flesh. Rub the remaining spice mixture over the skin.
6 Place the chicken on a wire rack in a baking dish. Pour 1 cup (250 ml/8 fl oz) water into the dish; this will keep the chicken moist while it cooks. Roast the chicken for 1 1/4 hours or until browned and tender. Transfer the chicken to a serving dish, cover loosely with foil and allow to stand for 5 minutes before carving.
NOTE: Mace is a spice ground from the membrane which covers the nutmeg seed. It has a more subtle flavour than nutmeg.

*NUTRITION PER SERVE (6): Protein 20 g; Fat 10 g; Carbohydrate 0 g; Dietary Fibre 0 g; Cholesterol 75 mg; 645 kJ (155 cal)*

SAFFRON
*Saffron is prized for the fragrance, subtle flavour and the orange colour it imparts to foods. The wiry, vivid red-orange saffron threads are actually tiny stigmas of the saffron crocus flower—each delicate bloom must be plucked by hand and its 3 thread-like stigmas removed and dried. It takes more than 150 000 fresh flowers to produce 1 kg (2 lb) saffron, which explains why it is the world's most expensive spice. Fortunately, only scant amounts are needed—1/4 teaspoon of loosely packed threads is sufficient to flavour and colour a dish to serve six people.*

*Above: Saffron Yoghurt Chicken*

# BURMA

The food of Burma reflects the influences of her many neighbours, especially the two largest, China and India. China's influence can be seen in the use of noodles and soy sauce, while Burmese curries are Indian in origin, though not as highly spiced. They are flavoured with lots of garlic, ginger, turmeric, chilli, onion and shrimp paste and served with bowls of home-made chutneys and pickles. Bowls of piping hot rice are served at every meal, though unlike in other Asian countries, the rice is boiled not steamed until it is soft and moist.

the garlic and cook for 2 more minutes. Add the turmeric and paprika and cook for a further 2 minutes. Drain on paper towels. Reserve the oil.

4 Place the blanched vegetables and the bamboo shoots, bean sprouts and cucumber in a serving dish and drizzle over 2 tablespoons of the reserved cooking oil. Add the onion and garlic and toss through the vegetables along with the salt and lemon juice. Scatter the sesame seeds over the salad and serve as an accompaniment to a curry.

*NUTRITION PER SERVE: Protein 5 g; Fat 25 g; Carbohydrate 10 g; Dietary Fibre 6 g; Cholesterol 0 mg; 1100 kJ (260 cal)*

### COCONUT PRAWN CURRY

*Preparation time*: 25 minutes
*Total cooking time*: 15 minutes
*Serves* 4

★

*750 g (1¹/₂ lb) raw prawns*
*1 teaspoon ground turmeric*
*1 cup (155 g/5 oz) roughly chopped onion*
*4 cloves garlic, crushed*
*¹/₂ teaspoon paprika*
*1 teaspoon seeded, finely chopped red*
*  chilli*
*pinch of ground cloves*
*¹/₄ teaspoon ground cardamom*
*1 teaspoon finely chopped fresh ginger*
*3 tablespoons oil*
*2 tomatoes, diced*
*1 cup (250 ml/8 fl oz) coconut cream*
*2 tablespoons fresh coriander leaves*

•

1 Peel and devein the prawns, leaving the tails intact. Toss the prawns with the turmeric.
2 Place the onion, garlic, paprika, chilli, cloves, cardamom and ginger in a food processor and process until a paste is formed.
3 Heat the oil in a deep-sided frying pan; carefully add the spicy paste (it will splutter at this stage), stir it into the oil and cook over low heat for about 10 minutes. If the mixture starts to burn, add a little water. When the paste is cooked it should be a golden brown colour and will have oil around the edges.
4 Stir in the prawns, tomatoes and coconut cream, and simmer for about 5 minutes or until the prawns are cooked. Stir in the coriander, season with salt and serve with rice.

*NUTRITION PER SERVE: Protein 25 g; Fat 30 g; Carbohydrate 5 g; Dietary Fibre 5 g; Cholesterol 235 mg; 1555 kJ (370 cal)*

### MIXED VEGETABLE SALAD

•

*Preparation time*: 25 minutes
*Total cooking time*: 15 minutes
*Serves* 6

★

*200 g (6¹/₂ oz) green beans, cut diagonally*
*  into 3 cm (1¹/₄ inch) lengths*
*¹/₂ small cabbage, finely shredded*
*2 medium carrots, sliced*
*3 tablespoons white sesame seeds*
*¹/₂ cup (125 ml/4 fl oz) oil*
*2 medium onions, sliced*
*3 cloves garlic, finely sliced*
*¹/₂ teaspoon ground turmeric*
*¹/₂ teaspoon paprika*
*1 cup (125 g/4 oz) bamboo shoots, sliced*
*1 cup (90 g/3 oz) bean sprouts, scraggly*
*  ends removed*
*1 cucumber, sliced*
*¹/₂ teaspoon salt*
*2 tablespoons lemon juice*

•

1 Place the beans, cabbage and carrot in separate heatproof bowls, cover with boiling water and leave for 1 minute then drain. Plunge into iced water, then drain again.
2 Heat a wok; add the sesame seeds and cook, stirring, over a moderate heat until they turn golden brown. Set aside.
3 Heat the oil in the wok; add the onion, and cook over a low heat until soft and golden. Add

*Above: Mixed*
*Vegetable Salad*

# FISH SOUP WITH NOODLES

•

*Preparation time*: 40 minutes
*Total cooking time*: 25 minutes
*Serves 8*

★★

750 g (1½ lb) firm white fish fillets
1½ teaspoons salt
2 teaspoons ground turmeric
3 stems lemon grass
4 tablespoons peanut oil
2 medium onions, finely sliced
6 cloves garlic, crushed
2 teaspoons finely chopped fresh ginger
2 teaspoons paprika
1 tablespoon rice flour
6 cups (1.5 litres) water
2 cups (500 ml/16 fl oz) coconut milk
½ cup (125 ml/4 fl oz) fish sauce
500 g (1 lb) somen noodles

•

*Garnishes*
4 hard-boiled eggs, quartered
½ cup (15 g/²/3 oz) chopped fresh
    coriander leaves
½ cup (60 g/2 oz) finely sliced spring
    onion
4 limes, quartered
fish sauce, to taste

4 tablespoons chilli flakes
½ cup (80 g/2²/3 oz) unsalted roasted
    peanuts, roughly chopped

•

1 Cut the fish into 3 cm (1¼ inch) cubes. Place the fish pieces on a plate and sprinkle with the salt and turmeric. Set aside for 10 minutes.
2 Trim the lemon grass stems to about 18 cm (7 inches) long. Bruise the white fleshy ends so that the fragrance will be released during cooking, and tie the stems into loops.
3 Heat the peanut oil in a large pan; add the onion and cook over medium heat for 10 minutes, or until soft and lightly golden. Add the garlic and ginger and cook for 1 minute. Add the fish, paprika and rice flour and combine well.
4 Pour in the water, coconut milk and fish sauce, and stir. Add the loops of lemon grass and simmer for 10 minutes, or until the fish is cooked. Cook the noodles in a large pan of boiling water for 8 to 10 minutes or until tender, then drain.
5 Place a mound of noodles in 8 warm individual serving bowls and ladle over the fish soup. Offer the garnishes in separate small bowls so the diners can add them to their own taste.

*NUTRITION PER SERVE: Protein 30 g; Fat 30 g; Carbohydrate 55 g; Dietary Fibre 5 g; Cholesterol 65 mg; 2410 kJ (575 cal)*

### BURMA'S NATIONAL DISH
*Seafood, the product of the country's extensive coastline, features prominently in Burmese cuisine. The national dish is moh hin gha, a spicy fish soup with noodles. In Burmese cities a 'take-away' family meal can be bought from street vendors who scoop steaming heaps of noodles into a supplied bowl then ladle over the soup (which traditionally includes banana heart).*

*Left: Fish Soup with Noodles*

## FISH IN BANANA LEAVES

•

*Preparation time*: 30 minutes
*Total cooking time*: 30 minutes
*Serves* 6

★

*3 large banana leaves (see note)*
*1 kg (2 lb) firm white fish fillets*
*½ cup (125 ml/4 fl oz) coconut cream*
*2 cloves garlic, crushed*
*1 small onion, finely chopped*
*1 tablespoon finely chopped fresh ginger*
*2 teaspoons sesame oil*
*2 teaspoons salt*
*1 teaspoon ground turmeric*
*1 teaspoon paprika*
*¼ teaspoon chilli powder*
*2 teaspoons rice flour*
*2 tablespoons chopped fresh coriander*
*  leaves*

•

1 Cut the banana leaves into 6 squares, about 25 cm (10 inches) wide. Cut the fish into 3 cm (1¼ inch) cubes. Place the banana leaf pieces in a heatproof bowl and pour boiling water over them. Leave for about 30 seconds, by which time the leaves should be pliable; drain.

2 Place the fish pieces in a large bowl and add the coconut cream, garlic, onion, ginger, sesame oil, salt, turmeric, paprika, chilli powder, rice flour and coriander. Using your hands, combine the ingredients well, making sure the fish is well covered with the mixture.

3 Divide the fish mixture evenly and place each portion in the centre of a banana leaf piece. Fold in the sides of each piece to form a type of envelope. Hold the leaf in place with a toothpick or wooden skewer.

4 Fill a large pan or steamer with 5 cm (2 inches) water. Place the fish parcels on a steaming rack and cover and steam for 10 to 15 minutes, or until cooked. Open one parcel to check that the fish is cooked before serving. Serve with steamed rice.

NOTE: If banana leaves are not available, cook the fish mixture in foil parcels.

*NUTRITION PER SERVE: Protein 30 g; Fat 10 g; Carbohydrate 0 g; Dietary Fibre 0 g; Cholesterol 100 mg; 925 kJ (220 cal)*

*FISH IN BANANA LEAVES*

*Soak the banana leaf pieces in boiling water until they are pliable.*

*Use your hands to combine the fish mixture well.*

*Place the fish parcels on a steaming rack.*

## FRIED PORK CURRY

•

*Preparation time*: 30 minutes
*Total cooking time*: 2 hours
*Serves* 6

★ ★

*2 cups (310 g/9¾ oz) roughly chopped*
*  onion*
*15 cloves garlic, crushed*
*4 tablespoons finely chopped fresh ginger*
*3 tablespoons peanut oil*
*1 tablespoon sesame oil*
*1½ teaspoons chilli powder*
*1 teaspoon ground turmeric*
*1.5 kg (3 lb) boneless pork, cut into 3 cm*
*  (1¼ inch) cubes*
*1 tablespoon vinegar*
*1 cup (250 ml/8 fl oz) water or stock*
*2 tablespoons fresh coriander leaves*

•

1 Place the onion, garlic and ginger in a food processor and process until a thick rough paste is formed.

2 Heat the peanut oil and sesame oil in a large pan; add the paste and cook it over medium heat for about 15 minutes until it becomes a golden brown colour and has oil around the edges. Add the chilli powder, turmeric and pork, and stir well for a few minutes until the pork is well coated with the mixture.

3 Add the vinegar and water, cover and simmer gently for 1½ hours or until the meat is tender. If necessary reduce the liquid by removing the lid and allowing the sauce to evaporate. Season with salt to taste (the dish will need more if you use water instead of stock) and scatter over the coriander. Serve with rice.

*NUTRITION PER SERVE: Protein 60 g; Fat 15 g; Carbohydrate 3 g; Dietary Fibre 2 g; Cholesterol 120 mg; 1675 kJ (400 cal)*

*Opposite page: Fish in Banana Leaves (top); Fried Pork Curry*

## BURMESE CHICKEN

•

*Preparation time*: 15 minutes
*Total cooking time*: 45 minutes to
   1 hour
*Serves* 4–6

★

1.5 kg (3 lb) whole chicken or chicken
   pieces (legs, thighs, wings, breasts)
2 tablespoons ghee or oil
2 medium onions, chopped
3 bay leaves
2 teaspoons ground turmeric
¼ teaspoon chilli powder
½ teaspoon ground cardamom
½ teaspoon ground cumin
½ teaspoon ground coriander
½ teaspoon ground ginger
1 cinnamon stick
2 stems lemon grass (white part only),
   chopped
6 cloves garlic, crushed
1 tablespoon grated fresh ginger
1 cup (250 ml/8 fl oz) chicken stock

•

1 If using a whole chicken, cut it into pieces.
2 Heat the ghee in a large pan; add the onion

*Below: Burmese
Chicken*

and cook, stirring, until the onion is soft. Add
the bay leaves, turmeric, chilli powder,
cardamom, cumin, coriander, ginger, cinnamon
stick, lemon grass, garlic and fresh ginger. Cook,
stirring, for 1 minute or until fragrant.
3 Add the chicken pieces and stir to coat with
the mixture. Stir in the stock and simmer,
covered, for 45 minutes to 1 hour or until the
chicken is tender.

*NUTRITION PER SERVE (6): Protein 25 g; Fat 10 g;
Carbohydrate 2 g; Dietary Fibre 1 g; Cholesterol 95 mg;
840 kJ (200 cal)*

•

## MIXED NOODLE
## AND RICE SALAD

•

*Preparation time*: 1 hour
*Total cooking time*: 40 minutes
*Serves* 6

★

1½ cups (300 g/10 oz) long-grain rice
120 g (4 oz) fine dried egg noodles
60 g (2 oz) dried mung bean vermicelli
120 g (4 oz) dried rice vermicelli
1 cup (90 g/3 oz) bean sprouts, scraggly
   ends removed
2 medium potatoes, peeled and sliced
3 eggs
½ teaspoon salt
1 tablespoon water
1 teaspoon oil
½ cup (125 ml/4 fl oz) peanut oil
4 large onions, quartered and finely sliced
20 cloves garlic, finely sliced
2 red chillies, seeded and sliced
¾ cup (25 g/¾ oz) dried shrimps, ground
   to a powder
½ cup (125 ml/4 fl oz) fish sauce
¾ cup (185 ml/6 fl oz) tamarind
   concentrate
2 tablespoons chilli powder

•

1 Fill 2 large pans with salted water and bring to
the boil. To one, add the rice and cook for about
12 minutes or until tender. Drain, rinse and set
aside. Add the egg noodles to the other pan and
cook them for a couple of minutes until tender.
Transfer the egg noodles to a colander, rinse
under cold water and set aside. Place the mung
bean vermicelli and rice vermicelli in separate
heatproof bowls, cover them with boiling water
and leave for 1 to 2 minutes until tender; rinse
under cold water and drain. Place the bean
sprouts in a heatproof bowl, cover them with
boiling water and leave for 30 seconds; rinse
under cold water and drain. Cook the potato in a

large pan of boiling water until tender, drain, then rinse under cold water and set aside.

2 Beat the eggs with the salt and water. Heat the oil in a small frying pan; add the egg and cook over moderately low heat, gently drawing in the edges of the omelette to allow the uncooked egg to run to the outside. When the omelette is cooked through, flip it over and lightly brown the other side. Remove the omelette from the pan and allow it to cool before cutting it into thin strips.

3 Heat the peanut oil in a large frying pan; fry the onion, garlic and chilli separately over a moderately high heat until crispy, adding more oil if necessary.

4 Arrange the assorted noodles, rice, potato and bean sprouts on a large platter; place the omelette strips, chilli, onion, garlic, dried shrimp, fish sauce, tamarind and chilli powder in separate small dishes. The diners then serve themselves the salad ingredients and garnishes.

NUTRITION PER SERVE: Protein 15 g; Fat 25 g; Carbohydrate 90 g; Dietary Fibre 5 g; Cholesterol 95 mg; 2750 kJ (655 cal)

## TWELVE VARIETIES SOUP

**Preparation time**: 45 minutes
+ 20 minutes soaking
**Total cooking time**: 20 minutes
Serves 8

★

300 g (9²/3 oz) pork liver or lamb liver
200 g (6¹/2 oz) chicken breast fillet
30 g (1 oz) dried Chinese mushrooms
3 tablespoons oil
3 medium onions, finely sliced
4 cloves garlic, finely chopped
1 teaspoon finely chopped fresh ginger
2 tablespoons fish sauce
¹/3 cup (40 g/1¹/3 oz) diagonally and thinly
   sliced green beans
¹/3 cup (40 g/1¹/3 oz) small cauliflower
   florets
¹/3 cup (30 g/1 oz) sliced button
   mushrooms
8 cups (2 litres) water
¹/3 cup (25 g/³/4 oz) shredded Chinese
   cabbage
¹/3 cup (20 g/²/3 oz) shredded spinach
¹/3 cup (30 g/1 oz) bean sprouts
3 spring onions, finely sliced
1 tablespoon fresh coriander leaves
3 eggs
1 tablespoon soy sauce
¹/4 teaspoon ground black pepper
wedges of lime, to serve

1 Cook the liver in simmering water for 5 minutes, cool and slice thinly. Cut the chicken into thin slices. Place the Chinese mushrooms in a heatproof bowl, cover with boiling water and soak for 20 minutes; drain well and slice.

2 Heat the oil in a wok, add the onion and cook over medium heat for about 5 minutes, until lightly golden. Add the slices of liver and chicken and stir to combine. Add the garlic and ginger and cook for another minute, then pour in the fish sauce and cook for 2 more minutes.

3 Place the Chinese mushrooms, beans, cauliflower, button mushrooms and onion mixture in a large pan. Add the water, bring to the boil and cook until the vegetables are just tender. Add the cabbage, spinach and bean sprouts and cook a further 5 minutes, until just tender. Stir in the spring onion and coriander.

4 Break the eggs into the boiling soup and stir immediately. (The eggs will break up and cook.) Add the soy sauce and pepper and serve immediately with the wedges of lime to squeeze into the soup.

NUTRITION PER SERVE: Protein 20 g; Fat 10 g; Carbohydrate 4 g; Dietary Fibre 2 g; Cholesterol 100 mg; 755 kJ (180 cal)

*TWELVE VARIETIES
SOUP*

Thinly slice the beans, cut the cauliflower into florets and slice the mushrooms.

Using a sharp knife, slice the liver thinly.

Add the cabbage, spinach and bean sprouts to the soup.

Above: Twelve Varieties Soup

2 Place the onion, garlic, ginger, turmeric, chilli and salt into a food processor and process until a paste is formed.

3 Heat the oil in a deep-sided frying pan; carefully add the spicy paste (at this stage it will splutter), stir it into the oil, lower the heat and cook gently for about 10 minutes. If the mixture starts to burn, add a little water. When the paste is cooked it should be a golden brown colour and have oil around the edges.

4 Remove the fish pieces from the fish sauce and add them to the pan, stirring to cover them with the spicy paste. Raise the heat to medium and cook for about 5 minutes until the fish is cooked through, turning it so it cooks evenly. Transfer the fish to a warm serving dish. If the remaining sauce is very liquid, reduce it over high heat until it thickens, then spoon it over the fish. Scatter the coriander over the fish and serve with rice and lemon wedges.

*NUTRITION PER SERVE: Protein 30 g; Fat 15 g; Carbohydrate 3 g; Dietary Fibre 1 g; Cholesterol 100 mg; 1085 kJ (260 cal)*

## BEEF, POTATO AND OKRA CURRY

*Preparation time*: 35 minutes
*Total cooking time*: 2 hours 25 minutes
*Serves* 4

★

*800 g (1 lb 10 oz) chuck or skirt steak*
*2 medium potatoes*
*200 g (6¹/2 oz) okra*
*1 cup (155 g/5 oz) roughly chopped onion*
*4 cloves garlic, crushed*
*3 teaspoons finely chopped fresh ginger*
*1 teaspoon ground turmeric*
*¹/2 teaspoon paprika*
*¹/2 teaspoon chilli powder*
*4 tablespoons oil*
*1 tablespoon sesame oil*
*1 teaspoon ground cumin*
*1¹/2 cups (375 ml/12 fl oz) water or beef stock*
*2 tablespoons garlic chives, finely chopped*
*1 lemon, cut into wedges*

1 Cut the beef into 3 cm (1¹/4 inch) cubes. Peel and cube the potatoes. Trim the okra; if large, halve it lengthways, otherwise leave whole.

2 Place the onion, garlic, ginger, turmeric, paprika and chilli in a food processor and process until a thick paste is formed.

3 Heat the oils in a large heavy-based pan; add the onion mixture and cook over a low heat for about 20 minutes, adding a little water if the

## DRY FISH CURRY

*Preparation time*: 20 minutes
*Total cooking time*: 25 minutes
*Serves* 6

★ ★

*1 kg (2 lb) firm white fish fillets, such as sea perch*
*2 tablespoons fish sauce*
*2 cups (310 g/9³/4 oz) roughly chopped onion*
*4 cloves garlic, crushed*
*2 teaspoons finely chopped fresh ginger*
*2 teaspoons turmeric*
*1 red chilli, seeded and finely chopped*
*1 teaspoon salt*
*3 tablespoons oil*
*2 tablespoons chopped fresh coriander leaves*
*lemon wedges, to serve*

1 Cut the fish into 4 cm (1¹/2 inch) cubes. Place the fish pieces in a shallow dish and pour over the fish sauce.

*Above: Dry Fish Curry*

mixture starts to stick or burn. When the paste is cooked it should be a golden brown colour with oil forming around the edges.

4 Add the beef and cook, stirring, for 5 minutes, until browned. Add the cumin and combine well. Pour in the water or stock and simmer, covered, for about 2 hours or until the meat is tender. Add the potato and okra in the last ¾ hour of cooking; remove the lid for the final 10 minutes until the sauce reduces and thickens. Season with salt to taste, sprinkle over the garlic chives, and serve with lemon wedges and rice.

NUTRITION PER SERVE: Protein 45 g; Fat 30 g; Carbohydrate 10 g; Dietary Fibre 4 g; Cholesterol 135 mg; 2070 kJ (490 cal)

## CHICKEN CURRY

Preparation time: 45 minutes
Total cooking time: 1 hour
Serves 6

⭐

1 kg (2 lb) chicken thigh cutlets
2 large onions, roughly chopped
3 large cloves garlic, roughly chopped
5 cm (2 inch) piece fresh ginger, roughly
   chopped
2 tablespoons peanut oil
½ teaspoon shrimp paste
1 teaspoon salt
2 cups (500 ml/16 fl oz) coconut milk
1 teaspoon chilli powder, optional
200 g (6½ oz) dried rice vermicelli

### Accompaniments

6 spring onions, diagonally sliced
⅓ cup (10 g/⅓ oz) chopped fresh
   coriander leaves
2 tablespoons garlic flakes, lightly fried
2 tablespoons onion flakes, lightly fried
3 lemons, cut in wedges
12 dried chillies, fried in oil to crisp
¼ cup (125 ml/4 fl oz) fish sauce

1 Wash the chicken under cold water and pat dry with paper towels.
2 Place the onion, garlic and ginger in a food processor and process until smooth. Add a little water to help blend the mixture if necessary.
3 Heat the oil in a large pan; add the onion mixture and shrimp paste and cook, stirring, over high heat for 5 minutes. Add the chicken, and cook over medium heat, turning it until it browns. Add the salt, coconut milk and chilli powder, if using. Bring to the boil, reduce the heat and simmer, covered, for 30 minutes,

stirring the mixture occasionally. Uncover the pan and cook for 15 minutes, or until the chicken is tender.
4 Place the noodles in a heatproof bowl, cover them with boiling water and leave them for 10 minutes. Drain the noodles and place them in a serving bowl.
5 Place the Accompaniments in separate small bowls. The diners help themselves to a portion of the noodles, chicken curry and some, or all, of the Accompaniments; the result will be as hot and tart as each person prefers.

NUTRITION PER SERVE: Protein 25 g; Fat 15 g; Carbohydrate 30 g; Dietary Fibre 0 g; Cholesterol 75 mg; 1485 kJ (335 cal)

Above: Chicken Curry

# SRI LANKA

Despite its size, this tiny, beautiful island has an amazing variety of food and cooking styles. Traders and conquerors have left their gastronomic mark, but there is also a huge range of distinctive indigenous dishes. In most Sri Lankan households the main meal will be rice with one or two curries, soup, vegetables and a selection of sambols. Popular breakfast foods include crispy coconut and rice-flour pancakes called 'hoppers'.

## TAMARIND FISH

•

*Preparation time*: 15 minutes
  + 1 hour marinating
*Total cooking time*: 15 minutes
Serves 6

✭

2 cloves garlic, crushed
2 tablespoons tamarind concentrate
1 tablespoon Ceylon curry powder
  (see page 126)
1/2 teaspoon ground turmeric
1 tablespoon lemon juice
2 red chillies, finely chopped
6 fish steaks (swordfish, cod or warehou)
  about 150 g (5 oz) each
3 tablespoons oil
1/2 cup (125 ml/4 fl oz) coconut milk

•

1 Combine the garlic, tamarind, curry powder,
turmeric, lemon juice and chilli.
2 Place the fish steaks in a shallow ovenproof
dish. Brush the garlic mixture over both sides of
the fish; cover and refrigerate for 1 hour.
3 Heat the oil in a large frying pan; add the fish
and cook over medium heat for 2 minutes on
each side. Stir in the coconut milk, cover and
simmer for 10 minutes or until the fish flakes
when tested with a fork.

*NUTRITION PER SERVE: Protein 25 g; Fat 15 g;
Carbohydrate 0 g; Dietary Fibre 0 g; Cholesterol 60 mg;
1045 kJ (250 cal)*

*Above: Tamarind Fish*

## LAMB WITH PALM SUGAR

•

*Preparation time*: 20 minutes
*Total cooking time*: 1 hour 40 minutes
Serves 4

✭

2 tablespoons oil
500 g (1 lb/16 oz) diced lamb
2 teaspoons chilli powder
1 tablespoon chopped fresh lemon grass
  (white part only)
1 tablespoon grated fresh ginger
300 g (9²/₃ oz) sweet potato, peeled and
  chopped
2 tablespoons grated palm sugar or soft
  brown sugar
2 tablespoons lime juice
1 cup (250 ml/8 fl oz) water

•

1 Heat the oil in a large heavy-based pan; add the
lamb in batches and cook over high heat until
browned. Drain on paper towels.
2 Add the chilli powder, lemon grass and ginger
to the pan, and cook for 1 minute.
3 Return the meat to the pan with the sweet
potato, sugar, lime juice and water; bring to the
boil, reduce heat and simmer, covered, for 1 hour.
Remove the lid and simmer uncovered for
30 minutes or until the meat is tender.

*NUTRITION PER SERVE: Protein 30 g; Fat 15 g;
Carbohydrate 20 g; Dietary Fibre 2 g; Cholesterol 80 mg;
1365 kJ (325 cal)*

# FRIKKADELS

•

**Preparation time:** 30 minutes
**Total cooking time:** 40 minutes
**Makes** 26

★

½ cup (45 g/1½ oz) desiccated coconut
500 g (1 lb) minced beef
1 clove garlic, crushed
1 medium onion, finely chopped
1 teaspoon ground cumin
¼ teaspoon ground cinnamon
½ teaspoon finely grated lime rind
1 tablespoon chopped fresh dill
1 egg, lightly beaten
1 cup (100 g/3⅓ oz) dry breadcrumbs
oil, for deep-frying
Yoghurt and Mint Raita (page 237),
   to serve

1 Spread the coconut on an oven tray and toast it in a slow 150°C (300°F/Gas 2) oven for 10 minutes or until it is dark golden, shaking the tray occasionally.
2 Place the coconut, minced beef, garlic, onion, cumin, cinnamon, lime rind and dill in a large bowl and mix to combine. Season with salt and pepper to taste.
3 Shape tablespoons of the mixture into balls; dip the meatballs in the egg and toss to coat in the breadcrumbs.
4 Heat the oil in a wok or deep-sided frying pan; add the meatballs in batches and deep-fry over moderately high heat for 5 minutes or until they become deep golden brown and cooked through. Drain on paper towels. Serve with Yoghurt and Mint Raita.

NUTRITION PER FRIKKADEL: Protein 5 g; Fat 5 g; Carbohydrate 3 g; Dietary Fibre 1 g; Cholesterol 20 mg; 260 kJ (60 cal)

FRIKKADELS

Combine the coconut, beef, garlic, onion, spices, rind and dill.

Use your hands to roll tablespoons of the mixture into balls.

Deep-fry the balls until they are golden brown, then remove and drain on paper towels.

Left: Frikkadels

## CHICKEN OMELETTE WITH COCONUT GRAVY

•

*Preparation time*: 20 minutes
*Total cooking time*: 25 minutes
*Serves* 4

★ ★

*½ barbecued chicken*
*1 large tomato, finely chopped*
*1 tablespoon chopped fresh dill*
*8 eggs*
*2 spring onions, chopped*

•

*Coconut Gravy*
*1²/₃ cups (410 ml/13 fl oz) coconut milk*
*½ teaspoon ground turmeric*
*2 cm (¾ inch) piece fresh ginger, grated*
*1 cinnamon stick*
*1 tablespoon lemon juice*

•

1 Remove the bones from the chicken and shred the meat. Combine the chicken meat, tomato and dill in a bowl. Whisk the eggs and spring onion together in a large jug.
2 Cook a quarter of the egg mixture in a lightly greased 25 cm (10 inch) nonstick frying pan. When the omelette is cooked, place a quarter of the chicken mixture in the centre, and fold in the 4 edges to form a parcel. Carefully transfer the omelette to a plate and repeat with remaining mixture. Serve with Coconut Gravy.

3 To make Coconut Gravy: Place all the ingredients in a small pan and simmer for 15 minutes, or until the gravy thickens slightly.

NUTRITION PER SERVE: *Protein 30 g; Fat 30 g; Carbohydrate 5 g; Dietary Fibre 0 g; Cholesterol 415 mg; 1770 kJ (420 cal)*

•

## WHITE VEGETABLE CURRY

•

*Preparation time*: 40 minutes
*Total cooking time*: 30 minutes
*Serves* 4 as part of a meal

★

*300 g (9²/₃ oz) pumpkin*
*200 g (6½ oz) potato*
*250 g (8 oz) okra*
*2 tablespoons oil*
*1 clove garlic, crushed*
*3 green chillies, seeded and very finely chopped*
*½ teaspoon ground turmeric*
*½ teaspoon fenugreek seeds*
*1 medium onion, chopped*
*8 curry leaves*
*1 cinnamon stick*
*2 cups (500 ml/16 fl oz) coconut milk*

•

1 Peel the pumpkin and cut into 2 cm (¾ inch) cubes. Peel the potato and cut into 2 cm (¾ inch) cubes. Trim the stems from the okra.

*Right: Chicken Omelette with Coconut Gravy*

2 Heat the oil in a large heavy-based pan; add the garlic, chilli, turmeric, fenugreek seeds and onion, and cook over medium heat for 5 minutes or until the onion is soft.

3 Add the pumpkin, potato, okra, curry leaves, cinnamon stick and coconut milk. Bring to the boil, reduce heat and simmer, uncovered, for 25 to 30 minutes or until the vegetables are tender. Serve with rice.

*NUTRITION PER SERVE: Protein 10 g; Fat 35 g; Carbohydrate 15 g; Dietary Fibre 5 g; Cholesterol 0 mg; 1705 kJ (405 cal)*

•

# SIMMERED BEEF
# IN COCONUT GRAVY
•

**Preparation time**: 30 minutes
**Total cooking time**: 2 hours 40 minutes
*Serves 4–6*

✸

2 kg (4 lb) piece blade steak
2 tablespoons oil
3 tablespoons Ceylon curry powder
  (page 126)
3 cloves garlic, crushed
2 tablespoons grated fresh ginger
3 tablespoons chopped fresh lemon grass
  (white part only)
2 medium onions, chopped

3 tablespoons tamarind concentrate
3 tablespoons vinegar
2 cups (500 ml/16 fl oz) beef stock
2 cups (500 ml/16 fl oz) coconut milk

•

1 Trim the meat of all fat and sinew and tie with string so that the meat holds its shape.

2 Heat the oil in a large heavy-based pan; add the meat and cook over high heat until it browns. Remove meat from pan and set aside.

3 Reduce the heat to medium; add the curry powder, garlic, ginger, lemon grass and onion, and cook for 5 minutes or until the oil begins to separate from the spices.

4 Return the meat to the pan; add the tamarind, vinegar, stock and coconut milk, and bring to the boil; reduce heat, cover and simmer for 1³/₄ hours, or until the meat is tender.

5 Remove the meat from the pan and keep it warm. Bring the liquid to the boil and cook it, uncovered, for 10 minutes or until a thick gravy forms. Slice the meat and serve topped with the gravy.

NOTE: If Ceylon curry powder is not available or you do not have time to make your own, ask for a curry powder blend made for meat at an Asian food shop.

*NUTRITION PER SERVE (6): Protein 75 g; Fat 40 g; Carbohydrate 5 g; Dietary Fibre 5 g; Cholesterol 175 mg; 2890 kJ (690 cal)*

*Above: Simmered Beef in Coconut Gravy*

*EGGHOPPERS WITH EGGPLANT SAMBOL*

*Process the toasted rice until it is finely ground.*

*Gradually whisk the yeast mixture and coconut milk into the rice mixture.*

*Cook the egghopper until the edges are crisp and golden.*

*Above: Egghoppers with Eggplant Sambol*

# EGGHOPPERS WITH EGGPLANT
## (AUBERGINE) SAMBOL

•

*Preparation time*: 40 minutes
+ 1 hour 30 minutes standing
*Total cooking time*: 2 hours 45 minutes
*Makes* 12–15

☆ ☆ ☆

7 g (¼ oz) dried yeast
½ cup (125 ml/4 fl oz) warm water
1 teaspoon caster sugar
1½ cups (330 g/10½ oz) short-grain rice
1½ cups (265 g/8½ oz) rice flour
2 teaspoons salt
4½ cups (1.125 litres) coconut milk
12–15 eggs

*Eggplant Sambol*
2 eggplants (aubergines), cut into 2 cm
   (¾ inch) cubes
¼ cup (60 ml/2 fl oz) oil
2 spring onions, finely chopped
1 teaspoon soft brown sugar
2 red chillies, finely chopped
2 green chillies, finely chopped
2 tablespoons chopped fresh coriander
   leaves
1 tablespoon lemon juice

•

1 Preheat the oven to moderate 180°C (350°F/
Gas 4). Place the yeast, warm water and sugar in
a small bowl. Put the bowl in a warm, draught-

free area for 10 minutes, or until foaming.
2 Spread the rice on an oven tray and toast in
the oven for about 15 minutes, until golden.
Cool slightly, transfer to a food processor and
process until finely ground.
3 Combine the ground rice, rice flour and salt in
a large bowl. Gradually whisk in the yeast
mixture and coconut milk and mix to a smooth
batter. Cover and set aside in a warm, draught-
free area for 1 hour.
4 Lightly grease a 23 cm (9 inch) nonstick frying
pan. Pour ⅓ cup (80 ml/2¾ fl oz) batter into the
pan or enough to thinly coat the base of the pan;
swirl the pan to cover the base. Crack 1 egg into
the centre of the pan, and cook over low heat for
5 to 10 minutes—time will vary depending on
the pan you use. When the edges are crisp and
golden and the egghopper is cooked, gently
remove it from the pan by sliding it out over the
side of the pan. Cover the egghopper and keep it
warm while cooking the remainder. Serve the
egghoppers with Eggplant Sambol.
5 To make Eggplant Sambol: Sprinkle the
eggplant with salt and leave for 20 minutes; rinse
and thoroughly pat dry. Heat the oil in a large
frying pan; add the eggplant, and cook over
high heat for 10 minutes or until golden brown.
Remove the eggplant from the pan and toss
through the onion, sugar, chilli, coriander and
lemon juice.

*NUTRITION PER EGGHOPPER: Protein 10 g; Fat 30 g;
Carbohydrate 35 g; Dietary Fibre 0 g; Cholesterol 180 mg;
1880 kJ (450 cal)*

# CASHEW NUT CURRY

•

**Preparation time**: 15 minutes
**Total cooking time**: 55 minutes
**Serves** 6 as part of a meal

★

1 pandanus leaf
3 cups (750 ml/24 fl oz) coconut milk
1 medium onion, chopped
1 tablespoon grated fresh ginger
½ teaspoon ground turmeric
3 cm (1¼ inch) piece fresh galangal
2 green chillies, seeded and finely chopped
8 curry leaves
1 cinnamon stick
250 g (8 oz) raw cashew nuts
2 tablespoons chopped fresh coriander
    leaves

•

1 Shred the pandanus leaf lengthways into about 3 sections, and tie into a large knot. Combine the coconut milk, onion, ginger, turmeric, galangal, chilli, curry leaves, cinnamon stick and pandanus leaf in a pan and bring to the boil. Reduce the heat and simmer for 20 minutes.
2 Add the cashew nuts, and cook for a further 30 minutes, or until the nuts are tender.
3 Remove the curry from the heat; discard the galangal, cinnamon stick and pandanus leaf. Sprinkle over the coriander and serve with rice and a couple of other dishes.

NUTRITION PER SERVE: Protein 10 g; Fat 45 g; Carbohydrate 10 g; Dietary Fibre 5 g; Cholesterol 0 mg; 2025 kJ (485 cal)

•

# RED PORK CURRY

•

**Preparation time**: 20 minutes
    + 1 hour marinating
**Total cooking time**: 20 minutes
**Serves** 4

★

4 dried red chillies
½ cup (125 ml/4 fl oz) boiling water
1 medium onion, chopped
2 cloves garlic, chopped
2 cm (¾ inch) piece fresh ginger, grated
1 tablespoon finely chopped lemon grass
    (white part only)
500 g (1 lb) pork fillet, sliced into
    medallions
2 tablespoons tamarind concentrate
2 tablespoons ghee or oil
½ cup (125 ml/4 fl oz) coconut milk

1 Place the chillies in a heatproof bowl, pour over the boiling water and soak for 10 minutes.
2 Place the chillies and soaking water, onion, garlic, ginger and lemon grass in a food processor and process until a paste is formed.
3 Place the pork in a shallow dish, add the chilli paste and tamarind, and mix to combine. Cover and refrigerate for 1 hour.
4 Heat the ghee in a wok; add the pork in batches, and cook over high heat for 5 minutes or until the pork browns. Return all the meat to the pan with any leftover marinade, stir in the coconut milk, and simmer for 5 minutes or until heated through. Serve with steamed rice.

NUTRITION PER SERVE: Protein 30 g; Fat 20 g; Carbohydrate 5 g; Dietary Fibre 0 g; Cholesterol 90 mg; 1240 kJ (295 cal)

Below: Red
Pork Curry

## SPICY SEAFOOD

•

*Preparation time*: 20 minutes
*Total cooking time*: 15 minutes
*Serves* 4

☆

500 g (1 lb) raw prawns
2 squid hoods
250 g (8 oz) mussels
3 tablespoons oil
2 medium onions, sliced
2 cloves garlic, crushed
1 tablespoon grated fresh ginger
1/2 teaspoon ground turmeric
1 teaspoon chilli powder
1 teaspoon paprika
1/4 cup (60 ml/2 fl oz) tomato purée
    (passata)
1 teaspoon grated palm sugar or soft
    brown sugar

•

1 Peel and devein the prawns. Cut the squid
hoods into 6 cm (21/2 inch) squares and score a
crisscross pattern lightly into the flesh with a
small sharp knife. Scrub the mussels and remove
the beards.
2 Heat the oil in a large heavy-based pan or wok;
add the onion, garlic and ginger, and cook over
medium heat for 3 to 5 minutes or until the
onion is soft.
3 Add the turmeric, chilli powder and paprika,

*Above: Spicy Seafood*

and cook for 2 minutes or until the oil begins to
separate from the spices.
4 Add the seafood to the pan and cook over high
heat for 3 to 5 minutes or until the prawns are
pink. Stir in the tomato purée and sugar and
stir-fry for 3 minutes or until the sauce is heated
through. Serve with rice or noodles.

*NUTRITION PER SERVE: Protein 20 g; Fat 15 g;*
*Carbohydrate 5 g; Dietary Fibre 2 g; Cholesterol 195 mg;*
*1025 kJ (245 cal)*

•

## FISH WITH FLAKED COCONUT

•

*Preparation time*: 20 minutes
*Total cooking time*: 50 minutes
*Serves* 4

☆ ☆

1/2 cup (45 g/11/2 oz) desiccated coconut
2 cups (110 g/32/3 oz) flaked coconut
500 g (1 lb) firm white fish fillets
1/2 teaspoon freshly ground black pepper
1 teaspoon turmeric
1 tablespoon lime juice
1 star anise
1 cinnamon stick
2 teaspoons cumin seeds
1 dried chilli
2 tablespoons oil
3 cloves garlic, crushed
3 medium onions, finely sliced

1 Spread the desiccated and flaked coconut on an oven tray and toast it in a slow 150°C (300°F/Gas 2) oven for 10 minutes or until it is dark golden, shaking the tray occasionally.
2 Place the fish, pepper, turmeric and lime juice in a frying pan, cover with water and simmer gently for 15 minutes or until the fish flakes when tested with a fork. Remove the fish fillets from the liquid and allow to cool slightly before flaking it into pieces.
3 Dry-roast the star anise, cinnamon stick, cumin seeds and chilli in a frying pan over medium heat for 5 minutes. Transfer to a food processor or a mortar and pestle and grind to a fine powder.
4 Heat the oil in a wok; add the garlic, onion and spice powder, and stir-fry over medium to high heat for 10 minutes or until the onion is soft.
5 Add the fish and coconut to the wok. Using 2 wooden spoons, toss the fish in the pan for 5 minutes or until heated through. Serve over rice.

*NUTRITION PER SERVE: Protein 30 g; Fat 40 g; Carbohydrate 5 g; Dietary Fibre 10 g; Cholesterol 90 mg; 2055 kJ (490 cal)*

## SRI LANKAN LENTILS

•

*Preparation time*: 15 minutes
*Total cooking time*: 1 hour
*Serves* 4

★

2 tablespoons oil
2 medium onions, finely sliced
2 small red chillies, finely chopped
2 teaspoons dried shrimp
1 teaspoon ground turmeric
2 cups (500 g/1 lb) red lentils
4 curry leaves
2 cups (500 ml/16 fl oz) coconut milk
1 cup (250 ml/8 fl oz) vegetable stock
1 cinnamon stick
10 cm (4 inch) piece lemon grass

•

1 Heat the oil in a medium pan; add the onion and cook over medium heat for 10 minutes, or until the onion is a deep golden brown. Remove half the onion and set aside to use as a garnish.
2 Add the chilli, dried shrimp and turmeric, and cook for 2 minutes. Stir in the lentils, curry leaves, coconut milk, stock, cinnamon stick and lemon grass; bring to the boil, reduce heat and simmer, uncovered, for 45 minutes. Remove the cinnamon stick and lemon grass and garnish with the reserved onion.

*NUTRITION PER SERVE: Protein 35 g; Fat 35 g; Carbohydrate 50 g; Dietary Fibre 20 g; Cholesterol 0 mg; 2800 kJ (670 cal)*

### SRI LANKAN CURRIES
*Unlike the curry powders of India, the spices that go into Ceylon curry powder—used in the black or brown curries that are characteristic of Sri Lanka—are roasted until dark, giving the mixture a completely different flavour and aroma. Dishes made with Ceylon curry powder have a distinctive deep colour. Chillies, ground or powdered, give red curries both their colour and heat, which can be scorching! White curries, on the other hand, are based on coconut milk and are usually fairly mild.*

*Above: Sri Lankan Lentils*

# DESSERTS

A burst of cooling sweetness is the perfect end to an Asian meal. Most Asian desserts make use of the natural sweetness of tropical fruits—coconuts, bananas and mangoes. Sticky rice, black or white, pancakes and semolina are often included to balance the tartness of the fruit, while ice creams and chilled custards refresh the palate.

*CASHEW
MERINGUE CAKE*

*Draw a circle onto each
piece of paper, using a
plate as a guide.*

*Fold the vanilla
esssence, vinegar and
ground cashews into the
beaten egg whites and
sugar.*

*Use a spatula to spread
the meringue mixture to
the edge of the circle.*

*Above: Cashew
Meringue Cake*

# CASHEW MERINGUE CAKE

•

*Preparation time*: 30 minutes + cooling
*Total cooking time*: 45 minutes
*Serves 8–10*

✷ ✷ ✷

*Cashew Meringue*
*300 g (10 oz) cashews*
*8 egg whites*
*1¹/₂ cups (375 g/12 oz) caster sugar*
*2 teaspoons vanilla essence*
*2 teaspoons white vinegar*

•

*Fillings*
*250 g (8 oz) unsalted butter, softened*
*1 cup (125 g/4 oz) icing sugar*
*4 tablespoons Crème de Cacao*
*2 cups (500 ml/16 fl oz) cream*
*1 tablespoon orange liqueur*
*2 teaspoons vanilla essence*
*chocolate curls and cocoa powder, for
    decoration*

•

1 To make Cashew Meringue: Preheat the oven
to moderate 180°C (350°F/Gas 4). Spread the
cashews on a baking tray and toast them in the
oven for 5 minutes or until golden, stirring
occasionally to turn them over. Check
frequently to make sure they don't burn.
Remove the cashews from the oven and allow
to cool. Place the cashews in a food processor
and process them in short bursts until finely
ground.

2 Reduce the oven temperature to slow 150°C
(300°F/Gas 2). Line 4 oven trays with non-stick
baking paper and draw a 21 cm (8¹/₂ inch)
diameter circle on each piece of paper.

3 Beat the egg whites in a large, clean, dry bowl
until soft peaks form. Gradually add the sugar to
the bowl, beating well after each addition, until
the whites are thick and glossy. Using a metal
spoon, fold in the vanilla, vinegar and ground
cashews.

4 Divide the mixture evenly among the 4 circles
and carefully spread it to the edge of each circle.
Bake the meringues for 45 minutes or until they
are crisp. Turn the oven off and allow the
meringues to cool in the oven, leaving the oven
door ajar.

5 To make Fillings: Place the butter, icing sugar
and Crème de Cacao in a bowl and beat until the
mixture becomes light and creamy. Set aside.
Place the cream, orange liqueur and vanilla
essence in a separate bowl and beat until soft
peaks form.

6 Place 1 meringue circle on a serving plate and
carefully spread it with half the butter mixture.
Place a second meringue circle on top and
spread it with half the orange cream mixture.
Repeat with the remaining meringue circles,
butter mixture and orange cream mixture.

7 The top of the meringue cake can be decorated
with chocolate curls and dusted lightly with
cocoa. Carefully cut into sections for serving.

*NUTRITION PER SERVE (10): Protein 10 g; Fat 55 g;
Carbohydrate 55 g; Dietary Fibre 2 g; Cholesterol 130 mg;
3230 kJ (770 cal)*

crepe pan. Pour 3 tablespoons of the pancake mixture into the pan and cook over medium heat until the underside is golden. Turn the pancake over and cook the other side. Transfer to a plate and cover with a tea towel to keep warm. Repeat with the remaining pancake batter, buttering the pan when necessary.

4 Cut the bananas diagonally into thick slices. Heat the butter in the pan; add the banana, toss until coated, and cook over medium heat until the banana starts to soften and brown. Sprinkle with the brown sugar and shake the pan gently until the sugar has melted. Stir in the lime juice. Divide the banana among the pancakes and fold over to enclose. Sprinkle with the toasted coconut and strips of lime rind.

*NUTRITION PER SERVE (6): Protein 5 g; Fat 20 g; Carbohydrate 65 g; Dietary Fibre 5 g; Cholesterol 60 mg; 1960 kJ (470 cal)*

## BANANA AND COCONUT PANCAKES
•

**Preparation time**: 10 minutes
**Total cooking time**: 30 minutes
**Serves 4–6**

✹ ✹

1 tablespoon shredded coconut, to serve
1/3 cup (40 g/1 1/3 oz) plain flour
2 tablespoons rice flour
1/4 cup (60 g/2 oz) caster sugar
1/4 cup (25 g/3/4 oz) desiccated coconut
1 cup (250 ml/8 fl oz) coconut milk
1 egg, lightly beaten
butter, for frying
4 large bananas
60 g (2 oz) butter, extra
1/3 cup (60 g/2 oz) lightly packed soft
    brown sugar
1/3 cup (80 ml/2 3/4 fl oz) lime juice
strips of lime rind, to serve

•

1 Spread the shredded coconut on an oven tray and toast it in a slow 150°C (300°F/Gas 2) oven for 10 minutes or until it is dark golden, shaking the tray occasionally. Remove the coconut from the tray to prevent it from burning and set aside.

2 Sift the plain and rice flour into a medium bowl. Add the sugar and desiccated coconut and mix through with a spoon. Make a well in the centre of the flour, pour in the combined coconut milk and egg, and beat until smooth.

3 Melt a little butter in a non-stick frying pan or

## COCONUT SEMOLINA SLICE
•

**Preparation time**: 20 minutes
**Total cooking time**: 55 minutes
**Serves 8–10**

✶

4 tablespoons sesame seeds
1 cup (125 g/4 oz) fine semolina
1 cup (250 g/8 oz) caster sugar
3 cups (750 ml/24 fl oz) coconut cream
2 tablespoons ghee or oil
2 eggs, separated
1/4 teaspoon ground cardamom

•

1 Preheat the oven to warm 160°C (315°F/Gas 2–3). Lightly grease a 28 x 18 cm (11 x 7 inch) shallow tin.

2 Toast the sesame seeds in a dry pan over medium heat for 3 to 4 minutes, shaking the pan gently, until the seeds are golden brown; remove from the pan at once to prevent burning.

3 Place the semolina, sugar and coconut cream in a large pan and stir over medium heat for 5 minutes or until boiling. Add the ghee and continue stirring until the mixture comes away from the sides of the pan. Set aside to cool.

4 Beat the egg whites until stiff peaks form. Fold the egg whites, egg yolks and cardamom into the cooled semolina mixture. Spoon the mixture into the prepared ovenproof dish and sprinkle over the sesame seeds. Bake for 45 minutes or until golden brown. Cut the slice into diamond shapes and serve with fresh fruit, if desired.

*NUTRITION PER SERVE (10): Protein 5 g; Fat 20 g; Carbohydrate 35 g; Dietary Fibre 0 g; Cholesterol 45 mg; 1500 kJ (360 cal)*

**THE SPICE TRADE**
*The spices of the East have long been keenly sought in the West. Laden caravans brought pepper from India and cloves and nutmeg from the Moluccas (now part of Indonesia) to the tables of the Roman Empire over routes controlled by Arab traders. In medieval times the merchants of Venice had a monopoly on the spice cargoes which arrived at Italian ports via the Holy Land. When overland routes became unsafe in the fifteenth century, navigators such as Columbus, Magellan and de Gama were dispatched to open up sea routes to the Spice Islands, as the countries of western Europe vied for the lucrative trade.*

*Above: Banana and Coconut Pancakes*

## STICKY RICE

*Sticky rice is also known as glutinous rice, though it does not contain gluten but a large amount of starch. It needs to be soaked before steaming. Usually served as a dessert, but some Asian countries (Laos) use it as an accompaniment to savoury dishes instead of white long grain.*

*Above: Sticky Rice with Mangoes*

## STICKY RICE WITH MANGOES

•

*Preparation time*: 40 minutes
  + 12 hours soaking
*Total cooking time*: 1 hour
*Serves 4*

✫ ✫

2 cups (400 g/12²/₃ oz) glutinous rice
1 tablespoon white sesame seeds, to serve
1 cup (250 ml/8 fl oz) coconut milk
¹/₂ cup (90 g/3 oz) grated palm sugar or
  soft brown sugar
¹/₄ teaspoon salt
2–3 mangoes, peeled, seeded and sliced
3 tablespoons coconut cream
fresh mint sprigs, to garnish

•

1 Place the rice in a sieve and wash it under running water until the water runs clear. Place the rice in a glass or ceramic bowl, cover it with water and leave it to soak overnight, or for a minimum of 12 hours. Drain the rice.

2 Line a metal or bamboo steamer with muslin. Place the rice on top of the muslin and cover the steamer with a tight-fitting lid. Place the steamer over a pot of boiling water and steam over moderately low heat for 50 minutes, or until the rice is cooked. Transfer the rice to a large bowl and fluff it up with a fork.

3 Toast the sesame seeds in a dry pan over medium heat for 3 to 4 minutes, shaking the pan gently, until the seeds are golden brown; remove from the pan at once to prevent burning.

4 Pour the coconut milk into a small pan; add the sugar and salt. Slowly bring the mixture to the boil, stirring constantly until the sugar has dissolved. Lower the heat and simmer for 5 minutes, or until the mixture has thickened slightly. Stir the mixture often while it is simmering, and take care that it does not stick to the bottom of the pan.

5 Slowly pour the coconut milk over the top of the rice. Use a fork to lift and fluff the rice. Do not stir the liquid through, otherwise the rice will become too gluggy. Let the rice mixture rest for 20 minutes before carefully spooning it into the centre of 4 warmed serving plates. Arrange the mango slices around the rice mounds. Spoon a little coconut cream over the rice, sprinkle over the sesame seeds, and garnish with the mint leaves.

*NUTRITION PER SERVE: Protein 10 g; Fat 20 g; Carbohydrate 115 g; Dietary Fibre 5 g; Cholesterol 0 mg; 2785 kJ (660 cal)*

·

# SPICY COCONUT CUSTARD
·

*Preparation time*: 20 minutes
*Total cooking time*: 35 minutes
*Serves* 6

★ ★

*2 cinnamon sticks*
*2 teaspoons whole cloves*
*1 teaspoon ground nutmeg*
*1 cup (250 ml/8 fl oz) water*
*1 cup (250 ml/8 fl oz) cream*
*1/2 cup (95 g/31/4 oz) soft dark brown sugar*
*1 cup (250 ml/8 fl oz) coconut milk*
*3 eggs, lightly beaten*
*2 egg yolks, lightly beaten*

·

1 Preheat the oven to warm 160°C (315°F/ Gas 2–3).
2 Place the cinnamon sticks, cloves, nutmeg, water and cream in a medium pan. Bring to simmering point, reduce heat to very low and leave for 5 minutes to allow the spices to flavour the liquid. Add the sugar and coconut milk, stirring until the sugar has dissolved.
3 Place the eggs and egg yolks in a small bowl and whisk to combine. Pour the spiced milk mixture over the eggs and stir to combine. Strain the mixture into a jug, discarding the whole spices.
4 Pour the custard mixture into 6 small dishes, each of about 1/2 cup (125 ml/4 fl oz) capacity. Place the small dishes in a baking dish; pour enough hot water into the baking dish to come halfway up the sides of the small dishes. Bake for 30 minutes. The custard is cooked when a knife inserted into the centre comes out clean and the custard is only slightly wobbly. Remove the custards from the baking dish. Serve custard hot or chilled.

*NUTRITION PER SERVE: Protein 5 g; Fat 30 g; Carbohydrate 30 g; Dietary Fibre 0 g; Cholesterol 210 mg; 1730 kJ (415 cal)*

# CHINESE FORTUNE COOKIES
·

*Preparation time*: 40 minutes
 + 15 minutes standing
*Total cooking time*: 50 minutes
*Makes* about 30

★ ★

*3 egg whites*
*1/2 cup (60 g/2 oz) icing sugar, sifted*
*45 g (11/2 oz) unsalted butter, melted*
*1/2 cup (60 g/2 oz) plain flour*

·

1 Preheat the oven to moderate 180°C (350°F/ Gas 4). Line an oven tray with baking paper. Draw 3 circles with 8 cm (3 inch) diameters on the paper.
2 Place the egg whites in a medium bowl and whisk until just frothy. Add the icing sugar and butter and stir until smooth. Add the flour and mix until smooth. Let stand for 15 minutes.
3 Using a flat-bladed knife, spread 11/2 level teaspoons of mixture over each circle. Bake for 5 minutes or until slightly brown around the edges. Working quickly, remove the cookies from the tray by sliding a flat-bladed knife under each. Place a written fortune message on each cookie. Fold the cookie in half to form a semicircle, then fold it again over a blunt-edged object like the rim of a glass. Allow to cool on a wire rack. Repeat with the remaining mixture.
NOTE: Cook no more than 2 or 3 cookies at a time, otherwise they will harden too quickly and break when folding.

*NUTRITION PER COOKIE: Protein 1 g; Fat 1 g; Carbohydrate 3 g; Dietary Fibre 0 g; Cholesterol 4 mg; 115 kJ (25 cal)*

*CHINESE FORTUNE COOKIES*

*Using a flat-bladed knife, spread the mixture over each circle on the baking paper.*

*Fold each cookie in half, then fold it again over a blunt-edged object like the rim of a glass or bowl.*

*Below: Chinese Fortune Cookies*

# TROPICAL FRUITS
Finish off your Asian meal with a delicious piece of fresh and cooling tropical fruit. Choose fruit in season and just slice it or tear it open to enjoy.

### MANGO
Ripe mangoes have a wonderful aroma and a rich, sweet, golden flesh. Ripen mangoes at room temperature, then store in the fridge and eat within 3 days. Mangoes are delicious on their own, puréed to make ice cream, or sliced and added to salads. The skin of a ripe mango will easily pull away from the flesh. Or cut the two cheeks from the mango, score the flesh in a criss-cross pattern, and gently push the skin upwards to release the flesh from the skin. Mangoes can also be eaten green, finely shredded in salads or made into chutneys and eaten with curries.

*NUTRITION PER 100 g: Protein 0 g;*
*Fat 0 g; Carbohydrate 10 g; Dietary Fibre 2 g;*
*Cholesterol 0 mg; 250 kJ (60 cal)*

### PAPAYA AND PAWPAW
Papaya and pawpaw are from the same family, but are not the same fruit. Papayas are usually smaller than pawpaws and have a slightly firmer texture. Both can be eaten green when finely shredded in salads or in curries. Ripen at room temperature until a soft orange colour with a pleasant aroma, then store in the fridge for up to 2 days. Cut in half lengthways and use a spoon to scoop out the seeds or remove the skin and slice or chop the fruit. Drizzle with lime juice and top with yoghurt.

*NUTRITION PER 100 g: Protein 0 g;*
*Fat 0 g; Carbohydrate 7 g; Dietary Fibre 2 g;*
*Cholesterol 0 mg; 120 kJ (30 cal)*

## COCONUT

Select whole coconuts that are heavy and shake them to confirm their liquid is still inside. To open a fresh coconut, pierce one of the eyes and drain away the coconut juice. Place the nut in a hot oven for 10 minutes, or until cracks appear in the shell. Transfer to a work surface and hit with a rolling pin to open. Coconut is delicious raw in salads, especially fresh fruit salads, or shaved, roasted and sprinkled onto curries.

*NUTRITION PER 100 g: Protein 3 g; Fat 25 g; Carbohydrate 4 g; Dietary Fibre 10 g; Cholesterol 0 mg; 1120 kJ (265 cal)*

## LYCHEE

Lychees grow in bunches of 3–20 fruit. The mature fruit has a deep red leathery skin and clear white flesh that surrounds a hard black stone. Lychees do not ripen after picking so must be fully ripe when harvested. Select fruit that is firm with no signs of splitting or decay; avoid fruit with brown skin as they are past their prime. Store lychees in plastic bags in the refrigerator. They are best eaten soon after purchasing. They have a sweet acidic flavour and can be eaten as a dessert with ice cream or in a fruit salad, in a salad with roast duck or as an accompaniment to stir-fries.

*NUTRITION PER 100 g: Protein 0 g; Fat 0 g; Carbohydrate 16 g; Dietary Fibre 1.3 g; Cholesterol 0 mg; 290 kJ (70 cal)*

## PINEAPPLE

Pineapple is one of the most popular tropical fruits. Select plump fruit that has a delicate, sweet fragrance and firm, fresh-looking skin and leaves. Store in a cool place out of direct sunlight or in the refrigerator. Once cut, store covered in the refrigerator. To prepare, cut off the top and base, and remove the skin using a sharp knife. Using a small sharp knife, cut on the diagonal around the pineapple to remove the little black eyes. Remove the core and serve sliced into rounds or cut into wedges. Pineapple is delicious mixed with mint and served with curries, in stir-fries or chargrilled and served with barbecued meat. Puréed pineapple is great for making sorbet or in a fruit punch.

*NUTRITION PER 100 g: Protein 0 g; Fat 0 g; Carbohydrate 10 g; Dietary Fibre 2 g; Cholesterol 0 mg; 160 kJ (40 cal)*

*From left: Mango; Pineapple; Lychees; Papaya; Pawpaw; Coconut*

# TROPICAL FRUITS

### GUAVA
Guavas have a thin, greenish yellow
skin; their soft pulpy interior can be
white, yellow, pink or red. They have
a sweet flavour and aroma. Select
firm, unblemished fruit which yield
to gentle pressure at the stem end.
Guava is high in vitamin C and a rich
source of pectin, making it ideal for
jam. Peel and slice in salads or purée
the flesh for granitas, sorbets or juice.

*NUTRITION PER 100 g: Protein 1 g;*
*Fat 0 g; Carbohydrate 3 g; Dietary Fibre 5 g;*
*Cholesterol 0 mg; 100 kJ (25 cal)*

### CARAMBOLA (STARFRUIT)
These can vary from delicately sweet
to a slightly tart lemon-pineapple
flavour depending on the variety and

ripeness. The thin waxy skin turns
golden yellow when mature and is
edible. Starfruit take up to 3 days to
ripen at room temperature and should
be refrigerated once ripe. Remove the
ends, trim the ribs of any brown marks
and slice into stars. Delicious served as
part of a fruit salad or a cheese platter.

*NUTRITION PER 100 g: Protein 1 g;*
*Fat 1 g; Carbohydrate 8 g; Dietary Fibre 1 g;*
*Cholesterol 0 mg; 150 kJ (35 cal)*

### MANGOSTEEN
Mangosteen has a tough, shiny skin
which is purplish red when ripe. The
pinkish white flesh is divided into 4 or
5 segments with a couple of small
black seeds. The fruit has a sweet,
slightly musk flavour and is best eaten

slightly chilled. To open, cut around
the skin using a sharp knife and peel
or twist away the skin. Break the fruit
into segments and remove seeds before
eating. Serve as part of a fruit salad or
purée for juice or to make ice cream.

*NUTRITION PER 100 g: Protein 1 g;*
*Fat 1 g; Carbohydrate 18 g; Dietary Fibre 1 g;*
*Cholesterol 0 mg; 320 kJ (75 cal)*

### SOUR SOP
The skin of a ripe sour sop, also
known as prickly custard apple, is a
light yellow-green colour and cream
between the nodules. Select firm
fruit, ripen at room temperature and
then refrigerate. The aromatic white
flesh is sweet and high in vitamin C.
The pulp is sometimes quite fibrous

and can be strained. Cut in half, remove the seeds (said to be toxic) and scoop out the flesh with a spoon. Great with breakfast cereal, or as a filling for strudel in combination with apple. The pulp freezes well and is good for ice cream.

*NUTRITION: No nutritional analysis available.*

## JACKFRUIT

Jackfruit is popular throughout Asia but many Westerners find its flavour strange at first. The fruit weighs about 5–6 kg (11–13 lb) and has a knobbly yellow-brown skin and a strong aroma. Usually it is picked while green and ripened in a cool place. Keep ripe fruit in an airtight container in the refrigerator. Oil your knife and hands before cutting to stop the sap sticking to them—cut the fruit in half and remove the flesh

from around the seeds. Often served in a fruit salad or mixed with warm coconut milk and brown sugar. The unripe fruit is cooked as a vegetable.

*NUTRITION PER 100 g: Protein 0 g; Fat 0 g; Carbohydrate 17 g; Dietary Fibre 3 g; Cholesterol 0 mg; 330 kJ (80 cal)*

## LONGAN

Often called the 'little brother of the lychee', but the delicate white flesh that surrounds the small brown seed has a musk, grape-like flavour and is sweeter than a lychee. Select fruit with a stalk attached and pale brown, unblemished skin with no cracks. Make sure there is no mould around the stalk. Peel and eat longans on their own or as part of a fruit salad.

*NUTRITION PER 100 g: Protein 0 g; Fat 0 g; Carbohydrate 15 g; Dietary Fibre 5 g; Cholesterol 0 mg; 240 kJ (55 cal)*

## RAMBUTAN

Egg-shaped rambutans grow in clusters and are sometimes called hairy lychees as their leathery skin is covered in long soft red hairs. They are bright red, yellow or orange when ripe, depending on the variety. Buy rambutans that are bright in colour with hairs that are fresh-looking, not brown and wrinkled. Rambutans contain a single seed surrounded by sweet acidic white flesh. To eat, simply slice in half and remove the seed. Rambutans are best eaten on their own or as part of a fruit salad.

*NUTRITION PER 100 g: Protein 0 g; Fat 0 g; Carbohydrate 16 g; Dietary Fibre 4 g; Cholesterol 0 mg; 300 kJ (70 cal)*

*From left: Guava; Carambola; Mangosteen; Sour Sop; Jackfruit; Longan; Rambutan*

**3** Add the sugar, cinnamon, cardamom and cream and cook, stirring, until the sugar has dissolved. Serve the pudding warm in small dishes, and sprinkle over the pistachios.

*NUTRITION PER SERVE: Protein 5 g; Fat 15 g; Carbohydrate 35 g; Dietary Fibre 1 g; Cholesterol 40 mg; 1220 kJ (290 cal)*

### SAGO PUDDING

*Preparation time:* 20 minutes + 1 hour soaking + 2 hours refrigeration
*Total cooking time:* 20 minutes
*Serves* 6

★

1 cup (195 g/6¹/₃ oz) sago
3 cups (750 ml/24 fl oz) water
1 cup (185 g/6 oz) lightly packed soft
   brown sugar
1 cup (250 ml/8 fl oz) water, extra
1 cup (250 ml/8 fl oz) coconut cream,
   well chilled

**1** Soak the sago in the water for 1 hour. Pour into a pan, add 2 tablespoons of the sugar and bring to the boil over low heat, stirring constantly. Reduce the heat and simmer, stirring occasionally, for 8 minutes. Cover and cook for 2 to 3 minutes, until the mixture becomes thick and the sago grains are translucent.
**2** Half fill 6 wet ¹/₂ cup (125 ml/4 fl oz) moulds with the sago mixture. Refrigerate for 2 hours, or until set.
**3** Combine the remaining sugar with the extra water in a small pan and cook over low heat,

### CARROT MILK PUDDING

•

*Preparation time:* 5 minutes
*Total cooking time:* 1 hour
*Serves* 6

★

4 cups (1 litre) milk
1¹/₂ cups (240 g/7¹/₂ oz) grated carrot
¹/₃ cup (40 g/1¹/₃ oz) sultanas
¹/₂ cup (125 g/4 oz) caster sugar
¹/₄ teaspoon ground cinnamon
¹/₄ teaspoon ground cardamom
¹/₃ cup (80 ml/2³/₄ oz) cream
2 tablespoons unsalted chopped pistachios

•

**1** Pour the milk into a large heavy-based pan and stir over medium heat until it comes to the boil. Reduce the heat to low and simmer until reduced by half, stirring occasionally to prevent it from catching on the base of the pan.
**2** Add the carrot and sultanas and cook for a further 15 minutes.

*Above: Carrot Milk Pudding*
*Right: Sago Pudding*

stirring constantly, until the sugar dissolves. Simmer for 5 to 7 minutes, until the syrup thickens. Remove from the heat and cool. To serve, unmould the sago and top with a little of the sugar syrup and coconut cream.

NUTRITION PER SERVE: Protein 0 g; Fat 10 g; Carbohydrate 60 g; Dietary Fibre 0 g; Cholesterol 0 mg; 1325 kJ (315 cal)

•

# COCONUT ICE CREAM

•

**Preparation time:** 10 minutes + freezing
**Total cooking time:** 15 minutes
**Serves** 6

★ ★

1¾ cups (440 ml/14 fl oz) coconut cream
1½ cups (375 ml/12 fl oz) cream
2 eggs
2 egg yolks
½ cup (125 g/4 oz) caster sugar
¼ teaspoon salt
1 teaspoon vanilla essence
¼ cup (15 g/½ oz) shredded coconut
fresh mint, to garnish

•

1 Place the coconut cream and cream in a medium pan. Stir over medium heat, without boiling, for 2 to 3 minutes. Remove from the heat, cover and keep warm.
2 Place the eggs, egg yolks, sugar, salt and vanilla in a large heatproof bowl. Using electric beaters, beat the mixture for 2 to 3 minutes until frothy and thickened.
3 Place the bowl over a pan of simmering water. Continue to beat the egg mixture while gradually adding the warm coconut mixture, ¼ cup (60 ml/2 fl oz) at a time, until all the coconut mixture is added and the custard has thickened. This process will take about 10 minutes. The mixture will be the consistency of thin cream and should easily coat the back of a spoon. Do not allow to boil or it will curdle.
4 Transfer the mixture to a cold bowl, cover and set aside to cool; stir it occasionally while it is cooling. When cool, pour the mixture into a shallow cake tin, cover and freeze for about 1½ hours or until half-frozen.
5 Quickly spoon the ice cream into a food processor and process for 30 seconds, or until smooth. Return the ice cream to the cake tin or place it in a plastic container, and cover and freeze completely.
6 Spread the coconut on an oven tray and toast it in a slow 150°C (300°F/Gas 2) oven for 10 minutes or until it is dark golden, shaking the tray occasionally. Remove the coconut from the tray to prevent it from burning and set aside to cool. Serve the ice cream in scoops with the coconut sprinkled over and garnished with the mint.

NOTE: Before serving the ice cream, leave to stand at room temperature for 10 to 15 minutes or until it has softened slightly.

NUTRITION PER SERVE: Protein 5 g; Fat 45 g; Carbohydrate 25 g; Dietary Fibre 0 g; Cholesterol 205 mg; 2160 kJ (515 cal)

*Above: Coconut Ice Cream*

PANDANUS LEAVES
*Also known as screwpine,
these long, flat, fragrant
leaves add colour and a
distinct flavour to both
savoury and sweet dishes
in Thailand, Sri Lanka,
Malaysia and Indonesia.
Before adding to the dish,
partly shred the leaf or cut
it into sections—this helps
to release the flavour—
then tie the leaf in a knot
to hold the sections
together. A short strip can
be added when cooking
rice. Available fresh or
frozen from some Asian
food stores, but more
widely available dried.*

## MANGO ICE CREAM

*Preparation time:* 20 minutes + freezing
*Total cooking time:* Nil
*Serves* 6

⭐

*400 g (12²/₃ oz) fresh mango flesh
¹/₂ cup (125 g/4 oz) caster sugar
3 tablespoons mango or apricot nectar
1 cup (250 ml/8 fl oz) cream
extra mango slices, optional*

1 Place the mango in a food processor and
process until smooth. Transfer the mango purée
to a bowl and add the sugar and nectar. Stir until
the sugar has dissolved.
2 Beat the cream in a small bowl until stiff peaks
form and then gently fold it through the mango
mixture.
3 Spoon the mixture into a shallow cake tin,
cover and freeze for 1¹/₂ hours or until half-
frozen. Quickly spoon the mixture into a food
processor and process for 30 seconds, or until
smooth. Return the mixture to the tin or a
plastic container, cover and freeze completely.
Remove the ice cream from the freezer
15 minutes before serving to allow it to soften a
little. Serve the ice cream in scoops with some
extra fresh mango if desired.
NOTE: Frozen or canned mango can be used if
fresh mango is not available.

*NUTRITION PER SERVE: Protein 4 g; Fat 20 g;
Carbohydrate 60 g; Dietary Fibre 4 g; Cholesterol 55 mg;
1710 kJ (405 cal)*

## STICKY BLACK RICE

*Preparation time:* 10 minutes
 + 8 hours soaking
*Total cooking time:* 40 minutes
*Serves* 6–8

⭐⭐

*2 cups (400 g/12²/₃ oz) black rice
4 cups (1 litre) cold water
2 cups (500 ml/16 fl oz) coconut milk
¹/₂ cup (90 g/ 3 oz) grated palm sugar or
 soft brown sugar
3 tablespoons caster sugar
3 fresh pandanus leaves, shredded and
 knotted
3 tablespoons coconut cream
3 tablespoons creamed corn*

1 Place the rice in a large glass or ceramic bowl
and add enough water to cover it. Soak the rice

for at least 8 hours or overnight. Drain the rice
and transfer it to a medium pan with the water.
Slowly bring it to the boil, stirring frequently,
and then simmer for 20 minutes, or until tender.
Drain.
2 In a large heavy-based pan, heat the coconut
milk until almost boiling. Add the palm sugar,
caster sugar and pandanus leaves, and stir until
the sugars have dissolved. Add the rice and stir
for 3 to 4 minutes without boiling.
3 Turn off the heat, cover the pan and let it
stand for 15 minutes to allow the flavours to be
absorbed. Remove the pandanus leaves. Serve
the rice warm with the coconut cream and
creamed corn.

*NUTRITION PER SERVE (8): Protein 5 g; Fat 15 g;
Carbohydrate 60 g; Dietary Fibre 0 g; Cholesterol 0 mg;
1630 kJ (390 cal)*

## ALMOND JELLY

*Preparation time:* 5 minutes
 + 1 hour chilling
*Total cooking time:* 5 minutes
*Serves* 4–6

⭐

*2 cups (500 ml/16 fl oz) cold water
¹/₃ cup (90 g/3 oz) caster sugar
2 teaspoons agar agar
²/₃ cup (170 ml/5¹/₂ fl oz) evaporated milk
¹/₂ teaspoon almond essence
3 fresh mandarins, peeled and segmented,
 or 300 g (9²/₃ oz) fresh cherries, pitted
 and chilled*

1 Place the water and sugar in a small pan.
Sprinkle over the agar agar powder. Bring the
mixture to the boil and simmer for 1 minute.
Remove the pan from the heat and add the
evaporated milk and almond essence.
2 Pour the mixture into a shallow 18 x 28 cm
(7 x 11 inch) pan to set. Chill for at least 1 hour.
3 Cut the jelly into diamond shapes, and serve
with the fruit.
NOTE: Agar agar is similar to gelatine but does
not need refrigeration to help it set. If it is
unavailable, use 3 teaspoons of gelatine
sprinkled over ¹/₂ cup (125 ml/4 fl oz) cold water
to soften. Stir the gelatine mixture into the water
and sugar mixture, bring to the boil, then
remove it from the heat—there is no need to
simmer. Proceed with the method as above but
refrigerate the jelly for 5 hours.

*NUTRITION PER SERVE (6): Protein 2 g; Fat 2 g;
Carbohydrate 20 g; Dietary Fibre 1 g; Cholesterol 10 mg;
450 kJ (105 cal)*

*Opposite page: Mango
Ice Cream (top);
Sticky Black Rice*

## SWEET WON TONS

•

*Preparation time*: 15 minutes
*Total cooking time*: 20 minutes
*Makes* 30

★★

125 g (4 oz) dates, pitted and chopped
2 bananas, finely chopped
½ cup (45 g/1½ oz) flaked almonds,
   lightly crushed
½ teaspoon ground cinnamon
60 won ton wrappers
oil, for deep-frying
icing sugar, to dust

•

1 Mix together the dates, bananas, almonds and cinnamon. Place 2 teaspoons of the fruit mixture into the centre of a won ton wrapper, and brush the edges lightly with water. Place another won ton wrapper on top at an angle so that the wrappers make a star shape. Place the won tons on a tray lined with baking paper. Repeat with the remaining ingredients, taking care not to stack the won tons on top of each other or they will stick together.

2 Heat the oil in a large pan until moderately hot; add the won tons in small batches and deep-fry for 2 minutes or until crisp and golden.

*Above: Sweet*
*Won Tons*

Drain on paper towels. Dust the won tons lightly with icing sugar before serving.

NUTRITION PER WON TON: Protein 3 g; Fat 5 g;
Carbohydrate 15 g; Dietary Fibre 2 g; Cholesterol 0 mg;
500 kJ (120 cal)

•

## EGG TARTS

*Preparation time*: 30 minutes
  + 15 minutes standing
*Total cooking time*: 15 minutes
*Makes* 18

★★★

**Outer Dough**

1⅓ cups (165 g/5½ oz) plain flour
2 tablespoons icing sugar
⅓ cup (80 ml/2¾ oz) water
2 tablespoons oil

•

**Inner Dough**

1 cup (125 g/4 oz) plain flour
100 g (3⅓ oz) lard, chopped

•

**Custard**

⅓ cup (80 ml/2¾ oz) water
¼ cup (60 g/2 oz) caster sugar
2 eggs

*Fold the Outer Dough over the Inner Dough so the short edges of the Outer Dough overlap.*

*Roll the dough in one direction into a long rectangle until it is about half as thick as it was before.*

*Cut out rounds of pastry using a fluted cutter and carefully place the rounds into the patty tins.*

*Fill each pastry case two-thirds full with the custard mixture.*

1 To make Outer Dough: Sift the flour and icing sugar into a medium bowl. Make a well in the centre. Pour in the combined water and oil. Mix with a knife to form a rough dough. (If the flour is very dry, add a little extra water.) Turn out onto a lightly floured surface and gather together in a smooth ball. Cover and set aside for 15 minutes.

2 To make Inner Dough: Sift the flour into a medium bowl. Using your fingertips, rub the lard into the flour until the mixture resembles coarse breadcrumbs. Press the dough together into a ball, cover and set aside for 15 minutes.

3 On a lightly floured surface, roll the Outer Dough into a rectangle about 10 x 20 cm (4 x 8 inches). On a lightly floured surface, roll the Inner Dough into a smaller rectangle, one-third the size of the Outer Dough. Place the Inner Dough in the centre of the Outer Dough. Fold the Outer Dough over the Inner Dough so the short edges overlap and the Inner Dough is enclosed. Pinch the edges together to seal.

4 On a lightly floured surface, roll the dough away from you in one direction into a long rectangle, until it is about half as thick as it was previously. Turn the dough 90 degrees so that the long edges are now horizontal to you. Fold the pastry into 3 layers by taking the left-hand edge over first, and then folding the right-hand

edge on top. Wrap the dough in plastic wrap and refrigerate for 30 minutes.

5 Preheat the oven to hot 210°C (415°F/ Gas 6–7). Brush 2 shallow 12-cup patty tins with melted butter or oil.

6 To make Custard: Place the water and sugar in a pan and stir without boiling until the sugar dissolves. Bring to the boil and simmer without stirring for 1 minute. Cool the mixture for 5 minutes. Place the eggs in a bowl and beat lightly with a fork. Whisk the sugar syrup into the eggs until just combined. Strain into a jug.

7 Place the pastry on a lightly floured surface. With one open end towards you, roll the pastry out to a rectangle about 2.5 mm (1/8 inch) thick. Cut out rounds of pastry using a 7 cm (2³/4 inch) fluted cutter. Carefully place the pastry rounds into the prepared patty tins. Fill each pastry case two-thirds full with the egg custard mixture. Bake for 15 minutes, or until just set. Take care not to overcook the custard.

8 Leave the egg tarts for 3 minutes before removing them from the tin. Slip a flat-bladed knife down the side of each tart to help lift it out. Cool the tarts on a wire rack, and serve warm or cold.

*NUTRITION PER TART: Protein 2 g; Fat 10 g; Carbohydrate 15 g; Dietary Fibre 1 g; Cholesterol 30 mg; 625 kJ (150 cal)*

*Above: Egg Tarts*

# INDEX

Page numbers in *italics* refer to photographs.
Page numbers in **bold** refer to margin notes.

# ACKNOWLEDGEMENTS

PHOTOGRAPHERS: Jon Bader, Paul Clarke, Joe Filshie, Andrew Furlong, Chris Jones, Ray Joyce, Andre Martin, Luis Martin, Reg Morrison, Andrew Payne, Peter Scott

•

STYLISTS: Wendy Berecry, Amanda Cooper, Georgina Dolling, Carolyn Fienberg, Mary Harris, Donna Hay, Di Kirby, Vicki Liley, Rosemary Mellish, Lucy Mortenson, Tracey Port, Suzi Smith

•

HOME ECONOMISTS: Myles Beaufort, Wendy Brodhurst, Rebecca Clancy, Michelle Earl, Jo Forrest, Susan Geraghty, Wendy Goggin, Donna Hay, Tatjana Lakajev, Michelle Lawton, Voula Mantzouridis, Melanie McDermott, Kerrie Mullins, Anna Paola Boyd, Tracey Port, Kerrie Ray, Jo Richardson, Tracy Rutherford, Maria Sampsonis, Stephanie Souvilis, Dimitra Stais, Alison Turner, Jody Vassallo

•

RECIPE DEVELOPMENT: Wendy Berecry, Wendy Brodhurst, Kerrie Carr, Laurine Croasdale, Jane Croswell-Jones, Michelle Earl, Wendy Goggin, Ken Gomes, Barbara Lowery, Rachael Mackie, Voula Mantzouridis, Rosemary Mellish, Sally Parker, Jacki Passmore, Jennene Plummer, Tracey Port, Jo Richardson, Tracy Rutherford, Maria Sampsonis, Christine Sheppard, Deborah Solomon, Dimitra Stais, Beverly Sutherland-Smith, Jody Vassallo

•

The publisher also wishes to thank the following for their help with the photography of this book:
*Corso De Fiori*, Shop 216, Sky Garden, Sydney; *Bamix*, Shop 205A, Westfield, Chatswood, NSW;
*House*, 249 King Street, Newtown, NSW; *East India Co*, Shop 5R, Glasshouse, Sydney;
*The Bay Tree*, 40 Holdsworth Street, Woollarah, NSW;
*Wedgwood*; *Accoutrement*, Queens Court, Queen Street, Woollarah, NSW.